RHODESIA

THE STRUGGLE FOR A BIRTHRIGHT

RHODESIA

THE STRUGGLE
FOR A BIRTHRIGHT

by

ESHMAEL MLAMBO

LONDON
C. HURST & COMPANY

First published in the United Kingdom by
C. Hurst & Co. (Publishers) Ltd.,
40a Royal Hill, Greenwich, London S.E.10

© 1972 by Eshmael Mlambo

SBN 90096672 6

Printed in Great Britain by
Billing & Sons Limited, Guildford and London

CONTENTS

N 1 0 6

MAP

PREFACE

This book has been written in the attempt to correct the misrepresentation of the African case on Rhodesia that has been going on since 1890. When Harold Wilson, then Prime Minister of the Labour Government, went to meet Ian Smith on the *Fearless* in 1968, he informed British television viewers that he was going as a representative and trustee of the Africans to solve the problem in their interest. Similarly, when Sir Alec Douglas-Home went to Rhodesia in 1971 to settle the independence problem with Smith, he claimed that he was doing so in order to halt Rhodesia's rapid movement towards apartheid. On his return he told the British Parliament that Africans would 'benefit from this more than anybody else'. In Rhodesia, Smith too puts up a façade of trying to help the Africans in their advance, and he is only the latest in a long line to claim that the Rhodesian Africans are the luckiest in the whole continent.

Whether or not the British and Rhodesian leaders are sincere in making these claims it is not for this book to judge; it can only say with certainty that in the eyes of Africans the claims appear false and dishonest.

Brititain has never faced a more difficult problem in all her history as an imperial power. Even the best-intentioned politician who tries to solve it soon finds himself sinking into a quicksand of moral contradictions. This is due to the racial nature of the problem, to which the British reaction is paternalism. In the latter half of the twentieth century it should be plain to any political leader that for white people to settle an African problem without the full participation of African leaders is psychologically impossible. Decisions made without regard to African opinion can only breed frustration, racial bitterness and strife.

This book puts forward the view that the racial resentment already felt in Rhodesia, and the Africans' determination to regain their birthright by any means, including violence, has been produced by the failure of white politicians in Britain and Rhodesia to recognise that the Africans are as much interested in shaping their destiny as are any other people in the world. Paternalism expressed in terms like 'mature', 'responsible', 'civilised', 'advanced' – which Africans must be before they can exercise power – only exasperates racial conflict; it does not solve any problem. The claims of Smith and his supporters abroad that chiefs are the leaders and that all Africans who oppose the Rhodesia Front régime's policy are Communists only increases the racial conflict.

It was therefore necessary in this book to look into the background of the problem, and review the political attitudes of Britain and the settlers, which have given rise to the Charter in 1889 and the 1898 and 1923 Constitutions. In none of these constitutional developments were Africans involved. Instead they were subjected to deliberate policies of discrimination, land deprivation and denial of political rights, while claims were made by those who benefited thereby that their progress was the best in all Africa.

The Africans in Rhodesia have done their best to achieve their freedom by using all the existing machinery at their disposal, internally and internationally. Their failure in this pursuit has been due mainly to British and settler intransigence. Despite the public quarrel between Britain and the settlers, they are firmly united in their desire to keep Rhodesia as a white man's land.

It is hardly necessary to repeat that a settlement that does not take cognisance of African feelings, such as that initialled by Ian Smith and Sir Alec Douglas-Home in November 1971, will not work. Racial strife will continue, and as the Africans' demand for the return of their birthright grows in strength, the settlers will feel ever less secure.

In continental terms, Rhodesia remains a land of hope. To the north is politically independent black Africa, to the south a country where only a blind optimist can see a peaceful end to racial domination of whites over blacks. Rhodesia lies uneasily between the two, prevented by history from ever belonging naturally in either camp. The Federation of 1953–63 was a false dawn for a polity based on non-racialism. As long as the 1971 'settlement' does not pass into law, hopes for a new and true dawn need not die.

Although this book expresses African feeling on some questions which, for various reasons, many European authors have left out of consideration, it does not claim to be equal to, or to approach the standard of work published by Professor C. Palley and Professor D. J. Murray, both my teachers at the University of Rhodesia. These two eminent scholars, together with Professor Colin Leys in his study *European Politics in Rhodesia*, have laid a foundation on which future generations will continue to build their studies.

I am exceedingly grateful to my former classmate at the University of Rhodesia and at Colorado State University, U.S.A., Leonard Kapungu, at present assistant professor of International Relations

at the University of Maryland, for his information on Sanctions.
The readiness of Mr. R. K. Maxey of Brentwood, Essex, England,
to supply me with the documents he has collected on Rhodesia
over a long period was invaluable to me, and the advice of Mr.
Kalayi Njini made the chapter on Education more complete than
it otherwise would have been.

My gratitude is due to Lesley Wynn-Davies for typing a difficult
project with a lot of foreign names. I express deep appreciation to
Mr. Richard Hall for reading and advising me on the manuscript,
and without Mr. Christopher Hurst's patience in working over my
English, the study would have taken a longer time to reach book
form than it has done.

Finally, I dedicate the book to my sons Eugene Kin and Khetha.
They and their generation will feel the effects of what is being trans-
acted now, for good or for ill, throughout their lives.

E. E. M. M.

London,
December 1971

CHAPTER I

APOSTLES OF CIVILISATION

(i) *The Constitutional Development of Rhodesia under Company Rule
1890–1923*

The Constitutional and political development of Southern Rhodesia
was reshaped by the revolt of the Ndebele and the Shona in 1896–7
against the rule of the British South Africa Company. Before this
bloody event,[1] the country was ruled under the Charter given to
the Company in 1889. Those who drafted the Charter, which was
issued on the basis of the Rudd Concession of 1888, were influenced
by the anti-slavery attitudes prevalent in Britain at the time. Its
ideals included 'promoting trade, commerce, civilisation and good
government', and it purported to create such conditions that the
lives of natives inhabiting the territories would be 'materially improved and their civilisation advanced.' Since the world was concerned with the abolition of slavery, it was found imperative to include a clause dealing with the end of slavery in Rhodesia. As the
abolitionists of the period understood by slavery what had existed in
the Americas earlier in the nineteenth century, it never occurred to
them that the colonialism which they were encouraging would in its
turn be construed as 'modern slavery'. Nineteenth-century philanthropists in fact believed that slavery could be halted by the protection of a 'civilised' European power. The people who set out from
European capitals for Africa were thought of as the apostles of
civilisation, and the colonisers believed the same of themselves.

The British Government cannot, however, have seriously intended to get these terms of the Charter enforced, since no provision
was made for 'the appointment of Imperial officers on the spot
who could either report on or intervene with the Company'.[2]

An examination of the Rudd Concession shows clearly that only
mineral rights were granted by Lobengula, but the Charter also
provided for administrative, legislative and judicial powers which
were not included in the Concession. The Charter further empowered the Company 'to improve, develop, clear, plant and cultivate
any lands', even though the concession had never allowed the acquisition of land.[3] All this was done before Cecil Rhodes had bought

the Lippert Concession[4] (later found invalid – after other grounds had been found for taking the land out of African ownership), in which Lobengula was said to have given away the rights to all land in his country. With the help of the Charter the Company entered and ruled Mashonaland from 1890. In 1893, after the Anglo-Matabele War, the British South Africa Company annexed Matabeleland. To appease humanitarians at home, the Anglo-Matabele War was claimed to be a crusade designed to end the 'slavery' imposed on Mashonaland by the Ndebele. The war, however, had motives other than humanitarian. After six years of Company rule in the country, both Shona and Ndebele revolted against white rule. Many died, black and white. The claim by the Company that their 1893 war was meant to save the Shona from the Ndebele was soon proved false because the revolt was co-ordinated by both Shona and Ndebele leaders, and resistance to the Company was more bloody in Mashonaland than in Matabeleland.[5]

The British Government's *laissez-faire* attitude to the Company's rule changed after the second revolt in 1896–7, which also cost many lives.[6] The Africans had taken advantage of the settlers' involvement in the Jameson Raid in the Transvaal in 1895 to start a revolt against Company rule, and the British Government was rudely awakened to the fact that Rhodes' policy was not as successful as had previously appeared. The revolt was viewed as an attempt by uncivilised men to revert to barbarism. Both witchcraft and the militarism of the Ndebele were blamed for it. A propaganda campaign was mounted in the United Kingdom to convince the public that natives wanted to destroy the nascent, imported 'civilisation' in Rhodesia.[7] The British Government thus introduced the 1898 Constitution which they believed to be fair to the Company, the settlers, and the Africans. This Constitution has been the basis of all subsequent ones, and its main provisions still remain in the present republican Constitution of Ian Smith. While the former British African colonies have substantially changed the structure of their constitutions, the Rhodesian republican Constitution has retained its late nineteenth-century structure with minority rule, a characteristic of colonial constitutions which was eliminated elsewhere by African nationalism.

A formal structure of government was set up, with a legislative council and administrative and judicial provisions. The policy of the British Government at this stage was to prevent a recurrence of the events that had led to the rebellion. This necessitated the presence of H.M. Government's representative in the person of a resident commissioner, whose main concern was to look after African interests. The details of the administration of African Affairs were embodied in a document entitled Native Regulations: Article 79 outlined how the administrator would appoint officials in consultation with the United Kingdom to run the department responsible for African interests. Article 80 outlawed any forms of disability to be imposed on Africans which did not equally apply to people of European descent, except in the case of arms, ammunition and liquor. The idea found its way into the 1923 Constitution under Article 42, and into the 1961 Constitution in a Bill of Rights. The intentions were honourable, but the provisions of the Native Regulations Act in 1898 turned out to be a foundation-stone for all the legislation oppressing the Africans.[8]

The Legislative Council of 1898 was made up of five nominees of the Company, four elected settlers, the Company Administrator as chairman with a casting vote, and the British Government representative – the Resident Commissioner – without a vote. The settlers obtained a say in the politics of the country, a lever which they later used to oust Company rule. Since the British Government, and indeed the whole world, regarded Africans as "uncivilised", no provision was made for their representation in the Legislative Council. It was inconceivable at the time that an African should sit side by side with a white man to consider political or economic problems.

In the 1889 Charter there had been provision for respect of African law and custom.[9] But there was no provision indicating how this 'respect' could be interpreted in practice. In 1898 machinery was set up for the protection of African law and custom. It included a provision for 'the assistance of one or two native assessors' in cases between Africans in the High Court and the magistrates' courts; but it has never been invoked. Even at the present time, when qualified African lawyers are available, no African is invited to sit with judges in cases involving Africans. Instead, white employees of the African Affairs Department participate in such trials as assessors.

The 1898 Constitution was a great improvement on the Charter of 1889. It was based on the following ideas: (a) preventing the recurrence of the 1896–7 revolt; (b) all matters concerned with African interests to revert to the British Government; (c) provision of a constitutional framework as a foundation for a future white dominion in Southern Africa. At this stage, Africans were looked on virtually as impoverished people with no rights to land and no property of their own.[10] Land was regarded as the property of the Company, which had got it by the Lippert Concession and by conquest. The British Government viewed its policies as humanitarian, designed to save a deprived people. In this policy it won sympathy from philanthropists, missionaries and liberals generally.

As soon as Rhodes died in 1902, the settlers' demand for self-government intensified, and both the British Government and the Company yielded a little to this pressure. The Government reduced the Company nominees by five in 1907, and gave a majority to the settlers who were confirmed in that position by an order-in-council of 1911.[11] Further agitation, and the prospect of further immigration, led the British Government to make a proclamation[12] giving elected settlers a maximum of fifteen in the Legislative Council. In 1907 the High Commissioner had promised the settlers Responsible Government by 1914, but when that year came, the Secretary of State did not honour the promise, on the grounds that the settlers had not sufficient financial security for Responsible Government. Their population was too small in comparison with that of Africans.[13] The fact that it was only eighteen years since the settlers has been nearly annihilated by rebellious Africans was not forgotten in Britain.

The settlers argued that continued Company rule stood in the way of progress, and prevented their case from being known in Britain; it also restrained the influx of immigrants because of land regulations, and, most important of all, Rhodesia could not be represented at the Imperial Conference because it was not a dominion. On the question of the smallness of the white population compared to the number of Africans, the settlers argued that more British immigrants would come to Rhodesia once Responsible Government was established and the laws improved, especially if land were owned by the State instead of by the Company.

In 1914 the Secretary of State for the Colonies gave the settlers a supplementary charter with the proviso that by an absolute majority, members of the Legislative Council could pass a resolution praying the King to provide for Responsible Government. The settlers had to show by October 1924 evidence of their capability of coping with the financial vicissitudes and other demands of Responsible Government. Once the Crown was satisfied that the settlers were capable of facing the pressure of Responsible Government, the Charter of 1889 and its Supplementary Charter of 1914 would be modified according to the requirements of Responsible Government. The election of 1914 had been centred on the end of Company rule. Most candidates regarded the Company as oppressive, especially in the way it handled the land question.[14] Because the settlers preferred to wait for Responsible Government until after the result of the land case then before the Privy Council, most candidates who advocated the *status quo* were returned with a large majority.

The First World War reduced the agitation for Responsible Government, but the end of the war, and the judgement of the

Privy Council, caused an intensification of the campaign, for which the current climate of world opinion was well suited. At the Versailles Peace Conference in 1919 the Trusteeship Committee chaired by Lord Milner had been persuaded by Smuts that the wealth and congenial climate of Africa south of the Zambezi, and the Kunene River in Angola,[15] were good for white settlement. General Smuts persuaded Woodrow Wilson and other leaders to designate that part of Africa 'white areas', hoping to attract mass emigration from Europe to settle and create an English-speaking African dominion similar to Canada, Australia and New Zealand. Smuts was regarded by world leaders at the time as the spokesman of all white settlers in Africa. His drafting of the Covenant of the League of Nations made a great impression on Woodrow Wilson, who commended his views to the others present. His paternalistic policies with regard to the African population dovetailed with the ideas of European leaders.

In Southern Rhodesia, speeches in the Legislative Council and in the Executive Council were now full of references to the need for Responsible Government. In these speeches the Company figured as an ogre to be attacked. The belief that Rhodesia would form part of the white dominion in Africa made negotiations easier for the settlers. Once their agitation gained currency, the pro-settler High Commissioner in South Africa, Lord Buxton, commissioned his Imperial Secretary, Herbert Stanley, later Governor of Southern Rhodesia, to draft a constitution for recommendation to the Secretary of State as a basis for a settlement.

The settlers were encouraged by a speech of Lord Buxton, who assured them that their case was going to meet with the British Government's approval. Lord Milner, worried by this assurance given without his approval, replied to the demand for Responsible Government by a telegram on 12 August, 1919, stating that the country was not yet equal to the financial burden it involved. He was also concerned at the small size of the settler population in comparison with Africans. He suggested that the settlers had three choices: incorporation into the Union, a provision which already existed under Clause 150 of the South Africa Act 1909; Responsible Government; and the continuation of Company rule.

The telegram met with shocked disapproval. Lord Buxton then contradicted his chief by telling a Bulawayo audience that Milner expressed his own and not the British Cabinet's opinion. This statement was published by the *Bulawayo Chronicle* and precipitated a demand from Milner for an explanation. Buxton denied the allegation that he had repudiated his chief's authority.

The result of the election of April 1920 was overwhelmingly for

Responsible Government. Of the 6,765 voters, 4,663 were in favour of it. The rest were as follows: for Responsible Government under the Crown, 420; for union with South Africa, 814; for continuation of Company rule, 868. One of the thirteen constituencies had no poll. Rhodesia at this stage had a population of 33,000 whites and 700,000 Africans, with 11,098 Coloureds and Asians. Only 51 were Africans, two born in Rhodesia. The election was followed by a resolution of the Legislative Council according to the specifications of the Supplementary Charter of 1914. R. A. Fletcher was the only one of the thirteen elected members who voted for it; one of the five Company nominees did so. The resolution provoked another telegram from Milner on 22 December, 1920, which stressed the need to maintain the *status quo* until another general election was held in 1923. Only after that could Responsible Government be granted before October 1924. The settlers became agitated over what they regarded as unnecessary delay, and Milner resigned from the Colonial Office.

Luck was always on the side of the settlers. Buxton retired from his position and arrived in Britain in time to be appointed Chairman of a committee, known as the Buxton Committee, to recommend constitutional changes for Rhodesia. Besides Buxton, the members were Sir Henry Lambert, Assistant Under-Secretary of State for the Colonies; R. M. Greenwood, responsible for the Treasury in the Solicitor's Department, Lieut.-Col. Sir E. M. M. Grigg and Major W. Waring, M.P.[16] They were to advise on (a) the date and the limitation of Responsible Government; (b) procedure for future constitutional changes; (c) the interim rule of the Company, and (d) the future of Northern Rhodesia. The recommendations were based on information from the memorandum to Lambert of Herbert Stanley,[17] then serving under the Governor-General of South Africa, Prince Arthur of Connaught; memoranda of the British South Africa Company, and resolutions of the Legislative Council. Neither Africans nor settlers were represented, but there is evidence to show that some of the Committee members were pro-settler.[18] A settlers' delegation led by Sir Charles Coghlan later went to London to talk with Winston Churchill, Secretary of State for the Colonies, about the constitutional settlement. They only discussed the question of land, and Coghlan obtained a promise that a land commission would be set up to review the land problem. But they created an impression in Rhodesia and with the British public that constitutional consultations had been held; yet the Constitution had been drafted by Herbert Stanley in South Africa two years previously.

No African had been consulted by the Buxton Committee, although there was a considerable body of articulate African opinion at the time.[19] Buxton was in a good position to implement the ideas of the Stanley memorandum, drawn up on his own instructions. The Committee's first recommendation was for a referendum, which was eventually held in 1922, 'to accept or reject Responsible Government'; the second was for annexation of Rhodesia following Letters Patent setting out Responsible Government or taking advantage of Section 150 of the South Africa Act of 1909.

The concept of Responsible Government differed from what is known in Africa today as 'self-determination' or 'independence'. The settlers were concerned primarily with getting rid of Company rule, which would mean their having control of the police and the armed forces. In essence this was all they obtained, as they already had powers to legislate for their internal affairs long before 1923. The political thinking at the time was for movement to dominion status, which had not long before been acquired by Australia, New Zealand and South Africa.[20] None of these had yet completely cut its ties with Britain. The settlers did not want to move nearer to that stage, but preferred the status given to Natal in 1893. This is what the Buxton Committee believed appropriate for Southern Rhodesia, agreeing that Rhodesia should have Responsible Government in all internal affairs.

The structure of the Constitution in fact changed very little from what had been embodied in that of 1898. The British Government's power to legislate, to intervene and to standardise legislation was withdrawn, except under entrenched clauses. The country became part of the dominions of the Crown, administered as a crown colony with a governor and a bicameral legislature with thirty elected members. The second chamber never came into being, being first introduced only in Ian Smith's republican Constitution. There was no provision for a prime minister with a cabinet until ten years later. The change did not affect the functioning of the judiciary.

Britain retained power to legislate for the colony by an Act or an order-in-council, and to revoke or suspend the constitution. This was confined to the entrenched clauses which could only be changed with the consent of the Secretary of State. They were those affecting constitutional amendments, any law setting up a legislative council, any law designed to change the land laws, and any law that imposed disabilities on Africans which did not apply to persons of European descent.[21] Other entrenched clauses referred to the administration of Africans by the Native Affairs Department and the British responsibility over African affairs.[22] This constitution governed the political activities of the country for thirty-seven years until it was replaced in 1961.

As Stanley had stated in his memorandum, the Committee joined the powers of the Resident Commissioner and the Administrator together into those of a governor appointed by the Crown. The reserved powers usually exercised by the Secretary of State through the High Commissioner and the Resident Commissioner were given to the Governor in respect of the police and armed forces. Previously it had been supposed that these powers were to be used only with the consent of the High Commissioner, but now they were to be used on the advice of the Rhodesian ministers. The Committee also recommended that the Governor be given power to disallow Bills which were not in accordance with the provisions in the Constitution.

The Buxton Committee believed that British responsibility over Africans should not be altered. The Constitution meant to leave the African population under British protection as in all other British African colonies. Paragraphs 61–6 of the Report declared that 'the natives are entitled to be secured in their existing position, and to be insured against discrimination or restrictions.' The position they confirmed was that provided for in the Order-in-Council of 1898 under the African Regulations: the settlers themselves did not oppose British responsibility for Africans, but some were upset at being thought incompetent to 'look after their natives'. F. L. Hadfield argued that the African population would not create difficulties because it was not as large as that of Kenya, Uganda or Tanganyika. In the end, even those who clamoured for taking over responsibility for African affairs accepted the imperial responsibility on all matters affecting Africans. Churchill argued that it was necessary for the protection of both black and white. Some of the participants in the rebellion were still alive, and the British Government remained fearful of a recurrence of the 1896–7 bloodshed. Article 46 of the Constitution was framed to provide for action by Britain against any future revolt.[23] The settlers' leaders believed it was necessary to accept the British policy of retaining control over African affairs. Sir Charles Coghlan told the Southern Rhodesian Legislative Council on 12 May, 1920:

> We could carry on the conditions given to us by the British South Africa Company, and we should submit to all the guarantees which the imperial government might choose to lay down in that respect. We should be content with the authority over the natives given to the British South Africa Company today.

The question of joining the Union was solved by a referendum which resulted in 8,744 votes for Responsible Government and 5,989 votes for union. Even though the British Government would have preferred to see Southern Rhodesia join the Union, they were more sympathetic to the arguments of the settlers than the settlers themselves realised. After Winston Churchill took over from Lord Milner in 1920 as Secretary of State, the settlers felt that they would receive a more sympathetic hearing.[24] Their feeling was correct. Churchill was impressed by the settlers' continued reference to their desire to remain as part of the British Empire; their loyalty was in sharp contrast to the attitude of the Nationalist Party in South Africa, which was opposing Smuts' policy of continued association with the Empire.[25]

After the draft constitution of the Buxton Committee had been made known in Southern Rhodesia, and the alternative of joining the Union had been rejected by the referendum, the Constitution came into force in 1923, at a time when the world's attitude towards black–white relations was still governed by nineteenth-century racial attitudes. Only Liberia and Ethiopia were free States ruled by black leaders, but even these were regarded as living examples of barbarism at the time. Acquisition of lands by conquest was still being seriously pursued – Italy was still bent on the capture of Ethiopia. In Europe itself, wars were still going on in the early 1920s: in Russia, between Greece and Turkey, and in the case of the French, invasion of the Ruhr of 1923. Ethiopia had to battle for its inclusion in the membership of the League of Nations. The British Government led those who objected to her inclusion because 'the character of the Ethiopian Government and conditions prevailing in that wild land of tyranny, slavery and tribal war were not consonant with membership of the League.'[26]

When Southern Rhodesia was granted Responsible Government, it did not occur to anyone that Africans should take part in that government with the settlers. It was clearly understood that the cultures of the two racial groups were incompatible. The provision left for the protection of the Africans was the best that could be envisaged at the time.

All the constitutional changes made by Britain in Africa before the Second World War took settlers' interests into account. While Britain could tolerate one of her own officials sharing responsibility with Africans, an ordinary settler was not expected to sit side by side with an African. The attitude was clear in the Central African and East African territories. Southern Rhodesia in 1918 was the only colony which had a white population of as many as 30,000. Its constitutional changes advanced beyond those of Nyasaland, which had fewer than 2,000 whites, and Northern Rhodesia, which had 2,000 at that time. The Rhodesian settlers obtained anything they demanded from the British Government. In East Africa, Ken-

ya's constitutional development advanced beyond that of her neighbours, Tanganyika and Uganda. By 1918 Kenya's settler population was 9,000, the second in size only to Southern Rhodesia in all
Africa outside South Africa. The African population stood at
2,500,000 while there were 25,000 Asians. Constitutional changes
in Kenya by 1918 introduced a legislative council of thirty members;
eleven elected Europeans, two elected Asians and seventeen members nominated by the Governor. Two nominated missionaries
represented African interests, Africans themselves only entering the
Council in 1944. As in Rhodesia, power was given to the settlers,
while the Africans, with all their large numbers, were left out of
power. In Uganda and Tanganyika, where there were 1,000 and
2,000 settlers respectively, there was little racial conflict, and power
remained in the hands of the governors and officials.

In West Africa there were no white settlers, and constitutional
development before the Second World War was even smoother.
In Nigeria Africans were represented by six chiefs out of thirty-five
members of the Legislative Council, while in the Gold Coast (Ghana)
there were six Africans in the Legislative Council, comprising three
chiefs and three 'middle-class' Africans from coastal towns. The
remaining fourteen were officials. The population of the Gold Coast
was 2,000,000 Africans and 1,500 white officials, missionaries and
traders.

At the Southern Rhodesian constitutional talks of 1923, the
question of African representation was not considered; Britain
believed that Rhodesia was going to be part of South Africa, and
that it was the first British possession in Africa, colonised in the
nineteenth century, to be created a dominion; and they thought
that Kenya and Northern Rhodesia were going to follow the Southern Rhodesian example.

(ii) *The Franchise*

The franchise legislation has been changed only five times since
1898: in 1912, 1951, 1957, 1961 and 1969. The basic aim of the
governments responsible seems to have been to minimise the
African presence on the voters' roll to the point of insignificance.
This must be why it is based on property and educational qualifications. Today the education requirement is no longer the prohibitive factor to the Africans that it was in 1898 when it was first
introduced; it is the financial requirement that continues to be the
barrier to African franchise.

The electoral laws of Southern Rhodesia were based on the old
Cape franchise, which was itself based on property ownership.
Like most political institutions, the franchise was introduced in the

1898 Constitution. The five amendments were made necessary by the growth in income of the African population. Once Africans appear to have enough wealth to qualify for the franchise, the qualification is raised.

The first elections held in Rhodesia in 1898 were heavily weighted in favour of the interest of miners and farmers (most settlers at the time had these occupations). Settlers were always considered first in any electoral laws that followed. At no other time in history has Britain given such an advanced constitution to such a small population as it gave to Southern Rhodesia in 1898. Power was given to only 13,365 people. Britain, and even the settlers, thought that the Constitution was in the interests of Africans and would prevent the recurrence of rebellion, but today the former claim is exposed as unreal. Nearly all the main areas were empty of white people; the Africans who dominated these areas then, as they still do, were deprived of their independence and placed under the paternalistic rule[1] of the British Government helped by the Native Affairs Department.

DISTRIBUTION OF POPULATION IN 1898
(from Director's report 31 March, 1898)

MASHONALAND

    Africans: 301,828

    Europeans: 2,500 in Salisbury, 1,330 in Umtali, 200 in Victoria, 500 in Melsetter.
                Total of Europeans, 4,500.

MATABELELAND

    Africans: 148,073

    Europeans: 8,000 in Bulawayo (the biggest settlement because of the siting there of road and rail routes), 800 in Gwelo, 35 in Tuli.
                Total of Europeans, 8,835.

Up to 1923 the two-member electoral districts conducted their elections under the franchise qualification based on the Cape system. This required the would-be electors to be males of twenty-one years of age, British subjects by birth or naturalisation, to have taken an oath of allegiance, and to have occupied a house of £75 p.a. rateable value for six months. An alternative was that any male who owned a mining claim would qualify. Another qualification was for males whose wages were more than £4 3s. 4d. a month (£50 p.a.) The literacy requirement was simpler than what followed in 1912 and thereafter. All the claimant was required to do was to write his name, address and occupation. The power to vary the franchise was vested in the Secretary of State through the High Commissioner.

The franchise seems simple enough, yet it was a complicated one for those days. The people who fashioned it were well aware that Africans could not qualify. No African owned a farm, a mine or a house worth £75 p.a. at that time. They were mainly labourers on the farms and in the mines, earning between 10s. and 30s. a month.[28] It took Africans three months of labouring in the mines and on the farms to be able to raise the money for the hut tax, which was 10s. up to 1904 and £1 after that date.[29] Yet, by 1906, fifty-one Africans had registered as voters. These were missionaries and teachers who were being brought into the country from South Africa by white churches. Some of them were Fingos who came with the first settlers in the 1890s. These fifty-one were then regarded as a threat, and desperate attempts were made to introduce a law which would exclude the registration of African voters altogether in the future. This could only be achieved with the co-operation of Lord Selborne, then High Commissioner, but after confidential consultation with him, the idea was dropped.[30] Fourteen years of a secret franchise war against Africans culminated in a victory for the settlers in 1912 when the franchise settlement was ultimately raised to double its 1898 level. The change affected the monetary qualifications rather than any other requirement, as changes still do. The value of the house to be occupied for six months prior to registration was doubled from £75 to £150 p.a., and wage requirements were doubled from £50 to £100 p.a. The mining claims provision remained the same. Instead of writing only his name, address and occupation, according to the 1912 requirements, the claimant filled a form in for himself. One would have thought those qualifications were adequate to keep power in the hands of the whites, even up to the present day. But, even then, the settlers were determined to get rid of the 'native franchise' altogether.[31]

At this time African income had not improved much from the levels of 1898. Wages were between 1s. and 1s. 4d. a day, and 6d. a day for boys under fourteen years of age. This franchise lasted from 1912 to 1951[32] which means that the income of Africans remained far below £100 p.a. for thirty-nine years. Only in 1955 had it risen to an annual average of £72.

Four sectors of the economy dominated the voters' roll, with 7,089 out of 9,502 in 1914: industry (1,921), farming (1,824), commerce (1,811) and mining (1,533). The rest of the voters were in government service (625), police and volunteers (431), religious orders (107), professional (458), railways (634) and miscellaneous (158), a total of only 1,413. The need for cheap African labour in

the first four sectors of the economy explains why they, and especially farmers and miners, dominate Rhodesian politics up to this day.

The Land of Milk and Honey

In discussing the constitutional problems of Rhodesia the issue of
immigration cannot be left out. It is central to the whole issue, as
it is the immigrant race that holds political, economic and social
power. The opening of Rhodesia to immigration was established
as one of the aims of the Charter of 1889.[33] Lobengula had never
conceded to Rudd the right of settlement, any more than he had
signed away his land rights. Yet the idea of making Rhodesia a
white man's country was spread in Britain even before Lord Salisbury and his colleagues gave Rhodes the Charter. *The Times* of
15 October, 1889, likened the country to Canaan after the wilder-
ness, because it was 'flowing with milk and honey'. It further declared that

> its numerous rivers are either flowing, or have plenty of water
> in them; there is, too, abundance of cattle and corn and wood,
> and, above all, it is very rich in gold, copper, iron and other
> minerals. Fever is unknown and white children could be reared,
> which is a *sine qua non* in a country if it is to be colonised by white
> men.

Glorious pictures of the country were drawn from time to time by
visitors to Matabeleland such as F. C. Selous, Lieutenant Maud
and Lieutenant Haynes; the last-named had said the country
was 'the best land in South Africa' and 'healthy for Europeans'.
Selous had written about the country in the *National Geographic
Society's Magazine* in 1880, describing its beauty, and in the book he
published after his visit to the country in 1878 he was even more
romantic.[34]

The spirit of the pioneers must have been inspired by the type of
publicity which made them feel that Rhodesia was another Canaan.
The growth in the number of immigrants was faster than in any
other British colony in Africa. Until 1920 an intensive campaign
was conducted by the British South Africa Company to attract
settlers to Rhodesia. This policy was continued by the Responsible
Government after 1923. The settlers in Rhodesia insisted that 'an
increase by British immigration of the white population is a vital
matter to the progress of Rhodesia.'[35] Mrs Jollie wrote:

> What we want is to take the men who are crowded off the land
> in the small, well populated British Isles and put them on the
> land in the sparsely populated, vast Dominion.[36]

South Africans, like other Europeans, were not very much wanted because of the resurgence of Afrikaaner nationalism during and after the First World War, and also because their quality was said to be poor in comparison with the Briton, 'brought up in the cold, invigorating British climate and without the influences inseparable from a country with a black population.' The cry was 'We want more British blood.'[37]

The demand for settlers up to 1920 could have been due to a genuine desire to increase the white population in order to accomplish dominion status. Even the British Government supported and encouraged this policy. Lord Milner believed that the 'steady influx' of immigrants would bring about the successful creation of a white dominion in Africa. What was more, the great majority were soldiers demobilised after the First World War. By 1920 the population stood at 32,000 whites and 750,000 Africans, with 11,000 voters. But, as the following table shows, emigration was as heavy as immigration, a tendency which remains up to this day, when the intake is politically inspired to boost white numerical power against that of Africans.[38]

	Immigration	Emigration	Net Loss	Net Gain	British troops
1916	14,412	15,288	876	—	—
1917	20,470	19,212	—	1,258	244
1918	19,305	17,479	—	1,826	131
1919	23,881	22,969	—	912	236

Thus the policy was not a success. Most of those who came into the country did not stay long. The present composition of the population in Rhodesia indicates quite clearly that the policy failed, but failure was only realised by British Governments in the 1930s. The United Kingdom's responsibility for troops in the process of demobilisation was satisfied by sending them to Southern Rhodesia; Milner said they were to be consulted about constitutional changes.

The growth of the white population slackened over the next twenty years, growing between 1920 and 1940 by only 35,000 to a total of 65,000, while the Africans became 1,390,000. The Second World War came at a time when it had become obvious that a white dominion could not be formed in Southern Africa. The growth of Afrikaner nationalism and the stability of the Rhodesian Government led Sir Godfrey Huggins, later Lord Malvern, to rule out any idea of a federation with South Africa. Instead, there was a great demand among settlers for a federation with the northern territories of Northern Rhodesia and Nyasaland, with Southern Rhodesia as senior and dominant partner.

In all Southern Africa, there is a general sense of racial insecurity among the European population, hence the anxiety to increase the rate of immigration. South Africa is now concentrating on the continent of Europe, especially Holland, Germany, France and Italy. English-speaking people are accepted with reservations because of their tendency to join the United Party. However, both in Rhodesia and South Africa all new residents are immediately absorbed into the white community united in the fight for the survival of 'civilisation'.

(iii) *The Land Problem*

The land problem is one of the most acute of all the problems of Southern Rhodesia, and has been so since 1900. Once the gold fever, which was a preponderant cause of the occupation of 1890, had subsided (it being realised that there was very little gold), the settlers turned to farming. As more settlers came into the country, agitation for land increased. The Company claimed the right to ownership of land. This right was challenged by settlers, and the Anti-Slavery and Aboriginal Protection Society (A.P.S.) also challenged it on behalf of the Africans. The resulting case was heard in London by the Judicial Committee of the Privy Council (it was brought in 1914 but only decided in 1918 owing to the war).

Judgement was given that 'the ownership of the land in Southern Rhodesia is not vested in, and has never been acquired by, the British South Africa Company.'[39] The power to dispose of the land was possessed by the Company by virtue of the authority conferred upon it as a governing body in the territory. This entirely predictable decision deprived the Company of power and conferred the land on the British Crown. The settlers benefited from the decision because they immediately rushed to buy the unalienated land, which was selling at between 13s and 14s per acre.

The significant point is that Africans were left out of land ownership altogether. The Privy Council declared that 'whoever owns' the lands not yet sold to white settlers, 'the natives do not.'[40] This decision was based on the English law of ownership and conquest, which had no relevance whatsoever to the African system of land tenure, a correct version of which had been given to the Privy Council by Leslie Scott, K.C., M.P., counsel representing the Africans in the Land Case. Ignoring this, the Privy Council discovered that the Company had no right to the ownership of land; and yet the Charter of 1889 had provision 'to grant lands for terms of years or in perpetuity, and either absolutely or by way of mortgage or otherwise.'[41] This had, of course, been drafted before the Lippert Concession of 17 November, 1891, and before the Matabele War of 1893, as a result of which the Company and the British Government claimed ownership of land by right of conquest. The decision of the Privy Council was based on this right, assuming that any form of conquest in Rhodesia was on behalf of the Crown.

The repercussions of this decision upon the Africans were serious. They ceased to be on their land by right, and the land which was ultimately reserved for them under the Order-in-Council of 1920 was held to be a favour for which they were supposed to be grateful. The setting up of the Native Reserves Commission in 1915 and the inclusion of its findings in the 1923 Constitution under the entrenched clauses, was regarded by Britain as an act of good statesmanship and humanitarianism for which Africans were expected to be grateful for many years to come.

The establishment of the Land Commission under Morris Carter, and the Land Apportionment Act of 1930, brought the maximum satisfaction to Rhodesian and British politicians as well as to missionary bodies. In Chapter II an attempt will be made to show why their satisfaction was misplaced, and why the reverse of their intentions was achieved. The Order-in-Council only legalised the allocation of land that had already been carved out since 1890; the fertile areas were taken over by whites before the First World War.

The only advantage that Africans gained from the Privy Council decision was that the rent which the Company had levied on African farm squatters was discontinued, but the settlers buying land obtained the right to levy rent on the Africans who had been living on it already. Heavy rents were sometimes imposed for permission to remain on land now suddenly owned by settlers; a single kraal was charged up to £300 for permission to remain in its ancestral home.

Ignorance of the nature of the social, economic and political life of the Africans accounted for those errors in decision and judgement, made in Britain and by settlers in Rhodesia, that were not simply the result of human selfishness. Even the missionaries and the officials of the African Affairs Department who claimed to know the Africans made errors of judgement. The fact that Rhodesia remained the only British colony in Africa and rebelled against the Crown is sufficient evidence that errors were made in its constitutional development.

The Land Apportionment Act highlights the errors made in the days before African nationalism had come to the surface. Even a leading socialist of the day, Lord Passfield (Sydney Webb), was prepared as Colonial Secretary in the MacDonald Government to compromise his egalitarian philosophy to appease settlers who wanted more land than the Africans, despite the disproportion in the population. After the Land Apportionment Act was passed in 1931 the allocation of land stood as follows:

	1931 (acres)	1962 (acres)
European areas	49,149,000	35,384,000
Native reserves	21,600,000	21,020,000
Native purchase areas	7,465,000	4,216,000
Special native areas	—	19,150,000
Unassigned or unreserved	17,793,000	5,416,000
Wankie Game Reserve	—	3,324,000
Forest area	591,000	6,650,000
Undetermined	88,000	—
TOTALS	99,686,000	96,610,000

REFERENCES

1. T. O. Ranger, *Revolt in Southern Rhodesia 1896–7*, Heinemann, London, 1967. See also the remarks of F. C. Selous, *Sunshine and Storm in Rhodesia*, Cassell, London, 1896, that the rebels were 'monsters in human shape, that ought to be shot down mercilessly like wild dogs or hyenas, until they are reduced to a state of abject submission to white man's rule'. This white attitude has been maintained up to the present day.

2. C. Palley, *The Constitutional History and Law of Southern Rhodesia*, p. 33.

3. Article 24, Subsections VI, VII and VIII. The argument does not seek to dispute the legality of the Concession, but to question the basis for the British Government's assumption that it could confer such powers on the British South Africa Company. As to the Lippert Concession, the Report of the Judicial Committee of the Privy Council declared in 1918 that it was valueless as a commercial title to land. See the Anti-Slavery and Aboriginal Protection Society pamphlet *The Colonial Office and Native Policy* by J. H. Harris.

4. For details of this Concession see Stafford Glass, *The Matabele War*, Longmans, London, 1968, pp. 31–3.

5. T. O. Ranger, *Revolt in Southern Rhodesia*; and F. C. Selous, *Sunshine and Storm in Rhodesia*.

6. For numbers of those killed, see Leys, *European Politics in Southern Rhodesia*, Clarendon Press, Oxford, 1959, p. 7.

7. F. C. Selous believed that the deceit of spiritualist mediums contributed to the revolt, cf. *Sunshine and Storm in Rhodesia*.

8. The same Act has been amended several times to meet the changing

political exigencies of the times to control the Africans in 1902, 1910, 1928, 1959 and 1964.

9. Articles 50 and 51 of the 1898 Constitution. The impounding of cattle from the Ndebele following the 1893 conquest interfered with the *lobola* custom, in which cattle were used both in Mashonaland and Matabeland in marriage negotiations. It was believed that the impounding showed a lack of respect for African custom, and that this was one of the causes of the revolt.

10. Part I, Section 6, of the Southern Rhodesia Native Regulations Proclamation No. 4 of 1902, and No. 55 of 1910, read: 'Reserve means lands the property of the British South Africa Company set apart for the purpose of native settlements exclusively'.

11. There were seven elected and five nominated members. The Company's administrator had a casting vote.

12. Order-in-Council No. 47 of 1914.

13. In 1912 the white population stood at 24,000, and the African population was estimated at 750,000.

14. Natal had gained Responsible Government in 1893 with a population of 47,000 whites, 41,000 Indians, and 456,000 Africans, and managed well until the Union in 1910; Rhodesia, it was argued, could do the same.

15. Beer, *Some African Questions at the Peace Conference*, Macmillan, New York.

16. Committee from 17 March to 12 April, 1921, Director's Report, 31 March, 1922.

17. Stanley to Lambert, 21 July, 1920. The Buxton Committee referred even details to Stanley. The Southern Rhodesia Letters Patent 1923 are almost identical to the memorandum. ('Rhodesia Committee much impressed with your memorandum of July 21, 1920, especially reference to 1. safeguards for natives, 2. dealing with land.' C.O.417/658.)

18. Buxton's speech in Salisbury and Bulawayo. At the Colonial Office Sir Henry Lambert was actively hostile to representatives of the Africans See Chapter II.

19. T. O. Ranger, *The African Voice in Southern Rhodesia*, Heinemann, Nairobi, 1969.

20. The framers of the Southern Rhodesia Letters Patent of 1923 hoped that Rhodesia would one day join the Union of South Africa.

21. Southern Rhodesia Constitution Letters Patent, 1 September, 1923, Articles 28–31.

22. Ibid., Articles 39–47.

23. Article 46 read: 'In case of a revolt against the Government, or other misconduct committed by a native chief or tribe, the Governor in Council may, with the approval of the High Commissioner, impose a reasonable fine upon the offender.'

24. F. L. Hadfield declared at a public meeting in Bulawayo that 'so far I have not heard any weighty objection to our proposal', *Bulawayo Chronicle* 5 February, 1921. He went on to say that Churchill was 'easier than Lord Milner'.

25. Brian Bunting, *The Rise of the South African Reich*, Penguin, 1960. The

Nationalist Party had just been founded, and their paper *Die Burger* attacked Smuts for being an 'imperialist lackey'.

26. W. S. Churchill, *The Gathering Storm*, Cassell, London, p. 149.

27. The Chief Native Commissioner's Report of 31 March, 1898, said: 'The natives, generally speaking, are exceedingly well behaved, but like children, require careful watching to be kept well in hand, and firmly but justly treated.'

28. See C.N.C. Report on African in the Director's Report, 30 September, 1897.

29. Colin Leys, op. cit., p. 101.

30. For methods and tricks devised to exclude Africans from the franchise, see Palley, op. cit., p. 170.

31. Palley quotes their leader, who told the Southern Rhodesia Legislative Council in 1912 that the first act of Responsible Government in the country would be to take away the franchise from the natives. Op. cit., p. 171.

32. Details of the subsequent franchise amendments will be discussed in Chapter IV.

33. One of the aims declares 'and to the opening up of the said territories to the immigration of Europeans'; and Article 24, subsection vii reads: 'to settle any such territories and lands as aforesaid and to aid and promote immigration'.

34. F. C. Selous, *A Hunter's Wanderings in Africa*, Macmillan, London, 1881.

35. Ethel Colquhoun Jollie, *The Future of Rhodesia* (pamphlet), Melsetter, 1917, p. 8.

36. Ethel Colquhoun Jollie, p. 9.

37. *British Policy on Responsible Government*, memo to the B.S.A. Co., 22 December, 1920, C.O. 417/653.

38. See Chapter VI.

39. *Mr. Podsnap and the Sacred Trust*, Aborigines Protection Society, 1918, p. 1.

40. *Mr. Podsnap and the Sacred Trust*, op. cit.

41. Article 24, Subsection VIII.

CHAPTER II

THE LAND QUESTION AND THE EARLY POLITICAL PRESSURE GROUPS

(i) Farmers

Up to the present, land has always been the most sensitive issue in Rhodesian politics, and no party can win an election without enjoying the support of Rhodesian farmers. Almost all Rhodesian prime ministers and leading cabinet ministers have been farmers,[1] and the land question has affected most of the racial laws that have been passed since the Land Apportionment Act of 1930. This chapter seeks to view the political history of land, and so to establish the basis of African grievances.

Until 1918, land was purportedly owned by the British South Africa Company by right of the Lippert Concession and conquest. The Company distributed and sold land to settlers, Africans and missionary institutions as it chose. Africans got poor areas as reserves. The soils in most of these areas were infertile and poorly watered, and they were infested with deadly insects and wild animals. After the defeat of the Ndebele in 1893, a Commission of Inquiry set up in 1894 by Rhodes arranged that the areas round Gwaai, Tsholotsho and Nkai should be declared Ndebele reserves. The Ndebele were later asked to leave the Matopo areas because Rhodes had made it his farm, naming the most beautiful part of it 'World's View'. The Africans in areas around Isiza, Fort Nixon, Filabusi, Gwanda and Belingwe were moved from pillar to post, and the same was done in Mashonaland.

Even the settlers felt a sense of injustice on their own account over the land question. It was their grievance over land more than any other factor that caused the settlers to demand the end of Company rule. In 1908, only six years after the death of Rhodes, the settlers started to question the basis of the Company's right to land,[2] feeling, as the Africans had long felt, that the Company was making money on land it did not lawfully own.

European methods of farming in the first twenty years of settlement were not fundamentally different from those of the Africans.[3] As soon as whites took the land reserved for them by Company authorities, they farmed the products on which the Africans lived; they produced maize in Mashonaland, and engaged in cattle-ranching in Matabeleland. Their trade interests therefore clashed with those of the Africans, who had previously been supplying European centres with these foodstuffs. The whites demanded African markets.

'In Matabeleland, where land was drier and the European farms were larger, the competition [between black and white] for grazing areas was much fiercer.'[4] This led to an African exodus from European land – in 1908 when rent was imposed on Africans living on unalienated land, in 1910 when locations were provided, and in 1912 when companies with farms in Matabeleland imposed rents on Africans.

Summary changes were liable to occur to the areas comprising the African reserves. Since the land issue became controversial after 1908, the land originally reserved for Africans in 1902 was reduced to meet white agitation. In 1907 Chikwana Reserve and Gutu District had their 258,200 acres reduced to 140,330. Exchanges, reductions and, in some cases, increases were carried out between 1907 and 1914. This happened sometimes if a mine or rich soil had suddenly been discovered.[5]

At that time it was preferred that Africans should remain on the land sold to farmers, and rent the land by their labours, or by payments in cash. About half the African population then lived on the 73,000,000 acres of 'European land'. According to the Native Reserves Commission of 1915, 405,376 Africans were in the reserves, while 327,777 were on the 22,385,182 acres alienated to whites, and the 47,825,668 acres yet to be so alienated. In Matabeleland especially, the land problem was acute. Out of the total African population of 152,227, the number that lived in areas designated as European was 86,996. These paid a total of £30,000 a year in rent to absentee landlords.

For it was the land with most Africans on it that sold best. Europeans simply bought land and disappeared back to Europe, leaving agents to collect their rents. A farmer with 5,000 acres occupied by 500 to 600 Africans, charging £1 per head, could make up to £600 a year, even without the additional benefit of causing the Africans to plough his farm. The Africans were paying the money just to keep their families in their own homes. Farmers continued to harass the Matabele tenants up to 1912–14, and when the east coast fever broke out, resulting in the Government imposing restrictions on the movement of cattle, landowners found it opportune to raise rents to pay for the construction of dipping tanks. Others ordered the Africans to leave, 'an impossible demand at such a time',[6] when firm restrictions had been imposed on the movement of cattle. If people were forced to go, they had to leave their cattle behind. As well as these rents, African people were still subjected to an administrative hut tax of £1 per head, plus 10s. for each wife in the case of those with polygamous marriages, a tax clearly designed to force Africans into the money economy. At this time the average African wage was between £6 and £12 per year. 'It is quite evident therefore that in Matabeleland there was very little security of tenure for Africans living outside the reserves, a fact which was soon to have political repercussions.'[7]

By August 1914, the differences between the settlers and the Company had come to a head, and the case was submitted for adjudication by the Judicial Committee of the Privy Council. The latter concerned itself only with the land that had not yet been sold out, technically referred to as 'the unalienated land'; this included even the 'native reserves' where Africans had been temporarily settled. 'Alienation' meant disposal to white settlers.

The settlers' grievances were based not on taxation but on the price of land. They compared that charged by the Company with prices in the Transvaal, Natal, Northern Rhodesia and New Zealand.[8] All these countries were selling at a lower price than the 13s. to 14s. per acre charged in Rhodesia.

Four parties were thus involved in the Land Case: the Crown, the settlers and the Africans all challenged the Company's title. The representatives of the settlers in the Legislative Council argued that the land belonged administratively to them as the potential government of the country.[9] Leslie Scott, representing the Africans, who had been briefed by the Anti-Slavery and Aborigines' Protection Society (A.P.S.) in London, argued that the land the Africans occupied had been theirs from time immemorial, that they never alienated the ownership themselves, and that neither the British Crown, the Company, nor the settlers had any right either by concession, or under any existing legislation, to dispossess the entire race of all ownership of land. Indeed, he said, no such colossal and complete act of expropriation had ever before been perpetrated in British Colonial history.

The Crown claimed that Queen Victoria had assumed complete rights and powers over the territory. The Company claimed that it had a title under the Lippert Concession, and by occupation in their own right and as successors to the full rights of King Lobengula in the lands which he had lost by conquest.

The case revealed some of the aspects of the British occupation of the country that up till then had not been generally known. In particular, the Victoria Agreement had a devastating effect on the Company's claims. Leslie Scott was determined to reveal the fraudulent way the Company had obtained the land. The Victoria document, of whose existence even the shareholders of the Company were unaware, had been signed by Sir Starr Jameson and given to those sent to invade Matabeleland in 1893. First each of the 700 men was given the right to purchase 3,000 morgen of land at £3 per morgen, a much lower price than land was fetching in Britain or South Africa: an attractive bait. Moreover, the invaders were also promised a share of 'the loot' (sic), cattle or money that Lobengula was believed to possess. The account of the 1893 war that had previously been put about was that it had resulted from Ndebele aggression; that the occupation of Matabeleland was a humanitarian mission on the part of the Company, designed to save Shonas who were often raided by the Ndebele. (The Victoria Agreement was produced by Joshua Nkomo and the late Paul Mushonga to the U.N. Special Committee on Colonialism in 1962 to prove how their people had been abused from the beginning.) The hearing also revealed the worthlessness of the Lippert Concession.

The Company lost the case. The Privy Council declared that conquest was no basis for private ownership of land occupied, and that the Lippert Concession could not be upheld. It found, predictably, that the Crown held dominion over the lands, and that the Company was only administering the country on behalf of the Crown. However, the Company was entitled to be reimbursed for the money spent on administering the country from 1890 to 1923.

The verdict brought jubilation to liberals, missionaries, philanthropists and socialist reformers in Britain and Rhodesia. The *Manchester Guardian* of 30 July, 1918, declared: 'The natives have gained the important point that their reserves are no longer in danger of being cut up and sold in the interests of the Company's shareholders.' What most of them did not realise was that the Africans did not greatly benefit from the decision. The verdict merely transferred the land from the Company to the settlers' administration. The Africans had hoped that land would be returned to them, Company rule being regarded as invalid from the start. They were upset to find that the court reverted to the principle of native reserves, which meant yet more removals of Africans to poorer areas. In Matabeleland, the Nyamanda National Home Movement became stronger after the judgement. The fact that these well-meaning people had made the British Government appoint the Native Reserves Commission in 1915 made them

B

believe that Africans would then have land of their own where no settlers would buy them out. African representation of the Africans' case at the Reserve Commission was inadequate. There were, of course, no African representatives; but suitable people such as the Rev. John White, A. S. Cripps,[10] or even independent observers, were never considered. The British Government made a compromise with the Company, and put on the Commission people who were obviously going to recommend what was acceptable to it. The Commission's secretary, H. S. Keigwin, was one of the most reactionary men in the African Affairs Department.

The error made by the white people who represented the Africans emanated from their ignorance of the actual problem and the thinking of the Africans at the time. This trend towards misrepresentation of the African viewpoint continues even in contemporary politics.[11] Up till the 1930s the Africans – particularly the Ndebele, as was shown by the Nyamanda movement – clearly wanted a national home of their own, free from foreign rule. They preferred to rule themselves as they had done before 1893, or as Basutoland, Swaziland and Bechuanaland were being ruled at the time. The concept of reserves, which philanthropists were advocating, was entirely foreign to the Africans. The British spokesman for African interests had in mind the example of the American Indians, and the policy Britain had followed at the end of the nineteenth century of creating pockets of land called reserves: this policy led to the establishment of the Transkei in the Eastern Cape, Zululand in Natal, and the three Protectorates mentioned above. In 1905 Lord Milner had recommended the application of this policy in South Africa.

The Africans themselves were in fact fighting against both the settlers and the Company for their land. Before the First World War the Company had sent all the legitimate heirs of the Matabele kingdom to South Africa to forestall the possibility of any political influence being exercised in future by the royal sons. In 1910, Njube, the pretender to the Matabele throne, had died, and his brother Nguboyenja had decided never again to speak to anyone.[12] The leadership of Matabeleland had then been taken over by Nyamanda, the eldest son of Lobengula,[13] who had twice personally experienced being evicted from his home, each time because it had been turned into a white farm. Nyamanda was followed by the former *indunas* of his father, most of whom had been at the *indaba* of 1896, and had felt dissatisfied with the decisions made there. Nyamanda believed that he and his *indunas* could raise enough money to buy back the whole of Matabeleland and re-establish their old rule. In the struggle he sought the support of the educated Ndebele, such as clerks, teachers and church ministers. He eventually obtained the aid of solicitors in Pretoria and Johannesburg, and sent representatives to the Peace Conference in Paris, and to the British Government.[14]

Nyamanda's tactics of pressurising the British Government by correspondence and petitions suffered many set-backs. Philanthropists abroad, including the A.P.S., had made the Ndebele feel that the King of England was prepared to listen to their grievances over land, and the Ndebele were determined to make the King see their point of view. An opportunity arose in August 1921 when Prince Arthur of Connaught, the new High Commissioner for the Rhodesias and the Protectorates, also Governor-General of South Africa, visited Bulawayo.

Nyamanda invited other Ndebele leaders to accompany him to put their case before the Prince, who happened to be the King's cousin. The gathering was attended by between 700 and 800 people. Many Government officials were present, and 300 chiefs came, most of them participants in the 1893 war, the revolt of 1896–7 and the *indaba* with Rhodes in 1896. Nyamanda and Madhloli were among them. Manjinkila Mkhwananzi,[15] son of Dhliso, who had led the revolt in the Matopo area, spoke on behalf of the Ndebele. His theme was that Nyamanda should be made king and 'dwell among us as son of King Lobengula and be a representative of our grievances'.[16] The Ndebele believed that their coming to meet Prince Arthur was a demonstration of solidarity in their desire to have their own king.

However, Prince Arthur showed that the High Commission was following the lead of the Rhodesian African Affairs Department rather than instructing it to carry out British policy. He told the *indunas*:

'You must accept what I say as a final utterance. I also hear complaints of lack of land. I must tell you that although I have not seen your reserves with my own eyes, I am kept informed of all matters concerning your wellbeing. I know that those of you who have been living on white man's land do not like removing your homes. But the reserves are wide and fertile. They were carefully selected and with very few exceptions they contain good supplies of water.'[17]

This speech revealed the blindness of British policy. It was designed to please the whites rather than the Africans. For Prince Arthur to say 'The reserves are wide and fertile' and then to admit that he had not seen them with his own eyes proved the correctness of A. S. Cripps' and the A.P.S.'s argument that the High Commissioners were not informed about the Africans. His warning to Nyamanda was a reiteration of Company policy:

> 'It is well that people should revere the memory of their past rulers. But I must tell you, as though I were a father speaking to his children, that you cannot go back; that you must go forward. This you can only do under the rule of the Government under which you live, and that rule cannot be a divided one. While the family of your late king will be taken care of, I must tell you quite plainly that this wish of yours cannot be granted, and I wish the Kumalo family, some of whom I am glad to see here today, to realise this.'

This policy was followed to its logical conclusion by the introduction of the Native Affairs Act in 1927.

The effect of all this was to frighten whites in several rural areas. A farmer, J. Wallston, wrote to the Prince on 16 October, 1921: 'Despite Your Excellency's recent utterances of warning to the native chiefs of this territory at Your Excellency's meeting with them in the Matopos, natives Madhloli and Nyamanda of the Kumalo family are again collecting moneys to obtain a kingdom of their own.'[18] Wallston claimed that all the agitation by the Ndebele was due to a fall in the prices of grain and cattle, which was all blamed by the natives on 'the evil machinations of the white men'.

The settlers were concerned by the sense of solidarity which made the Ndebele even refuse to be witnesses in cases where black and white were involved. What was more, several Ndebele still carried guns. There was also continued reference to the notorious death of Major Alan Wilson and his patrol at the Shangani River in the 1893 war. The settlers believed that Nyamanda could easily raise 1,000 to 1,500 men, who might march on Bulawayo at short notice. Prince Arthur demanded an inquiry into the allegations. It was found that many Africans indeed had guns, according to Section 2 of the Native Regulations 198 of 1897, which provided that Africans could have guns 'subject to good behaviour'.

The meeting with Prince Arthur did not pacify the Ndebele. They pressed forward with raising money for the 'purpose of establishing a black king, with blacker kingdom'.[19] Soon after the meeting, £20 was collected to pay their attorney, Msimanga, whom they believed would further their request for more land. The official view over the Matabele National Home was that Nyamanda was being encouraged to do all this by the educated South African Africans, especially the Zulus' lawyers in Johannesburg.[20] This belief stemmed from the attitude that the Africans in Southern Rhodesia were not as advanced as those in South Africa, and so not able to put forward learned and articulate political opinion. This attitude made the British Government suspicious of any petition or representation from the Africans. This, in fact, was a misunderstanding of African society, as often occurs today. The case of Africans in this period has recently been aptly put as follows: 'Whites often said that during this period there was no African voice at all. Conservatives maintained the Africans were silent because they were contented; Liberals complained of the heavy responsibility of acting as spokesman because the Africans could not speak for themselves.'[21] This concept was held more firmly by the British Government than by anyone else. With this in mind, it showed suspicion and disapproval of any ideas expressed by the Southern Rhodesian Africans. Once they had convinced themselves that Nyamanda was being helped by a South African attorney, they ignored all representations from him. It can be seen in retrospect that the Africans were well organised, and were in fact following the political trends in the country and in the world. They pressed for their political rights through many organisations, such as the African Welfare Association, Gwelo Native Welfare Association, the African Workers' Voice Association, the Bantu Benefit Transport Society, the Rhodesia Bantu Voters' Association and the Industrial and Commercial Workers' Union.[22] When Rhodesia obtained a Responsible Government constitution in 1923, the number of Africans employed in commerce and industry exceeded that of the entire European population, as 38,700 Africans were employed, compared to a white population which had reached 33,000 in 1924. Yet all the representations made by their leaders were ignored by successive British governments, a trend still followed today.

Similarly, representations from African ministers, evangelists, teachers and trade unionists on questions of land and constitutional changes were ignored because they were thought to have been inspired from outside by people such as the Rev. A. S. Cripps and John White, who had long been discredited in British official circles for making the Africans demand more than they were thought able to shoulder without the help of the Native Affairs Department. Although the Nyamanda and Matthew Zwimba[23] movements in Matabeleland and Mashonaland respectively were concerned with problems of land, the educated African leaders were concerned with constitutional changes as well: they preferred a continuation of British rule to being surrendered to the settlers. On 9 December, 1920, twenty-five Africans scattered all over Southern Rhodesia sent a petition to Winston Churchill, the Colonial Secretary, protesting against the constitutional changes which they believed to have been geared only to white interests. In the petition they also objected to the Land Commission's recommendations, because Africans had been assigned to 'sandy and rocky' and 'very dry and barren' soils. These soils were unsuitable for cultivation. They pointed out that this was true of Bubi, Wankie, Gwaai, Manzimnyama and Sabi reserves. They argued that the policy of the Reserve Commission of 1915, which had been given effect by the Order-in-Council of 9 November, 1920, was lacking in foresight because it ignored the growth of the African population.

Now, after the Order-in-Council, the British authorities regarded themselves as having accomplished a feat, because they believed that they had caused the landless Africans to have reserves of their own. Most important of all, they thought they had prevented British speculators from buying both the land and the Africans on it. The Africans who did not want to stay and pay rent for European lands were free to move to the reserves, but they could not conceive of a situation where the land on which their ancestors had been born had suddenly become a white man's farm. Even worse than that was the idea that they too had become a source of revenue for the absentee landlord, who charged them £1 per head for staying on the land where they were born. The petition added:

> We are thinking about the future as well. Our people are increasing in numbers and we fear that in a few years they will not be able to find land for agricultural purposes. We would remind your Lordship too that there are many thousands of people outside the reserves who will have to move inside when the land is taken up by white people. Where are these people to find land to plough?[24]

Churchill was suspicious of the authenticity of the petition, doubting whether the Africans had drawn it up of their own accord. He suspected John White of organising them, especially as most of them were teachers and ministers of his church; since Africans were believed incompetent to organise themselves to produce a petition, some one like White had to be responsible. It was Churchill's job to reply to the petition; he referred it to Prince Arthur in South Africa, pointing out that all matters raised in it were dealt with by the Reserve Commission.[25] Then, not replying at all to the petitioners themselves, he directed their petitions back to the C.I.D. in Rhodesia; and a report sent back to Churchill by the C.I.D. reveals the harsh treatment the petitioners received for their political beliefs. Churchill had asked the C.I.D. to find out their country of origin, religious background and employment situation. The C.I.D. went to them in their homes and interrogated them at about 4 o'clock in the morning. It was reported to Churchill that the signatories were leaders of the Bantu Vigilance Society, which aimed at being in time the representative of all Bantu peoples in Northern and Southern Rhodesia. As some of them had been associated with the Ethiopian Church,[26] 'their aims may be mischievous'. The report went on to say that 'as far as can be ascertained, the signatories represent the alien element only in European settlements, and are in a false position in attempting to represent the indigenous and native of the territory.' Churchill felt that this C.I.D. report freed him from the obligation to answer the petition. It only confirmed his long-held belief that Rhodesian Africans were contented, and that those who objected to the land policy or to constitutional changes were foreign, or an element which had been seduced into objection by radical missionaries.

By 1930 Nyamanda's movement had failed. Most of the chiefs who had seen the good old days of Lobengula were dead. Furthermore, two new factors had come into the situation: the penalties imposed by the Native Affairs Act of 1928 were having an effect on African protest similar to that of the Law and Order Maintenance Act of today; and, more important, an educated leadership had come into politics.

(ii) The Anti-Slavery and Aborigines' Protection Society

The main supporters of the African cause abroad were the Anti-Slavery and Aborigines' Protection Society (A.P.S.), and if they had been taken seriously, the present impasse might never have come about. With the help of some of the missionaries, they had conducted an intensive campaign for African land rights ever since the land question came under scrutiny twenty years after the occupation of the country. As a pressure group, their role was similar to that played today by United Nations, the Organisation of African Unity and the Commonwealth.

Their interest in the Rhodesian land case was provoked by the publication in Belgium in 1913 of a book by Professor Henri Rolin. The British South Africa Company and the British Government had made other European colonial powers believe that their native policy in Rhodesia was the best in the world. The Belgian Government, therefore, commissioned Professor Rolin to study Rhodesia in order that Belgian colonial civil servants might learn from his findings. His study[27] revealed something which the British Government and the Company did not expect. He formulated a theory that Southern Rhodesia was divided into two castes: 'Property-owners and white capitalists form one, and the black proletariat is the other. The electoral law was made so as to deprive the latter of all real influence.'

He demonstrated that the attempt by settlers to get rich quickly on arrival in the country led to many atrocities. The Company had confiscated the minerals and the land, and had placed the natural riches in the hands of European capitalists instead of leaving them to those who occupied the soil. He said that the influence of black nurses on white babies created a race of little white tyrants un-accustomed to manual labour, with diminished energy, whose frame of mind tended to resemble that of the slave-owners of old. He argued that the Company's native policy was capitalistic in all essentials and made a native a hired servant; the Company had not evolved any social policy in the interest of the Africans. He showed how the British Government's franchise of 1912 was designed to exclude the Africans from the vote in practice, while the right to vote was admitted in theory. He observed the beginning of the disintegrating African kinship system, and the fact that the chiefs were in the pay of the Government to maintain law and order.

The book provoked great interest among church leaders and philanthropists in Europe. John H. Harris, Secretary of the A.P.S., took it upon himself to study the Company's activities. The result of his study was the publication of a book called *The Chartered Millions*.

Rolin's book was obviously a shock to the British Government and the Company, especially as, even before the Russian Revolution, it was couched in Marxist terms. A further cause of antagonism was that the author had been given royal treatment, being housed in the Administrator's residence during his stay in Rhodesia. Most important of all, their critic was a representative of the Belgian Government, whose colonial policy had been condemned all over the world. In Belgium, however, he earned himself a respected place. He was to be his country's representative on the Mandate Committee in Paris in 1919, and later at the Trusteeship Committee of the U.N. in 1946. For the Africans in Rhodesia, his book helped immensely in that it brought on to the scene the A.P.S., who played such a major part in improving their plight, briefing Scott as counsel to represent them before the Privy Council when it was clear that no official representation would be forthcoming for them.

The *Manchester Guardian* published an interview with John H. Harris on 29 July, 1918, after the publication of the Privy Council's judgement of the Land Case. He declared:

> It is clear that the situation cannot remain as it is left by the decision, and it is hoped that the Secretary of State will give to the Matabele and Mashona natives a secure and adequate title such as will prevent the tendency to move the natives on some-where else in order to sell the lands they have developed.

The A.P.S.'s main concern had been to dispossess the Company of its claim to the right to all land in the country on the strength of the Lippert Concession and conquest, in which they had been successful. The Privy Council had taken away that claim, and the A.P.S. were then left with another task, that of ensuring that the Africans got a fair share of the 73,000,000 acres still unalienated to Europeans, and representation in the Government. The land was to be divided into farms for whites, 'native purchase areas', and reserves. The British Government needed little persuading to provide native reserves. This was something they understood, from the experiences of America and South Africa. It was thought that the same could be done in Rhodesia, leaving enough land for future white settlement.

In this second stage of their fight, the A.P.S. was briefed by the Rev. A. S. Cripps, John White and the Lloyds of St. Faith Mission, Rusape. Their methods covered writing pamphlets, letters to the Colonial Secretary, briefing M.P.s and addressing meetings in Britain on colonial matters about which they felt strongly. One of their pamphlets, entitled *An Appeal to the Parliament and People of Great Britain, the Dominions, and the Dependencies,* gave a vivid account of how the Africans were deprived of their land rights. The plight of the Africans at the time was given a great deal of publicity. The A.P.S.'s activities were making it unpopular with ministers in the Government because the latter believed that with its wild demands for native rights, the Society was making their task of 'civilising' the natives impossible. L. S. Amery, then Under-Secretary of Staff for the Colonies, did not disguise his contempt for their principles. A meeting between Amery and a seven-man delegation from the A.P.S. led by Lord Henry Cavendish-Bentinck, T. W. H. Inskip, M.P., and John H. Harris revealed the Under-Secretary's hostility towards them and towards the Africans. In that Amery was the man to whom the British Government entrusted African matters, his hostility could also be accounted the hostility of the British Government as a whole. The meeting ended with tempers frayed. Amery took exception to the A.P.S. plan 'to raise money from all native communities of Africa under the British Crown through chiefs, missionaries and political organisations', and, predictably, to their claim that 'the money was intended for the Africans of Southern Rhodesia suffering under British oppression'. He told them that their action was a 'monstrous and criminal one'. The A.P.S. replied that the appeal was intended for chiefs of Southern Rhodesia, but it was dropped at the request of Lord Harcourt, then Colonial Secretary, for fear that it might incite Nyamanda to rise against the settlers. The British Government preferred that the A.P.S. should raise money in Britain rather than go and stir the Africans against

the Crown, especially by telling them that 'their kind' in Southern
Rhodesia were oppressed following the decision of the Privy Council.
The Government said this was tantamount to 'a blackmail – to
frighten the Colonial Office in view of the trouble which might be
incurred in those territories'.

When that indefatigable exponent of their principles, John H.
Harris, wrote to the Prime Minister, Lloyd George, requesting a
meeting to discuss African rights, he was directed to Lord Milner
because the Prime Minister could not see the A.P.S. delegation
owing to 'pressure of work'.[28] The truth was that Amery had urged
the Prime Minister to refuse to see the deputation. The A.P.S. had
hoped to raise objections to the composition of the Cave Commission,[29] because the membership was reactionary and would favour
the British South Africa Company against the Africans. They
intended to put forward suggestions that it should be composed of
the principal religious missionary bodies, political parties and
philanthropic organisations; and they wanted to stress to the inquiry
that the Africans 'lost all indigenous ownership rights to their land
to such an extent that no single native owns a square yard of land;'
yet this expropriation was founded upon a concession which, after
twenty-five years of controversy, had recently been authoritatively
declared a worthless piece of paper.[30]

By this stage, their arguments had attracted a great deal of
attention. Churches and philanthropic organisations joined in the
cry for African land rights. This forced Lloyd George to reply to the
A.P.S.'s letter, despite Amery's discouragement. He had to explain
to the Africans the reasons why the Government continued to hold
their land, and why it was found necessary to give Africans a mere
19,500,000 acres instead of all 96,000,000. The reply pointed out
that there were 'no less than 19,500,000 acres especially reserved
for natives in Southern Rhodesia, and since they were only 770,000,
there was considerable acreage per head.' It further said that
Africans were encouraged to reside on land sold to Europeans on
'labour agreements with white settlers, or to stay on as rate-paying
tenants'. The reply missed the core of the matter, which was that
Africans had long believed that the land had been extracted from
them by deceit.

In addition to the problem of African land rights, the question of
constitutional changes was interwoven with land allocation between
black and white. On this issue the A.P.S. argued that the Privy
Council decision had established a principle upon which the Africans
should be treated in the same way as their white fellow-taxpayers.[31]
In the fight for African political rights, the A.P.S. believed that
Britain should confer Trusteeship on the Africans, as in the High

Commission territories – Basutoland, Swaziland, Northern Rhodesia and Bechuanaland. But progress towards Responsible Government would end British protection over the Africans in Rhodesia. The A.P.S. was determined to see this retained after Responsible Government status had been attained. They evoked the principle, enunciated by the Secretary of State for the Colonies in February 1906, that 'there is an Imperial responsibility for the protection of the native races not represented in the legislative assemblies.' They demanded that Lord Milner should adhere to this principle for unrepresented African races, with special reference to the grant of citizen rights and the protection of land rights. They insisted on getting assurances that no political change would be permitted which would place the Africans in a worse position than had been theirs under the Company's rule. On the franchise, they returned to the usual British formula that it should be accorded automatically to all 'civilised natives' on the same conditions as to the settlers.[32]

Unlike the land problem on which the A.P.S. received replies that were sometimes vague and sometimes insulting, Milner cheerfully replied to it on the question of African political rights, assuring them that the principle of imperial protection of Africans would be 'the basis of the constitutional change in Southern Rhodesia.' That is indeed what it became, underlying Articles 39–47 of the Southern Rhodesia Letters Patent of 1923.

After Responsible Government was conferred on Southern Rhodesia, the A.P.S. turned its efforts to fighting oppressive legislation, and to making successive British governments implement their responsibility over the Africans according to the provision of the 1923 Constitution. Three years later the legislature introduced a Bill enacted as 'the Native Juvenile Employment Act, 1926'. This provided for passes to enable boys over the age of fourteen years to seek employment, and for powers of guardianship over destitute African boys of under fourteen years. The Native Commissioners were to be given the power to indenture into the labour market all such boys, as well as children under fourteen, and the power summarily to whip boys 'with a light cane not exceeding ten strokes' for refusing 'to obey any order of a Native Commissioner'.[33] The A.P.S. protested to the Secretary of State for Dominion Affairs, objecting to the Bill, and particularly to the powers given to the Native Commissioners. It expressed its aversion to the drastic powers given to the Native Commissioners under Section 6 of the Bill, which allowed for them to contract a juvenile 'for a period of service not exceeding six months to any fit and proper person willing to engage him'.[34] In a letter to the Secretary of State in the Dominion Office, the Society's secretaries, T. Buxton and John H. Harris, argued that

the Act would enable, if it did not force, youngsters to seek employment without their parents' consent, and that the Native Commissioners stood in danger of becoming labour recruiters, being
enabled to dispose of black youths as they thought fit. They
wondered whether in a country where tribalism prevailed there
could really be any friendless or destitute children. They referred to
the objections, raised in the report of 1911, that Government
employees should be involved in recruiting African labour. The law
clearly imposed disabilities on Africans which did not apply to
people of European descent, thus clearly violating Section 28 of the
1923 Constitution, which prohibited such laws. They called upon
the British Government to disallow the Bill according to its reserved
powers.

The Dominion Office replied that 'the Act was designed primarily in the interests of the native juveniles themselves, in order
inter alia to protect them against such evils as loafing, undesirable
employers, and undesirable companions and surroundings.'[35] The
Minister avoided mentioning the basic issue, namely that the law
was not applicable to white juveniles who were affected by similar
conditions. The labour history of the country justifies the stand
taken by the A.P.S. African births are not registered, and it is
doubtful whether the children were all in fact fourteen years old
when they were recruited into these jobs. In retrospect it is also
possible to see the intention to control and trace back to the parents
a boy who deserted from work or who was accused of petty theft,
hence the clause about whipping.

Within the same year the Prime Minister, who was also the
Minister of Native Affairs according to the Constitution, introduced
in the Southern Rhodesia Legislature the Native Affairs Act (1927),
the real purpose of which was to control Africans who were
organising themselves against oppressive laws. The Nyamanda
movement had then been joined by several educated young men,
and the urban Africans were beginning to take an interest in the
politics of the country. Most important of all, the British General
Strike of 1926 had evoked a reaction in South Africa, and the
Rhodesian authorities wanted to forestall the possibility of it
spreading to Rhodesia by introducing restrictive legislation.

This matter too the A.P.S. took up with the Secretary of State
for the Dominions. It objected to all the principles in the Bill,
especially Section 17, which gave power to the Native Commissioner
to try to punish 'any native who shall have been guilty of insolent
or contemptuous behaviour to, or of failing promptly to obey and
comply with any lawful or reasonable order, request or direction
of, [the] Native Commissioner.' The Bill was designed to strengthen

native regulations introduced by the High Commissioner in 1898 by authorising the Commissioners to try cases of contempt in their own courts, increasing the punishment for juvenile offenders to a maximum of fifteen strokes with a cane, and allowing the trials to be held wherever the Native Commissioner felt to be necessary.

Two principles were being violated by the Bill: first, its application to Africans only violated Section 28 of the Constitution; secondly, it violated the provisions of the Colonial Laws Validity Act 1865 which provided for metropolitan standards of justice in the colonies. That the Native Commissioners were to act as complainants and as judges in their own cases created conditions in which there could be miscarriages of justice. The A.P.S. called upon the Secretary of State to exercise his reserved powers, but as with the Juvenile Employment Act, it failed. The Bill became an Act. The A.P.S. believed it obnoxious for the British Government to allow the passage of laws that would have the incidental effect of turning chiefs into constables over their own people, and that their tenure should depend on good behaviour, a provision which would interfere with the hereditary principle and make them mere government nominees. The most absurd idea contained in the Bill was that of whipping children. The A.P.S. believed the idea to cut across the principles of British justice and civilisation.

(iii) *The Church as a Pressure Group*

The Southern Rhodesian Missionary Conference, founded in 1906, was listened to with particular respect by the philanthropic organisations in the United Kingdom and by the British Government over all matters affecting the Africans; it thus became an effective pressure group. More than any other institution it could claim first-hand knowledge of the Africans. The church in Rhodesia was caught in a cleft stick. On the one hand, it recognised the need to deliver Africans from oppression, yet on the other it could not possibly countenance an African government. Its basic attitude towards black people was different only in degree from that of the ordinary settlers. It denied equality to the African, practised racialism, lived within the settler community and worked hand-in-glove with the Native Affairs Department. Most of the labour and pass laws were enacted with its approval. The church occupied land freely given by Rhodes, and some missions and missionaries owned farms. It was as unpleasant for the church as it was for the Company when the Africans, the A.P.S. and other overseas humanitarian organisations questioned the ownership of land.

Land interests among churchmen were reflected in their political stances. Missionaries could be divided into conservatives and radicals. The conservatives, who were in agreement with the settler government, made up the majority. They were consulted by the British and settler governments, and encouraged to put forward views on how best African interests could be served.

The radicals were led by the Rev. A. S. Cripps, John White and the Lloyds of St. Faith Mission Farm, Rusape. The radicals clashed with their fellow-missionaries, the British Government, the Company and the Responsible Government authorities, putting the Africans' case by means of pamphlets and letters, and briefing British M.P.s, especially those of the Labour Party, whose numbers increased at every election after the First World War. These missionaries worked with the A.P.S. and shared its unpopularity in official circles.

The reaction of the British authorities to the policies of the radical missionaries needs examination. When talk of Responsible Government was at its height in 1920, A. S. Cripps preached a sermon at his Marondamashanu[36] church which sparked off a controversy. He told his African congregation that the church had to fight five-fold evils in Rhodesia: 'forced labour, land grabbing, colour predjudice, the pass law oppression and the failure of men to speak for the under-dog'. The text of the sermon was published in Britain and met with a reaction from the British South Africa Company, whose Secretary, A. P. Millar, wrote to the Bishop of Southern Rhodesia, President of the Missionary Conference, stating that the pass laws were approved by the church, but adding that the Company was prepared to amend them if the church made necessary recommendations. The Bishop, then on leave in England, replied to A. S. Cripps' sermon through an article in *The Times*, accusing both A. S. Cripps and the A.P.S. of publishing 'false ideas' through the press about the ill-treatment of the Africans at the hands of the Company and the European settlers. He paid tribute to 'the sympathetic treatment which our natives receive at the hands of the administrative officials and the white population'.[37] The Bishop's reply was forwarded by Millar to the Colonial Office, who accepted it as a more dependable 'testimony' than Cripps' statement.[38] Meanwhile, contemptuous letters were sent to Cripps, to which he replied that 'the arrest of natives for not having their certificates of registration upon them at all times or seasons, should not be allowed; to have to carry them about in the wet season on pain of fine or imprisonment is surely a hardship.' On the day he dedicated the church at his mission, he told the congregation that he was prepared to give up his farm in the interests of the Africans. This was more than an ordinary Christian sacrifice, and forced the British and Rhodesian officials to visit the farm, because the claim meant that other churches might follow suit.

Sir Drummond Chaplin, the Company's representative, visited Cripps' farm, and in a report portrayed Cripps as a man who was teaching Africans to be lazy. He said there were no roads and no work for the Africans, and that conditions on the farm were primitive. He told the directors of the Company that Hope Fountain Mission was a better place, and 'more civilised'.

Yet Cripps had been able to provoke interest in, and discussion of, the land issue among church leaders in Britain. Resolutions and letters of protest were sent to the Colonial Office from many parts of the country, expressing 'profound anxiety at the manner in which the African native is being deprived of his land rights'. Other districts insisted that they were protesting against 'the complete expropriation of the land from the natives of Southern Rhodesia'.[39] Other demands pressed the British Government to exercise its powers of trusteeship in order to ensure that the Africans got a square deal. The officials of the Colonial Office were so overwhelmed with letters that they decided on a standard reply to any inquiry.[40] The answer, in the form of a stereotyped memorandum, stated: 'There is no question of natives of Southern Rhodesia being dispossessed of their land by the Southern Rhodesian administration.'

The attitude of the British Government against the pressure groups became firmer after the publication of the Reserve Commission Report, rejecting the policy of the A.P.S. and of Cripps and John White in challenging the way land had been acquired by the Company settlers. The Government believed that such claims incited Africans to attack the white population. The British Government had believed that the Report, by recommending that the Africans should have 19,000,000 acres reserved for them, would satisfy those who wanted the Africans to have land of their own without anyone buying it away from them.

Cripps led the attack on the Reserve Commission Report. He objected to its recommendations for depriving Africans of 291,000 acres from the Sabi Valley; he could not see why the Crown should not give the Africans some of the unalienated land since, according to the Privy Council judgement, the land had reverted to the Crown. He objected to the British Government depending on information from the British High Commissioners, who were ignorant of the facts relating to the natives, and creating an oligarchical and isolated class of settlers. He repeated his previous pledge that he was prepared to surrender his farm in the interests of the Africans.[41] Cripps' objections to the report were supported by African leaders in Gwelo, Selukwe, Fort Victoria and Somabula. Even Chaplin, the Company's administrator, realised that the Commission had been unfair to Africans, but no one would admit this publicly. Chaplin noted in a memorandum in March 1920 that 'it appears certain that some of the reserves as defined by the Native Reserves Commission will not be large enough to accommodate all the natives who might naturally be expected to live in such reserves.' The memorandum further stated that considerable numbers of natives would eventually be unable to remain where they were or to find accommodation in the neighbouring reserves.[42]

Letters from the Bureau International des Ligues de Defense des Indigènes in Geneva, the National Council of the Evangelical Free Churches, and the Archbishop of Canterbury touched the heart of the problem.[43] They questioned the integrity of the members of the Reserve Commission and accused them of carrying out the Company's policy. The Archbishop's points were carefully answered by Milner.[44] He pointed out that the 19,000,000 acres recommended amounted to twenty-six acres per head; but he overlooked the fact that this did not refer to arable or pasture lands only. It included rocks, mountains, rivers and other terrain not useful to an individual African farmer.

The Native Reserve Commission, whose findings were rejected by African leaders, recommended that the area of the African reserves be altered to 20,491,151 acres. On the aggregate it proposed that 5,610,595 acres be added, and 6,673,055 deducted, giving a net reduction of 1,062,460 acres. Reductions were made in Matibi, Gwaai and Shangani Reserves. It can be seen today that the African opposition to the findings of the Commission were justified. According to Palmer, 'its personnel, its *modus operandi*, its assumptions and its conclusions were all open to question.'[45] Its chairman Robert Coryndon, later Governor of Uganda, had been an employee of the British South Africa Company until 1907; the second member, Atherstone, was the Company's surveyor-general and had always favoured the reduction of the reserves by 4,000,000 acres; the third member, Garraway, while more inclined to sympathise with the Africans, finally endorsed the recommendations of his colleagues. The British Government ignored persistent demands for the inclusion of a missionary or an official of a philanthropic organisation in Britain for fear that the Company might object (a state of mind which perists over constitutional matters today).

The Commissioners said in defence of their Report that the reserves they had arranged would be much easier to supervise and control than areas from five to ten times larger; that tribalism, with all its objectionable and retrogressive features, would thus be more effectively broken up; and that material progress and education of the natives would be more rapid and thorough if they were kept in closer touch with the surrounding white population. The labour supply would be more evenly distributed and more rapidly developed by closer contact with the source of demand; the tendency to segregation – which they believed to be a futile and even dangerous principle in native administration – would be avoided; a more equitable division of the various types of country and soil would be made possible, according to the different requirements of the native and the white settlers; and the areas would still be sufficiently large to allow the natives to retain their feeling or independence and ownership.

(iv) *The British Civil Service as a Pressure Group*

Throughout the early constitutional development of Rhodesia, the British civil service played a major role in frustrating and obscuring the African case. Paternalism, ignorance, and the general belief that the civilisation of white people placed them in a position of unassailable superiority over Africans, influenced British civil service thinking on Rhodesia. The 1923 Constitution was the brain-child of Buxton and Stanley, and Tait and Lambert were largely responsible for the memoranda which confused people seeking to ascertain the Africans' position with regard to the land.[46] Their replies to such people showed that they were ignorant of African custom and law. It was correct that the Africans never had a title, in the European sense, but not that Africans never had any right to their land. Nearly all the High Commissioners in South Africa were in favour of the settlers at the expense of the Africans. In his time Milner had attempted to be fair, but Gladstone, Grey, Selborne, Buxton and Prince Arthur of Connaught were less so.

Lord Buxton, the High Commissioner who had shaped the constitutional development of Southern Rhodesia, believed that Africans in that country were better off than those in any other country of Africa. This belief was also held by the British Government, the Company, the missionaries and the African Affairs Department. From this premise, Buxton's ideas found their way into the Constitution of 1923. It is difficult to understand, however, why he and the British Government rejected the idea of African representation in the Southern Rhodesian Legislative Assembly, while in the Legislative Councils of the Gold Coast and Nigeria there were already African members. In Kenya, Africans were represented by a missionary, a course suggested by John White for Rhodesia but rejected by the British Government.

The British officials took a pro-settler line, and followed a paternalistic policy toward the Africans; for their information and policy they depended on the Native Affairs Department. The policy was based on the belief that Africans wanted to revert to their 'barbarous life', and it was in their own interests that they should be restrained, by an iron fist if necessary, from going back into darkness. The policy, as we have seen, was clearly stated by Prince Arthur at his meeting with the Ndebele in 1921.

The first Governor of Southern Rhodesia, Sir John Chancellor (1923–9), was responsible for restraining the British Government from using its veto. He defended the Native Juvenile Employment Act of 1926 and the Native Affairs Act of 1928, the effect of which still demoralises Africans today. He believed that segregation was necessary for the comfort and happiness of black and white, and also that Rhodesian Africans were better off than those in South Africa, because they had 21,000,000 acres of reserves.

The pressure of Company officials also added to the Africans' difficulties. They had the extra advantage of being able to criticise their opponents in the A.P.S. and the church on the grounds that most of these had never been to Rhodesia, which made the Company's selfish policies appear more practical that the philanthropic ideas of their opponents.

(v) *The Role of J. C. Smuts in the Political Development of Southern Rhodesia*

J. C. Smuts was respected not only by the British Government but by world leaders. This Afrikaner politician was paternalistic towards Africans, hence he was aligned with the missionaries and the Native Affairs Department. He was respected by the British for forgetting the horrors of the Boer War, in defiance of his fellow-Afrikaners. He was the champion of all the settlers in Africa, speaking for them at the Versailles Peace Conference in 1919, and at imperial conferences. As a member of the Imperial War Cabinet, he had spoken on African matters with authority, supporting settlers in the Rhodesias, Kenya and South Africa,[47] and speaking of the Empire generally with a British sentiment.

The British Government recognised that no constitutional changes could be made in Southern Rhodesia that were unpalatable to Smuts. He was consulted on every detail of the constitutional draft. The native policy introduced into the constitution by Stanley was in essence that of Smuts. Churchill even persuaded the Responsible Government delegation from Rhodesia to accept the idea of joining the Union so that they could be helped by Smuts on native policy.[48] Smuts hated German imperialism because, before the First World War, it had armed the Africans. He declared that British policy 'always tended to study the natives' interests', adding: 'No impartial person can deny that, so far from exploiting the natives for military or industrial purposes, the British policy has on the whole had a tender regard for native interests, and the results have been beneficial to the natives in their gradual civilisation'.[49] His policy was to guide the British Government in Basutoland, Swaziland, Bechuanaland and the Rhodesias. The A.P.S., however, attacked him for his failure to realise that British policy denied the Africans 'self-determination'.[50]

REFERENCES

1. Only Sir Charles Coghlan, 1923–7, the first Prime Minister, was not a farmer. H. U. Moffat (1927–33), Sir Godfrey Huggins (1933–53) R. S. Garfield Todd (1953–58), Sir Edgar Whitehead (1958–62), Winston Field (1962–64), and Ian Smith (1964–) were and are farmers.

2. In 1908 the settlers, under the leadership of Sir Charles Coghlan, asked the Company's lawyer, Bourchier Hawkesley, and Sir Starr Jameson to produce the Company's title deeds. The lawyer replied: 'I am not here to be challenged upon my title.' *Manchester Guardian*, 15 April, 1918.

3. R. H. Palmer, 'History of the Land Apportionment Act 1890–1936' (unpublished thesis, University of London), p. 135.

4. Ibid.

5. In 1911 in the Mtoko district, where no reserves had been defined, 100,000 acres were marked out for European occupation, after the discovery of gold and the resulting influx of miners to the district. Palmer, op. cit., p. 164.

6. Op. cit., p. 177.

7. Op. cit., p. 177.

8. Jollie, *The Future of Rhodesia*, p. 11.

9. According to the 1889 Charter, this was due for revision in 1914, and advancement of the Charter towards Responsible Government was expected.

10. A. S. Cripps, brother of Sir Stafford Cripps, went to Rhodesia as a missionary of the Church of England. Later disowned by the church on account of his radical views, he founded his own mission at Marondamashanu. During the early period of constitutional development in Rhodesia, he was active on behalf of African interests.

11. See the *Tiger* document of 1966 and the *Fearless* document of 1968.

12. L. H. Gann, *A History of Southern Rhodesia: Early Days to 1934.* Chatto and Windus, London, 1965, pp. 231–4.

13. By Ndebele custom, the heir to the throne was the first son born after his father became king. Nyamanda was born before 1870, when Lobengula inherited from Mzilikazi.

14. T. O. Ranger, *The African Voice in Southern Rhodesia*, Heinemann, London, 1970, pp. 64–87.

15. Manjinkila was the father of the present Chief Ngungumbane of Belingwe. Ngungumbane was removed from the Essexvale area with his people to the Belingwe area in 1922, only a year after the meeting at the Matopos with Prince Arthur.

16. C.O. 417/664.

17. *Bulawayo Chronicle*, 13 August, 1921.

18. Letter from Wallston to Prince Arthur, C.O. 417/664.

19. Ibid.

20. 'There appears to be every reason for believing that Msimanga has stimulated Nyamanda in the course followed by him.' H. J. Taylor's letter to the Administrator, 19 November, 1921, C.O. 417/665. A Colonial Office memo remarked: 'A native attorney in Johannesburg is responsible for all this.'

21. Introduction to *The African Voice* series, Heinemann, 1970.

22. T. O. Ranger, *The African Voice in Southern Rhodesia*, 1898–1930, pp. 119–38.

23. Zwimba had organised an independent church in Mashonaland which opposed white rule.

24. Petition of Africans to Lord Milner, 9 November, 1920, C.O. 417/664.

25. Churchill to Prince Arthur, 25 February, 1921, C.O. 417/664.

26. The British Government was even more hostile to Africans who had come from South Africa, most of whom were missionaries, teachers and leaders of the Ethiopian Church.

27. Henri Rolin, *Les lois et l'administration de la Rhodésie*, Emile Bryland, Brussels, 1913.

28. Letter from the Prime Minister's Private Secretary, 27 March, 1920, C.O. 417/655.

29. Set up under the chairmanship of Lord Cave to audit the accounts of the British South Africa Company with special reference to their costs in administering the country during their period of rule.

30. A.P.S. letter to Prime Minister, C.O. 417/655.

31. A.P.S. letter to Under-Secretary of State for the Colonies, 12 January, 1920, C.O. 417/656.

32. In almost all of its correspondence with the British Government, the A.P.S. included the theme that 'for the first time in British history a whole people had been dispossessed of all land ownership rights upon the basis of a concession admitted to be valueless.' Letter to Lord Milner, 17 July, 1920, C.O. 417/656.

33. Papers relative to the Southern Rhodesia Native Juveniles Employment Act, 1926, Cmd. 3076, p. 8.

34. Cmnd. 3076, p. 16.

35. Cmnd. 3076, p. 23; Amery's letter to the A.P.S., 13 May, 1927.

36. Shona for the Five Wounds of Christ.

37. *The Times*, 11 June, 1920.

38. Government memo, 29 June, 1920. C.O. 417/655.

39. C.O. 417/656, No. 17319, 18 March, 1920.

40. Minute from Tait to Lambert, 17 March, 1920. C.O. 417/656, No. 13521.

41. *The Times*, 9 March, 1920.

42. Palmer, op. cit., p. 257.

43. The Secretary of the National Evangelical Free Churches demanded to know why Africans who had 'never disposed of their title to anyone' should buy back the land from the Company. Letter to Amery, 14 May, 1920, C.O. 417/656.

44. Minute of Colonial Office, 417/656 No. 27632. Before Milner replied, the official had decided to take a tough line on their pestering letters. One of them said: 'We could tell them the truth, that the natives never had any title and never had any right. . . . Titles are derived from a system of law and rights from rent and labour, and it is precisely because of the absence of these among the natives that only two have been able to purchase land in the last twenty years. That a very generous part of land in the reserves has been made available to the natives and that H.M.G. does not propose to interfere.'

45. Palmer, op. cit., p. 179.

46. Tait and Lambert framed the ready-made memorandum on land which said 'Why don't we tell them the truth? The native never had any title and never had any right.' C.O. 417/656.

47. G. Bennett, *Kenya – A Political History: The Colonial Period*, pp. 41, 46,

48. J. P. R. Wallis, *One Man's Hand*, Longmans, London, 1950.

49. Lecture on German East Africa to the Royal Geographical Society. 28 January, 1918, reported in the *Manchester Guardian*, 29 January, 1918.

50. Letter in the *Manchester Guardian*, 29 January, 1918, from J. H. Harris.

CHAPTER III

COMMUNITY STRUCTURES AND THE ROLE OF CHIEFS IN RHODESIAN POLITICS

(i) *The Department of Internal Affairs*

The role of chiefs in Rhodesian politics is closely related to their position in the Constitution. They are administrative instruments of the Department of Internal Affairs[1] used in the controlling of Africans in the Tribal Trust areas.[2] This Department had previously been known as the Department of Native Affairs, but the amendment of the African Affairs Act in 1962 brought about a number of changes, one of which was to get rid of the word 'native' in official titles because the Africans resented it. The new titles were the Ministry of Internal Affairs, the Secretary for Internal Affairs (previously the Chief Native Commissioner), the Provincial Commissioners, and the District Commissioners. The Act divided the country into fifty administrative districts, each comprising several chieftaincies. Almost all the officers other than the chiefs are Europeans, from the District Commissioner to the tax collector. Africans are employed merely as messengers and interpreters, as originally provided in the Native Regulations of 1898. Indeed, the only changes from the 1898 situation are that the word 'native' has gone, and the messengers wear a different uniform. The white officials do not properly represent African interests, although they are accepted by Europeans as people who 'know the African way of life.' Even the British Government believed, up to the 1960s, that the Department truly worked for African interests.[3]

The reorganisation of the Department of Native Affairs in 1962 resulted in the separation of three functions: Rural and Urban African affairs; and the former functions of the Department of Internal affairs, such as registration of births, marriages and deaths and the probate of wills, under one permanent secretary; and the administration of national parks and antiquities. The racial limits of this department remain distinct. Only the administration of wills, migration, births and deaths is compulsory, but does not affect Africans except in a haphazard way.[4] The main preoccupation of the Department remains the administration of the many acts regulating African life: the African Affairs Act, African Councils Act of 1957, Councils of Chiefs and Assemblies Act, African Registration and Identification Act, African Tribal Trust Land Forest Produce Act, African Cattle Marketing Act, African Development Fund, Land Husbandry Act, African Marriages Act, African Beer Act, African Wills Act, and African Law and Courts Act, 1937; and the Tribal Trust Lands and Native Purchase Areas. All these Acts operate in the areas specified as African areas according to the Land Apportionment Act.

The original idea of the Land Apportionment Act was that cities, towns and commercial centres were white establishments; it was never accepted that Africans would at any time live in them. The creation of African urban areas was done by the amendment of the Land Apportiontment Act in 1941, dividing the whole country into four sections, European Areas, Native Areas, Forest Areas and Unreserved Land. By 1950 the Native Areas had been further divided into Native Special Areas and reserves, the Special Areas being subdivided into Native Purchase Areas and Native Township Areas. In the Purchase Areas, Africans can acquire land of their own, as opposed to the reserves, or 'Tribal Trust Land', where it is owned in common. In the Native Townships, Africans can build houses of their own and establish an African commercial centre without white residents. These areas are sometimes found within twenty miles of white cities: e.g. Seke Township near Salisbury and Ntabazinduna near Bulawayo.

(ii) *Chiefs as African Representatives*

In order to understand whether or not African chiefs play a political role, it is necessary to view the social and economic aspects of both rural and urban areas designed for Africans.

The Tribal Trust Land, with 40,115,712 acres of land, had a population of 3,199,000 people in 1966. They are under the control of District Commissioners, who are answerable to the Provincial Commissioners, who in turn are answerable to the Secretary of Internal Affairs and the Minister.

Although the Tribal Trust Lands have been protected under the Constitutions of 1923 and 1961, and now under the Tribal Trust Lands Act of 1969, they have always been open to the activities of mining speculators, who, on successfully establishing a mining claim, are free under the Mining Act to make compulsory purchases from the Government and so expropriate tribal land from the

Africans without compensation. Examples are the emerald mines of Sandawana, in Belingwe, the Buswa iron mines near Shabani and the chrome mines near Musume Mission. This derives from the Rudd Concession of 1888, lasting for 100 years, which the Rhodesian Government acquired from the British South Africa Company in 1948. In these Trust Lands there were 225 chiefs and 379 headmen 'recognised' and 'appointed' by the Government.[5] The Government appoints chiefs if they co-operate with the administration, and it is the duty of the District Commissioner of the area to find the most loyal candidates. The appointment of chiefs is easier in Mashonaland because of the collateral system of succession prevailing there, and the District Commissioner is able to play off one eligible candidate against the other, insisting on loyalty to the Government as a prerequisite. In Matabeleland it is more difficult because the primogeniture method is used, and the first son of the chief takes over the responsibility of chieftaincy. Here, once the prospective candidate becomes 'insolent' or 'disobedient' to the régime, it is difficult to sidestep his claim without provoking the hostility of his followers. The collateral system is responsible for the advanced age of some Mashonaland chiefs. From 1966 thirty-three chiefs and fifty-six headmen, the majority Shona, died out of a total of 225 chiefs and 379 headmen. Two of those who died in 1967 were reputed to be centenarians, Chief Sampakarume being 106 years old and Chief Bushi 100. Since the amendment of the African Affairs Act, thirty-one chiefs and thirty-seven headmen have been appointed, or upgraded from the position of headmen. Chiefs are paid according to regulations made in 1965,[6] which put them into two categories. The first category have a following of more than 500 people and earn £420 p.a. The second category have a following of less than 500 people and earn £240 p.a. In addition to the normal salaries, a chief is rewarded in cash for 'personal attributes, his administrative ability, co-operation with the administration, tribal importance, leadership, control and authority over the people'. This bonus is paid to fifty-one out of 225 chiefs, the majority of whom are members of the Chiefs' Council or the Senate, or are 'senior chiefs'. The District Commissioner in the areas where the chiefs live has the power to assess their qualities for extra pay.[7] Only the chiefs who co-operate with the policies of the Government qualify.

Not more than five chiefs are used for all the propaganda work which claims that Africans are represented by chiefs for all political activities. In Matabeleland, the chiefs are Simon Sigola and Kayisa Ndiweni; and in Mashonaland Zwimba, Wata, and now Chitanga after Wata's death. These chiefs have incurred a great deal of hostility both from other chiefs and among the African people in general for agreeing to be used as stooges by successive settler régimes. The stooge chiefs dominate the Government institutions. One finds Kayisa in the Constitutional Council, the Senate, Mpilo Hospital Committee, and the Council of Chiefs. He was a member of Sir Edgar Whitehead's constitutional delegation in 1961 and the Whaley constitutional commission in 1967–8, and he went on the chiefs' tours in 1964 and 1965 to Europe and South Africa. Likewise, honours and jobs have proliferated for Zwimba and Sigola just as, before their deaths, they did for Wata and Mugabe. Each time British politicians and officials visit Rhodesia, the same people are produced to repeat the parrot-cry that 'chiefs and people stand by the Government's policies.'

During the 1961 constitutional talks, the chiefs as a whole stood behind the nationalists. Indeed, the choice by the Government of Chief Kayisa as a chiefs' representative at the conference caused resentment among the other chiefs, especially in Matabeleland. At a meeting held in the Ntabazinduna council hall in January 1961, Kayisa was warned that he was junior both in age and position, and told that the chiefs disapproved of the suggestion of removing the reserved powers. The chiefs wished Kayisa to associate himself with the United Federal Party, whose delegation he had joined, and not claim to represent the chiefs. His confidant, Chief Simon Sigola, sat on the fence without indicating either support for, or opposition to, Kayisa. Chief Dakamela openly said that the chiefs were prepared to accept Nkomo as their spokesman,[8] but the white politicians, having inserted their own nominee Kayisa, took no notice.

Sir Edgar Whitehead's policy was to reduce the number and powers of chiefs because he did not see the usefulness of retaining the African Affairs Department to supervise them. The Department had been subjected to nationalist onslaughts ever since 1951 because of its involvement in the Land Husbandry Act. Whitehead had accepted the *Indaba*'s recommendation in 1960 that it should be abolished because of its backward-looking attitude. On the other hand, the racially-minded Rhodesia Front were determined to revive it, because its reactionary and paternalistic attitude is ideal for imposing policies with a racial bias. The chiefs, with their vested interest in obedience, are the best instrument to employ in forcing the African back into his past.

As soon as the Rhodesia Front took power in 1962, it set itself to increase the number of chiefs and headmen. The 1963 delineation resulted in the elevation of five headmen to chiefs' status, and the creation of twenty-five new headmen. The process continues with great intensity, especially in areas where nationalist activity is suspected. Curiously, their policy is in accordance with the Constitution. When the Native Affairs Department was created by the British Government in 1898 on the instructions of Joseph Chamberlain, chiefs were given the same status as constables, the express purpose being to use them to maintain law and order, administer justice, collect taxes and help to recruit Africans for European employment, thus avoiding a repetition of what had happened in 1896–7.

The Department's administrative concept is to ensure that the Africans are subservient to the whites. When the Nyamanda movement seemed to be threatening the white man's power in the 1920s, the Government strengthened the 1898 regulation. The explanation given then to the Secretary of the Dominions was that 'there is a growing disobedience in matters for which no express penalties are provided, and an increasing disrespect towards officials and Europeans generally.'[9] For this reason, the Southern Rhodesian Legislature was allowed to pass the Native Affairs Act in 1928 without its being vetoed according to Britain's reserved powers. The fears of Moffat over Nyamanda in 1927 are the fears of the Rhodesia Front over African nationalism today. W. J. Carry, M.P., even invoked the 1896 settler spirit while addressing a meeting in 1963, calling upon whites to be ready to do what the pioneers had done in 1896. In the struggle between black and white, the Rhodesia Front takes comfort from the chiefs, especially the five favourites who repeat to them conscience-soothing stories of African 'loyalty to white rule'.

The organisation of chiefs runs from the 'kraal heads' to Parliament. The structure set up by the African Affairs Act was: the kraal heads, the headmen, the chiefs, the Reserve Council, the Provincial Assemblies, the Council of (twenty-four) Chiefs, the Legislative Assembly, including eight M.P.s elected by the College of Chiefs, and the Senate, including ten chiefs elected by the Council of Chiefs.

The ten chiefs in the Senate are also members of the Chiefs' Council, of whose twenty-four members three represent Mashonaland North, four Mashonaland South, three Matabeleland North, four Matabeleland South, three Midlands, five Victoria and four Manicaland. The chiefs on the Council toured Europe and the South African Bantustans in 1964 and 1965. Only five other chiefs joined the European tour. The 1964 group was more representative than that of 1965, but the same 'leading chiefs' were in both groups.

The Chiefs' Council's functions are prescribed by the Councils of Chiefs and Provincial Assemblies Act 1961, which was introduced by Sir Edgar Whitehead, to legalise the holding of regular Provincial Chiefs' Assemblies, which was insisted upon by Duncan Sandys, then Commonwealth Relations Secretary. The chiefs assemble about two or three times a year.[10] The purpose of the Chief's Council is to make representation to the Minister of Internal Affairs about the needs and wishes of the tribesmen living on Tribal Trust Land, to consider any representation made to it by the Provincial Assemblies, and to review and comment on any matters referred to it by the Minister of the Tribal Trust Land Board of Trustees. These powers are purely advisory: the Minister is not obliged to accept them if they cut across government policy.

The Chiefs' Council meets at least twice a year to discuss matters referring to government apart from the role of chiefs in the administration of the country, the control of land in the tribal areas and the judicial system. Such discussions are said to have the purpose of reviewing Bills before Parliament. What actually happens is that an official of the Department of Internal Affairs speaks to the Council on the Bills on African matters which are before Parliament. Those chiefs who understand them comment, and usually comment favourably on the Bills, which are then returned for passage in Parliament. The intention of this ritual is to make the white population believe that the policies of the Government have African backing; yet the backing is really that of the officials of the Department of Internal Affairs. Every Council meeting ends with the chiefs' declaration of loyalty to the Government. The meeting which took place from 20 to 22 May, 1963, was attended by the Minister of Internal Affairs, the Prime Minister Winston Field, the Minister of Agriculture and the Chairman of the Natural Resources Board. The 1969 meeting was attended by officials of the Government, the Secretary of Internal Affairs and his Deputy, three Provincial Commissioners and the Deputy Secretary for Information, Immigration and Tourism, and the discussion was centred on the policy of the Government in the reserves. It is natural for the chiefs, who are mostly ill-educated and all on the Government's payroll, to back the Government in the presence of such important personages.

In 1961, after the constitutional conference, 203 chiefs and 331 headmen met at Fletcher High School near Gwelo to discuss the Constitution and the land settlement, which was due for discussion in Parliament in mid-May. The meeting was held in secrecy, with police posted at the gates. Sir Edgar Whitehead came to the meeting himself, with H. J. Quinton, Minister of Native Affairs, and R. M. Cleveland, Minister of Local Government and African Education. The official report stated that chiefs had decided to form a Chiefs' National Council, to ban nationalists in the reserves and to accept the constitutional proposals. This was two months before the referendum in which the European electorate voted for the Constitution. The chiefs who were supporting Nkomo at Ntabazinduna were completely silenced, and Kayisa Ndiweni's approving voice preponderated over all others.

The policy of the Government on land, conservation of natural resources, education and constitutional changes was given to the chiefs for discussion. The 1965 Council met the British Secretary of State for Commonwealth Relations, Arthur Bottomley, and the Lord Chancellor, Lord Gardiner. Afterwards a policy statement was released by an official of the Internal Affairs Department to the effect that the chiefs supported the Government's policy of seeking independence under the 1961 Constitution.[11] Likewise officials of the Internal Affairs Department released a statement in 1965 after the Chiefs' meeting with Harold Wilson in Salisbury. The officials of the same department criticised Mr. Wilson for not paying attention to them but rather concentrating on Z.A.P.U. and Z.A.N.U.[12] After U.D.I. the Chiefs' Council met on 20 December, 1965, and in the presence of W. J. Harper, Minister of Internal Affairs, 'expressed their satisfaction over the firm action taken by the Government'.

The Secretary of Internal Affairs' Report of 1965 defended the chiefs against the accusation that they were paid servants of the Government, claiming that they are in the same position as the Leader of the Opposition, Members of Parliament and judges. He ignored the fact that these people earn their salaries on the basis of 'departmental administration' and qualities such as 'personality' and 'co-operation with the administration'. Judges are appointed by the Government, and do not claim to represent anybody: similarly, the Leader of the Opposition in a democratic state is paid, but he is chosen by his own party and they are not subject to a departmental discipline.

Successive Rhodesian governments have not hesitated to deal firmly with chiefs who defy their policies. Chief Mangwende of Mrewa suffered deposition during the legal existence of the African National Congress (1957–9). Chief Shumba, a former teacher who was president of the Chiefs' Council in 1963, signed an anti-minority -independence petition organised by J. M. Chinamano and N. M. Shamuyarira, and after publication of the story in the *Daily News*, he was forced to resign.[13] The case of Chief Shumba to some extent revealed how chiefs are used for party political ends. The Government Information Department said that chiefs refused to participate in the Chiefs' Council as long as Shumba remained president because he had involved himself in politics; the chiefs did not want

their Council to be associated with politics. Since Shumba had indicated his disapproval of independence under the 1961 Constitution, he had committed his Council against their will to supporting
the African nationalist cause!

Meanwhile, according to the reports of the Secretary of Internal
Affairs in 1964 and 1965, chiefs gave unanimous support to the
Government for its stand 'in demanding independence under the
1961 Constitution'. The 1965 report said that chiefs were impressed
by the firm stand the Government had taken. The obvious interpretation of the reports is that chiefs dislike African politics but approve
of Government politics because they are conducted by whites. It is
difficult to believe these reports as they come from the Government
and not from the chiefs themselves.

The African Affairs Department is unacceptable to most Africans
because of its history. They cannot be expected to forget the system
of forced labour, the passes, de-stocking and all the removals still
carried on today under the District Commissioners. Since its beginning the Department has been run by people who believe in racial
segregation. C. Carbutt,[14] N. H. Wilson, H. J. Taylor and others
who held high posts in the African Affairs Department, were arch-
segregationists.

The Permanent Secretary of Internal Affairs since 1963, W. H.
Nicolle, has been responsible for the current racial attitude in his
ministry and the policy of sending chiefs on trips abroad was his.
The trips ended in South Africa, where they spent most of their
time visiting Bantustans and educational and other institutions for
Africans. After such trips he makes speeches in which he claims to
speak for the chiefs. The Department of Internal Affairs never
allows the chiefs to speak for themselves. This is done instead by
their white 'spokesmen'.

The way chiefs are manipulated for political ends was comically
shown after the talks on board H.M.S. *Fearless*. Following their
tradition of 'consulting' chiefs, the Smith Government sent the
Minister of Internal Affairs to perform this task. After the meeting
he held a press conference to the effect that the chiefs had supported
the *Fearless* talks – for at this stage the régime had hoped to accept
the settlement. When they finally decided against the settlement,
Nicolle stated that the chiefs had *not* accepted the *Fearless* settlement. Smith, disturbed by this obvious confusion, decided to tell
the public himself that the chiefs had not accepted the *Fearless*
settlement.

During the 1969 referendum campaign, Nicolle appeared on
radio and television, and even held a press conference, in support of
government policy. This is not in accordance with the 'civilised'

state system of administration, which adheres strictly to the principle of separation of powers. Dr. A. Palley told Parliament that the behaviour of the Secretary for Internal Affairs was not in keeping with the Rhodesia Front's claim to maintain 'civilised' standards because the use of a civil servant for political comment was not conducive to sound administration.[15] Some M.P.s declared that Nicolle's policy was one of imitating the South African policy as applied in the Transkei.[16]

(iii) *African Councils*

In their political activities, the chiefs invite comparison with councillors in local government. Like local councils, Chiefs' Councils are meant to implement Acts already passed by the legislature. The councils were so envisaged in the 1923 Constitution, whereby it had been hoped to create a local forum only for discussion of district matters of common interest; they were not then regarded as institutions that might indulge in the discussion of national political matters. But no positive step was taken to implement these aspects of the 1923 Constitution until the Native Councils Act No. 38 of 1937 was passed. This version too did not envisage power going to the councils. G. M. Huggins, then Minister of Native Affairs, told Parliament that the aim of the Native Councils Bill was to 'try to induce a little responsibility into the native people'.[17] It was believed then that Africans were too widely scattered geographically to form a central council; but small and powerless councils dotted all over the country would make a resonable start.[18] This could be achieved by using the chiefs and headmen who, he admitted, had very little authority left; he said that the effect of the legislation passed since 1891 had reduced the chiefs and headmen more or less to 'glorified policemen'.[19] The Act of 1937 was the culmination of the persistent demand for this sort of outcome by the Rhodesian Agricultural Union.[20] The farmers blamed the Africans for all the soil erosion taking place in the country, and pressed the Government to do something to change African methods of agriculture. The 1937 Councils Act empowered the Native Commissioners to act as executive officers to supervise Africans in carrying out the following kinds of work: the conservation and augmentation of water supplies, the construction of roads, bridges, dams, contour ridges, afforestation and the care of existing forests, soil conservation, improvements in methods of agriculture, agricultural husbandry, veld management, prevention of overstocking in pastureland and reduction of surplus stock, suppression of disease, destruction of noxious weeds and improvements in the marketing of produce. Most of these were praiseworthy measures, and were to be carried out by the councils. But no council was set up as a result of the Act until 1942, in Mashonaland. Instead, the Native Commissioners were responsible for implementing the Act, and where it related to forced labour, they carried it out as soon as it was introduced. People were forced to build roads, dams, etc., under forced labour conditions. In some cases nominal fees were paid to those who did the forced labour. The District Commissioner recruited the people through the chiefs. It was the aspect which dealt with the prevention and reduction of overstocking which brought unrest in the reserves in the 1940s. In 1947, a combination of destocking and removals of Africans caused resistance in the Filabusi, Gwanda, Belingwe and Shabani districts. B. B. Burombo organised a movement which finally brought the matter of destocking to the High Court.[21] The chiefs co-operated with those who resisted destocking. From 1937 to 1957 the Native Councils operated in a crude form in a few areas of the country.

By 1957 it had become clear to the settlers that Africans would not remain contented with the political situation as it existed. Although the African National Congress was operating only in Matabeleland, the militant Youth League was already active in Salisbury from 1955. The implementations of the Land Husbandry Act 1951 was then causing irritation among Africans in the Tribal Trust Lands: agitation against the Act was heard from Mrewa, Sipililo, Gwanda, Nakai and other places.

The Government of R. S. Garfield Todd decided to reintroduce the idea of the Native Councils Act 1937 into the African Councils Act 1957. The 1957 Act gave much more generous powers to the councils than the 1937 version had done; it covered the whole scale of African local government. This was due to two factors. First, Todd believed that the Africans needed some form of responsibility in the running of their own affairs, and secondly, at this stage white people had accepted that Africans could be good city-dwellers like anybody else. The 1957 Act assumed that the Africans in the various areas would be willing to take responsibility for their own affairs, the element of willingness being intended to induce support for the councils among the educated Africans in the reserves and townships. The lack of general support from Africans in the previous ten years, 1942–52, was thought by the Todd Government to be due to the concentration of responsibility in the hands of the Native Commissioners and the chiefs. Todd knew that these two groups were often reactionary, and unpopular with the educated Africans.

The 1957 Act, which with a few amendments still operates today, provided for the institution of an African Councils Board consisting of the Secretary for Internal Affairs, one other officer of the Ministry of Internal Affairs chosen by the Minister, an official of the Treasury nominated by the Minister of the Treasury, and a person nominated by the minister responsible for local government. All these are white officers. The functions of the African Councils Board are no different from those of any other body dealing with local government authorities.[22] The Act empowers the Minister to establish the African Councils in Tribal Trust Land, African Townships and Special Native Areas under the Land Apportionment Act of 1941. The Minister can only do so in areas outside municipalities or Town Management Boards. Once the Minister has established the Council, power is transferred to the Secretary of Internal Affairs who determines its composition and powers and the scope of its by-laws, and all its other local government functions. He has powers to appoint chairmen and the rights to exclude some chiefs from the position of vice-president[23] and to prevent headmen from being councillors.

The number of elected councillors varies. The District Commissioner is *ex-officio* president and adviser to all the councils in his area. The councils of the African Purchase Areas have no chiefs or headmen; and individual farm owners work together to administer the area.

Councillors hold office in rotation for three years, with those that have served longest retiring first, and the District Commissioner has the power to fill the vacancies with his nominees. The duties and responsibilities of the chiefs and headmen, apart from those of serving as councillors, are to publish by-laws and notices of the councils, to arrest and apprehend persons breaking the by-laws, to collect rates and other payments, and to supply labour promptly for mine undertakings. These powers are part of the law and apply to all chiefs and headmen.[24]

The revenue of the council is drawn from rates, and a large variety of other sources, including various fees, interest on investments and grants from the Government, the African Development Fund, the Tribal Trust Land Fund, the Natural Resources Board, etc. The number of councils rose from fifty-five in 1962 to eighty-eight in 1968. Several have collapsed entirely and others have done so in all but name.

Councils are used as instruments for implementing the Rhodesia Front policy of community development (which is based on the belief that there are racial groups in the country whose culture and social interests are irreconcilable). Smith, however, stated in 1966 that his policy on community development was to promote organised communal self-help and enterprise on two levels. The first level is that of community development: community boards might be recognised in local government legislation and would be able to organise and operate in their own way with the utmost flexibility, provided their activities did not infringe upon or affect other communities. The other level is that of local government, where formal statutory local government councils would operate under the normal disciplines. This concept is expressed in the word 'apartheid' in South Africa, and 'separate development' in Southern Rhodesia. The policy in both countries finds its origin in British colonial rule, which was responsible for the creation in 1905[25] of the areas of South Africa now called bantustans. It was also responsible for the Land Apportionment Act 1930 in Rhodesia and the White Highlands in Kenya. Britain has of course since dropped this as official government policy. In Rhodesia, however, it is being revived, and in South Africa it is being implemented with all the Afrikaner ruthlessness and stubbornness. In Kenya, it was killed by African nationalism. Its colonial origins and unfortunate modern development explain why community development is disliked in Rhodesia, although it is acceptable in independent Africa.[26] By providing money and officers to the councils, the Rhodesian régime succeeds in getting some of its policies carried out. In an attempt to get people to accept the policy, potential leaders are brought to the Domboshawa Training Centre, where 'treasurers', 'secretaries' and 'leaders' for community development are trained. Leadership seminars, home economy courses for the women's group, liaison officers and women's clubs are organised. The seminars are also attended by council chairmen, councillors, tribal leaders, school leaders and the staff of various ministries connected with rural African problems. School boards have been created, with chiefs holding full executive responsibility. Officials believe that there is a sign of weakening opposition to these policies, yet Africans' resistance to the implementation of the community development scheme was noted even by parliament.[27] There were still 150 areas without councils out of a potential total of 300. Despite the vigorous drive by the régime to establish councils, success is not in sight.

The failure of separate development policies is construed by whites as being due to the inability of Africans to do things for themselves. The Africans, on the other hand, believe it is due more to the success of their boycott policy.

Most African states follow the policy of community development to deal with their social and economic problems. Rhodesia's policy in this area is not a new phenomenon developed by the Rhodesia Front Government; in 1962 the Whitehead Government dedicated itself to the 'philosophy, principles and practice of community development as the basis of district administration, local government and technical development'.[28] This declaration was immediately followed by a grant of aid for community development from the U.S. Government, who sent their experts in the field to work in Rhodesia. Community development was defined – by Ian Smith in reference to Rhodesia – as 'the process by which people of each community are given responsibility for their own development through communal organisation, formally and informally, for democratic planning and action. These bodies of communal self-help make their own plans to meet their needs and solve their problems, and execute their plans with maximum reliance upon resources found within the community, supplemented when necessary with administrative and technical advice and assistance, and financial and material aid from government and other agencies outside the community.'[29] Since 1962, the policy has been implemented in conjunction with the African Councils Act 1957, the primary intention of which was to foster the principles of self-help and responsibility and to bring out any latent African capacity for self-management in local affairs. The policy is in practice in certain more backward European countries such as Italy, Greece and Turkey, and in Iran, India, Pakistan, Tanzania, Nigeria, the Philippines and many other countries.

The old ambitions of the United Federal Party in this matter have not been achieved. The Rhodesia Front policy of separate development caused Africans to resist the implementation of community development, because Africans see in it nothing more than apartheid in disguise. The use of the District Commissioners, who have for years been regarded by African people as instruments of oppression, increases suspicion of the Government's motives. Most important, the fact that Parliament is unrepresentative makes it difficult for Africans to believe that its legislation is in their interests. This was true even during Sir Edgar Whitehead's time. The chiefs and other Africans who work for the Government in furtherance of this scheme, and even those who supinely accept community development, are accused of being stooges. Yet in African countries ruled by the majority, community development is accepted as a normal part of life, and indeed the governments of such countries are pressed by their people to provide facilities for it. Although the fostering of community development could have hastened the diminution of paternalistic authoritarianism, African people cannot trust the Government to give them the sort of aid they would give to European-run institutions, such as municipalities, town management boards, peri-urban town councils and rural councils. Since they do not possess a vote to force a government to act according to the wishes of the African majority, scant attention has been paid to

African councils. The result, as we have seen, is that several of them have collapsed, and as usual, the régime blames this on the inability of Africans to take on responsibilities.

In the urban areas community development has followed a study of the community organisation and structure, a delineation exercise designed to study the neighbourhood units which exist in the township, and a social analysis aimed at gaining an overall understanding of life in the communities. This has been undertaken at Dzivaresekwe, Highfields, Kambuzuma, Luveve, Inyazura, Zimunya and other places.

(iv) *Africans in the Urban Areas*

As noted earlier, the Land Apportionment Act 1930[30] was drawn up in the belief that Africans would never live in urban areas. Only a few years later, with the growth of industries, the number of Africans had increased in Bulawayo and Salisbury until by 1936 the total African population in the main urban centres was 45,550. Twenty years later the figure had nearly doubled.

Already in the 1920s urban conditions needed attention. The attempt by Moffat's Government to master the African problems in the towns was rebuffed by the Native Affairs Department and by the missionaries, who felt that these problems were their province.[31] Moffat had set up two commissions of inquiry to look into the conditions of Africans living in the locations of Bulawayo and Salisbury, but the idea was abruptly dropped, leaving the Africans at the mercy of the church and the Native Commissioners.

By the time Parliament introduced the Native Councils Act 1937,[32] it had become acceptable in principle, although not in practice, that some Africans would have to live in the urban areas originally intended for Europeans only. Two factions guided the government of the day: in the reserves, administration of Africans was based on trusteeship (paternalism), and in the cities (European areas) it was under the principles of adaptation, free from paternalism. Only two urban townships were in existence then as homes for Africans, Luveve in Bulawayo and Highfields in Salisbury. Africans working in the nascent industry of the country were housed in locations in Makokoba in Bulawayo and Harare in Salisbury. These were regarded as accommodation for 'unmarried' workers, and provided by employers according to the Labour Laws[33] which required all employers of African labour to provide or rent accommodation for their employees in private premises or in native townships set aside by the Land Apportionment Act 1941. The 1951 amendment of the African (Urban Areas) Accommodation and Registration Act 1966 placed upon local government authorities the responsibility for equipping and maintaining any African urban area established under the Land Apportionment Act. The municipalities are expected to provide both single and married accommodation. The Act provides for fixed rents for all sizes of houses, to be paid by the employer on behalf of the employee.

Africans living under these conditions are supposed to have passes for identification showing that their occupation is legal. Vaccination, medical examination and treatment is covered by the Act; unemployed or self-employed Africans may live in the city for years, without going through the stipulated medical requirements whereby an African, as soon as he finds a job, undergoes a medical examination. Bulawayo city operates a private employment exchange for Africans, and next to its office there is a doctor waiting to examine those who have found employment. As soon as a man finds a job he is issued with a pass book for which the employer pays a shilling a month to the City Council.

African work-seekers are expected to live in hostels established by the Native Registration Act of 1937. The hostels were established as half-way-houses where job-seekers could spend nights and then seek work the following morning. They are open shelters made of corrugated iron. No one takes the responsibility for tidying them or making them sanitary, and people thus often avoid them, preferring to stay with friends. But this is illegal, and the hosts in these cases are the victims of pass raids.

Pass laws are rigidly enforced in Salisbury, Gwelo and Gatooma, while Bulawayo is more reasonable than most of the urban centres. The rigidity of the pass laws causes a bitter reaction even from the less articulate African M.P.s. Sir Edgar's government was slowly reducing the burden of passes between 1958–62, but since the advent of the Rhodesia Front, the Salisbury City Council has resorted to their extensive use. Africans living in its municipal areas are expected, if they want to visit places outside Salisbury, to report to the location superintendent, who has the power to prescribe the period of the visit, or to refuse wives the right to visit their husbands. A child born in Salisbury municipality cannot go to school elsewhere without the risk of having its name struck off its father's card, which would mean children ceasing to be residents within the municipal area, and thus subject to the Juvenile Employment Act 1926 by which the District Commissioner can indenture a child to employment. Girls over the age of fifteen years could be cancelled from the household card in this way, which would mean their being immediately exposed to police raids as they would be deemed to have forfeited the right to live with their parents. The laws make it impossible for people to visit their relations in other African townships after 4 p.m. because by that time the pass office will have closed. Husbands are compelled to leave their *situpa*[34] with their wives while they are at work in order for their wives to be able to produce it to the police on demand.[35]

Under the African (Registration and Identification) Act of 1957, provision is made for a class of Africans who are 'fit and proper' to obtain an identity card which exempts the holder from the obligation to hold a *situpa*. This 'fit and proper' person does not have to cope with the voluminous municipal by-laws which require other Africans to carry their passes at various times of the day. However, he is not exempted from producing it on demand from the police, from an employer or at a bank. Failure to produce it to the police can lead to criminal prosecution. Police often waylay buses travelling between cities to inspect passes and to intercept travellers without them.[36]

Large building companies (e.g. Sir Richard Costain and Johnson and Fletcher), manufacturers and mines provide, though to a lesser extent than in the past, their own accommodation for 'unmarried boys'. In this accommodation, no person not employed by the company can spend a night without a written permit from the compound manager. The companies employ policemen who often carry out raids to find unauthorised tenants. The latter sleep with their employment passes under the pillow in order to prove the legality of their tenancy during the night when raids occur. The *sipekitsheni* (raids) are conducted on the instructions of the compound manager, and their frequency depends on his character. In Gwelo, the compounds owned by Rhodesia Alloys, the Bata Shoe Company and Rhodesia Castings are subjected to constant raids. This was also true of those in Bulawayo and Salisbury. In most cases the wives of tenants are found, arrested and fined for trespassing.[37] People who lose their jobs lose their accommodation at the same time, a rule which has often been used against African nationalist families.[38] Often there are four bunks with two to three beds in each room. Eight to twelve people would sleep in them at a time. George Hartley, M.P. for Victoria, a former administrator of the African townships of Salisbury, told Parliament that he knew of a case where twenty-five people lived in a room meant for four. It was often almost impossible to add illegal tenants, but this still happened quite frequently, as prosecutions revealed. The trespassers turned out to be wives, relations and friends of the legal tenants.[39]

The laws of accommodation are being made by people who believed that Africans are incapable of looking after their own money, a belief expressed in the Rhodesia Front policy of 'civilised and responsible hands'. The employer is given the responsibility for providing accommodation, food in form of rations, and sometimes uniforms. Mines and large companies sometimes built their own accommodation.[40] People are turned out of these, not only if they lose their jobs but also if they are prosecuted under such laws as the Sedition Act, the Law and Order Maintenance Act, Harmful Liquids Act, the Native Pass Act or, before 1957, for possessing 'European' liquor. In accommodation where Africans pay their own rent, ejection could be effected for three arrears. Up to the end of the 1950s, 80 per cent of accommodation in townships was for single people. They got their rent paid by their companies, and this ensured payment to the city councils. Accommodation provided by the city councils was often unpopular with employers because it was far away from the places of work.[41]

The growth of the African urban population was accelerated by the economic boom under the Federation. In 1955 the Todd Government raised £1,000,000 from the Colonial Development Corporation for a total of 4,993 married quarters in Mpopoma and New Highfields: these were called home-ownership schemes. At this stage some white people had accepted that Africans were permanent residents of the cities, and that they were responsible enough to pay their own rent. The houses were sold at an average price of £337, on ninety-nine-year leases at £2·15 per month, with a monthly rate of £1·15 for water, sewerage, roads, dustbin collection, etc. The new scheme provided for lodgers, whose rent payments helped the owners in paying their mortgages. This accommodation did not necessarily apply to domestic workers because they often had rooms provided for them at the backs of their masters' homes and because of their poor wages.

The policy of urbanisation of Africans developed after the Second World War in Southern Rhodesia. In 1940 the Prime Minister, Sir Godfrey Huggins, employed nearly 15,000 Africans (including Coloureds) in the Rhodesian African Rifles and 9,000 whites to fight in the Rhodesian Army. The African troops proved their capability as fighters.

By 1941 Huggins was forced to drop his old policies of 'two pyramids'. He started talking about 'blood brotherhood between black and white',[42] thus causing a number of whites a great deal of surprise. It was even more surprising when a man like Frank Johnson, who at the age of twenty-four had led the first settlers into Rhodesia in 1890, now pressed Huggins for the representation of Africans in Parliament by whites. Huggins by this time had accepted the fact that Africans were in the towns to stay. The total African urban population in the six municipalities of Salisbury, Bulawayo, Gwelo, QueQue, Gatooma and Umtali had risen from 45,550 in 1936 to 99,341 in 1946. Small towns such as Fort Victoria, Shabani, Selukwe, Shamva, Umvuma, Marandellas and Gwanda, together with several other small centres and mines, were getting more and more urbanised. The growth of cities after the Second World War was a phenomenon observable in most of Africa.[43] In addition to these factors influencing the change of political attitude towards Africans, there was the strength and impact of the Fabian Society in the United Kingdom which often prodded the British Government in the 1940s to advance the colonial peoples. Huggins was aware that he could no longer get away with policies which preached the difference between racial types.[44] Some of his admirers were disillusioned at his change of heart. By 1941 he had accepted that Africans in the cities needed accommodation just like anyone else, and in 1944 he introduced into Parliament the Native (Urban Areas) Accommodation and Registration Act, which was passed in 1946.[45] The Act provided for married accommodation, and channels for communication of grievances by the setting up of an African Advisory Board on local government politics. The Board was supposed to have three Africans in each African area, and a white chairman. These provisions applied only in municipalities and town management boards, but not in government townships such as Old Highfield or Luveve.[46] The Government administers these through township managers appointed by the Ministry of Local Government and Housing. In some cases the townships are managed by the District Commissioners.

By 1946, the new policy of the Government allowed for schools in the African townships (*see* Chapter IV). Primary schools were built in Bulawayo, Salisbury, Gwelo and Umtali in the 1940s and early 1950s. Maternity homes were built at Mpilo in Bulawayo and Harare in Salisbury. Before that date the married status of African women in towns had been disregarded, and little attention was given to their maternity requirements; they were even regarded as prostitutes.[47] However, the amendment of the African (Urban Areas) Accommodation and Registration Act in 1951 provided for urban housing for Africans with wives.

(v) *Urban African Administration*

The Land Apportionment Act of 1941 and the African (Urban Areas) Accommodation and Registration Act of 1946 are the principal laws which guide African administration in the towns and cities. Since their enactment, ancillary legislation has been passed either to amend them or as independent intruments to cope with the changing environment of the 1950s and 1960s.

The Land Apportionment Act provided for Africans to acquire

freehold land only in the Native Purchase Areas or in the townships of the Special Native Areas, such as Seke, Tabazinduna or Zimunya. Africans could not purchase land adjacent to European townships. Because of the restrictions on land ownership, houses had been acquired by Africans on leasehold at Mpopoma, Bulawayo, Ascot, Gwelo and New Highfields, Salisbury.

The Whitehead Government amended the Land Apportionment Act 54 of 1960 to enable Africans to own land in the towns adjacent to Europeans. Bulawayo City took advantage of the Act to allow Africans to purchase 292 houses in Barbourfields, and some Africans immediately improved the four-room houses by adding one or two extra bedrooms. Families with teenage children of different sexes had been living under embarrassing conditions. The change in the law helped those who could afford to add a bedroom, a bathroom or w.c.s, or to build extensions. In Salisbury the amendment opened opportunities for the development in 1961 of Marimba Park and in 1963 of Kambuzuma, where Africans could obtain freehold titles, a facility provided in most of the African townships built after 1960.

The new system appears progressive, but it has its disadvantages built in over a long period in which racial practices have become entrenched. Claire Palley warns that 'quite apart from legislative provisions which make it impossible for Africans to acquire land in many areas of Southern Rhodesia, particularly in the urban areas, an extensive practice of inserting racially restrictive title-deed conditions has been established.'[48]

The Smith Government's legislation is nullifying the small advances made under previous Acts. All the legislation passed by the Rhodesia Front régime since 1963 on urban African affairs has been intended to curtail the movement towards a non-racial society. The Property Owners (Residential Protection) Bill, first introduced into Parliament in 1967, is designed to force even Coloured and Asian people away from European areas. In the 1923 Constitution, Coloureds and Asians were classified as Europeans. The Land Apportionment Act 1930 gave them the same privileges as whites, whose facilities they were in theory free to use. In practice, prohibitive labels such as 'whites' or 'Europeans' were put on entrances to lavatories, swimming baths, hotels, etc., to keep the Coloureds and Asians from mixing with Europeans.

By 1960 a few measures had been introduced by Sir Edgar Whitehead's Government to get rid of some of these pinpricks, but the Rhodesia régime has systematically reintroduced them; they have in fact gone further, making it even more difficult for Coloureds and Asians to retain the few privileges they enjoyed before 1962. The Property Owners (Residential Protection) Bill is aimed at those two racial groups, Africans being dealt with under a myriad of laws and under the Land Apportionment Act. The Bill provided for a petition from fifteen Europeans resident in the area in question to the Minister of Local Government objecting to the presence of other races. In response to the petition, the Minister would require persons of other races occupying property within that area to vacate their property or surrender it to cumpulsory purchase. The legislation is worse than its South African counterpart, because it leaves residents free to impose their whims upon others; and fifteen people hardly form a majority of any sort. In South Africa, it is the government which takes action without waiting for a petition from white residents. J. H. Howman, Rhodesia Front Minister of External Affairs, and Peter Nilson, M.P., told a party meeting during the election on 25 March, 1970, that the reference to Asians and Coloureds as Europeans in the Constitution did not matter, because once the Rhodesia Front was elected, they would make sure that no Asian was allowed to buy a house in any European area. When one of the audience wanted assurance from the Rhodesia Front that, once elected, they would introduce legislation to protect European schools from infiltration by children of other races, Howman agreed.[49]

The Municipal Act 1952 was originally intended to enable the seven municipalities[50] to administer the areas within their jurisdiction; however, it was amended by the Rhodesia Front in 1967 to codify the racial practice that had been going on in the towns and cities. The first Municipal Act of 1930 did not recognise that Africans could live in the towns, so no provision had been made in the pass laws to deal with those Africans not living in hostels provided by private companies; the latter were provided for under the Native Urban Location Act of 1906, the Native Passes Act, Ch. 77 of 1939, and the Native Passes Consolidation Amendment Act 14 of 1933. The indignities of passes and shortage of accommodation suffered by Africans were lessened by the Native (Urban Areas) Accommodation and Registration Act. No. 6 of 1946 and its amendment in 1951, which reduced the effect of tying passes to employment and accommodation, but did not get rid of the passes, or of police arrogance over passes. Even the Pass Laws (Repeal) Act. No. 50 of 1960 reduced the number of passes carried by each individual but left the burden as cumbersome as before. The 1952 Amendment was significant because it spelt out the details of how the powers of municipalities over Africans resident within their jurisdiction should be administered. The Act made the municipalities responsible for providing housing and welfare and sports facilities for their African residents.

Until 1946 housing and sporting activities had been the responsibility of private companies, welfare being left to the Native Commissioners. Before 1950 welfare was mostly concerned with marriage problems and stranded persons. People who were incapacitated or destitute were given travel warrants by bus or train from the city to the tribal areas. Disabled immigrants were simply repatriated to Malawi, Zambia, Mozambique or wherever they had come from. The Act also gave power to erect schools, hospitals, public entertainment facilities, etc. Thus in a large measure facilities which had been confined to European residents under the Municipal Act of 1930 were extended to the Africans in municipal areas. In this respect the Act brought about an improvement in the lives of Africans, and councils with 'liberal' ideas took advantage of it to establish facilities for Africans in their areas. In reactionary areas such as QueQue, Gatooma and Fort Victoria, no significant changes were made from the situation in the 1930s and 1940s.

The Land Apportionment Act 1941 provided that land might be leased or owned by an African in an African township.[51] The 1961 amendment empowered the Governor after consultation with local authorities to proclaim that some land within the township's vicinity could be acquired, leased or occupied by Africans. The amendment emphasised industrial areas, that is, areas within the seven municipalities and the twenty town councils.[52] The intention of the Act was to enable some Africans to operate their businesses without difficulty in the cities. Before this amendment it had been almost impossible for African lawyers, doctors or businessmen to operate in the towns other than the Native Townships provided under the Land Apportionment Act or the Native Urban Locations Act.[53] In some cases Africans operate their businesses regardless of the prohibition and the possibility of harassment, often with a political motive. When the lawyer, H. W. Chitepo, arrived back in the country in 1954, he could not work with other lawyers in chambers in Salisbury, because for an African this was not legally possible. The only place he could have established his office was Old Highfield, because it was the only native village settlement set aside for Africans under the Native Locations Act 1906. Harare or Mzilikazi in Bulawayo were ruled out because they were municipal establishments under the 1941 amendment of the Land Apportionment Act, which did not deal with African business facilities. The laws in Rhodesia seem to contradict each other. During the time when Africans were not allowed business facilities in municipalities and town councils, thousands of them operated without fear of prosecution, or other forms of government action. The number of African businessmen increased from 1,586 in 1931 to 3,616 in 1940.[54]

The 1961 amendment also provided for multi-racial schools, clubs, hotels and associations in European areas for the promotion of good race relations through cultural, religious, recreational, sporting or welfare activities. The amendment permitted occupation of land in the European area by an African who was in employment, engaged in religious or business activity, teaching, being educated or trained or doing research etc. But the opening of business areas to all people regardless of race has been halted by the Rhodesia Front. Although they have not amended or repealed the 1961 amendment to restore the old provision, they have introduced instead the Municipal Amendment Act No. 371 of 1967 with the purpose of implanting an apartheid spirit into it. It achieves discrimination against Africans by an administrative approach. The spirit of the 1961 amendment is killed by the delegated legislation given to municipalities and town councils to discriminate against Africans at their discretion. The Act is a subtle manoeuvre by the régime to avoid opposition by African M.P.s and the adverse reports of the constitutional council, yet achieve the aims of the Rhodesia Front without resort to parliamentary legislation. In theory the Municipal Amendment Act of 1967[55] is void of discrimination. But its implementation via delegated legislation reveals quite clearly that it is designed to discriminate against Africans. Provision was made to force employers of African domestic servants to stop them using accommodation within or at the backs of their yards, and a notice was sent to all employers to remove employees so that they should find accommodation in the congested townships. In 1963 there were 16,679 African families accommodated in Salisbury, yet there were 9,553 waiting for houses. Thus the position remains as it was in 1963 in most towns and cities. The new measure of removing Africans from accommodation provided by employers only worsens the accommodation problem.

An isolated effect of the Municipal Amendment Act 1967 was the collecting of all Africans in the European suburb of Greendale into an African township created as an enclave within it. The new township, known as Tafara, is meant for 2,000 families, and 830 units have already been built and occupied there by Africans with a government loan of £600,000. Separate African townships are now to be developed *within* the suburbs originally meant exclusively for Europeans – Hatfield, Greendale, Highlands, Mabelreigh, Marlborough and Mount Pleasant in Salisbury, and suburbs of the same type in Bulawayo. All these suburbs have always contained more Africans than Europeans – living in their masters' back yards.

The Municipal Amendment Act 1967 increased the power of the régime to control municipal by-laws which do not conform to the

spirit of government policy. In areas where local government authorities have powers over Africans, the régime may intervene and make
regulations affecting the lives of the Africans within the jurisdiction
of the local authority.[56] The Act is designed to forestall the possibility of liberal laws being introduced by local government. The
same Act authorised service charges for the occupation of immov-
able property; the policy of the régime was to make the African
houses in government, municipal and town council areas 'economic'.
Africans would have to pay despite the fact that their income has
not risen for some time. Only 1 per cent of the nearly 60,000 families in urban areas had an income of over £36 per months in 1964;
most received less than £20 a month. This situation has changed
little up to the time of writing.

The policy of the régime on European housing is to leave it to
private enterprise while assisting as much as possible where difficulties arise. The National Housing Advisory Committee, which
was established to deal with European housing in 1968, was disbanded, and in its place a Committee was set up under the chairmanship of the Deputy Secretary of Housing and Works. The Committee has representatives from many professional organisations
connected with the building trade and finance, but no African organisation is represented, because Africans are not permitted to own
houses built by private enterprise in the same way as whites.

The building of African houses is often financed by loans made
available to the municipalities and town councils by the Government. Even in the Marimba Park scheme, where thirty-three privi-
leged Africans can own houses worth on average £4,000 each,
the Government provides the loan. This is designed to prevent
Africans from claiming the same privileges as whites, such as representation on the local government councils or qualification for the
vote. Berween 1968 and 1969 a total of 4,096 new houses were
built for Europeans in the seven municipalities. This kept pace with
demand because of a 'reduction in the European migration drain
from 6,954 in 1968 to 5,030 in 1969.'[57]

Africans in the urban areas are regarded as different from those
in rural areas because they are separated from a tribal structure, and
independent from chiefs' or headmen's control. African urban administration is in the hands of the elective Advisory Boards, with permanent municipal employees – called superintendents – who
exercise great power over the lives of the Africans. These officers
are under the overall control of the Director of African Administration. The superintendent is responsible for collecting rents,
rates and payment for other services such as water and electricity.
Until the late 1950s few houses in African townships had electricity.

In Bulawayo nearly all major townships – Mzilikazi, Barbourfields, Mpopoma, Njube, Luveve and Nguboyenja – got electricity after 1960. In Mambo, at Gwelo, most married accommodation had electricity from 1951 when it was built. However, it was confined to lighting. One bulb was placed in a gap in a wall, to cast light into two rooms. The four rooms in a house were thus lit by two bulbs. Reading by this method was virtually impossible. The power went out automatically at midnight after burning for six hours. Families experienced great hardship when children fell sick after midnight.

The Government African township of Highfields, Salisbury, has no domestic lighting – only street lights, intended to stop crime. Nearly all the 7,000 houses, with between 70,000 and 80,000 inhabitants, are without electricity, despite the abundance of it from the Kariba hydro-electric power station. Similarly, water distribution to Africans is parsimonious. Water pipes as well as electricity cables are always strategically placed so that any African insubordination can be quickly dealt with. In cases of strikes or political demontions, water and electricity in the homes is cut off until the protesters give in. Water is often communally distributed, and few taps are found inside the houses. In Mambo and Monomotapa at Gwelo, as well as Barbourfields and Mpopoma, drinking water is drawn from taps connected directly with pipes supplying the lavatories and bathrooms. At Mzilikazi and Harare, in Bulawayo and Salisbury respectively, families collect water from taps centrally placed within a square. The same places have communal bathrooms even today. In Barbourfields no bathrooms at all are provided, and families are left to devise their own means of taking a bath. The standard houses in the African locations have four rooms – two bedrooms, a living room and a kitchen. In Mpopoma–Bulawayo, Highfields – Salisbury and Mambo–Gwelo, the lavatory is used as a bathroom. A big hole in the middle of the floor is washed by a flush tank tucked in a corner of the room. Beside the pipe leading into the flush tank stands a pipe that carries the shower cap. Hot water facilities are completely non-existent. The user of the bath directs the cold water that runs down his body into the hole of the lavatory. No seat is provided for the lavatory. The water, instead of accumulating on the floor, runs into the same drainage as that from the flush tank.

The roads running through these locations are dust roads except for the main ones down which city officials, mayor, councillors, government officials and visitors from Europe (especially British ministers and M.P.s) are driven. That is the one beautiful road into and out of the location. On rainy days the dust roads become quagmires, with water sometimes stagnating for days in the many pools that lie between houses. In African townships with clay soils, such as Mambo and Monomotapa in Gwelo, and where there are loam soils, as at Tshabalala and the Rhodesia Railways compounds in Bulawayo, life is unbearable. Children spend days in mud, parents find it difficult to peddle their bicycles to work, and there is no hot water on tap to wash it off.

These houses are valued at £250–499 while European houses cost between £4,000 and £20,000, and they are virtually the only ones an African is allowed to buy. In Marimba Park, Salisbury, African families own European-style houses. The area has been converted into a tourist attraction and propaganda site, and the overseas tourists who visit Salisbury and are taken there to be shown 'how the European governments have worked hard to advance Africans.' The visitors are told that as soon as Africans have advanced to this stage they can have equality with whites. Sometimes the same overseas visitors are shown the poverty in the Tribal Trust Land and are told that when Africans remain in that stage of poverty it is because they are 'lazy'. Then sad stories are told of how some white people have lost their lives in their desire to help Africans. No one ever mentions to tourists such details as African wage-rates and job-availability, or takes them to see the conditions in which all urban Africans – except for thirty-three families – have to live.

Even in towns where Africans are regarded as detribalised, welfare schemes such as care for the old, the blind, the physically handicapped and the unemployed are mostly left to the tribal structure, in that families look after their own invalids. Bulawayo does operate Jairos Jiri Centre for the physically handicapped, but this is the only scheme of its kind in the entire country. Facilities for this aspect of welfare work operate in several forms in the European community, because the Government provides for them. Schemes such as clinics (in urban areas), nurseries or nursery schools for African children are not thought of as a government responsibility. Some voluntary organisations such as that run by Miss Barbara Tredgold in Harare, Salisbury, or that of the Y.W.C.A. at Mpopoma, are run on a voluntary basis.

The Africans in the towns are in some respects luckier than their brothers in the rural areas. The presence of hospitals and clinics helps to check infant mortality. Births and deaths are booked, whereas in the country they are not. Vaccination is carried out, and an outbreak of a disease gets quicker attention in the urban areas for fear that it may spread to white areas. Africans in the urban areas have recreational amentiies, beer halls and even public televisions. These facilities are unknown in rural areas, or in rural African

Government townships such as Beitbridge, Inyanga, Macheke, Mashaba Mtoko Dett, etc. Mines sometimes provide schools and recreational and welfare facilities.

TOWN POPULATIONS 30 JUNE, 1970[1]

	Africans	Europeans	Asian	Coloured	Total
Bulawayo	210,000	51,800	2,470	6,000	270,000
Fort Victoria	9,000	2,600	150	210	12,000
Gatooma	21,000	2,000	140	190	23,000
Gwelo	40,000	8,500	340	710	50,000
Marandellas	9,000	2,200	30	10	11,000
QueQue	33,000	3,400	300	220	37,000
Redcliff	7,000	1,500	—	—	8,000
Salisbury	310,000	102,900	4,130	5,450	423,000
Shabani	15,000	1,600	40	60	17,000
Sinoia	12,000	1,600	210	30	14,000
Umtali	40,000	8,700	530	450	50,000
Wankie	19,000	2,400	—	—	21,000

Urban population as a percentage of national total

Europeans	79·2
Asians	90·7
Coloureds	83·0
Africans	14·4

[1] *Rhodesia Digest of Statistics*, December 1970.

REFERENCES

1. Part I, Section I, of the Southern Rhodesia Native Regulations, 1898, 1902 and 1910 says 'Chief' means a native appointed by the Administrator-in-Council to exercise control over a tribe. See Cmd. 3076, p. 78. This is the position up to the present day. See the African Affairs Act as amended 1927, 1959 and 1964.

2. Native reserves according to the 1923 Constitution; this title came into use following the 1961 Constitution. The lands are now controlled by the Tribal Trust Lands Act, 1969.

3. D. J. Murray, *The Southern Rhodesian Government System*, Clarendon Press, Oxford, 1970, p. 282.

4. Registration of births and deaths is compulsory for whites, but not for Africans.

5. Secretary of Internal Affairs Report, 1966, p. 3.

70   RHODESIA: STRUGGLE FOR A BIRTHRIGHT

6. Government notice 479 of 1965.

7. The Minister of Internal Affairs told Parliament that 'this is a departmental assessment'. S.R.L.A. Debates, Col. 970, 17 May, 1967. In 1969, Kayisa earned a total of £1,329·50 in the form of allowances for serving on various government committees.

8. *The Daily News*, 31 January, 1961.

9. A memorandum from the Solictor-General to the Governor, to be forwarded to the Dominions Secretary, 9 September, 1926.

10. Claire Palley, *The History and Constitutional Law of Southern Rhodesia 1888–1965*, Oxford University Press, London, 1966, pp. 670–4.

11. Secretary of Internal Affairs Report, 1965, p. 4.

12. Ibid.

13. J. P. Barber, *Rhodesia: the Road to Rebellion*, Oxford University Press, London, 1967, p. 238.

14. Carbutt, once Chief Native Commissioner, publicly advocated segregation when he was in retirement. L. H. Gann and M. Gelfand, *Huggins of Rhodesia*, Allen and Unwin, London, 1964, p. 130. See also R. H. Palmer's chapter on segregation.

15. Palley's speech on a motion of censure to the Government. S.R.L.A., 2 July, 1969, Col. 258.

16. I. H. Samuriwo likened the methods of manipulating chiefs for political ends to those of Hitler. S.R.L.A., 2 July 1969, Col. 1969.

17. S.R.L.A., 29 October, 1937, Col. 2386.

18. Huggins said: 'We must keep the power in our hands.' Ibid., Col. 3290.

19. Ibid., 22 October, 1937, Col. 2059.

20. Noaks, a representative of the Rhodesian Agriculture Union, told Parliament that the Act was a result of the recommendation of the Committee of the Rhodesia Agricultural Union, 29 October, 1937, Col. 2391.

21. H. E. Davies, later a M.P. representing African interests in the Federal Parliament, defended the Africans who resisted destocking.

22. G. C. Passmore, *Local Government Legislation in Southern Rhodesia up to 30 September, 1963*, U.C.R., Salisbury, 1966, pp. 36–42.

23. All chiefs appointed under the African Affairs Act Amendment, Cap. 92 are *ex-officio* vice-presidents to the District Commissioner in the area.

24. The duties were originally conferred upon the chiefs by Orders-in-Council of 1898, 1902 and 1910. See Part V, Sections 30–5, for chiefs, and Part VI, Sections 36–43, for headmen. Part VIII, Section 47, says: 'Every chief, headman, head of a kraal or other native failing or neglecting without reasonable excuse to carry out any of the duties enumerated in Sections 44, 45 and 46 hereof shall be deemed guilty of an offence and shall upon conviction be liable to the penalties prescribed under Section 50 of this Proclamation.'

25. A. Atmore and R. Oliver, *Africa since 1800*, Cambridge University Press, London, 1967, p. 189.

26. Official explanation for the opposition is expressed in the Secretary for Internal Affairs' Report 1965: 'Opposition is not so much directed

against what the government is doing and what it wants to do as against the nomenclature employed. The words "council" and "community development" are anathema to many people.' Secretary of Internal Affairs Report 1965, p. 6.

27. Kandengwa, M.P., asked the Minister of Internal Affairs about the progress of his policy since Africans 'refuse to co-operate in the establishment of the councils'. S.R.L.A. Debates, Col. 905, 12 May, 1967.

28. G. C. Passmore, op. cit., p. 11.

29. G. C. Passmore, op. cit., p. 11.

30. The paradox of the policy followed by the British Labour Government in 1930 was that they ignored the fact that in 1928 there were 70,572 Africans who lived as workers in urban areas.

31. D. J. Murray, *The Government System in Southern Rhodesia*, Clarendon Press, Oxford, 1970, p. 315.

32. See Huggins' speech, S.R.L.A., 22 October, 1937, Col. 2060.

33. The Natives (Urban Areas) Accommodation Act, No. 2 of 1946, Subsections 5 and 6, and the Land Apportionment Act No. 11 of 1941, Subsections 36 and 38.

34. Meaning 'pass', derived from Sindebele word for 'thumb'.

35. When the Director of African Administration, R. Briggs, was asked by P. J. D. Rubatika, then M.P. for Harare, about this rigid enforcement of pass laws, he replied that 'some of the pinpricks would be dealt with.' *Rhodesia Herald*, 7 April, 1970.

36. The bus travelling between Salisbury and Kariba is inspected at every point it passes a police station for 'terrorists'.

37. Mr. and Mrs. A. C. Dlomo, teachers at Mambo School, Gwelo, were invaded in their bedroom in 1954. The two were embarrassed, but no amount of explanation could make the police leave them alone.

38. Morgan Khumalo was detained at U.D.I. and when released in mid-December 1965, found his house sold and his family forced to stay with friends.

39. S.R.L.A., 5 September, 1967, Col. 8.

40. Shabani and Wankie Mines have good single and married accommodation, but other mines take very little interest in their African workers. *See* T. Franck, *Race and Nationalism*, New York, 1960, p. 139.

41. Bulawayo City Council housed people in Mpopoma, Mzilikazi, Nguboyenja, Tshabalala and Barbourfields, and Salisbury City Council in Harare National Mabvuku, Mufakose, etc., which are not as close to the factories as Makokaba hostels at Voodoo and Harare hostels at Matrapi, Marengenya and Magaba, which are at walking distance.

42. L. H. Gann and M. Gelfand, op. cit., p. 173.

43. Thomas Hodgkin, *Nationalism in Colonial Africa*, Muller, London, 1965, p. 67.

44. Murray, op. cit., p. 301–2.

45. The Native (Urban Areas) Accommodation and Registration Act No. 6 of 1946.

46. There were thirty-three African Government townships by 1964. The number grows every year.

47. Huggins said in Parliament on 2 April, 1937: 'Natives bring a few girls to towns to use them for earning enough money for tax. . . . This must stop. . . . It is up to the white people to treat them as children.' S.R.L.A., Col. 589.

48. Palley, op. cit., p. 640.

49. *Rhodesia Herald*, 26 March, 1970.

50. Bulawayo, Salisbury, Gwelo, Umtali, Gatooma, QueQue and Fort Victoria. The structure of local government under white management is divided into three parts: municipalities, town councils, rural councils, local boards and local committees.

51. This meant in any of the townships formerly known as Native Urban Areas or Native Urban Locations if they were established under the Native Urban Locations Act, or in the Native townships established in the Native Purchase Areas under the Land Apportionment Act 1930.

52. See Appendix for lists.

53. For example, an African accountant, J. Mahlanga, M.P. for Mpopoma, was expelled in 1971 from Bulawayo Exchange Building, where he had been in business since 1963 under the Land Tenure Act. P. J. Chanetsa, a farmer and ex-M.P., was expelled in 1970 from offices which he rented in the centre of Salisbury. Yet African lawyers continue to practise in similar buildings. These expulsions invariably result from complaints by European competitors. African buses plying between the reserves and the European shopping areas of Bulawayo, Salisbury and other towns, bring valuable African custom to these areas, hence no objection is raised to their presence.

54. Native Commissioner Reports, 1931–40.

55. Local Government Act, No. 27, 1967.

56. Local Government Act No. 27, 1967.

57. Report of the Secretary for Local Government and Housing, 1969, p. 19.

CHAPTER IV

AFRICAN EDUCATION IN
RHODESIAN POLITICS

(i) *History of African Education*

To follow current progress in African education in Rhodesia, it is necessary to review its historical development before the present régime took power in 1962. In that time, only two prime ministers, H. U. Moffat and R. S. Garfield Todd (who had missionary backgrounds), had any interest at all in African educational development, but their careers did not last long enough for their policies to be properly implemented. Huggins, who was in power for more than twenty years, was inimical to African interests, as is Smith today; none of the other prime ministers lasted in power for longer than six years,

African education in Rhodesia took shape only after 1907, when the British Government passed the first order-in-council on African education. This came as a result of pressure for such an ordinance from the Southern Rhodesian Missionary Conference, founded in 1906 by fifteen Christian church bodies. At this stage of British rule, African education was regarded as a missionary responsibility because of the belief that education was a constituent of Christianity. Jesus, after all, had taught, healed and preached, and His true disciples had to follow His example.[1] In most of British Africa these functions, which in independent countries now belong to the state (apart from preaching), were left to missionaries until after the Second World War. Rhodesia was no exception. This put the missionary in a strong position in relation to both the Africans and the Government. Everywhere in Britain's African colonies, including Rhodesia, the European missionaries regarded themselves as spokesmen for the African. Both the British and the Rhodesian Governments accepted this claim of the missionaries and, because they were believed to have intimate contact with the African people, consulted them on all matters concerning Africans. Their claim to this right did not, however, depend on African support but on the assumption that, since the Christian church was responsible for educating, evangelising and healing Africans, it had the right to speak for them as well. African teachers were believed to be inarticulate.

Up to the passage of the Native Education Ordinance of 1907, there were only fifty recognised schools in Southern Rhodesia, with 4,319 pupils. These gave primary education to only a fraction of those wanting it. The education ordinance set up boarding schools for Africans under the supervision of missionaries, and other primary schools teaching courses of up to four years. By 1913 the number of primary schools had grown to 193, while the number of pupils had reached 15,723. The demand for education grew rapidly during the First World War: enrolment nearly trebled within the seven years 1913–20, at the end of which period the total of pupils was 43,084, in nearly 700 schools.

This growth in African education was certainly not due to any effort by the Government to improve the system. On the contrary, the effort was made by the Africans themselves under the supervision of the missionaries. African parents had by then started to appreciate the need for education, and were taking responsibility themselves for the building of schools; but it was the young adult, rather than the child, for whom they sought this education. In most cases, indeed, pupils were family men who either left their wives behind to come to school, or brought their wives as well to learn in school beside them. The Government's part was to consent to the starting of schools when asked, to give land for them to be built on, and to create the inspectorate. In 1920 the Government's expenditure on African education was £10,016, which worked out at 5s. 3d. a head for the year.[2] Although there were only eighty European schools by 1918, and an enrolment of 5,408 in 1920, expenditure on white education in 1920 was £187,831, or £34 15s. per head. Much of this sum was spent on recruiting teachers from South Africa and Britain. In 1920 there were 229 teachers in European schools, of whom thirty-two were university graduates. Neglecting African education and spending revenue contributed by Africans for education on something else is no new phenomenon in Rhodesia. Yet, despite the oppressive policies followed by the settlers at that time, British statesmen were impressed by the way their administration dealt with Africans in Rhodesia.

In 1919 the A.P.S. attacked the British South Africa Company for exploiting and oppressing Africans. This attack found support in the British press, and as a result the British Government was forced to defend the way in which it had allowed the Company a free hand in Rhodesia. Both L. S. Amery, Under-Secretary of State for the Colonies, and Lord Buxton, High Commissioner in

South Africa responsible for Southern Rhodesia, repudiated the claims of the A.P.S. and paid tribute to the settlers' 'reasonable attitudes' towards Africans. Amery told the House of Commons on 26 April, 1920, that the attitude of the white people in Southern Rhodesia was a model 'not only in Africa but for any part of the world where you have the very difficult problem of white settlers living side by side with the native'. When the testimony of Amery and Buxton failed to impress the critics of British policies on Rhodesia, the British South Africa Company and the Rhodesia Agricultural Union pressed the Missionary Conference and the Native Affairs Department, both organisations respected in Britain as true spokesmen for the Africans, to contradict the statements of the A.P.S. The Anglican Bishop of Southern Rhodesia, at the time President of the Missionary Conference, happened to be on leave in England and took the opportunity to endorse the settlers' policies, and to denounce the A.P.S. and A. S. Cripps for their allegations.[3] The Missionary Conference at its annual conference in Salisbury in the same year protested to the A.P.S. in strong terms, and passed a resolution dissociating itself from their allegations. It attacked Cripps and the Rev. John White for encouraging Harris, the secretary of the A.P.S., to visit the country and collect information about the problems of the Africans there.

In the period before the spread of nationalism in Africa, African leaders and chiefs were ignored. Some missionaries believed the Government to be contemptuous of Africans. African pastors, teachers and evangelists resented the Southern Rhodesian Missionary Conference's misrepresentation of African opinion to the Government of the country and abroad – a resentment which led to the formation of the Native Christian Conference in the 1920s, under the Rev. D. T. Samkange, which was later recognised by the European Missionary Conference in 1926 'as an integral, though subordinate, part' of its own organisation.[4] This gesture came from the Rev. John White, then President of the Missionary Conference.[5] At their biennial gathering, the Missionary Conference discussed matters concerning African welfare such as housing, education, hospitals and marriage. In most cases they had in mind Christian Africans and not all Africans. Yet, in spite of this show of concern, the European Conference comprised Christian principles in order to meet the wishes of the settlers when they denied Africans participation on equal terms even in church affairs. Most of the missionaries were, after all, settlers themselves, with much the same interests as other settlers; and a master-disciple relationship is inherent in a missionary situation. Christianity, which teaches obedience and humility, is a useful religion in a colony.

The missionaries had an advantage in the context of Rhodesian politics because there were people in responsible and influential positions who were sympathetic to them. H. U. Moffat, a minister in 1923–7 and prime minister in 1927–33, was the grandson of the famous missionary Robert Moffat, confidant to King Mzilikazi in the 1860s. Similarly C. H. Tredgold and W. S. Thomas were related to Moffat, and each held an influential position: Tredgold as attorney-general and a judge from 1903, and Thomas as a lawyer in public service in the 1920s. F. L. Hadfield, a M.P. in the 1920s, had been a founder member of Dadaya Mission for the Church of Christ, a New Zealand sect. He continued to associate himself with missionary interests although elected to Parliament as a Labour member. These leading figures shared the fashionable zeal for spreading Christian 'civilisation' to the Africans, and assisted missionary effort wherever possible. In the double capacity of missionary and M.P., Hadfield in 1924 led a commission of inquiry into the improvement of African education. The commission depended largely on recommendations made by European missionaries, while African leaders and chiefs were deftly left out in the belief that their ideas were not representative.

The Commission recommended in 1925 that there should be an advisory board of education, and that the Department of Education should be separate from the Native Affairs Department. This was an attempt to diminish the powers of the Native Affairs Department, which was a state within a state, the dominance of the Native Commissioners in African matters being resented by other departments as well as by missionaries. Progressive and able educationists such as H. Jowitt found it intolerable that education should be subject to restriction for political motives, as was then the practice among the civil servants in the African Affairs Department.

After the death in 1927 of Sir Charles Coghlan, Prime Minister and Minister of African Affairs, who had been ignorant of what was happening in the Department, Moffat took over. He was responsive to the demands of the missionaries, and immediately acted on the recommendations of the Hadfield Commission in creating an Education Advisory Board, the Native Education Department, and the Department of Native Development. The departments were at first headed by Jowitt,[6] who attempted to follow the principles of education practised elsewhere in the world at the time, of teaching all pupils at least the Three R's. There was reduced interference from the African Affairs Department between 1928 and 1930, because the Chief Native Commissioner, H. K. G. Jackson, was from a missionary family and shared missionary ideals. Yet, even with this rare government co-operation, the missionaries did not adopt a thoroughgoing radical education policy, as had happened, for example, in East Africa. Yet Moffat's Act of 1929, although it owed its existence to missionary politics, had some useful facets – e.g. teacher training schools and the introduction of eight years education – introduced through Jowitt's administrative skill.

Jowitt was optimistic about the ability of Africans to benefit from education like anyone else. He believed that, given the same chance as European children, they could learn and contribute to the development of their country. His policy was inspired by the declarations made at the regional conferences on education of the British East African dependencies at Dar-es-Salaam, held in March 1929, which all the eleven colonies in East, Central and South Africa (except Northern Rhodesia, where there was a railway strike) attended. South Africa, a dominion at the time, also attended. One of the conclusions of the conference was that 'the economic and educational development of the African is not only justified by the needs and potentialities of the African, but is definitely in the interests of the European populations.'[7]

A feature of the Rhodesian political system stemming from its Company antecedents is that power lies in the department rather than with the minister. If the permanent head of a department is illiberal, the minister in charge often has a difficult task implementing his policies when they conflict with those of the head. This is clear in the departments which affect Africans, as is shown by the way Nicolle dominates the Department of Internal Affairs today.

During Jowitt's directorship, Moffat, the minister, left him to put his ideals into practice, and those propounded by the conference at Dar-es-Salaam. The 1929 Act prescribed the conditions on which grants-in-aid could be made, authorised loans for the erection of buildings, and stated the fees payable by pupils.[8] The previous categories into which schools had been divided became six: teacher training, boarding, central day schools, kraal schools, evening schools and special schools. The Act made provision for poor pupils to pay their fees with labour done during the vacation when the other pupils had left the institution if it was a boarding school, or after school hours if it was a day school. The provision of fees by labour should not be misconstrued as a harsh Act, for up to 1946 the average school age was 18·8 years, so in most cases it was not a matter of child labour. And it was a useful means of ensuring the continued schooling of gifted pupils who could not otherwise have attended school for lack of money.

The introduction of teachers' training schools and the aiding of special schools were two significant innovations of this Education Act. It ended the old system whereby missionaries made teachers out of anybody who knew the Bible well, but who did not necessarily have much acquaintance with the Three R's. The teachers' training schools produced teachers equipped to teach the Three R's, with less emphasis on the Bible. The standard of teachers was still by no means high, but it was an improvement on the position during the three decades before 1929. These teachers started training after Standard IV, i.e. after their sixth year at school, doing Standards V and VI concurrently with the two years of their teachers' training. These teachers are the people who taught most of the African university graduates of today in the 1940s and 1950s.

Special schools were Morgenster Mission School for the deaf and dumb, Kapata School for the blind, run by the Dutch Reformed Church of South Africa, and another school for the deaf and dumb run by the Roman Catholic Church at Loreto Mission. Under the Act, the Government provided a grant-in-aid to these three institutions. Before 1929 they had been run out of church funds, with the result that very few deserving individuals could be taken into them. After that year, places could be given to many more needy pupils.

Before 1929, the Government had specialised in educating Africans in industrial skills at their often-cited 'model' schools of Domboshawa in Mashonaland and Tjolotjo (Mzingwane) in Matabeleland. Industrial training was confined to an elementary knowledge of agriculture, carpentry and building. There was no attempt to make the pupils of these schools acquire the same advanced knowledge as whites, for fear of opposition from white workers.

The power to control African education, according to the Act, was vested in the Advisory Board of fifteen members, comprising the Minister of African Affairs *ex-officio*, the Prime Minister, the Attorney-General, the Chief Native Commissioner, the Director of Education, the Medical Director, a Native Commissioner, an Inspector of Schools, and eight missionaries. At their first meeting on 27–8 November, 1929, they uttered the most liberal sentiments, and this progressive policy lasted up to the end of Moffat's administration and the resignation of Jowitt.

The opportunity was soon lost. In 1930 a racialist Chief Native Commissioner, C. L. Carbutt, replaced Jackson and the system changed. Carbutt was able to disorganise not only the education system, but also the Missionary Conference. The Anglican Church supported Carbutt in reversing Jowitt's liberal policies; although the Roman Catholics preferred the Jowitt line, they were too few to count, and Jowitt, finding himself largely isolated, resigned. After his departure, Moffat's interest in African development could prevail only as far as Carbutt and the missionaries were prepared to allow it. In 1930 Moffat made education compulsory for white children, but he did not consider extending the compulsion to African children; this division has remained up to the present day. The next year he passed the Public Service Act, which specifically excluded Africans and other non-whites from recruitment to the civil service. This closed a possible career to the ambitious African, thus discouraging him from seeking more and better education.

The denominational difference within the Missionary Conference on educational policy damped Moffat's interest, and in 1933 G. M. Huggins took power with a 'two-pyramid' policy designed for parallel development of racial groups, very much along the lines of the present Rhodesia Front policy and indeed of Afrikaner Nationalist policy in South Africa.

Between 1933 and 1940 the government attitude to African advancement was hostile. Huggins and his Chief Native Commissioner, Carbutt, were fearful of educated Africans, and struggled to prevent the emergence of a white-collar proletariat open to political influences through the written word; ability to read (or to write) pamphlets with revolutionary ideas was a major preoccupation. They were prepared to train medical orderlies, agricultural demonstrators, laboratory assistants and dispensers, but not the academics who were going to question the Government's methods of administration.

Huggins was adept at speaking with his tongue in his cheek and suiting his words to his audience. In England, he spoke of how the British people had helped the African to struggle out of his ignorance and poverty. In Rhodesia, depending on the particular constituency where he was speaking at the time, he uttered some outrageous things about Africans, yet at other times his utterance were unpleasant to European ears. In 1936, for example, he said that the country's economic development could not be achieved while the Africans remained in poverty and ignorance, arguing that the Government ought to provide elementary and technical rather than advanced academic education.[9] Knowing that the statement was unpalatable to whites who had rejected the Moffat approach, preferring his own of two pyramids, he added that educated Africans should not go to towns to compete with white men; instead, they should give uplift to their people in the reserves. This policy of protecting the whites against African competitors was translated into the Industrial Conciliation Act No. 10 of 1934, and its amendment in 1937, and the Maize Control Amendment of 1934.

Despite the shortcomings of their education policy, the missionaries in Rhodesia made an immense contribution to the educational progress of the Africans. But, measured against what other mission-

aries did in East and West Africa, those in Central Africa lagged far
behind – the reason for this being that they were caught up in
settler politics more than in their missionary work: they were
impelled to abandon the right course of their work among Africans
to accommodate settler politics. Their hostility to radical missionaries such as John White and A. S. Cripps, who are today proved
correct, is a measure of their failures and lack of foresight.

(ii) *The Situation in other Parts of British Africa*

Until after the Second World War, African education, which was
then largely under missionary control, was to all intents and purposes
in hostile hands. In a sense, this missionary attitude also prevailed
in Northern Rhodesia and South Africa, because the same churches
operated in these three countries. Nyasaland was in a different
position, because it was dominated by the Presbyterian Church of
Scotland, which always felt a special responsibility for African
welfare there.[10] The churches adopted this paternalistic attitude to
the Africans because, like the settlers and the British Government,
they believed that Southern Rhodesia, South Africa and, until
1924, Northern Rhodesia were white men's countries, in which
education was dispensed to Africans as a favour. The lack of large
settler populations in East and West Africa, and the progressive
attitude of the Christian missionaries there, opened the way for
early advancement of African education.

In East Africa, missionary influence was preponderant in political
institutions as well as in education. Missionaries fought and put an
end to the conscripted labour system, while in the Central African
territories of Southern Rhodesia, Northern Rhodesia and Nyasaland
they turned a blind eye to it, in some cases even justifying it on the
grounds that it taught the Africans how to earn a living. But Arch-
deacon Owen of Kavirondo fought against Indian and European
immigration into Kenya because he believed that it hindered African
advancement. The East African churches led the way in pressing
for Africanisation and social integration;[11] their African priests did
not suffer radical discrimination, and as a result there was an
African Roman Catholic bishop before the Second World War, an
Anglican one after it and an African cardinal in Tanganyika in the
1950s before the country attained independence. East African
churches had free elections on an equal basis in their synods and
assemblies, with large numbers of Africans participating, before
political democracy was ever talked about.

In Tanganyika, the Germans and their missionaries had provided
better education than in any British colony: by 1914 there were
100,000 African school pupils. In Uganda, half the African children

attended school, and 8 per cent obtained five years of education. The country got a high school as early as 1906; Kenya had Alliance High School in 1926. Neither Northern Rhodesia nor Southern Rhodesia had a single secondary school for Africans before the Second World War.

The British Government itself took a positive step towards African education in East and Central Africa in the 1920s. Even then the policy was not one of direct government intervention, but of encouraging the missionaries to step up their own education of Africans,[12] and it did not immediately yield the desired results for, up to the Second World War, only one-third of the children of school age in this large area attended school, and the average length of attendance was only four years.

Most colonies, except for the Gold Coast and Nigeria, had an annual output of fewer than 100 secondary schoolchildren. The British Government contributed to the mission schools by providing an inspectorate and subsidies; they trained teachers and prescribed syllabuses. Nigeria was alone among colonies in Africa in having rather more than a dozen secondary schools before 1939; these were confined to the Eastern and Western regions, leaving the North without secondary education. The products of the few secondary schools in the Gold Coast and Nigeria were able to further their education overseas. However, both colonies had African lawyers and doctors even before the First World War. After that war, some of the West African intellectuals, led by J. E. Caseley Hayford, a Gold Coast lawyer and member of the Legislative Council, formed the 'National Congress of British West Africa' with the aim of achieving self-government for all British West African territories. The then Governor of Nigeria, Sir Hugh Clifford, could talk of them as a 'self-selected and self-appointed congregation of educated African gentlemen who collectively style themselves the West African National Conference'[13] – at least the education is admitted.

In East or Central Africa there was no educated African, in Sir Hugh's sense, to be found. South Africa was the only country at that time outside West Africa with African lawyers and doctors. These were involved from 1913 onwards in the African National Congress, whose lawyer, Richard Msimanga, helped the Ndebele leaders in Southern Rhodesia. For, in the latter country, there was a deliberate policy of excluding educated men who were potential leaders. Njube and Nguboyenja, sons of King Lobengula who had obtained some education, were not allowed by the British South Africa Company to come back into Rhodesia. Nguboyenja was forced to drop his legal studies in London, and eventually returned to Rhodesia, where he took no part in affairs. The political activities in the country before the Second World War were led by chiefs and industrial leaders;[14] no university graduate was involved at the time.

It can thus be seen that the efforts of missionaries in Southern Rhodesia did not reach the standard of those in many other colonies.

(iii) *Southern Rhodesian Education before the Rhodesia Front*

The structure of African education in Southern Rhodesia improved little in the 1930s after the advent of Huggins. Enrolment in the schools had increased, but not as fast as in other African colonies. In 1929 there were 1,549 schools for 96,403 African pupils, a figure which then declined for fourteen years, as a result of Huggin's policy, implemented by the Chief Native Commissioner, Carbutt, until it picked up in 1943.

By way of comparison, we see that in Northern Rhodesia there were 110,368, pupils enrolled in schools in 1930 out of a total population of 1,300,000. They had 2,500 teachers in 1931.

Rhodesian expenditure on education in 1930 was £44,736 18s. 1d., and yet the African contribution to Government revenue by direct taxation[15] had reached £357,301. The kraal (village) schools, which enrolled more pupils, got only £12,169 per annum. The Government claimed that 58 per cent of African children were attending schools that year out of a total population of 931,842, of which 20 per cent (186,000) were children. This claim does not appear to be founded on fact because the size of the African population has never been satisfactorily estimated.

In 1938 Huggins claimed that more than 30 per cent of Africans aged from five to fifteen years attended primary school. It was argued that this was the highest figure in British Africa, the figures for other leading territories being: Gold Coast, Nigeria and the Sudan, under 5 per cent; Kenya and Bechuanaland, 10–15 per cent.[16] Like the claim made in 1930, this one is difficult to believe. Apart from the lack of accurate census figures, it appears to have been made in ignorance of the fact that in 1938 no African child went to school at five years old.[17] Only white children attended school at that age. The average primary school age, which we have already seen was 18·8 years in 1946, only dropped to 17·9 years in 1950, and to 16·5 in 1951. At present, African children start school at seven years. At this time, Nigeria, the Gold Coast, Kenya and the Sudan had secondary schools producing university material, but there were still no secondary schools in Rhodesia. In 1938 Northern Rhodesia had more African pupils in schools than Southern Rhodesia: the latter had 1,322 schools with an enrolment of 109,588 pupils, while the former had 122,065 pupils. The Southern Rhodesian annual increase was 1,000; in Northern Rhodesia it was 2,000.

In Southern Rhodesia, the Government had responsibility only for two trade schools, in Northern Rhodesia in the 1930s, it was responsible for all urban education. The children in or around the Copperbelt – at Luanshya, Mufulira and Broken Hill – were taught in government schools. Town management boards had their own council schools in 1938, at a time when the Government in Southern Rhodesia had not accepted the principle that Africans would live in the cities. Only mission schools operated in a restricted sense in the towns.

The Northern Rhodesian Government was already subsidising the building of teachers' training colleges at Mapanza, Mbereshi, Lubwa, Cosenga, Johnston Falls and Senga Hills, while in Southern Rhodesia a block grant was given to missionaries who were responsible for all primary education and teachers' training without it being tied to particular projects as in Northern Rhodesia. It was Northern Rhodesia which led the way in the training of nurses by 1935, to be followed by Southern Rhodesia in 1937. The Northern Rhodesian Government authorities saw the need for training Africans for responsibilities in the local authorities and chiefs' courts. The schools at Chipembi and at Kasama trained African clerks for various jobs in the Government. The Lusaka Post Office already trained African telephonists in the 1930s.

African secondary education was introduced at long last into Rhodesia in the decade 1949–50. In fifty years of European rule, not a single African secondary school had been founded in the country, although there were European secondary schools in all the main town areas, and boarding schools in the country areas such as Plumtree. Africans in Southern Rhodesia had one expedient not available to those in Northern Rhodesia: although there were no secondary schools in their own country for them, they were able to go to South Africa for secondary education; Northern Rhodesia was surrounded by countries no better endowed than itself with secondary school facilities.

Teachers with some secondary education were imported from South Africa between 1910 and 1940, and the 1930s saw a number of talented young men going to secondary schools in South Africa run by the same churches as operated in Southern Rhodesia. Very few girls were allowed by their parents to leave the family roof to do this, which meant that secondary education was virtually closed to them.

The South African schools taking Rhodesian pupils were the following: a Roman Catholic school at Marianhill, Natal; two Anglican schools, St. Matthew's in the Cape and St. Peter's in the Transvaal; two Methodist schools, Hilltown in the Cape and Kilnerton in the Transvaal; the London Missionary Society school at Tiger Kloof in the Cape; the Lutheran School at Dundee, Natal; the American Board School, Adams College in Natal; and the African Methodist Episcopal school at Wilberforce in the Transvaal. Other churches which did not have denominational facilities arranged with these for their students to attend secondary schools of their choice. The Brethren in Christ sent their students to Tiger Kloof and Kilnerton. Adams College was the most enlightened of all, students belonging to other churches being admitted entirely on merit. The majority of the present Southern Rhodesian African leaders in politics and education went through Adams College. Joshua Nkomo studied there, as did Dr. M. A. Wakatama, at present associate professor in education at the City University, New York, Professor S. T. J. Samkange of Harvard University, U.S.A., and G. N. S. Khumalo an inspector of schools in Rhodesia; all are Methodists. Another inspector of schools, P. S. Mahalangu, of the London Missionary Society, and H. W. Chitepo, an advocate and leader of Z.A.N.U. in Lusaka, an Anglican, were educated at Adams College. (A. J. Luthuli, later Nobel Peace Prize Winner and leader of the A.N.C., was among its teaching staff.)

In the 1930s, the Government had provided bursaries for gifted pupils to proceed with their education in South Africa, restricted to ten a year. The rest were paid for by their parents, who might sell their cattle to send their children to South Africa. Some pupils went after they had worked and saved the money themselves. Nkomo had worked as a carpenter and a driver, saving enough money to see him through two years of secondary education; he did the rest by private study up to degree level. Nkomo often talks about his embarrassment in class at twenty-seven years of age, while the next oldest pupil was sixteen. He nearly left Adams College but for his friends Khumalo and Moses Siqalaba, who advised him against it, as he was in fact the brightest 'boy' in his class.

Marianhill Roman Catholic College was the second choice for Southern Rhodesian African students. It followed a policy of giving priority to Catholics from Rhodesia, but as in the case of Adams College, a number of leading citizens of Rhodesia studied there. Among these are Lawrence Vambe, former editor of African newspapers and Secretary, under the Federation, to the High Commissioner in London. The most illustrious Southern Rhodesian scholar to be produced by Marianhill is Dr. B. T. G. Chidzero, now working for U.N.C.T.A.D. in Geneva. Others are in education, such as S. Mlala, an inspector of schools, A. Masukusa, a headmaster, and T. G. Silundika, a leading official of Z.A.P.U.

Those who had obtained the matriculation certificate at these

South Africa institutions in the late 1930s and early 1040s became either teachers or ministers of religion, the only careers open to the educated African at the time. The civil service was closed to them, industry practised a colour bar, and the police force paid very badly and was suspicious of educated Africans. Hence to most Africans teaching or the ministry were the only professions open.

Huggins' African policy changed somewhat during the war. Several factors played a part: the participation of Africans in the Second World War in larger numbers than in 1914–18; the world-wide change of racial attitudes at the end of the war; pressure from the British Government, who had also changed their attitude towards Africa; the increase in the growth rate of the African population in the rural and urban areas from 2·7 per cent in 1940 to 4·16 per cent in 1945; and, most important, the upsurge in South Africa of hostile Afrikaner nationalism which persistently supported Hitlerism and opposed Smuts' policy of co-operation with Britain in the war. These factors made the Rhodesian settlers wish to have the African, *faute de mieux*, as an ally. This alliance, they thought, could be achieved by attending to their most pressing problems, education and urban accommodation. During the war no anti-African law was passed, rather the Land Apportionment Act was amended in 1941 in favour of the Africans. The tendency of Rhodesian politics is for recent immigrants to be further to the right, and for whites who have stayed there longer to be less rigidly hostile.[18] From 1940 to 1945 only 5,030 immigrants came into the country. Political power and influence remained with the older settlers who had come between 1890 and 1940. Huggins could become more 'liberal' without fear of electoral reprisals from the white electorate. Thus his Government announced in 1942 that they would take responsibility for African education in the urban areas at the same time as they introduced the provision of married accommodation in these areas.

Although the announcement was made during the war, the provisions were not carried out until 1946. Two years after the announcement, the Government took over the church schools in the Salisbury township of Old Highfields, Senga in Gwelo, Luveve and Victoria Falls. And the first Government African secondary school in Southern Rhodesia was built at Goromanzi, near Salisbury, in 1946. In 1946 and 1949 they built Lobengula and Mzilikazi schools in Bulawayo – but some mining managements had already felt it necessary to provide schools for African children during the war. It was then that Shabani Mine and Wanderer Mine built African schools.

Salisbury City Council contributed £25,000 towards the construction of schools in 1942. The Government further demonstrated its seriousness of purpose by increasing the budget for African education, but with the increased number of pupils in the 1940s the budget was still lamentably insignificant. Enrolment had risen from 113,379 in 1941 to 163,949 in 1945, and 232,689 in 1950. In the 1940s African education in Southern Rhodesia overtook that of Northern Rhodesia in enrolment and structure.

In Southern Rhodesia, meanwhile, the churches had diversified their field of education and founded industrial schools on the lines of Domboshawa and Mzingwane, and nursing schools in some mission hospitals. The Government trained nurses and orderlies at Memorial Hospital, Bulawayo, and General Hospital, Salisbury. There were six church industrial schools in the 1940s at Chikore, Waddilove, Inyathi, Empadeni, Mt. Silinda and Tegwani, each with an average of 200 boys and offering argicultural, carpentry and building courses. By 1942 there were thirteen church teachers' training schools all over the country.

Following the Government's new policy, the missions started three-year courses in secondary schools leading to a junior certificate at St. Augustine, Dadaya, Kutama, Hartzell, Tegwani and Gakomere. These secondary schools enrolled, on average, 200 junior and thirty senior students by 1949.

The advent of Goromanzi secondary school in 1946 was a landmark in the history of Southern Rhodesian African education. In 1949, when the number of secondary school pupils was nearly 600, Goromanzi alone took 254, of whom fifty-three were girls. The first principal, G. M. Miller, ran the school on English public school lines. Apparently the African parents like this; Miller was (and remains in retrospect) one of the most respected heads of African schools ever appointed. The staff had high qualifications, and the school's examination results were excellent, with thirty-three passes out of thirty-four candidates for the first Cambridge Overseas school certificate ever to be attempted by Africans in the country. Within the two years 1949 and 1950, Goromanzi had produced seventy-one pupils who obtained the Cambridge certificate. This brought many surprises for the white community, who had never believed that Africans could obtain the same certificates as their own children, with as much ease.

Secondary schools helped to improve the standard of teachers and the quality of teaching in the 1950s and 1960s. In 1951, out of a total of 6,812 teachers, 2,284 had the primary teachers' certificate, 272 had junior certificates, seventy-nine had matriculation, and fifteen had university degrees. At this stage of development, the presence of these fifteen African university graduates with degrees from South African universities teaching Africans marked a tremendous advance if one remembers that Zambia, Malawi and Botswana had no graduates at all at the time.

Many other Southern Rhodesian African students achieved their education by private study. In 1948 alone there were 716 private students, a hundred more than were enrolled in the regular secondary schools.

The system of giving teacher training concurrently with their school work to pupils in the last two years of their primary school education had ceased in 1940 – the primary teacher's certificate (P.T.C.) being introduced at this stage to replace 'elementary teacher's certificate' introduced by Jowitt in the early 1930s. The P.T.C. was taken two years after the finish of primary education at Standard VI. These teachers were restricted to teaching children doing their first five years of schooling, and thus handled the great majority of pupils because most children spent only five years in school.

Like most Africans in the country, these teachers were poorly paid, their salaries rising from £36 p.a. in 1940 to £60 p.a. in 1950. In addition to the P.T.C. teachers, there were untrained teachers, whose own education had not gone beyond Standard V or Standard VI, who served as assistants to the trained teachers. There were eighteen P.T.C. training schools in the 1940s, all of which were run by the churches.[19]

The growth of secondary schools towards the end of the 1940s necessitated the development of a higher teacher's certificate (P.T.H.). It was started by the Roman Catholics at Kutama, the Church of Christ under Garfield Todd at Dadaya, the Anglicans at St. Augustine, the Dutch Reformed Church at Morgenster and the Methodists at Waddilove. In 1952, while the P.T.C. schools were producing an annual output of 400 teachers, the P.T.H. output was below 100. P.T.H. teachers specialised in teaching Standard IV-VI between the ages of fourteen and sixteen. The pupils in these grades were found in the schools often referred to as upper primary schools.

A third group of teachers' training schools were for training domestic science teachers: the result was a tremendous improvement in the system of training African women in domestic work, a useful process if not exactly education. Missions, too, introduced 'homecraft schools' where women could improve their methods of cooking, housewifery, dress-making, etc. Many married women spent six to twelve months doing this form of training.

The history of educational development in Southern Rhodesia between 1933 and 1950 might give the impression – a false one – that the authorities were taking an interest in African education

D

and development. The Government's part in the process was one of inadequate concessions usually made for selfish motives. The development was influenced by the social and economic dynamics of the period throughout the world, with the growth of towns and industries drawing large numbers of families to the cities. In 1936, still believing that Africans were doomed to remain interminably in the rural areas, Huggins passed the Native Registration Act 1937; it had been instigated by his Chief Native Commissioner, Carbutt, who shared his belief that giving Africans innumerable passes would reduce offences arising from 'the impact of an uncivilised people with our civilisation'.[20] Huggins and Carbutt (the latter by this time had African education in his grasp) were determined to put European interests above those of Africans. Huggins arrogantly asked M.P.s. whether they wished

> 'our municipal areas to be polyglotted with a happy mixture of black and white, or to proceed with the policy of segregation envisaged in the Land Apportionment Act and keep our towns as white as possible; that is to say that the native is a visitor in our white towns for the purpose of assisting the people who live in towns, and no other native should be present in the towns unless of some assistance to the white people inhabiting those towns.'[21]

The hostile attitude of this speech indicates the Huggins Government's incapacity to plan an education system suited to the Africans' needs.

The progress of African education in 1933–50 was due mainly to Africans themselves. Many of them spent the little they earned on educating their children. The majority of mission schools were in the rural areas, and buildings, school equipment, books and even pencils and rulers, as well as the fees, were paid for directly by the parents. Even then the Government did not make the situation easy for African parents, in that it destroyed cattle, reduced arable land and, worst of all, removed Africans from 'European lands' to the reserves. This meant that some children ended up in areas where there were no schools. Some of the parents thus removed started new schools, with all the problems of raising more money and, sometimes, finding new teachers. Children shifted from one environment to another were inevitably affected by the instability which this entails.

Another disadvantage which African education now suffered was the weak direction of G. Stark, who had taken over from Jowitt. He submitted to the machinations of the Africans Affairs Department, and principles of education were compromised to accommodate the policy of the Huggins Government. The result of this was, as always, that the African got education only to the extent that the European community was willing to allow it. Although there was no actual legislation inimical to Africans during the war, administrative decrees continued to follow the tone of the 1930s. If Stark had followed the progressive policies of Jowitt, secondary schools could have come at the end of the 1930s, the education budget could have been increased, and government interest in African education could have come earlier than it did. But Stark toed the line drawn by the Chief Native Commissioner, and it was not to be.

(iv) *New Approach to Education*

Any improvement in the development of African education as it stood in the early 1960s can be attributed to the policy of Todd's Government of 1953–8. In 1951 the Huggins Government had appointed the Kerr Commission,[22] which recommended that African education should be taken over by the Government, especially in the towns. The Commission found the policy of leaving African education to the voluntary effort of the missionary agencies unworkable. Between 1951 and 1953 Huggins was far too busy with the building of his Federation to attend properly to education, and the recommendations of the Commission were left in abeyance until Todd came to power in 1953.

Todd's policy of involving the Government in African education improved the enrolment considerably. From 1955, education was separated from the African Affairs Department, and like the other departments, was administered as a unit on its own under a Secretary of Education. Todd wrested this responsibility from a reluctant Sir Patrick Fletcher, then Minister of African Affairs. Fletcher resented this action, which he regarded as interference, and three years later, he led a revolt against Todd by all the other ministers. He explained to the approving United Federal Party Congress, which deposed Todd in February 1958, that Todd's policies encouraged Africans to demand more than the country could afford. By this he meant that to advance African education could create too many African agitators and upset the *status quo*. Yet it appears that Todd was the only prime minister Southern Rhodesia ever had who sincerely and consistently believed that the education of Africans was an asset and not a threat to the settlers. His policies were fast showing signs of progress. The number of Government primary schools rose from under twenty at the start of his leadership to forty-six in 1960, two years after he left power. When Sir Edgar Whitehead took power in 1958, he did not alter Todd's arrangements. He was not enthusiastic about Todd's education policies, but nevertheless he did not reduce their content; they were too useful as Federation propaganda.

Todd's education policy was aided by the equally progressive approach of the Director of Education, H. C. Finckle. Improvements were made in the secondary schools. Mission schools were given grants to help in introducing four-year courses in secondary schools, and in urban areas secondary schools were planned, three with 508 pupils being started by 1960. Fletcher High School, the second Government secondary school teaching up to university entrance level, was opened in 1957. A Government teachers' training college and a technical teachers' training college were built at Umtali and Luveve respectively during Todd's rule. A school of secretarial service was attached to Fletcher High School, but this was later closed down by Sir Edgar's Government under pressure from white settlers, who feared that their children would have to compete for secretarial posts with the school's African pupils.

Despite its shortcomings, the system of education in Southern Rhodesia[1] was loudly hailed during the campaign for the Federation as the best in Africa. This claim continues to be made up to the present day, although the very opposite is true. As soon as Sir Edgar Whitehead became prime minister in 1958, he put about the claim that Southern Rhodesia spent 12·5 per cent of its Budget on African education, boasting that 86 per cent of all children of school age were attending school. The boast was proved false by the census conducted by Sir Edgar's own Government in 1962, and published in 1964 during Smith's rule. The analysis of the census figures showed that a mere 60 per cent of children of school age (seven to sixteen years) were attending school. It further showed that 46·6 per cent of males and 58·7 per cent of females born after 1947 had never been to school at all.[23] These ought to have been in school between 1952 and 1962, a period covering the whole of Sir Edgar's premiership (1958–62): educating the country's children had been his ultimate responsibility. But no one seemed to notice the discrepancy. The propaganda put about by the Southern Rhodesian Government was taken up and spread all over the United Kingdom. The Federation even hired a public relations firm, Voice and Vision Ltd., to put its case to the British public. The claim was used by the British delegates to the U.N. in defence of British policy in Rhodesia in 1962. After Lord Butler had visited the Federation in May 1962, he told the British press of his impression of African education in Rhodesia: it was the same old story.[24] The false claim was repeated yet again in Kenneth Young's book, *Independence and Rhodesia*.[25]

When all these claims were being made, Rhodesian secondary education was not much different from that of Nyasaland and Northern Rhodesia. In 1959–60 the secondary school enrolment figures were: Southern Rhodesia, 3,300; Northern Rhodesia, 2,108; Nyasaland 1,300. The total enrolment of white children in all the secondary schools in the Federation in the same year was 21,671. The budget for all pupils was (per child per year): white children, £103; Southern Rhodesian African children, £8; Northern Rhodesian African children, £9; Nyasaland African children, £3. In Ghana, secondary education had reached the 1971 Southern Rhodesian level in the 1940s.[26]

(v) *The Rhodesia Front's Education Policy*

The Rhodesia Front admires and wishes to emulate the South African Bantu Education policy. It is determined to revive the the restrictive policies followed by Huggins in the 1930s and earlier 1940s because it believes that the African must acquire the type of education that he can use to serve his own segregated society within the Tribal Trust Lands. Heavy emphasis is laid on the conflict of culture between black and white, with the implicit notion that African culture is inferior to that of whites. All achievements in technology are arrogated to the 'white man's civilisation' as its exclusive property.[27] African education must therefore be at a lower level than that of whites.

This cutting-back of the vigorous yet unfostered growth of African education is to be achieved by organising African society into local governing bodies (see Chapter III), to take over the responsibilities of education from religious bodies – as was achieved by the South African Bantu Education Act No. 47 of 1953.[28] The Rhodesia Front has not passed any new education Acts, the last being that of Sir Edgar Whitehead in 1959. While they administer education according to South African theory, they are not achieving much success, because their policies are meeting with resistance.

In 1966 a new plan was announced, extending education for everybody 'for seven years primary education'. In this, the emphasis remains on literacy and 'pre-vocational' secondary education, the stated purpose being the establishment of a relationship between the school and the area in which it is situated. The schools should be able to provide the labour to meet the demands of industry. In rural areas it would be essential to link the two final years of schooling to agricultural activities.

It is clear from this educational policy that the future of the African in the country is today still conceived of as lying very largely within his own community, that his main contribution to the good of the state is in providing an efficient labour force and a growing domestic market. He is not conceived of as setting up alongside the European in professional, managerial, administrative or capitalist capacities.

The provisions of the 1966 Plan are as follows:

(a) a full seven-year primary course for all children commencing in 1969;

(b) a two-year secondary course leading to the Rhodesia junior certificate, and directed towards the type of employment which will probably be available. It is in commerce, industry and agriculture that work must be sought. These schools were to begin opening in 1969 with, as their target, an intake of approximately 37 per cent of these leaving primary schools by 1974.

(c) a four-year course of formal secondary education for approximately 12 per cent of those completing their primary education; this is to be followed by

(d) a further two-year course for those suitable to proceed to university entrance;

(e) correspondence courses, supervised by a teacher based at a school for the 50 per cent who cannot be accommodated in secondary schools, the cost of this course to be met by the pupil.

It was laid down, however, that the Government's financial contribution to this expanded education programme would be pegged each year to a sum equal to approximately 2 per cent of the gross national product. Any shortfall would be met from local government sources, by school fees, or by any other appropriate means. Capital costs would be reduced by communities building their own schools, and recurrent costs would be kept low by letting voluntary agencies shoulder much of the burden. To cut costs further, the Government proposed a severe measure of economy, with a scheme whereby only four teachers would be allocated to teach a single five-year stream from Grade I to Grade V – a scheme which, it acknowledged, would involve a degree of double sessioning in the primary course, with one teacher teaching two classes in one day

The Plan is held to be progressive on the following counts: the extension of education given to all children from five-year to a seven-year period is clearly commendable; provision of secondary education for 50 per cent of primary school leavers is an advance on earlier patterns in which only some 20 per cent were admitted; a secondary education scheme allowing for differing aptitudes and abilities is better than one which is exclusively academic; and the attempt to link school to work is altogether desirable.

All this, considered *in vacuo*, may be true, but the Plan has equally fundamental limitations. It is based on the assumption that African development will take three forms: (*a*) within the Africans' own culture and designated areas, improved productivity; (*b*) within their own areas, the development of professional and skilled services as doctors, teachers and administrators; and (*c*) outside their own areas and within a national economy, an increasingly efficient labour force.

What is assumed here is that, while society is conventionally classified horizontally as, for example, professional–administrative, technical–executive, skilled, etc., in Rhodesia, according to the Rhodesia Front, it can be divided vertically into three strata: Africans, non-Africans and 'National'. While Africans cannot enter the top echelons of the non-African or National strata, Europeans have free mobility. The consequence of this limitation in the 1966 Plan is that African schooling is tightly controlled to allow access to higher qualifications only to that number of Africans estimated as being required once the non-African pool of ability has been drained.

Another serious limitation to the 1966 Plan is that only those portions of it will be implemented that can be paid for out of 2 per cent of the G.N.P. It is suggested that 'other sources' should make good any deficit; but the stark fact is that unless the G.N.P. is rising at a healthy rate from year to year, the burden on these 'other sources' will rapidly become impossibly heavy. In that event, the rate of implementation will be slowed down, and parts of the Plan may have to be shelved. Most likely to be affected are the two-year secondary courses, since in any case the responsibility for building the schools has been placed on the Community Councils, and where these councils have neither the means nor the initiative, no schools will be built.

The rise in G.N.P. inevitably continues to be restricted, mainly owing to sanctions; at the same time, predictions on population growth were far off the mark, and thus the percentage of annual wastage in the schools was badly under-calculated. Present demographic trends show that in 1975 there may well be over 200,000 children seeking school places. However, the 1965 prediction for the Grade I intake in that year is only 161,300.

Every year in Rhodesia a significantly high percentage of children fail to return to school the following year. Many commissions have investigated education all over Africa in the last eighteen years and have reported that the lower primary schools are so poorly equipped and incompetently staffed that there is a large-scale withdrawal from them of bored, untouched children.

Because of the nation-wide demand for education in Rhodesia the annual wastage is likely to continue to drop. How marked this will be is impossible to predict, but in the ten years 1956–66 it fell by half, from 16 to 8 per cent. In 1968 it was 7·1 per cent. What is particularly noteworthy in the 1968 figures is that wastage in the lowest three classes was 6·3 per cent, while in the upper two 'Standards' it was 12·05 per cent. Clearly education is being priced out of the reach of many children, but if there were any significant reduction in school fees, or rise in average African income, the wastage rate would drop rapidly.

Fees at Government schools were fixed in the 1966 Plan as follows:

Sub A – Std. 1	£2·85 p.a.
Std. 2 – Std. 3	£3·40 p.a.
Std. 4 – Std. 6	£4·30 p.a.
Day secondary schools	£9·00 p.a.

There are wide variations in the methods of assessment and in the amounts charged by the voluntary agencies. There is, indeed, not merely a variation from mission society to mission society, but in some instances even from school to school within the same society. Fees in mission primary schools are generally lower than those in Government schools. They vary from £0·62½ to £2·50 between Grade I and Grade VII. In addition there are contributory funds in mission schools for buildings, books, writing materials and uniforms. These form an increasingly heavy burden as the child progresses up the school.

The probability is that to send a child to school may cost the parents, at the lowest estimate, from £1·50 for the first few years and thereafter, in the rural areas at least, not more than £5 p.a. These sums sound very small; but the more remote the area, the nearer to subsistence level is the economy, and the less easy is it to find the school fees.

The phrase 'Seven-year education for everybody' suggests that primary education is free, but it is only so for those who can afford it. If education were free, the Grade I intake would rise sharply, and the annual wastage would be dramatically cut. This in turn would mean that a very much increased annual supply of teachers, and a considerable expansion in the present number of classrooms, would be needed. Both annual capital expenditure and annual recurrent expenditure would rise steeply.

The total cost of African education is extremely difficult to calculate, since many items, as we have seen, such as building, maintenance, administration and even teaching, are provided by voluntary agencies, the community or parents.

The 1966 Plan envisaged that entrants to junior secondary schools would be 5 per cent of the 1969 primary school leavers in 1970, 10 per cent of the 1970 leavers in 1971, 20 per cent in 1972, 30 per cent in 1973 and 37½ per cent from 1974. These projections are based on the assumption that intakes into grades would increase annually over the entire period at a constant 2·9 per cent. The population growth rate, however, rose between the 1954 and 1962 censuses from 3·0 to 3·5 per cent and there is no reason to doubt that it is still rising. Even if it remained constant, against all logic, at the 1962 figure, the 1966 projections are such that every year a higher percentage of children reaching school age will not be provided with school places. The percentage of children excluded from school will increase if the population growth rate goes on rising. Clearly, then, more reliable predictions will take account of a rising population growth rate and not assume that it will remain stable.

The 1966 projections are calculated on the basis that, standard by standard, year by year, natural dropping-out will reduce class sizes by 8 per cent. Even if one accepted the fixed nature of this figure, already too high in 1968, it is absurd to apply it to the imposed cut-off, between primary and secondary schooling for example. The 1966 predictions first apply the 8 per cent wastage formula and then allow admissions to be fixed on a percentage of the remainder. One must surely assume that 12·5 per cent of the primary school leavers means precisely that, not 12·5 per cent of 92 per cent primary school leavers. The wastage is bound to continue to drop as teaching efficiency increases and the value of education generally is appreciated; a cautious estimate is that it will decline by 0·2 per cent each year. There is evidence from the 1962 census figures that hardly 70 per cent of children of school age ever attended school; from the same source, 145,000 children were expected to reach school age in 1969, but even the projected intake into Grade I in 1969 (135,000) was not reached.

It is clear then that a far higher percentage of African children than is usually claimed never attend school. If the weaknesses we have examined in the 1968–78 enrolment projections were removed, there would be 200,000 more children at school by 1978 than were forecast in the 1966 calculations, and almost 9,000 more teachers than expected would be needed in that year.

The Select Committee on Education presented its third report to Parliament on 16 April, 1969. A general conclusion was that all education should be directed towards developing the greatest potential of any pupil so that he should be equipped, within his capacity, to take his place in society at the end of his period of formal education, and compete to the best advantage in employment.

On organisation, 'your Committee then took evidence and came to the unanimous conclusions that the structure was outdated, unnecessarily complicated and extremely difficult to operate', one of the main faults of the existing structure being the lack of a clear-cut chain of command. Numerous examples were given.

*   *   *

To conclude, we will look at some individual topics in the education area: teacher training, university education, employment, the civil service and the education budget.

The training of African teachers had been a missionary function until Todd introduced Government schools at Umtali and Luveve,[29] and the Gwelo Teachers' Training College which was completed in the time of Sir Edgar's Government. Until the early 1950s, African education was dominated by untrained teachers, but the provision of these two colleges improved teachers' qualifications in the 1960s.

Enrolment of teachers in training schools was given a fillip by Todd's education policy. By 1960, 2,565 were registered. This average was maintained until the advent of the Rhodesia Front Government at the end of 1962, which then pursued a deliberate policy of emasculating the education system. Within a year of its coming to power, a downward trend in teacher training had begun, and enrolment had declined from 2,883 in 1964 to 1,624 in 1969. Several methods are being used for this systematic destruction of African education. The major one is reduction of the budget. In 1963 the money allocated for government teachers' training was £153,337; by 1965, after two years of Rhodesia Front rule, it had been cut to £106,541. There was a slight subsequent increase, until it stood at £132,268 in 1969. Before the Rhodesia Front came to power, there were about twenty teacher training colleges scattered throughout the country. From 1969 all teacher training colleges formerly run by missionaries were unified into one college called the 'United College of Education', situated near Bulawayo, where 710 students were registered in T4 and 520 in T3.[30] Other students, about 614, are registered at the Government's Gwelo and Umtali colleges, where they are doing T1 and T2 respectively. The teachers trained for secondary schools are on the increase, because the University College of Rhodesia and the Gwelo Teachers' Training College are producing an unprecedentedly large number of graduates. Also, the squeezing out of African graduates from industry and the civil service has helped the staffing of secondary schools, though among these teachers the valuable sense of vocation is probably missing.

The 1959 African Education Act, which is still operating today, introduced pensions and a gratuity for all teachers retrospectively from January 1947. Before 1959, only teachers in Government schools qualified for pensions and a gratuity, while the bulk of teachers in Government-aided or mission schools did not so qualify. In practice it means that all teachers are now paid and controlled by the Government instead of by the church, a matter of the fire rather than the frying-pan. They are subjected to political control: for example, they are refused the right to participate in politics, which they were free to do under the previous arrangement. To this end they are subjected to the same disabilities as the civil servants but, except for those with university degrees, they are not given the same advantages of contributory pension rights and higher salary, for fear that they would qualify as voters.

The Act divides teachers into 'standard' and 'non-standard', i.e. those with university degrees or equivalent diplomas, and those without. The sixty 'standard' teachers in 1960 were given civil service privileges, but the bulk of teachers were left out. Today, more than 500, mainly university-trained, work under the system. The reason for giving the 'standard' teachers the same advantages as the white civil service was to encourage Britain to allow the Federation to continue, because it could be argued that everyone with a high standard of education got the same salary regardless of race. It was also hoped to keep the African university men from joining the nationalist movement. It has to be noted that the Act was passed immediately after the banning of the A.N.C. – several teachers had been swooped upon at the same time as the A.N.C. leaders. The salary scales of the 'non-standard' teachers were left in the old range, causing great disunity in the teachers' organisation, the African Teachers' Association, in 1961. The entire A.T.A. executive, which was composed mainly of 'standard' teachers, was sacked at one of the annual meetings held at Fletcher High School. The organisation became, and continues to be, weak. The system, established in 1961, of equal salaries for white and African graduate teachers was reversed in July 1971. Schoolchildren who protested on behalf of the demoted African teachers were caned by the police.

The Education Act of 1959 was also designed to reduce any form of nationalist influence in the schools. Section II of the Act was meant to deal with schools suspected of nationalist indoctrination of African children. In 1964 the Rhodesia Front Government introduced higher school fees, with the result that school attendance dropped. Police were sent to schools in African townships to deal with children who stayed away or showed any form of protest – though education is not, and never has been, compulsory for African children. The thinking on this occasion was exceedingly muddled. The children in Community School in Highfield, headed by J. M. Chinamano, were accused of having nationalist sympathies, and the school was closed down, the headmaster, a well-qualified teacher, being sent to the concentration camp at Gonakudzingwa. When the Act was at the planning stage in early 1959, there had been several demonstrations by children of school age in Gwelo and Salisbury, which explains why the Act was loaded with punitive clauses. Using the same Act, the Rhodesia Front Government has been able to refuse African pupils admission to privately-run white schools.[31] In the administration of African education the Rhodesia Front has achieved what the Nationalist régime of South Africa has done for African education there since 1953; the system which had been built there with so much toil, mainly by Africans, since the nineteenth century, has been destroyed in less than twenty years.[32]

As we have seen, the majority of university-trained Africans in the 1940s and 1950s in Southern Rhodesia were educated in South African and overseas universities. In the 1950s a large number of university graduates got their degrees by private study. Some students started with private study and finished at Fort Hare University College or at Pius XII University College at Roma in Basutoland. Among the students who studied privately are two nationalist leaders, Joshua Nkomo and the Rev. N. Sithole. Similarly, a man like Robert Mugabe, with four degrees, did them all by private study. Edson Sithole had left school after only five years' education, and did the rest, up to the LL.M. of London University, privately. Many graduates by private study are found in the teaching field. The University of South Africa, with a well-organised private tuition system, contributed immensely in the development of African education in Rhodesia.

African medical doctors, except for a few trained in Britain, West Germany, India, Israel and Canada, were mostly trained in South Africa. The University of Witwatersrand produced the distinguished Dr. Tichafa Samuel Parerinyatwa, who became Vice-President of Z.A.P.U. in 1962, but lamentably and mysteriously died in a car accident in August that year. Two others after him graduated from Witwatersrand in the 1950s. Natal University produced the majority of African doctors in Rhodesia.

It is significant that despite all governmental obstruction to African progress, African educational attainments were higher than in the neighbouring new independent states. By 1960 there were nearly twenty African doctors, while Zambia, Malawi and Botswana had fewer than ten in all. Today, if those living abroad are included, the number is nearly double that of 1960. There are only two African lawyers, K. Katsere and K. Sibanda, practising in Rhodesia. Edson Sithole was released from detention in March 1971 but he cannot establish a reasonable legal practice. The régime makes this almost impossible for African lawyers, and even for white ones who are opposed to its principles. Most African lawyers have left the country for Zambia, Malawi and Britain. Walter Kamba, David Zamtshiya and Simpilisio Mubako, all lawyers, have taken university teaching posts. Enoch Dumbutshena, Herbert Chitepo and John Shoniwa now live in other African countries.

Other African universities employ some of Rhodesia's African graduates as lecturers. The University College at Dar-es-Salaam took Nathan Shamuyarira; the University of Zambia took Dr. P. M. Makhurane in the Department of Physics, Dr. M. A. Wakatama in the Department of Education and S. Mubako in the Department of Laws.

The U.S.A. has been more considerate than Britain, which despite its legal responsibility prefers to keep the graduates at student status on scholarships; together with other 'non-partial' immigrants, they have difficulty in finding paid work suitable for their qualifications. Africans from Rhodesia with Ph.D. degrees in Arts and Social Sciences are employed on the teaching staff at several U.S. universities.

The African students in Canada are luckier than those in Britain and Australia, because like the U.S.A., Canada offers appropriate employment to those with qualifications. It is difficult to make an estimate of the number of Rhodesian African students at universities abroad and of the number who graduate, but the numbers have increased considerably since 1960.[33] A total of 964 African students have graduated from the University College of Rhodesia in the last ten years. The enrolment there rose from 232 students of all races in 1960 to 1,084 in 1970. The annual output of graduates has risen from thirty-seven in 1960 to 952 in 1969. Nearly half of the 1969 graduates were Africans. Yet African students find it difficult to gain entrance at the University because there are only four schools in the country, two of them founded in 1971, with facilities to teach for university entrance qualifications, compared to forty-seven for whites. There was a total of 16,000 white Rhodesian students at South African universities in 1968. In 1953 the South African Government obstructed the admission to their universities of African students from Rhodesia but the Todd Government entered into an agreement admitting six African students from Rhodesia each year to the medical school at Natal University until the

University in Salisbury was ready. No limit was put on white students.

(vi) Employment Problems

African education policy under the Rhodesia Front Government is meant to ensure that African education does not make Africans dangerous to their European rulers.

Seven years' education leading to Grade V in primary schools is just about the tolerable maximum. The majority of the pupils in mission schools end in this grade. These obtain employment in private domestic service as 'garden boys', waiters, cooks, cleaners or bedmakers. Between 3,000 and 4,000 of them enter employment annually, at an average wage that was £112 p.a. in 1965 and had risen to £122 p.a. in 1969. The rest of this group of Africans, including those who never went to school at all, join the migrant labourers in mines, on farms, roads, dams, sewage and other works, at incomes sometimes lower than those of private domestic workers.

The rest of the early school leavers continue to Grade VII or Standard VI (thirteen to fourteen years). The annual output of these averages 40,000. This group of students spends eight years at school, and they are often an irritant to Rhodesia Front supporters who rub shoulders with them at work in industry, where they operate as factory hands. Other typical occupations are as drivers or as clerks in banks and insurance companies, the wholesale and retail trade, and government and municipal services. They are semi-skilled and can perform accurately the jobs which their white bosses also do. The white worker is always reminded that his job could easily be done by the black worker, if the latter were given the opportunity to improve his skill. Often the black workers ask polite but awkward political questions of their embarrassed white bosses, who are sometimes less well-informed than they are. They read the newspapers, listen to the radio and television, and at lunch breaks they talk politics with their African colleagues behind the backs of the bosses. Their numbers vary from industry to industry.

The industrial sector, which takes the semi-skilled Africans with at least eight years' schooling, is that which also employs the greatest number of whites. It is these whites who most fear African competition. In the three major sectors – manufacturing, wholesale and retail, and transport and communications – African employment increased by only 26,200 between 1965 and 1969; yet 175,664 African pupils left primary school in that period. On the other hand, white workers employed in those industries increased by 2,760 in the same period.

	African.		European·	
	1965	*1969*	*1965*	*1969*
1. Manufacturing	71,000	92,600	16,130	18,690
2. Wholesale and Retail	31,700	35,900	18,260	18,000
3. Transport and Communication	16,300	16,700	10,260	10,720
	119,200	145,200	44,650	47,410

Out of the 638,000 Africans in employment in 1965, 124,300 were employed in these three industries. The situation is more significant for white workers. Out of a total of 89,800 whites employed in 1965, nearly half, or 44,650, were employed in these three industrial sectors.

The third set of primary school-leavers go to secondary schools, and become teachers, medical orderlies, nurses or agricultural demonstrators, or take government jobs as clerks in schools, hospitals, the Post Office, the railways, etc. A few go to university. This set is small in comparison with the first two. Until 1958 it was possible to absorb all the African school-leavers in these three categories into the economy without much difficulty. Since 1960 the situation has been changed by population growth, economic sanctions, and the racial policies of the Rhodesia Front. More than half the African population is under sixteen years of age, and the yearly increase rate of 3·5 per cent is among the highest in the world. The failure of the economy to absorb all the school-leavers spells danger for the white supremacist policies of the settlers, and indeed, for the stability of the whole country.

Africans are recruited in the Rhodesian Civil Service under the scheme which Sir Edgar Whitehead, under pressure from the British Government, introduced in 1960. A liberal lawyer, J. B. Pitman, introduced the motion in Parliament as a backbencher, and it was passed with little opposition. The new Act amended the Public Services Act 1931, which had made it clear that the public services should not be open to 'any native or coloured person'. Pitman's Act, the Public Service Amendment Act No. 42 of 1960, abolished this disability and theoretically opened the civil service to the non-white population. Some Rhodesian Africans had been employed by the Federation as nurses, doctors, broadcasters and information officers, who were made civil servants after 1956. But Southern Rhodesia itself had maintained the 'old tradition' of whites only until 1960. Although in theory the racialism of the public service was abolished, the practice remained as rigid as before. In 1962 Africans were promoted by Sir Edgar's Government to the education inspectorate, and were taken into the information service on a civil service basis. But Africans still could not hope for promotion in other ministries. The Ministry of African Affairs carefully chose a few as clerks, but restricted their duties to issuing passes, hardly the summit of anyone's ambition. The Ministries of Agriculture, Finance, Welfare and Local Government remained a white preserve. Despite this carefully two-faced policy, Sir Edgar found himself under strong attack from the white electorate. The white civil servants in the African Affairs Department were especially hostile. Sir Edgar was unsuccessful in persuading the whites to accept African civil servants, just as he failed to make them accept African voters. In 1963, three years after Africans had been taken into the civil service, only ninety-three were employed out of a total of 2,247 civil servants. The end of the Federation resulted in the Africans originally employed by the Federal Government joining the Rhodesian Government. In 1965, two years after the end of Federation, there were 1,652 Africans, all in subordinate positions, out of a total of 9,905 officers.

Under the Rhodesia Front régime, however, the situation has been radically changed. The régime's policies doggedly reflect the feeling of the whites. It was determined to meet white objections to the inclusion of Africans in the civil service by reducing the number of those that had been recruited already. Six years after the first intake, there were 1,700 Africans in various posts in the civil service, but by the end of 1969 the number had been reduced to 802, and continuous efforts are being made to reduce it still further. African salary scales in 1966 were as follows: 1,280 earned between £240 and £420 p.a.; 450 earned between £440 and £1,280, and forty earned over £2,000 as doctors or school inspectors. In 1966 the average for white civil servants was £1,385 p.a.[34]

The Rhodesia Front recognises that there is a shortage of skilled labour in the country, but it hopes to supplement the short supply by white graduates of the two technical colleges in Salisbury and Bulawayo and by immigration from Western Europe.[35] The Government's policy was attacked even by the Association of Rhodesian Industries at their Congress in August 1970. One industrialist, C. W. Dewhurst, said that industry was being held to ransom to pay wage rates to whites far in excess of those laid down by National Industrial Councils for unskilled work. He preferred to employ Africans in that sort of job. Another industrialist, B. H. Watts, wondered where Rhodesia hoped to get its next generation of artisans. He suggested: 'We must train and use the resources [of Africans] we have got.' The resolution calling on the Government to train Africans for the jobs generally reserved for whites was unanimously passed. In the context of Rhodesian politics, such an attitude on the part of industrialists is regarded as unpatriotic.

Countries north of the Zambezi have a national budget for all departments without racial considerations. Rhodesia and South Africa are the only countries in Africa with separate education budgets for Africans and non-Africans. Clearly discernible in both countries is the preference given to European education over that of Africans. Believing, as they do, that education is the mother of nationalism, both Rhodesia and South Africa have devised a system of education which, they hope, will keep Africans away from the influence of the U.N., the O.A.U., the Commonwealth Conferences, and other international institutions hostile to apartheid, racialism and colonialism.

Rhodesia is systematically following in the footsteps of South Africa's Bantu Education Act of 1953, but the Smith régime came to power too late to be able to make lightning changes. It found the present system already established, and cannot make changes as quickly as it would like because of its own instability.

Both countries have education policies designed to nip African nationalism in the bud. In South Africa this is achieved by teaching through the medium of vernacular languages such as Zulu, Xhosa, Sotho and Tsonga; some of these languages have not kept pace with the present scientific and technological development of the world – thus Africans are reminded of their deficiencies.[36] In any case, scientific language is not regarded as necessary for Africans, who should not aspire to that sort of knowledge. Yet even in African-ruled countries, advanced teaching is still invariably carried on in English and French, the languages of the former colonial rulers.

In Rhodesia, although subjects to be taught in African schools are carefully selected, and syllabuses are drawn up to fit into the framework of the policy, the methods are more direct. Education is emasculated by reducing the employment of teachers at an average rate of 700 a year. There were 22,900 African teachers in 1966 and 20,300 in 1969. Conversely, this has affected the enrolment of pupils, which is declining from 713,170 in 1968 to 703,729 in 1970,[37] while, in contrast, the birth-rate is rising all the time..

Bottlenecks are created at Grades V and VII (children of eleven to fourteen years) to control the numbers of those who get to the top of their pyramid. In primary education 113,941 children began their education in 1960 at Grade I (seven years). Five years later, in Grade V, only 85,160 were left. The same batch was reduced to 36,262 when they did Standard VI in 1967. The secondary schools only took 6,754 of the pupils who had begun their schooling in 1960. In European schools, 5,379 pupils were registered as beginners in 1960. Five years later, 4,697 remained, and seven years later, when they completed their primary education, there were 4,241. Secondary schools enrolled 4,468 pupils following their completion of primary school in 1966. This shows consistency; the small variations are due to migration. African education is relatively expensive, and when parents keep children away from school, it is mostly because they cannot afford to pay the fees.

The education policies in the independent African states are based on the belief, shared by most countries of the world, that their manpower must be educated to keep pace with the world's economic advance, and to grapple with modern industrial and agricultural techniques. Education is viewed as a benefit which, with the money available, all citizens must receive for the good of their country – to say nothing of their own happiness in achieving their full potential as individuals. African states plan to achieve universal literacy within twenty years of their independence.

Only four years after the Universities of Malawi and Zambia were started in 1964, their enrolments were respectively 642 and 541 in 1967–8 and 989 and 704 in 1968–9. Rhodesian enrolment (of all races), after thirteen years of operation, stood at 700 and 894 over the same period.[38] African students at the University of Rhodesia are limited in their choice to the few faculties which are acceptable. Engineering and other technical subjects are not yet available for fear that if Africans take them they may cause embarrassment in employment, and white Rhodesian students do these subjects in South Africa and the United Kingdom.

The rise in the budget for African education – from £503,811 in 1950 to £8,172,901 in 1969 – sounds a lot, yet it works out at £9 per child, while £103 is the amount spent on each European child. The education budgets for both races are nearly the same, but there are more than five times the number of African pupils to be paid for out of it. More money is spent for each European child than in Britain, where the state spends £88 per child per year. South Africa spends £77 on each white child.

One of the conditions of the Anglo-Rhodesian Settlement Proposal of November 1971 was to provide such 'additional facilities for the education and training of Africans in Rhodesia as will enable them to develop their capabilities'; it was believed that this would equip them for greater employment opportunities to qualify for the vote. The British Government was going to provide £5,000,000 a year for ten years while Rhodesia provided an equal amount. This policy was framed in London by people who had no conception of Rhodesia Front policies. The party had come to power to stop this very development .What was being attempted here by Britain was the imposition of a totally new policy on the Rhodesia Front, one diametrically opposed to that which it actually professed.

Only with the vote can the Rhodesian Africans influence the policies that govern them, and so ensure that their Government fulfils its duty to educate them.

REFERENCES

1. Almost all mission stations in the country ran schools, hospitals and churches. Some failed because of lack of staff, and inadequate support from their countries of origin.

2. Most of the money contributed by Africans as tax was spent on the Native Affairs Department.

3. The Bishop wrote in a letter to *The Times*: 'I can unhesitatingly endorse the recent high tribute of our High Commissioner [Lord Buxton] to the sympathetic treatment which our natives receive at the hands of the administrative officials and the white population.' *The Times*, London, 11 June, 1920.

4. Murray, op. cit., p. 281.

5. In the early 1930s, two African representatives were allowed to sit as observers at the European Conference. At the same period in East Africa, all pastors sat together regardless of race.

6. See Jowitt's Annual Reports presented to Parliament between 1928 and 1931. These show a belief that African education was an asset which the country needed, rather than a threat to white supremacy.

7. Report of Director of Native Education and Development, 1929.

8. Government Notice 676 of 1929.

9. Gann and Gelfand, *Hugisns of Rhodesia*, London, 1964, p. 135.

10. The Presbyterian missionaries had persuaded the British Government to protect Nyasaland against slave traders and a German take-over during the scramble for Africa in the nineteenth century, and thus were concerned to keep control of a situation for which they had been responsible.

11. A. J. Hughes, *East Africa*, Penguin, 1969, p. 19.

12. In 1925, Ormsby-Gore, Under-Secretary of State for the Colonies, invited the Governors of East and West Africa to London to discuss education policy. *See* Oliver and Atmore, *Africa Since 1800*, Cambridge, 1967, p. 164.

13. Kalu Ezera, *Constitutional Developments in Nigeria*, Cambridge University Press, 1964, p. 24.

14. Ranger, *African Voice in Southern Rhodesia*, London and Nairobi, 1970, p. 138.

15. Direct taxation (in 1933) meant: African poll tax, £331,072; African dog tax, £15,440; duplicate registration certificates, £1,041; contract of services, £9,932; working passes, £16. Total, £357,501.

16. Gann and Gelfand, op. cit., p. 136.

17. The author was refused admission to school at six years old in 1938 because he was regarded as too young.

18. See article by E. Mlambo in *The Times*, London, 17 March, 1971.

19. The Roman Catholics had the most with five, followed by the Dutch Reformed Church with three; the Anglicans and Methodists had two each, and the other missions had one each.

20. Speech of Huggins as Minister of Native Affairs in Parliament, 2 April, 1937, Col. 582–4. The same Chief Native Commissioner, Carbutt, blamed African agitation against laws such as the Land Apportionment Act on educated Africans, and advised Huggins in 1934 to remove them to Northern Rhodesia to free the Government from the responsibility of considering the interests of educated Africans. Ranger, *The African Voice*, p. 186.

21. S.R.L.A., 2 April, 1937, Col. 582–4.

22. The Government was responsible for an insignificant number of African pupils at the time the report of the Kerr Commission was written. Progress of government participation in the education of Africans was, and still is, slow. In 1946 the five primary schools which were government responsibilities in Bulawayo and Salisbury had an enrolment of 2,970. In 1950 the figure was 4,489. In 1954 it was 10,706, which included pupils at two new primary schools in Umtali (built 1953) and Gwelo (built 1954). Till 1960 the Government catered for the education of $8\frac{1}{2}$ per cent of the African pupils.

23. Census Report, 1964, Paras. 86–90.

24. Patrick Keatley, *The Politics of Partnership*, Penguin, 1963, p. 316.

25. Young gave U.N.E.S.C.O. as his source of information and declared: 'Rhodesia eads the rest of Africa – South Africa apart – as well as the Latin Ameŗrican and Far Eastern countries in having 91·5 per cent of its school-age (five to fourteen years) population at school, a percentage representing 627,806 Africans and 35,770 European children in this age group enrolled at Rhodesian schools.' (P. 17.)

26. Between 1880 and 1914 there were more secondary schools in the Gold Coast than in all the rest of Africa (excluding Arab lands and South Africa) put together.

27. The Mayoress of Salisbury told students at the University in 1969 that it was wrong to lay much emphasis on university education for the Africans.

28. As amended in 1954, 1956, 1959 and 1961.

29. Luveve Technical Teachers' Training College was closed in 1963 by the Rhodesia Front Government, partly because it was against their policy, and also because its graduates had no employment prospects.

30. T4 teachers are expected to teach pupils doing Grades I and II (seven to nine years). T3 teachers teach pupils of Grades III to VII (ten to fourteen years); T2 teachers have pupils in junior secondary schools (fourteen to sixteen years) and the T1 teachers and the university graduates teach pupils of sixteen to eighteen years in the senior secondary schools.

31. 'Regulations issued under the African Education Act relating to

conditions of service of African and European teachers employed by the Division of African Education and the regulations providing for the exclusion of African children from schools if their fees are unpaid have also been found discriminatory.' Palley, op. cit., p. 614.

32. L. M. Thompson, *The Republic of South Africa*, Little Brown, Boston, 1966, pp. 105–12.

33. *Financial Times*, 3 June, 1971.

34. E. Mlambo, *Rhodesia: the British Dilemma*, p. 18.

35. Speech by 'Minister of Mines', Ian Dillon, reported in the *Rhodesian Herald*, 1 August, 1970.

36. The progression to vernacular teaching in, for example, Senegal (*The Times*, 18 May, 1971) is a totally different thing, a deliberate fostering of national consciousness.

37. Rhodesia Digest of Statistics, 1970.

38. Inter-University Council for Higher Education Overseas, '*Overseas Universities*', February 1970, p. 12.

CHAPTER V

STRUGGLE FOR THE BIRTHRIGHT

(i) *Protest Movements*

White rule was never accepted without resistance in Southern Rhodesia. From the time of the Rudd Concession of 1888, Africans had always believed that they were being cheated of their land. Their preoccupation has always been, and still is, how to regain their lost birthright. The settlers, on the other hand, liked to believe that their rule was acceptable to the Africans because it was peaceful, civilised and Christian, and, most important of all, had brought wealth to the African. What the settlers regard as acceptance of their rule is the failure of the Africans effectively to rid themselves of it. This chapter seeks to explore the methods that have been used by the Africans to fight for their birthright, and their successes and failures in that struggle. Many methods have been tried: the traditional method of fighting, the conscience of the church, and economic, social and political methods.

As they came to feel the effect of the conflict of cultures in the first ten years of Company rule, both the Shona and the Ndebele people fought in an attempt to regain their independent nineteenth-century way of life. For the Ndebele, the power rested in the King, Lobengula, through the regiments (*amabutho*), some of which had been defeated in the 1893 war; but the regiments in Gwanda, Filabusi and the western part of Bulawayo had not been affected by this war. These became the source of the Ndebele spirit of resistance in the later 1890s. Among the Shona, power was in the hands of the chiefs of the old Munhumutapa empire, a power sanctioned by the *Mwari*, or God, at the Matopo Hills. The Shona leaders revived the independent spirit of va-Rozwi of the Mambo dynasty, the one clan which had remained powerful after the collapse of the Munhumutapa empire, which had flourished in the sixteenth and seventeenth centuries, and part of the eighteenth century. The combined efforts of the Ndebele and Shona leaders resulted in the bloody revolt against the Company's rule, which was only contained with the help of British troops rushed into the country from the United Kingdom,

Cape Colony and Bechuanaland.[1] The chief and ultimate effect of this revolt was that it created feelings of fear among whites. The laws, the institutions and the administrative arrangements the settlers made after the revolt were meant to protect them against possible revolts in the future.

Some of the leaders of the revolt in Matabeleland continued making attempts to regain their lost freedom up to the 1920s. They were helped in their struggle against settler rule by South African lawyers, teachers and church leaders.[2] In Mashonaland, the settlers and the British Government had together destroyed nearly all the leaders of the resistance in 1896–7. New chiefs had been created to replace the rebels. The effect of the defeat in this area was complete bewilderment, and passive acceptance of the new way of life.

The second phase of African resistance to foreign rule was organised by the African-sponsored churches. The people could make their protest by supporting the foreign churches, such as the African Methodist Episcopal Church, which clearly opposed current settler policies. This church, which had been founded by American Negroes in Philadelphia in 1818, aligned itself with the Ndebele in their political struggle. Zacharia Makgatho, a Mosotho from the Northern Transvaal, knew and advised Nyamanda during the days when the latter was trying to regain the Ndebele national home. Another foreign religious movement with influence in Rhodesia in the 1920s was that of the Jehovah's Witnesses, brought by immigrant labour from Nyasaland and Northern Rhodesia. It confined itself, politically, to organising labour, especially in the mines such as Wankie, Que Que, Shabani and Shamva. The strike at Shamva mine in 1927, involving 3,500 workers, was organised and co-ordinated by Jehovah's Witnesses; as the first industrial action ever seen in the country, it gave the Government a great shock.

Foreign African churches were soon superseded in the strength of their influence by indigenous African churches such as the Zionists, the Vapostori Movement and the Church of the White Bird, whose activities were concentrated more in the rural areas of Mashonaland than in the towns, where the Jehovah's Witnesses had operated. These resisted Government tax-collectors, opposed the implementation of the Land Apportionment Act in the early period, and sometimes spread anti-Government information.

African political protests also came through 'welfare associations'. Although these seemed on the surface like all welfare organisations as they are generally known, they were in fact political. They had various names, depending on the areas in which they were situated. They were local rather than national in scope, unlike the revolt of 1896–7 or the nationalist movement today. One example was the

Gwelo Native Welfare Association, led by C. Gwebu and Alfred Maliwa Zigode, which concentrated its activities within Gwelo and the Midlands towns, protesting against passes, the colour bar in hotels, restaurants, railway stations and trains, bad housing, poor wages, and the laws which they regarded as inimical to African interests. The Welfare Associations worked with the help of the A.P.S. to protest against the Land Apportionment Bill, and often put forward well-thought-out arguments against injustice.[3]

Some of the African political organisations fought between the wars for the enfranchisement of Africans. The most famous, whose aim was to get Africans on to the voters' role, was the Rhodesian Bantu Voters' Association, a movement entirely designed to create privileges for the 'educated Africans' who qualified for the vote. None among its members ever thought of speaking for all Africans, or of making today's demand of 'one man, one vote'. In fact, they believed that the educated African, or, more especially, those with votes, should be treated differently from those who still lived according to the traditional basis of African society, and they would presumably have agreed with the present Rhodesia Front policy of dividing Africans into rural dwellers in the Tribal Trust Lands, and those in the towns and cities.

None of the African movements in Central, East or South Africa at the time was thinking of taking over the reins of government from the white settlers. Even in South Africa, the sizeable black middle-class movement already in existence concentrated on fighting the wrongs done by the Government, not on taking control. The actual power struggle in South Africa was between the pro-British Smuts and the anti-British Afrikaner nationalists. In Kenya, the struggle was about land grievances, as it was in Rhodesia and in South Africa.

West African influence was too remote to reach the populations of the countries in the rest of Africa where the settler minorities monopolised power. Black leaders were more articulate in Paris, London and New York than in the capitals of African countries. The West Indian Negro, Marcus Garvey, preached the return of his people to Africa, but never suggested a formal structure of how Africa would be ruled; W. E. B. DuBois, a black American, was impressed at this time by the policies of assimilation into the colonising community practised by France and Portugal. Black leaders rejected the British policy of racialism as it was reflected in the legislatures of the British colonies. As for the European press in African countries, it did not heed African political opinion, nor did it even record the injustices done to the Africans. The League of Nations was paternalistic, and had, in any case, become moribund soon after its foundation. Its international machinery for remedying grievances in colonies was not as clearly defined as it is in the United Nations today.

In the 1930s and 1940s Africans in Rhodesia had moved from the haphazard joining of protest movements to attempting to secure representation on official bodies, and starting their own organisations in the urban areas. Since the Government still believed that Africans were mere visitors in the towns, incapable of representing themselves, African grievances or suggestions were supposed to be channelled through their kraal heads, headmen and chiefs up to the Native Commissioners and those officials of the Native Affairs Department who were appointed to represent them. This put the Africans in the towns in a difficult position, because, to get anything done, they would have to return to the reserves, sometimes 300 to 400 miles away from their places of employment or the source of their grievance.

The organisations now formed by Africans were named according to the area or language of origin.[4] The African National Congress was started in Bulawayo in 1934 by Aaron Jacha on the same pattern as in Northern Rhodesia, Nyasaland and South Africa, but it did not spread much to other parts of the country. At this juncture it was more of a Matabeleland organisation than a national one.

Even those Government-sponsored organisations which covered aspects of the economy embracing African interests, such as the Cattle Advisory Board, the Grain Marketing Board, the Maize Control Board and the Native Labour Boards, did not include African representatives. Yet these official organisations were meant to promote the welfare of the people who produced and sold cattle and grain in the country. Africans were, and still are, grain-producers, but they were not only left off these boards, but those whites who did belong to them put pressure on the Government for protection against African competition.

European political organisations operated freely, and the groups looking after sectional interests were recognised and listened to by the Government. Members of the Rhodesia National Farmers' Union, the Chamber of Commerce, the Chamber of Mines and the Chamber of Industries were elected to Parliament, and sometimes rose to be ministers in their areas of interest.[5]

Africans were officially represented by the African Advisory Board, set up by the African (Urban Areas) Accommodation and Registration Act of 1946. This was the first Act to provide for elected African representatives in urban areas, and it laid down the rules under which Africans were, and are, elected to participate in township affairs, and to assist the local white authority in the administration of Africans. The Act compels all local authorities to establish advisory boards, and defines the objects of such boards, as being to consider and report to the local authority, or through the local authority to the minister, on any by-laws, or laws from the central Government, to be implemented by the local authority; also to consider any subject specifically affecting the interests of Africans in the area upon which the board might consider it desirable to report. By-laws were to be made by the white local authority and passed to the advisory boards for their comments. The boards have no legislative powers of their own, their powers being confined to recommendation to the city councils on matters they regard as important to the Africans in the area, such as provision for roads in townships, schools, beer halls, street lighting, etc. The city councils are not bound in any way by the recommendations. Indeed, a location superintendent or a municipal official has higher powers than the advisory board. The boards, the number of which depends on the number of African townships under the jurisdiction of the white council, sit under the chairmanship of a white councillor on the day of presenting the items to the main council. This chairman is usually *ex-officio* a member of the African Affairs Committee in the European council of the district. For example, in Bulawayo, the chairman of the Housing and Amenities Committee is *ex-officio* chairman of the African Advisory Board.

The advisory board system originated in South Africa, and was established in Southern Rhodesia in 1930 as a result of the Commission of Inquiry into matters connected with the African location in Bulawayo. In 1940, after a ten-year lag, the Bulawayo City Council set up its own advisory board. In the African Urban Accommodation and Registration Act of 1946 the Government was able to introduce a clause which made the creation of an Advisory Board for each African township compulsory throughout the country. As these boards originated from a local arrangement in Bulawayo, other municipalities were reluctant to implement the measure, for Bulawayo was, and still is, considered too liberal in its treatment of Africans.

Between 1946 and 1956, the boards in due form expressed the feelings of Africans in the townships, for the white councils to act on or not as they decided. Membership of a board conveyed prestige, and leaders of the Welfare Associations and trade union movements of the 1920s and 1930s now fought for election to them. From time to time members were invited to multi-racial social gatherings with the mayor of the city, the white councillors, and sometimes even with M.P.s.

The situation changed in the late 1950s with the rise of modern nationalism. The prestige of the advisory boards was destroyed by the African nationalists who demanded direct representation on the actual municipal councils. The ten years 1946–56 saw the prelude to the African political re-awakening in Southern Rhodesia. The politics of Huggins had changed from the 'two pyramid' policy to that of attempting to create 'partnership between black and white' in the country. The motives that led to the change of policy have been explained rather differently by Gelfand and Gann in their book *Huggins of Rhodesia* on the one hand and by B. V. Mtshali in *The Background to the Rhodesia Crisis* on the other. The first two authors believe that Huggins had never been a hard-line right winger after becoming prime minister, and that his change of policy could have been motivated by a desire to create the Federation, which had been the ambition of all white settlers in Rhodesia since the turn of the century. On the other hand, Mtshali believes that essentially Huggins did not change at all. All he did was create a façade of liberalism designed to woo the British Government into accepting the creation of the Federation, and to insulate the settlers in Southern Africa against the onslaught of African nationalism emanating from West Africa (the victories of Nkrumah from 1948 onwards could not go unnoticed by settlers in white-dominated African countries).

Both arguments are plausible in terms of Huggins' politics and personality, for he was adept at extracting the maximum of profit from any situation that presented itself, even if this entailed contradictions in policy. Whether or not the policy of partnership was simply the old racial policy of the 1930s and 1940s in disguise is debatable, but it is significant that both the British Government and the settlers allowed Huggins, with the help of Sir Roy Welensky, to create the Federation, which lasted for ten years.

Once the Federation was established, it followed policies of the Southern Rhodesian Governments, both past and contemporary. Every aspect of the life of all the people of Central Africa, social, economic and political, was arranged to benefit the settler minorities. The franchise was restricted so as to enable the settlers in all the territories to dominate the electoral roll. The salaries of white workers in all territories continued to be ten times those of Africans, only African doctors qualifying for white salaries on leaving the university. African nurses were started at a low scale and raised higher on a promotion system based on 'good conduct', which meant after recommendation from white matrons, who might be influenced by factors other than professional skill. Although the health service was the function of the Federal Government, African orderlies were paid salaries on the territorial scale, which meant that they were poor. In the general field of employment, the Federation brought to the Africans no improvement whatever on their previous position.

On the other hand, the Federation brought prosperity for whites. The merging of the economies of the two Rhodesias increased employment opportunities for them, and immigration, especially into Southern Rhodesia, was never higher than during the good Federation days between 1953 and 1958.

African representation in the Federal Parliament consisted of two Africans for each of the three territories from 1953 to 1958, and four for each territory after 1958. There were also three Europeans, each representing Africans in one of three territories. The European representatives of Northern Rhodesia and Nyasaland, respectively Sir John Moffat and the Rev. A. Doig, a Presbyterian, were progressive and acceptable to Africans. The Rev. P. Ibbotson, a British Methodist, of Southern Rhodesia, followed the paternalism of the old Southern Rhodesia Missionary Conference, of which he was a member. After his sudden death, a lawyer, H. E. Davies, now Mr. Justice Davies, was elected as a United Federal Party member to represent African interests. He was contemptuous of the Africans, and in a debate on the Federal Franchise and Constitutional Amendment Act of 1957, even referred to them as 'savages'. The amendment was opposed by the African Affairs Board, which had been set up as a constitutional safeguard to protect African interests, and which was mainly composed of people representing Africans, including Davies himself. But he abandoned the role for which he had been chosen – of looking after African interests – and supported the contrary policies of his own United Front Party.

Between 1953 and 1958, racialism was still as strong in the two Rhodesias as before the Federation. The paucity of whites in Nyasaland made the degree of racialism there less severe than in the other two constituent countries of the Federation. For example, passes were not as rigorously enforced in Nyasaland as in the other territories. However, in all three territories, Africans continued to be denied the right to use hotels, restaurants, public lavatories, and public facilities on the railways. Up to 1957, they were not allowed to drink that dangerous liquid, European beer; and the right to drink spirits was only given to them in 1959 as a sop to please those Africans who bemoaned the ban on the Southern Rhodesian African National Congress – which throws an interesting light on the way the settlers' minds worked in the land of the sundowner.

Towards the end of the 1950s even the so-called African 'moderates' were expressing their misgivings about the Federation. The African nationalists[6] had already come to the conclusion that it had been founded purely for the purpose of curtailing the progress of the Africans towards independence. The African nationalists of the

three territories were by 1958 in touch with each other to discuss
the need to end the Federation.[7] At the All-African People's Conference in Accra in December 1958, a decision was taken to work
for the end of Federation.

By the time of the Monckton Commission on the future of the
Central African Federation, the African nationalists had long
accepted in principle that the Federation must end. The banning
and arresting of African leaders of the Zambia National Congress
led by Kenneth Kaunda, the Nyasaland A.N.C. led by Dr. Hastings
Banda and the Southern Rhodesia A.N.C. led by Joshua Nkomo
did much to harden the African attitude towards the Federation.
The Africans suspected Sir Roy Welensky of bullying the Governors
of the two territories, and the Prime Minister of Southern Rhodesia,
Sir Edgar Whitehead, into banning the three movements in order
to lessen opposition to his Federation.

African determination to oppose both European rule in general,
and the Federation in particular, was spurred by the downfall of
Garfield Todd. Todd's policies, although not very radical in
practice, frightened the settlers, who imagined what they augured
for the future. He had, in fact, made several liberal speeches, but
little had been translated into legislation. The most significant of
his liberal policies was the Five-Year Education Plan, designed to
increase the enrolment of African pupils, provide technical education
and increase the salaries of African teachers. Todd also believed in
solving political problems by talking to African leaders. He spoke
to Nkomo, who had asked for a meeting to clarify certain points
after Todd's threats to legislate against the Congress's activities,
especially its opposition to the Land Husbandry Act 1951. Because
the two men had simply met and talked, Todd was called 'a kaffir
prime minister'. He argued that he was not prepared to depend on
one section of the community for votes. He had refused to amend the
Immorality Act 1904 to make intercourse between a white man and
a black woman a punishable offence, and to increase sentences
under the Act; he had said that any change in the Act should rather
be its complete repeal, and the consequent legalising of inter-racial
intercourse. He had also made it legal for Africans to drink the
alcoholic beverages previously restricted to whites. He was accused
by Fletcher, his Minister of Native Affairs, of being a dictator, and
his policies were put to the U.F.P. Congress for 'testing'. The first
round of voting gave Todd 129, Sir Edgar Whitehead (a former
Minister of Finance in the Huggins Cabinet, but at that time Federal
Representative in Washington) 122 and Fletcher 73. The second
vote, after Fletcher's elimination, gave Sir Edgar the 73 votes from
Fletcher and thus a majority.

Critical reappraisal of Todd's policies of 1953–8 shows that he was no different from other white prime ministers, apart from the present Rhodesia Front leadership. He was responsible for the African (Registration and Identification) Act of 1957, which gave 'advanced' Africans an identity card – for which they had to pay £1 – giving better, though still limited, rights. Pressure from the white electorate had forced Todd to amend the Subversive Activities Act 1950 in 1956, and to introduce the Public Order Act in 1955. These laws were a prelude to the suppression of freedom of speech. They forbade such things as inciting to riot and criticism of the police. The freedom to incite a riot is perhaps not all that desirable, but the wording of such Acts, being vague, can be used to inhibit opposition generally. It is the way they are used, and the accusations stemming from them, which ultimately are more important than their intentions. George Nyandoro told a meeting that a circus elephant did not know her own power; if she did, she would not submit to her trainer. This metaphor was construed as incitement to riot, and Nyandoro was arrested. On another occasion, he was charged under the same Act for saying (the truth) that African policemen were housed in worse conditions than European policemen.

Todd's franchise law introduced the two-tier system now being used by the Rhodesia Front to entrench permanent racial divisions in the country. The Southern Rhodesia Franchise Amendment Act of 1957 established a lower voting qualification for the 'Special Roll', under which Africans could marshal only 20 per cent of the total European voting power. The franchise qualification for the Ordinary Roll (accounting for 80 per cent of the total voting power) increased, making it difficult for people of low income to qualify. The Native Councils Act of 1957 was another Act which remains unpopular with Africans up to the present day, and yet it was passed by Todd. The labour laws and those concerning education were left unfinished until they were completed by Sir Edgar Whitehead in 1958 as the Industrial Conciliation Amendment Act 1959 and the African Education Act 1959 respectively. In dealing with African strikers at Wankie in the Rhodesia Railway, Todd was as ruthless as Sir Edgar Whitehead or Ian Smith. He did not hesitate to use force to maintain law and order.

His success with the Africans resulted from the intention of his policies and not from their implementation. Most important of all for the Africans was the way he was crucified by whites for his policies, and this made them receive him with open arms.

(ii) *Modern Nationalism*

The African National Congress in Southern Rhodesia was born

during the days of Todd's Government, on 12 September, 1957. Before this date it was a proto-nationalist movement, operating mainly in Bulawayo, where it had been started by Aaron Jacha in 1934. Between that year and 1956 it never had any intention of taking over the government of the country. Its members were school teachers, clerks, ministers of religion and social welfare workers. Its activities were no different from those of other quasi-political movements such as the Gwelo Welfare Association, or the Matabele Home Society. The political fight was confined to securing privileges for the educated Africans in matters such as exemption from pass laws, liquor laws and curfew laws, and securing the right to travel by rail and be served in hotels. Implicitly it acknowledged the superiority of the white man by seeking to obtain his privileges, and by claiming to have attained to a similar degree of education and a similar type of 'civilisation'.

In the 1950s, especially towards the end of the decade, an upsurge of nationalism came to the surface, catching the European unawares. The new form of nationalism sought equality of opportunity in the economic, social and political institutions of the country. Its policies and principles were a challenge to white rule. Most important of all, it demanded the implementation of universal adult suffrage in the Rhodesian political system. The organisation had evolved from the A.N.C. centred in Bulawayo and the Youth League centred in Salisbury, which had been formed in 1955, after the Huggins horse and rider speech,[8] by George Nyandoro, James Chikerema, Duduza Chisiza and Edson Sithole. It was an all-black organisation, mostly concerned with urban problems, and following a militant line as yet unknown in Rhodesian politics. Two years later, these two organisations combined to form the Southern Rhodesia African National Congress.[9] In 1956 the Youth League had registered a success when it staged a municipal bus boycott in Salisbury against increased fares. Todd used all the forces of law and order he could marshal to suppress the boycott, which culminated in riots. The merger, which was achieved on 12 September, 1957, was first suggested by J. W. Msika of Bulawayo, who was at the time chairman of the Bulawayo A.N.C. He called for a nation-wide organisation which would build up pride in themselves among the Africans.

The leaders in the A.N.C. in 1957 were Joshua Nkomo, President; J. R. D. Chikerema, Vice-President; G. B. Nyandoro, General Secretary; J. Z. Moyo, J. W. Msika, Francis Nehwati, Peter Mutandwa and Peter Mudikwane as committee members. When the conference was convened, Nkomo was in Lusaka on business, but he flew in to participate. He had been active in the politics of the country since 1947, serving various committees and representing

Matabeleland at the Federal talks in 1952. Nkomo's early identification with the black masses of Rhodesia – the only African graduate who did not take the soft option of a 'European' job – was to be decisive in the split of Z.A.P.U. in the early 1960s.

The first concern of the A.N.C. was to fight all forms of discriminatory practice and legislation which 'affected the social, economic and political progress of the underpriviledged.'[10] Their first congressional year, September 1957 to September 1958, was devoted to the examination and exposure of laws based on racial discrimination and racial differences. The conclusions arrived at were that

> 'the franchise laws intended to bar Africans from participating in government are the chief cause of our sufferings. All our present misfortunes and the decaying dignity of our race are directly or indirectly produced by such laws which have subjected the African to the position of a serf both physically and mentally. The greatest crimes are committed by the rulers of this country, through the legislative monopoly and power which they have, and regulations that are of a discriminatory nature.'[11]

The settlers, by corrupting democratic institutions, had destroyed human values in themselves, believing that only they as a race were capable of ruling the country. The report attacked the Native Land Husbandry Act 1951, which was being implemented during the time of the Todd Government, the system of identity cards as compared to the ordinary passes known since 1895, and other forms of racial discrimination.

Of all the three Rhodesian nationalist movements, A.N.C., N.D.P. and Z.A.P.U. before the split, the A.N.C. had the most clearly-defined policies. On the problem of land, it aimed to get rid of the Land Apportionment Act and its offspring, the Native Land Husbandry Act; it was determined to abolish the Native Affairs Department because it had always followed a 'policy of spying on the progress, attitude and the general development of the African people'.[12] The A.N.C. believed that it was this department which was responsible for the African Affairs Act in 1928, and its amendment in 1958, which gave *carte blanche* to the native commissioners in order to enable them to deal with the members of the A.N.C.[13] Similarly, on the question of the chiefs, the policy was clearly enunciated. Chiefs and headmen were to remain 'our chiefs' for they had shown co-operation with Congress in 1957–8, despite 'indoctrination and intimidation' by the Government.

The A.N.C. sought to achieve its poliices by negotiating with the government of the day. In 1958 it attempted several times to influence the Government to change its education policy by presenting its own education **Plan**; this the Whitehead Government superciliously turned down.

Its policy on the Federation followed that of other movements in Northern Rhodesia and Nyasaland. They all regarded it as a failure because, in their opinion, it had increased racial discrimination, and it did not stick to the principles of its own preamble. Deportation of African leaders from Southern Rhodesia made the Federation a sham; and the refusal by the Federal Government to grant passports to African leaders, and interference by the Federation in the constitutional changes of the territories, showed that the settlers were bent on controlling the political destinies of the three territories in perpetuity.

The policy of the A.N.C. on self-government was less clear-cut than that of the movements that followed it – the N.D.P., Z.A.P.U. and Z.A.N.U. On this aspect, it simply stated: 'What Congress wants is self-government for all the inhabitants.' The policy statements, and the utterances of its leaders, in themselves ushered in a new era in Rhodesian politics. But nothing was explicit about self-determination; the struggle was on discrimination. It challenged white supremacy as perhaps never since the revolt of 1896–7, and within a few months of its formation, it received spirited encouragement from sister-organisations in Northern Rhodesia and Nyasaland.

The A.N.C. recruited mainly in the urban areas, and especially in the four towns of Bulawayo, Salisbury, Gwelo and Umtali. Many factors encouraged Africans to join: the implementation of the hated Native Land Husbandry Act, continuing racialism, suspicion of the Federation, the visible successes of African nationalists in other countries, and the downfall of Garfield Todd.

As shown in Chapter II, the land issue has been a source of racial conflict ever since the white people settled in the country. The Land Apportionment Act was amended in 1951 when the Land Husbandry Act was passed: the official explanation of the purpose of the Act was that it would improve African agriculture in the Tribal Trust Lands, an explanation which was swallowed whole by the British Labour Government in 1951. On 20 March, 1951, the A.P.S. wrote to Patrick Gordon Walker, then Secretary of State for Commonwealth Relations, asking him to veto the Native Land Husbandry Bill in Southern Rhodesia. It brought to Gordon Walker's attention Clause 47, authorising District Commissioners to put any unemployed African on forced labour for two months. Gordon Walker replied: 'The Bill is one which is subject to my approval and I had in fact seen it in draft.'[14] He believed that the measures in the Bill were wise and in the general interest of the African inhabitants,

E

because they would check social evils arising from the practice of migratory labour. As far as the British Government was concerned, the Act would avert malnutrition and conserve the soil; and its labour regulations were, they thought, according to the provision of the International Labour Office Convention of the proposed U.N. Covenant on Human Rights.

Like other British Governments before it, the Labour Government depended on the report of the Chief Native Commissioner, hardly an unbiased source, for its information on the utility of the Bill. At the time, 1947–50, B. B. Burombo was campaigning relentlessly in Southern Rhodesia against the measure, but it never occurred to the Labour ministers to talk to him. Gordon Walker's claim that the Bill would check the evils of migratory labour shows that he was simply ignorant of the facts.

In Rhodesia, only the white migrants were allowed to own and cultivate land. African migrant labourers never own land; they work on farms and mines, and then return to their own countries when their contracts expire.

African opposition to the Land Husbandry Act did, however, lead some in Britain to question the wisdom of the British Government in allowing the Act to pass through the Southern Rhodesian Parliament. The A.P.S. accused the British Government of pro-white tendencies by allowing discriminatory legislation to be enacted in Rhodesia without vetoing it. Some of the arguments were published in the press. They argued that the failure to use the veto was due to the fact that the policy on Rhodesia was discussed 'between white men who come to a happy compromise. The black man is thus pushed off his land in a more or less wholesale way or forbidden more or less drastically to defeat his position in the labour market.'[15] Colin Leys, a prominent student of Rhodesian politics and author of *European Politics in Rhodesia*, supported those who attacked the British *laissez-faire* policy on Rhodesia, especially on the discriminatory laws. He disputed the arguments of those who said that the Africans benefited from discriminatory laws such as the Land Apportionment Act or the Native Husbandry Act. He pointed out that the land assigned to Europeans under the Act was occupied by Africans who were not confirmed in their occupancy, but on the contrary had been gradually removed from it as it had been taken up by Europeans. The Europeans cultivated only 3 to 4 per cent of the land alienated, and the rest was 'grossly under-farmed'.

On the other hand, there were those who supported the white man's case, like G. H. Baxter, an assistant Under-Secretary of State for Commonwealth Relations in the Churchill Government in the 1950s. He said that critics of settler policies in Rhodesia saw nothing good in 'our Rhodesian kinsfolk and manufacture opportunities to traduce them.' To Baxter, the land laws were not one-sided, and that was why the British Government did not veto them. The Land Apportionment Act, he argued, confirmed the Africans in the exclusive occupation of lands they were occupying before the white man came into the country.

The opposition mounted by the A.N.C. from 1957 to 1959 was largely ignored by the British Government. In the countries with less white concentration, the British Government was prepared, also in the days of the A.N.C., to discuss the grievances of the African organisations.

In reality, the Native Land Husbandry Act was one of the most racialist laws on the statute book. It imposed restrictions on the rights of African peasants in the reserves. Sections 5 and 7 of the Act provided for the punishment of those who exceeded the per-mitted number of cattle: if the offenders were convicted three times, their permits were to be cancelled. An African family, according to the Act, was entitled to five head of cattle and eight acres of land, but of course no limitations were placed on even a newly-arrived immigrant white. The District Commissioner, and not the chief, had the right to allocate land or to refuse the allocation altogether. The Africans who had more than five head of cattle when the Act was passed were compelled to sell them at prices stipulated by Govern-ment regulations, which were different from the prices applicable to white-owned cattle of the same breed. As it would be rare to find another African as a purchaser, the effect was that those with surplus cattle were compelled to sell, at an artificially low price, to the white authorities. Africans could not transfer their grazing or cultivation rights without the consent of the District Commissioner, who even had the power to refuse a deceased man's rights to his heir, so that fathers could not feel certain that their children could inherit from them. In this way the Act violated the African law of inheritance on which the Ndebele and Shona customary law is identical. Most important of all, the right to both grazing and culti-vation permits did not entitle the African holders to qualify for the franchise unless the land was in the African Purchase Area.

Armed with these sweeping powers, the District Commissioners developed an even more overbearing attitude, exasperating to Africans. In some areas, the officers of the African Affairs Depart-ment ran a racket in permits: in 1955 an African Federal M.P. for Matabeleland, M. M. Hove, made an investigation, and established that some officers in Belingwe District were charging Africans for permits. These culprits were convicted.

The African leaders, particularly George Nyandoro, capitalised on the Act, obtaining many recruits in the reserves as well as in the towns. As Nathan Shamuyarira says,[16]

> These were dark days for the African people. But the A.N.C. leaders saw themselves making progress fast at the level of Southern Rhodesia. The example of Burombo was remembered. There was great scope for winning support in rural areas where the Land Husbandry Act was unpopular. The cases it [the A.N.C.] took to court, defending farmers' rights against loss of land or cattle under the Land Husbandry Act, brought political consciousness into rural areas.

The areas most affected were Mrewa, Gwanda and Spilolo. Here people joined the A.N.C. in large numbers. Nkomo said that the conclusions the Congress formed after a study of the Act in 1957–8 were that it was 'a vicious device whose primary aims and objectives are to uproot, impoverish and disperse the African people.'

The racial practices and laws of Rhodesia were a cause for great concern in the 1950s. Africans had become critical of all facilities provided for distinct racial groups. The labelling of facilities for 'Europeans only' was questioned, especially as white and African M.P.s were sharing similar amenities in Parliament. They decided to put to the test whether or not 'partnership' was a reality by trying to use restaurants, hotels, sports fields, railways, etc. Africans sometimes demanded service in places which had been unquestionably white in the 1940s. But 'partnership' proved a sham: they were refused service. Some cases ended with a fracas or the intervention of the police.

In a sense, the Federation contributed to the political awareness of the African people. The constant attacks on European Federal ministers by African members like W. M. Chirwa, M.P. for Nyasaland, and D. Yamba, M.P. for Northern Rhodesia, caused the Southern Rhodesian Africans to expect their own Federal M.P.s, J. Z. Savanhu and M. M. Hove, who took a milder line, to do the same. Pressure was put on the African M.P.s of Southern Rhodesia to resign from the Federal Parliament, especially after they had voted for the Bills that amended the Federal Constitution and the Electoral Act in 1957. At a meeting in Harare, Hove and Savanhu were shouted down after they had voted for these Bills, and Davies was attacked for his speech in the Federal Parliament representing the Africans as 'savages'.

Contact with the Congresses of the other two territories of the Federation gave inspiration to the Southern Rhodesians. Early in 1958 they had a joint conference in Lusaka to exchange information: there they discussed political tactics and agreed on a joint policy of the Federation as a whole.

Ghana had become an independent African state in 1957. The appearance of Nkrumah dancing with the Queen at the independence ball, and then his appearance at the Commonwealth Conference, spurred the African nationalist movements in Rhodesia. The whole continent of Africa was seething with pressure for independence. The French African colonies had (all but Guinea) voted for independence within the French Community. There were indications that Africans would rule themselves throughout Africa between 1957 and 1958.

It would be misleading to give an impression that as soon as the A.N.C. was born all Africans turned to it. The African population at the time could be divided into three groups. First there were those with professional education – teachers, ministers of religion, clerks and businessmen – who in general were members of the Welfare Associations, and believed that the Federation would involve a policy of genuine partnership, with equality for black and white. The Federation was four years old, and these 'moderates' had not yet lost hope. Most of them were voters, and gained preferential treatment as 'emergent' Africans. These rejected the leadership of the A.N.C. Some of them admired Nkomo because he was educated, but they failed to understand why he spent his time with semi-educated subordinates.[17] These moderates preferred to go along with the Federalists.[18]

The second group, mainly businessmen, consisted of people who did not care which side won, the Federalists or the nationalists, seeing gain in both policies.

Thirdly, there were the workers. In the reserves it was those people who suffered under the Native Land Husbandry Act, and it was among them that Congress found its supporters. Nkomo had been a trade union leader for some time, and he was known in that capacity. When he turned to the A.N.C., people saw him as intending thereby to achieve the economic advancement of the Africans. It was not unusual for people who had been sacked from their jobs, or been evicted from non-tied accommodation for defaulting on rent payments, coming to the A.N.C. offices to report. At meetings, speakers dealt with a wide range of subjects, from the lack of a vote to the lack of a job or poor accommodation. A myriad of grievances were explained in terms of the political situation. Up to 1954, educated Africans had believed that, by joining European organisations, they could influence Europeans to improve the lot of the Africans generally. Nkomo was a member, and Bulawayo chairman, of the white-led Federation of African Welfare Societies.

Professor S. T. J. Samkange, the lawyer E. Dumbutshena, the trade union leader L. C. Mzingeli and others were members. Some of the African members even served on the Executive. At the same time, Nkomo was General Secretary of the anti-Federal African Convention, and Samkange had been General Secretary of the old Congress General of 1934, his father being its chairman. Some African organisations such as the Capricorn African Society and the Inter-Racial Association were multi-racial, yet the more the Africans supported them the less the Europeans were inclined to do so. Such organisations, except for their white chairman, were black rather than multi-racial.

(iii) *The Fall of Todd*

With educated Africans dragging their feet, the A.N.C. was faced with a formidable task. It found itself exposed to ridicule and the fears of Government officials. Of the old Youth League leaders, Nyandoro was constantly harassed under the Public Order Act for critical attacks on discrimination in the police force, and Chikerema was arrested and fined £100 for his speech against Sir Patrick Fletcher at the Extraordinary General Conference of the A.N.C. during the Todd crisis, when Fletcher's own freedom of speech had been remarkable.

The fall of Todd in February 1958 came when the African hope of political salvation via the multi-racial organisations was declining, and for the A.N.C. it proved a blessing in disguise. The 'moderates' and neutrals were shaken out of their shells. As soon as the result of the United Federal Party Congress was announced, some U.F.P. branches in the African townships disbanded, and the members joined the A.N.C., which held its own Congress on 18 March to review the reasons for the Todd crisis. This extraordinary general meeting was attended by 2,000 delegates, the largest political gathering of Africans ever seen in the country, and speeches centred on an analysis of the policy of partnership. The resolutions passed at the conference were more militant than those of the previous year when the A.N.C. was founded. Nkomo told the meeting that the African people were horrified and distressed at Todd being crucified by his colleagues' caucus and the Congress of the U.F.P. for implementing the policy of partnership.

Even in the reserves, the reaction to Todd's departure was useful to the A.N.C. In Wedza and Chiota reserves, African voters met at Marandellas and expressed their concern at the way Todd had been deposed. They argued that the claim that Todd was advancing the Africans too fast was unfortunate, commenting: 'What was good for Europeans was good for Africans.' They passed a vote of no-confidence in their local white M.P., N. W. Wingfield, for not supporting Todd. Now they expressed their interest, not in the U.F.P., but in the A.N.C., and told a meeting on 24 February, 1958, that 'the European politicians of Southern Rhodesia, particularly Sir Patrick, have opened the eyes of the Africans to the fact that their salvation is in their own hands, and they can only trust themselves.'[19] Suspicion between black and white increased. The resolutions passed by African organisations after Todd's downfall showed that they were fast becoming militant.

At the subsequent General Election, held on 4 June, 1958, 2,000 Africans on the voters' roll voted for Todd's new party, the United Rhodesia Party. The majority of the 52,000 European voters voted for the Dominion Party, giving their preferential vote to the U.F.P. of Sir Edgar Whitehead. The election was the most hotly contested in the history of the country. It had been caused by the defeat of Sir Edgar Whitehead at the Hillside, Bulawayo, by-election when, having secured the reversion of the leadership of the U.F.P., he attempted to get a parliamentary seat in order to exercise it.

It was believed in Britain at the time that the Europeans in Rhodesia were more liberal than in South Africa, where Dr. H. F. Verwoerd had just become Prime Minister following the death of J. G. Strydom. The belief was that Sir Edgar Whitehead would be elected to power, and Todd would go into opposition in the three-cornered fight; the Dominion Party, then led by Sir Ray Stockhill, was regarded as too extreme for the Rhodesian British white population because of its inclination towards the South African racial approach.

Both the U.F.P. and the D.P. were hostile to the policies of Todd. The U.F.P. differed from the D.P. only when it talked of gradually accepting the emergent African. When Todd was dismissed from the U.F.P. and the Cabinet, six other leading U.F.P. men went with him, mostly professional men who believed in the rightness of the policy of advancing Africans. The U.F.P. was thus denuded of its most liberal element.

The election, fought with extraordinary racial acrimony, showed that the electorate was bent on bringing to power a party that would halt any form of African advancement. When it was called, the state of the parties was: U.F.P. (Whitehead), 17; U.R.P. (Todd) 7; D.P. (Stockhill), 5; Independent Labour (Jack Keller), 1. At the time there were 55,148 people on the voter's roll, made up of about 52,000 Europeans, 2,000 Africans and 1,500 Asians and Coloureds. The electoral reforms introduced by Todd in 1957, designed to increase the number of African voters, managed to collect only a little over a thousand. It was discovered when Africans started to register that the qualifications were higher than they had been previously, when an income of only £20 per month had been sufficient. So the Africans' desire to help Todd could not be fulfilled, as there were too few of them to be effective.

At the first count on the straight vote, the results showed that the white people intended to follow a party (the D.P.) with policies designed to suppress the Africans' political aspirations. The U.F.P. was saved by the preferential vote system, which had been introduced in 1958. The election result showed that the majority of the white people chose the D.P. first and the U.F.P. second.

Parties	First Vote	Second Vote	Preference	Seats
D.P.	18,314	18,142	172	13
U.F.P.	17,516	16,840	1,224	17
U.R.P.	3,991	4,663	199	nil

The 1958 election drew a dividing line between the races. The Africans discovered to their utter horror that the white population was squarely behind the white supremacist leaders. Further analysis of the results showed that the majority of the Africans and the Asians had voted for Todd. Todd received a total of 3,991 votes on the first count. As there are 3,500 non-white voters, it could be presumed that only about 400 white people had given Todd their first vote. There must have been U.F.P. supporters to the left of their colleagues who had given their second vote to the D.P.[20] The D.P. supporters were instructed not to use their second vote,[21] yet Todd told his supporters to give their second vote to the U.F.P. and the indications were that they did so; some D.P. supporters did the same, but the majority of the D.P. voters obeyed instructions and cast only one vote.[22]

The victory of the U.F.P. was due to the second vote from the African and Asian voters, a fact which Sir Edgar Whitehead forgot once he was in power, when he worked hard to entice voters from the D.P. This tactic was to spell disaster for him in December 1962. The framers of the 1961 Constitution failed to appreciate that the black and white population had been gradually drifting apart since 1958 because of the deposition and eventual elimination of Todd in that year. The Africans had lost faith in the integrity of the white leadership, and there was a general belief among them that the election results were rigged. They also lost faith in the usefulness of the qualified vote, because they had seen its futility in the Todd fiasco. After the election, no African could be unaware of the settlers' intentions, and the boycott of the 1962 election should be seen against this background.

Most political commentators tend to emphasise that racial

polarisation in Rhodesia came about after the 1962 General Election, which brought victory for the Rhodesia Front. It was, in fact, the 1958 election which was decisive. Racial fear, suspicion, tension, hate and unrest increased after the victory of Sir Edgar Whitehead. To the white people, he was a middle-of-the-road leader, and indeed a compromise between Todd, the 'kaffir prime minister', and the extreme racial policies of the D.P. Africans viewed him otherwise. The difference between him and Stockhill and later W. J. Harper, leaders of the D.P., was one of degree, not of policy. A racial gulf had been created which up to the present has not been bridged.

In 1958 all people elected to the African Advisory Boards were members of the A.N.C. rather than of the European-led parties. The Highfield Trust Board and, in Gwelo, the Advisory Board for Mambo/Munhumutapa were captured by A.N.C. supporters. The civic associations such as residents' and ratepayers' associations were also taken over by Congress members. On the councils there was a general demand for representation of Africans by Africans. After a year of struggle between the A.N.C. members on advisory boards and the six municipalities in Rhodesia, Salisbury was prepared to give in. Leslie Pocket, Mayor of Salisbury, agreed in principle to the African demand for representation on the municipal councils. He thought that since the African Councils Act 1957 was meant for the rural areas, it was time Africans were represented in the urban areas.[23]

The A.N.C. lasted from 12 September, 1957, to 25 February, 1959, exactly one year, five months and fourteen days, and during that time it made a great impact on the Africans. This was enough to scare the white population, and the settlers pressed Sir Edgar to take action to end its activities. More upsetting for them were the numbers of Africans who attended A.N.C. rallies. The special Congress held after the deposition of Todd was attended by 2,000 delegates; there were 5,000 at the meeting addressed by Dr. Hastings Banda after the Congress in Accra in 1958, and 3,000 at the meeting addressed by John Stonehouse, the British Labour M.P., in the Cyril Jennings Hall. In comparison with later N.D.P. and Z.A.P.U. meetings, these were small gatherings, but at that time they were the largest political rallies held by Africans that the settlers had ever seen. They could not understand in what way the minds of the previously 'contented natives' might be working. There was a demand by whites, especially the Dominion Party M.P.s in the Federal and territorial Parliaments, for the banning of the A.N.C.[24] After the Stonehouse meeting, the cry became louder.

Organised by the A.N.C., schoolchildren in Gwelo marched to demand places for Standard IV (10–12 years). In Chiota reserve the A.N.C. had plans for a fifty-mile march to demand places from the Minister of Education. The atmosphere all over the country was charged with protest. In Northern Rhodesia, Kenneth Kaunda had just broken from the N.R.A.N.C. to form the Zambia African National Congress, an organisation regarded as more extreme than the N.R.A.N.C. Overnight, H. Nkumbula and the A.N.C. became the darlings of the white settlers in Northern Rhodesia, while Kaunda and his associates became the villains. In Nyasaland, Dr. Banda had taken a harder line than before, after his ban from Rhodesia for addressing a political rally in Salisbury.

Whether Sir Edgar Whitehead had taken the six months since coming to power to plan his assault on the A.N.C. or whether it was a sudden decision, it is difficult to tell. But his attack on the Congress leaders when it came, was not unexpected, because the election results and his recall from Washington had indicated that the white electorate wanted a leader with an iron fist for the Africans. In the state of emergency which he declared throughout the country, 500 leaders were arrested.[25] This included all branch officials and some militant trade unionists such as J. T. Maluleke. The state of emergency was declared under Section 24 of the Public Order Act 1955 (passed by Todd), which gave powers to the Governor to stop acts which endangered public safety, disturbed or interfered with public order, or interfered with the maintenance of any essential services. However, the declaration was not warranted by any of those clauses; nothing was endangered except white morale, which was declining as a result of the upsurge of nationalism. The state of emergency was followed by similar declarations in Northern Rhodesia and Nyasaland.

The reasons put forward by all the Central African Governments was that the three banned organisations had planned a general massacre of all white people.[26] In a national broadcast Sir Edgar further said that the nationalists were disregarding the authority of the Government and ruining the scheme of development, and that they had planned violence. These statements were made without explanation. People were left to guess what he meant. In the Africans' minds, the 'authority of the Government' meant the arrogance of the African Affairs Department, and the 'schemes that were ruined' could have been the implementation of the Land Husbandry Act, which was universally opposed in all parts of the country.

In Britain, and more especially in the eyes of the British Government, Sir Edgar was a model of liberalism. Most British people who care about the political situation in Rhodesia often chide the Africans for their failure to support his liberal policies, which they think would have brought peaceful transition to majority rule. It is not uncommon even to hear responsible members of British Governments, both Labour and Conservative, claiming that the Africans missed their opportunity by not helping Sir Edgar to victory by registering as voters and voting for him in 1962. This is seen as lack of foresight on their part, and indeed Nkomo is regarded as the worst leader in all Africa for not realising this. This attitude of mind comes from people who followed the 1962 General Election with little attention to what had been happening in the country under Sir Edgar's leadership from 1958 up till 1962. Sir Edgar may indeed have been a liberal in the European sense, but Africans believed him to be a repressor of their rights. The complete stifling of freedom of speech was achieved by Sir Edgar with his legislation restricting meetings of African political organisations.

An examination of Southern Rhodesian politics between 1958 and 1962 explains why a polarisation between the races had been established by the 1960s. As has been shown, Africans had ceased to be impressed by European-led organisations by about 1954. Some, like J. Z. Savanhu, C. Chipunza, P. J. Chanetsa and R. C. Makaya, continued to associate themselves with the U.F.P. and the Central African Party. Up to 1960 the African intellectuals were in the Central African Party, led by Todd and Sir John Moffat, a Federal M.P. representing African interests of Northern Rhodesia. Professor S. T. J. Samkange, W. J. Kamba, a lawyer, Edward Ndlovu, and the Rev. Ndabaningi Sithole were members of the C.A.P., Samkange being the Party's second vice-president. The C.A.P., with its intellectual and liberal image, did not appeal to the white electorate in general, but it was supported by some prominent Rhodesian-born whites such as H. H. C. Holderness, the Haddons, Ben Baron and his son Marshall, some professional white people and some farmers such as the brothers Ralph and Eric Palmer. The policies of the C.A.P. were nearer to those of the African Nationalist parties, except that they believed in a qualitative franchise and the retention of white leadership. Their desire to stamp out racialism and hasten the social and economic development of the Africans was impressive and genuine. The African members of the C.A.P. were not subjected to the ostracism which the U.F.P. Africans suffered among their own communities. Their meetings did not need police protection, as did those of the U.F.P. and the D.P.

Sir Edgar's party was supported mostly by businessmen and part of the conservative middle class. It lacked the intellectualism of the C.A.P., but it was better than the D.P. because its membership included university men such as Sir Edgar himself and the lawyers J. B. Pitman, R. Knight, and J. H. Gasson.

The Dominion Party was supported mainly by farmers and

European workers. Paradoxically, had it been in a European country, it would have been a left-wing party. In the context of Rhodesian politics, the party is racialist because it protects the white workers against the advancement of African workers; the conflict of workers on racial grounds has brought about its apparent right-wing alignment. Because it is a workers' party rather than doctrinaire left wing, it is poorly endowed with educated supporters, being worse off in this respect than African parties.

On the other hand, the difference between the U.F.P. and the D.P., which was clear to the white population, was not at all clear to the Africans. The U.F.P. believed in the qualitative franchise in order to keep the government 'in responsible and civilised hands', and so did the D.P. Both parties believed in the increasing use of police power. Both thought that the African nationalist could only be controlled by detention, and in fact introduced legislation to put Africans in detention camps. They concerned themselves with appeasing 'the electorate' – in other words, white people, as African voters were insignificant.

Close examination reveals some facets of liberalism in the U.F.P. policies of Sir Edgar Whitehead which are difficult to find in the D.P. or, later, the Rhodesia Front. Sir Edgar believed in creating an African 'middle class', which would gradually be absorbed into positions of responsibility. He hoped to achieve this advancement of Africans by a change in the franchise system, expansion in African education, jobs for Africans in the railways and in the civil service, which had just been opened to them, and the ownership of land in the African Purchase Areas. As soon as he arrived from Washington D.C., Sir Edgar made a policy statement. He said there would be no retrogression over African advancement, which must be *pro rata* with economic advancement. He would press forward with the Land Husbandry Act of 1951, he would industrialise the urban areas, and the Industrial Conciliation Act would create multi-racial unions and encourage Africans to participate in European politics. He believed it fair that people should get the rate for the job. However, he was cautious lest Africans so advanced should upset the positions of Europeans. Africans could only get jobs where there was no European competition. He talked of not 'opening the floodgates', and of maintaining the standards – phrases obnoxious to Africans. His desire to recruit the Africans into the U.F.P. was genuine; he even addressed meetings in the African areas, a thing that the D.P. or the Rhodesia Front would never worry about. After opening the door of the civil service, he made sure that the Rhodesian information service should recruit educated Africans. After the 1961 constitutional referendum, he started 'Build a Nation' and 'Claim Your

Vote' campaigns, the aim of which was to create an understanding of the Government's policies and harmonious relationships among the races.

In all these policies he failed, and as the result he was defeated at the polls in December 1962. He had intensified the Africans' suspicion of his policy by the legislation he introduced after the declaration of the state of emergency in February 1959. The 'security laws' eliminated the last vestiges of freedom of speech which had remained after the laws introduced by Moffat under the Native Affairs Act 1928, the Huggins Sedition Act 1936, the Subversive Activities Act 1950 and Todd's Public Order Act 1955. Sir Edgar's legislation placed considerable restrictions on individuals. The Unlawful Organisation Act 1959 and the Preventative Detention Act 1959[27] respectively banned the A.N.C. and caused the detention of A.N.C. leaders.

The 1958 amendment of the African Affairs Act included Clause 4, which reinforced the old powers of government officers over the chiefs: thereby any chief who was insolent to a government officer was guilty of an offence. This was designed to deal with Chief Mangwende, who in aligning himself with the A.N.C. in opposing the Land Husbandry Act, had clashed with the Native Commissioner of his district. The chief was arrested under the Act and fined £50 only a few days after it was passed, and immediately afterwards he was deposed under the African Affairs Act of 1928.

The amendment of 1959 introduced Clause 52, whereby 'any native who is insolent to any officer of the Government or chief, or is guilty of any contemptuous behaviour or makes any statement, or does any act or anything that is likely to undermine the authority of any officer, chief or government department, is guilty of an offence and liable to a fine or imprisonment.' When it was first introduced in 1952, the Act defined the relationship between the government officers and the chiefs. The chiefs were the targets because they were acknowledged leaders of the people. The 1959 amendment introduced new features which acknowledged that leadership now came from people other than the chiefs. The chiefs as well as the officers of the departments were to be protected against exposure to contempt and ridicule by statements likely to undermine their authority. In this way, the chiefs were lumped together with District Commissioners as government officers, a change from the situation in 1928 when, although they were government officers, they were regarded as hostile to the District Commissioner.

The legislation was hurried through Parliament several days after the leaders of the A.N.C. had been arrested under the Public Order

Act of 1955. In democratic or (to use their language) 'civilised' countries, the laws that are passed after people are arrested do not affect their cases. Under Sir Edgar's Government, however, all these rules of law were ignored. The A.N.C. was banned, and its leaders were detained – respectively under the laws that were passed after they were arrested.

Africans looked for intervention on the side of justice from the British Government, which had full responsibility over matters of discrimination such as these, and especially over the Africans, who had enjoyed the status of British-protected persons under the 1923 Constitution, which still applied. Nkomo, who was attending the Afro-Asian people's solidarity council in Cairo, went to London to plead with the British Government on behalf of the African leaders. His plea to Sir Alec Douglas-Home, then Secretary of State for Commonwealth Relations, went unheeded. The British public were not shocked by the arrest of the African leaders, but they were horrified that an Englishman, Guy Clutton-Brock, had been arrested together with the Africans. Lord Malvern, addressing the House of Lords, found intense hostility over a white man being arrested with Africans. He tried to explain that even the liberal Todd had warned Clutton-Brock against his association with the African nationalists, but he was unable to placate British opinion. Within a few days, Clutton-Brock was released, but the Africans in Rhodesia waited in vain to ascertain the British Government's reaction to the arrest of African leaders.

Instead of encouragement and assistance from the British Government, what eventually came from London was a disheartening speech from Sir Alec. He said that the crisis in Central Africa was caused by friction generated from 'civilised Europeans living with the Africans who were originally nomadic tribes' – in which he showed ignorance, for none of the Central African tribes were nomadic. The Ndebele under Mzilikazi had fled from Shaka in Zululand in the early nineteenth century; the Shona had occupied their land for centuries. Europeans, he said, were responsible for the development, prosperity and civilisation of central Africa. He reverted to the 'kith and kin' argument, and reminded his audience that 'most of the Europeans in the Central African Federation are like us; translated into Africa, but with our instincts and our sense of fair play.'[28]

Sir Alec left many questions unanswered, a tendency which continues to this day in British politics. No one explains how a sense of fair play is to be squared with arresting and detaining people without trial in open court, and passing a law to hold them after they have been arrested.

In addition to the two items of security legislation mentioned above, Sir Edgar passed other measures to curtail future African political activities.[29] By the end of 1959, the statute book was heavy with repressive laws. It is sometimes argued that the British Government could not have vetoed the laws because they were not discriminatory, and that they were not meant for the Africans alone. The argument is unsound because, in the first place, the laws were repugnant to the British system of justice and contravened the Colonial Laws Validity Act 1865; also, the way they were implemented clearly showed that they were meant for Africans alone. Subsequent events proved that only Africans, and pro-African whites such as Todd, are affected by them.

The reaction of the Africans to the ban on the A.N.C. was one of bewilderment. At Kariba, out of 6,000 workers, 1,500 from Rhodesia went on strike. (Those from Malawi and Mozambique who were in the majority, remained at work.) In Highfields, more than 1,000 Africans came to a meeting called by the U.F.P. on 14 March, 1959. The speakers, all M.P.s, were Dr. Burrows, Mrs. Rosin and Chad Chipunza. Advertisements for the meeting said that the speakers were going to discuss the arrested A.N.C. leaders, but when they avoided mentioning the leaders, the speakers were shouted down, and within thirty minutes the meeting was a near riot. Police intervened and protected the speakers. P. J. Chanetsa, one of the leading U.F.P. supporters, was stoned, and his mother was knocked unconscious; and the houses of African U.F.P. supporters were stoned.[30] This was the first time that the Africans had attacked their political opponents, and a new era had been introduced into African politics. Yet when Garfield Todd arrived back from abroad, he organised a meeting in the Salisbury Athenaeum Hall, at which he addressed 7,000 Africans. Attempts by Sir Edgar's ministers to woo the Africans failed during the whole of 1959, and in the end, in January 1960, the Africans formed the National Democratic Party.

Sir Edgar received a great deal of support from the white electorate in banning the A.N.C.; white police reservists joined in the operation of arresting the A.N.C. leaders with great enthusiasm. Subsequent events proved them unwise because all they had succeeded in doing was to create national heroes out of Nkomo and his lieutenants Nyandoro, Chikerema, Msika, Nyagumbo, Edson Sithole and others, who were members of the National Executive or who held key positions in well-placed branches such as Highfield and Harare. The longer they stayed in detention, the more popular they became. Until they were released by Winston Field in February 1963, Nyandoro and Chikerema were second only to Nkomo in popularity, even after the present leaders of Z.A.N.U. had emerged within the ranks of the N.D.P. and Z.A.P.U. Nkomo himself realised that these people had built up both his name and the nationalist movement. As soon as they were released, he spent more time with Chikerema, Nyagumbo and others who had been released from Gokwe. Between January and March 1963 Nkomo travelled the length and breadth of the country with the ex-detainees, or 'prison graduates' as they were known. One of the trips ended in his arrest and that of the ex-detainees at Rusape.

There is no doubt that the coming to power of Sir Edgar White-head and his detention of African leaders created a watershed in the relations between black and white, and the failure of Britain to exert her constitutional obligation to restrain the settlers in 1959 made them believe that they could get away with anything. Sir Edgar's claim that he had the support of Africans was soon proved to be wishful thinking when there was a total African boycott of the election of 1962.

REFERENCES

1. T. O. Ranger, *The Revolt in Southern Rhodesia, 1896–7*, London, 1967.
2. T. O. Ranger, *The African Voice in Southern Rhodesia*, p. 71.
3. Ranger, *African Voice*, p. 178.
4. Murray, op. cit., p. 325.
5. Murray, op. cit., pp. 154–61, 163–97.
6. The Nyasaland African National Congress (N.A.N.C.), the Northern Rhodesia African National Congress (N.R.A.N.C.) and the Southern Rhodesia African National Congress (S.R.A.N.C.).
7. The three movements met in Lusaka early in 1958 and discussed political tactics, interchange of information and co-operation in order to fight the Federation at the conference in 1960.
8. Defining partnership as like a horse and rider going the same way – the African as the horse and the white man as the rider. Speech in the Federal Parliament, 1955.
9. Even before the Youth League and the A.N.C. were formed or merged there had been unco-ordinated opposition to the Land Husbandry Act. The Chief Native Commissioner's Report of 1954, p. 7, said that 'although some opposition was experienced in some districts when the movements were first organised, natives moved from Crown lands and other areas have in fact co-operated extremely well with the administration.' In the same year, 342 families had been moved on to farms under labour agreements. They lived as squatters on European farms under conditions which impose

criminal sanctions for the labourers who absent themselves from work without adequate reasons.

10. Nkomo's Presidential Address to the Second Congress of the A.N.C. 12 September, 1958.

11. Presidential report on the progress and expansion of the S.R.A.N.C. during 1957–8, p. 1.

12. Ibid.

13. Nkomo's contempt for the employees of the African Affairs Department was undisguised. He told the Congress that the department had failed to advance Africans into positions of responsibility. 'There is not a single African Native Commissioner or Assistant Native Commissioner in this country. Why? Instead we find that this Department has become a convenient hide-out for incapable, inefficient people; rejects of commerce and industries and other professions.'

14. Gordon Walker's letter to Greenidge, A.P.S. file H.1.

15. T. Fox-Pitt's letter to A. Creech-Jones, February 1957, A.P.S file H.1.

16. N. Shamuyarira, *Rhodesian Crisis*, André Deutsch, London, 1965, p. 48.

17. The Federal Information Service in London made capital out of this fact, showing that none of Nkomo's lieutenants had secondary education.

18. N. Shamuyarira, 'Tea Party Partners', chapter in *Rhodesian Crisis*, op. cit.

19. *Daily News*, 25 February, 1958. Sir Patrick Fletcher, Minister of Native Affairs and Deputy Prime Minister in Todd's Government, led the revolt against Todd.

20. Ten constituencies which went to the U.F.P. did not receive absolute majorities but were saved for it by the preferential vote.

21. On 21 May, when the election campaign was on, the D.P. petitioned the Governor to suspend the preferential vote. The Governor rejected the request.

22. To follow the machinery of the second vote, see discussion of the 1961 Constitution on pp. 289ff.

23. *Daily News*, 12 February, 1959.

24. Philip van Heerden, M.P. for Rusape, suggested that the Minister of Justice should ban the S.R.A.N.C. *The Daily News*, 12 February, 1959.

25. T. Bull, *Rhodesian Perspective*, Michael Joseph, London, 1967, p. 118.

26. The Devlin Commission investigated the claim and found the story to be without foundation.

27. Maxey and Christie, in *Rhodesian Outlook*, No. 1, April 1969, Minerva Press, says that 'a draft of the Preventive Detention Act of 1959 was provided for the Rhodesians by the Commonwealth Office in London'.

28. Speech at the dinner of the Institute of Public Relations. *The Daily News*, 16 March, 1959.

29. The Peace Preservation (Amendment) Act 1953, the Subversive Activities (Amendment) Act 1950, the Public Order (Amendment) Act 1959, the African Affairs (Amendment) Act 1958.

30. *Daily News*, 16 March, 1959.

CHAPTER VI

THE AFRICAN LEADERSHIP
1960–1962

The ban on the A.N.C. had created a clear definition of the political
stand of the Africans. Their general feeling was that they could no
longer count on European leadership. Although there were frequent
cries of 'one man, one vote' at the A.N.C. rallies, the main cry was
for the end of discriminatory laws. The ban on the A.N.C. had
proved that the white people were not only reluctant to end racialism,
but they were in fact determined to stamp out any African demand
for reforms.

The rest of 1959 was a time of bitter disillusionment for Africans.
Some joined the C.A.P., the only party left open to them of all the
three European-led parties. From March to 31 December, 1959,
there were three political parties that continued to operate in the
country. Of these the U.F.P. was the Government party both in the
Federal Parliament and in the three territorial parliaments. To the
right of the U.F.P. was the D.P., an all-white party forming the
opposition in the Southern Rhodesian and Federal Parliament. In
Southern Rhodesia it was led first by Sir Ray Stockhill, S. E. Aitken
Cade and W. J. Harper. To the left of both parties was the C.A.P.,
which merged with the U.R.P. to form the Central African Party
led by R. S. Garfield Todd.

To see how the Africans reacted to the political situation in 1960
it is necessary to examine the policies of the three white-led parties
in the period under consideration.

The policies of the U.F.P., the powerful party of the period, were
based on the concept of partnership. To African leaders at the time,
partnership followed Lord Malvern's definition: it was like the
relationship between a horse and rider, both going in the same
direction, but the horse (the African) carrying the burden of the
journey. This typical ambiguous Hugginsism of the early days of
Federation was not typical in other ways. The whites who supported
the policy had a different concept from Lord Malvern's. They were,
on the whole, paternalistic, believing that power must remain in

the hands of the whites, while there should be a gradual absorbtion of the emergent Africans. They believed that racial discrimination should be eliminated without upsetting the white people. Africans were to share the leadership of the white-led parties, but were not to rise above the white leadership. They hated the policies of South African apartheid, yet they also hated African nationalism and the African governments emerging north of the Zambesi.

U.F.P. policies were dictated by business interests. The leaders of the chambers of commerce, industry and mines actively supported the U.F.P., as did white-collar white workers. African businessmen who benefited from the tranquillity brought by the repressive laws supported the U.F.P. It was not an intellectual party but it attracted more educated people than the D.P.

While genuine in his desire to end racial discrimination, Sir Edgar was aware that the white people controlled the vote; he could only legislate against racialism to the extent that they were prepared to let him. He could not pass unpopular laws without the risk of losing the next election. The way Todd had lost power was a clear lesson to him. Pressure from the D.P. and the Southern Rhodesia Association – a pressure group, formed in 1960, dedicated to retaining the white man's privileges – fretted Sir Edgar's conscience. Attempts to woo Africans to join the U.F.P. were futile in view of their votelessness and the attraction of African nationalism.

Sir Edgar was only a liberal in the context of Rhodesian or Southern African politics. His attitude and philosophy were different from those of South Africa and in degree from that of Sir Roy Welensky, but to Africans he was just another oppressor. White liberalism had ended with Todd, who was deposed for 'advancing Africans too fast'. Sir Edgar spent all 1959 trying to win Africans to accept white leaders, and him in particular, but the meetings he addressed in African townships always had a rowdy conclusion. In Salisbury a hostile African meeting forced the Prime Minister to run for his life – the police opened a window for him and pushed him through it.[1] He was shouted down in Macdonald Hall, Bulawayo. His claim that Africans were intimidated by the nationalists not to join the U.F.P. was often proved false. In some cases Sir Edgar acted from inaccurate intelligence reports: his civil servants had made him believe that when the African political parties were banned, Africans felt relieved of the pressures of 'thugs and spivs'. The popularity of those who were imprisoned or banned disproved this view.

If Sir Edgar was called 'liberal', his cabinet could not qualify for that description. The two lawyers, R. Knight and A. R. W. Stumbles, together with C. J. Hatty, had been in Todd's cabinet and had revolted against his liberalism. R. M. Cleveland and H. J. Quinton were men of the establishment. They held no independent philosophy, but were prepared to follow where Sir Edgar led. A. E. Abrahamson had been in the cabinet Todd formed after sacking the rebels; he tried to appear as a liberal but Africans suspected him for joining Sir Edgar. Few of them ever took him seriously, especially as he had defeated A. D. H. Lloyd, who was respected in the African community for being a successful lawyer as well as a progressive politician. Barber's conclusion that 'all white Rhodesian politicians who were active in 1960 were right-wing and reactionary' was shared by many Africans.[2]

The Dominion Party did not disguise its racial attitude over Africans and its opposition to African advancement. It attacked the policy of partnership as too 'liberal' and because it 'endangered good race relations.' Even today, under its new name of Rhodesia Front, the D.P. has a curious concept of 'good race relations': if the Europeans are unhappy then race relations are in danger, but if the Africans protest, this is the work of 'agitators', 'communists' and 'unemployables'. Abolition of racialism in hotels, swimming baths and residential areas and the sharing of similar hospital facilities are regarded as upsetting the racial *status quo*. They refused to abolish the Land Apportionment Act on the grounds that it would spoil good race relations.

The D.P. was not interested in recruiting African members, although it had African candidates in Federal seats and got I. H. Samuriwo elected in 1958. When it had become the Rhodesia Front, it sponsored African candidates in the 'B' roll constituencies created in the 1961 Constitution. All the Rhodesia Front-sponsored candidates lost to the U.F.P. candidates. The inclusion of some Africans as Rhodesia Front candidates was rather surprising to Africans because its policy was never anything but hostile to African advancement.

The African Federal M.P.s at the time were C. Chipunza, M. M. Hove, J. Z. Savanhu and I. H. Samuriwo. Savanhu had been made Federal Parliamentary Secretary to the Ministry of Home Affairs in February 1959 as a gesture to show the world that the white leaders were serious in their aims.[3] None of these, not even Savanhu in his special capacity, could address public meetings without harassment by the African crowds. The African M.P.s were in a dilemma at this period of Rhodesian constitutional development. They made the whites believe that Africans supported them and the policy of the U.F.P., and yet they could not address meetings in their own constituencies. This dilemma was clearly shown by R. G. Mugabe on his return from Ghana.[4] He said that the Africans in the Federal

Parliament did not represent their own people who, being a hopeless minority on the voters' roll, were unable to influence their election. He declared: 'Most of these M.P.s never dared address meetings in their constituencies because as Africans know what Africans want but they do not bother to put their case before Parliament. If an African M.P. cannot address meetings in his electoral district, it's plain that his conscience makes him feel that he is unwanted by the masses. And a man in such a position cannot claim to represent the African people.'[5]

Mugabe's assessment of the African masses' attitude towards African M.P.s was correct: the Federal M.P.s were regarded as people interested in drawing good salaries for themselves rather than in representing Africans (which they knew they were not doing). The present Rhodesian African M.P.s are regarded in the same way. Even the cautious M.P. for Gwani, M. M. Hove, found it difficult to address African meetings for fear of being shouted down. At one of his meetings in Gwelo only sixty people turned up, but it turned out to be the roughest and rowdiest of meetings.[6] The police came to his rescue and the meeting ended with more police than audience.

Between February and December 1959, the European public was made to believe that African nationalism had been annihilated and that the comfortable 'good old days' of Lord Malvern had been resuscitated by his one-time cabinet minister. The African, it was thought, had become docile again.

The facts of the situation were different. African protest, simmering since the ban on the A.N.C., came to the boil again. By June, only four months after the ban, seventy-one people had been arrested under the Unlawful Organisation Act 1959, for attempts to reorganise the A.N.C. or to start a new party. The Act had been meant to forestall any future attempts to organise a nationalist movement similar to the A.N.C. This in essence meant that any African-led organisation with political objectives that included universal adult suffrage could be declared unlawful. During the remaining ten months of 1959, Africans were wondering whether to form another party or not. In Nyasaland, where the A.N.C. was banned together with the S.R.A.N.C., the Malawi Congress Party had been formed to replace the banned A.N.C. Orton Chirwa, a barrister and former inmate of Khami Prison, Bulawayo, where he was detained in February 1959 with 500 S.R.A.N.C. leaders, had formed the Malawi Congress Party which continued the fight, and in Northern Rhodesia the United National Independent Party (U.N.I.P.) had been formed to replace the Zambia National Congress. For months Southern Rhodesia had gone without an African nationalist movement. This gave credence to those who claimed that Africans stood by the U.F.P.'s policies and that the A.N.C. leaders had been forgotten.

One of the policies of the A.N.C. before it was banned in 1959 had been the sending of Africans to study abroad. One, Michael Andrew Mawema, who had been working as social welfare officer of Rhodesia Railways, was sent to Israel to study co-operatives; others went to India and Egypt. Mawema returned to the country ten months later, and was detained for questioning lasting several days about his study in Israel. In December 1959 he and E. J. Zvobgo,[7] T. G. Silundika, M. Malianga, Sketchley Samkange and E. Nkala formed the National Democratic Party which they launched on 1 January, 1960. It had the same aims as the A.N.C., although it avoided the latter's motto 'Forward ever, Backward never'. Its aims were majority rule under universal adult suffrage, higher wages and increased educational facilities for the Africans, the abolition of the Land Apportionment Act, improvement of social conditions in the urban areas and improved African housing. Africans feared from the start that it would be banned as the A.N.C. had been.

The formation of the N.D.P. had disproved Sir Edgar's claim that Africans were no longer interested in nationalism because he had received congratulations after banning the A.N.C. from hundreds of Africans through 'officials, private organisations or direct to the Government for regaining their freedom from the pressure of Congress'.[8] The N.D.P. made a forceful start. Before January was over, meetings had been addressed and branches started in Salisbury, Bulawayo, Gwelo and Umtali. Clandestine contact was maintained with Nkomo and the A.N.C. detainees; letters and messages from Nkomo were read to the audiences to demonstrate the A.N.C. link. Between January and May 1960 audiences averaged around 2,000, which had also been the average size of an A.N.C. audience a few months before it was banned.

The educational background of the N.D.P. differed little from that of the A.N.C. Mawema, who was interim president from January to September 1960, had the primary teachers' certificate and was an experienced teacher; he was an official of the Railways African Workers' Union. Silundika and L. Takawira had attempted university education, but neither had obtained degrees. Malianga had matriculated in South Africa; Sketchley Samkange had only two years' secondary education, while Nkala had no secondary education at all.

The university-trained Africans both inside and outside the teaching profession continued to pay lip service to nationalism during the first five months of 1960, as they had done two years earlier with the A.N.C., but they found refuge in the fiction (as far as Rhodesia is concerned) that civil servants do not participate in politics.[9] Africans in industry were in the C.A.P. To be associated with the African nationalists in some cases meant the end of one's job. Personal security was and still is preferred by some Africans to freedom.

One of the N.D.P.'s policies was to call upon the British Government to convene a conference of all political parties in order to provide a constitution which would allow African representation in Parliament. The N.D.P. had first to persuade the reluctant British Government to accept that it represented African nationalists; it had to fight against a hostile press in Rhodesia and Britain, and convince the British public that the N.D.P. was no different from U.N.I.P. in Northern Rhodesia, the Malawi Congress Party in Nyasaland, the Kenya African National Union (K.A.N.U.) in Kenya, T.A.N.U. in Tanganyika and those parties that had attained independence, or were about to do so, in West Africa. Most important of all, the N.D.P. had to convince the U.F.P. that the majority of Africans were not the U.F.P. African 'moderates', but were N.D.P. supporters.

From January to May the N.D.P. directed its campaign at the British Government, demanding that it should reassert the constitutional rights reserved to it for the protection of the Africans in the 1923 Constitution, which, in its life of thirty-seven years had been amended from time to time, without the British trusteeship being removed. The British right to veto laws which were discriminatory to Africans had been used only privately and restricted to instructing the Rhodesian Governments to delete certain clauses in Bills rather than calling upon them to drop entire Bills. Some discriminatory laws such as the Land Apportionment Act and the Land Husbandry Act, the Pass laws and other racial legislation in housing and education had been justified by pointing to racial and cultural differences.

In most cases the Rhodesian ministers convinced the British Government and public by saying the laws were good for Africans.[10] The N.D.P. set itself the task of convincing the British Government that the Africans were not different from those of other parts of Africa. The British public had been fed with propaganda that claimed Southern Rhodesian Africans to be the most fortunate on the continent; these stories were believed. However, the arrest of African nationalists in 1959 and the deportation of John Stonehouse, the British Labour M.P., at the same time as the ban on the A.N.C., had created doubts in the minds of some British people who had accepted the old propaganda. The N.D.P. sought to capitalise on these doubts over the settler Government's policies, the arrest of African leaders, the continued exile of Nkomo and, most important of all, the 'wind of change' in Africa.

It was during the first phase of the N.D.P. campaign for constitutional changes that the British Prime Minister, Harold Macmillan, visited the African Commonwealth countries and British territories to 'listen and learn'. On arriving at the airport in Salisbury on 18 January, 1960, he found himself surrounded by 1,500 white people, as though he had arrived at Heathrow. Attempts by Rhodesian Africans to display placards to Macmillan's car resulted in a scuffle with the Europeans. The Africans were beaten up and their placards destroyed.

During his stay in Southern Rhodesia, Macmillan was introduced to the leading Europeans and Africans. The latter were hand-picked from the editorial staffs of African newspapers – a recruiting ground for 'African moderates'.[11] They included U.F.P. African supporters and some businessmen. The N.D.P. leaders were ignored, ostensibly because the British Government was not convinced that the N.D.P. represented African political attitudes, especially as its formation had been announced only eighteen days before Macmillan's visit. Despite the plausibility of this argument, subsequent events showed that British Governments never paid much regard to African-led organisations.

The hostility shown to the N.D.P. by the British High Commissioner's office in Salisbury before and after Macmillan's visit left the African people with an impression that they had been responsible for their premier's failure to meet the African nationalists. This was demonstrated most clearly when the N.D.P. wanted to visit Lord Home at the Commonwealth Office in London in April 1960 to oppose Sir Edgar Whitehead's attempt to end Britain's veto powers, entrenched in the 1923 Constitution, over Southern Rhodesian legislation. When Mawema and Malianga approached the British High Commissioner with a request to arrange a meeting with Lord Home in London, they were told that he would not be in London at the material time. They nevertheless went to London, and found that Lord Home was there and ready to meet their delegation, which also included Paul Mushonga, Enoch Dumbutshena and Dr. B. T. G. Chidzero.

On returning to Rhodesia in May 1960, Mawema said that the British Government had recognised the N.D.P. as representing the African people, but the statement was rejected by the British High Commissioner's office as untrue. Only after much debate in the African newspapers, where Africans were being accused of exaggeration, C. M. A. Alport, then Minister of State for Commonwealth

Relations, made a statement in the House of Commons on 9 May, 1960, that African opinion would be consulted over future changes to the Constitution.

Following their policy of educating the British public, the N.D.P. sent Takawira and Malianga to tour parts of Britain and address meetings about the plight of Africans in Rhodesia. Their task was to destroy the myth that Rhodesia was independent and also that the Africans there had the best opportunities in all Africa. In this they were assisted by E. Dumbutshena, Paul Mushonga and Joshua Nkomo, who opened an office at 131 Golders Green Road in London. It was not easy to make the British public believe that Rhodesia could ever be ruled by Africans, an idea that had still not been accepted more than ten years later.

The press in Rhodesia, and more especially the *Daily News*,[12] gave the nationalists a formidable look. European-managed and African-edited, the *Daily News* was one of several papers intended for African readers. The *Daily News* distorted African opinion in that it expressed European opinion through African mouths. It supported the U.F.P.'s policies of multi-racialism without admitting its affiliation to that party. Since the A.N.C. days it had shown hostility to the African nationalists, giving space to articles written by 'Non-Congressite', which were intended to show up the A.N.C. as unreasonable.

On the day the A.N.C. was banned, 'Non-Congressite' supported Sir Edgar's policy, saying that the party had created a 'state of fear, suspicion, racial tension, hate and unrest'.[13] He sought to show that its emphasis on universal adult suffrage was unreasonable because it was not what the African people wanted. As far as the *Daily News* was concerned, African leaders ought to concentrate on the pressing issues such as 'clothes, employment, industrialisation, high standards of living, good wages, good housing, good food, etc.'. The fact that governments rarely if ever respond to the pressure of the voteless was ignored by the *Daily News*. This had clearly been shown in the case of Africans in South Africa and Rhodesia, and of Negroes in the U.S.A. When the Africans went on strike at Kariba Dam following the ban on the A.N.C., the *Daily News* commented that the strike was not in sympathy with the arrested African nationalists, but that it was a protest against the death of seventeen African workers at the dam. The paper blamed the fate of the A.N.C. on the leadership of Nkomo and the 'extremism' of Nyandoro and Chikerema. It encouraged Africans to support the Industrial Conciliation amendment in Parliament.

During the N.D.P. days it attacked Mawema's leadership. On 7 May, 1960, it said: 'African politicians have a tendency to exaggerate statements made by the Secretary of State in the past. If Mr. Mawema has made a similar exaggeration, he must be exposed; if he has not, it is up to Sir Edgar to explain why he has not told the people here about the pending conference.'[14] In fact Mawema was right, as the speech of Alport, referred to above, shows. The claim that Africans made exaggerations suggested that only white politicians could be trusted, which was strange for a paper which claimed to be the only one speaking for Africans.

Organising people for nationalist parties was nearly impossible in the country. In the reserves, meetings[15] were virtually banned except for those organised by Government officials. When the N.D.P. tried to organise meetings on constitutional issues in reactionary towns such as Gatooma, Marandellas, Rusape and Fort Victoria, the local authorities demanded such a large deposit to protect their property that it was impossible for rallies to be held. The town management board of Marandellas demanded a deposit of £10,000 for an N.D.P. rally to be held, and at Hartley £25,000 was demanded. The District Commissioner also asked for £10,000 for the hall at the African township of Seke. The banning of meetings in the Tribal Trust Lands was even condemned by the lukewarm African Federal M.P. for Gwani, M. M. Hove. The N.D.P. appealed to Duncan Sandys, Commonwealth Relations Secretary after Home, to revoke the ban on meetings in the reserves, but he would not embarrass the Whitehead Government.

Apart from the negative attitude of the African newspapers to African nationalism, the educated Africans in Southern Rhodesia did not ally themselves with nationalism as in other parts of Africa. Those in the professions joined the white-led parties or, in some cases, sat on the political fence. Many reasons are put forward to explain this. The strength of white power made some Africans resign themselves to the idea of a 'white man's country', and they decided to find their place within the system. This is true of some businessmen. The claim of the alarmists that African rule would revive the nineteenth-century law of the jungle was sometimes taken seriously by the educated Africans and the business interests. The concept of a multi-racial society was accepted as the best method of solving the problem despite the fiasco caused by the revolt against Todd's policies; Sir Edgar was regarded as equally liberal, and competent to implement the policies of partnership. The attack by nationalists on African businessmen and graduates who appeared to be compromising with white rule must have forced them further into the white man's arms.

The African élite in Rhodesia does not have to endure the vicissitudes of bad social conditions such as poverty, urban overcrowding, unemployment, rural discontent and differences in standard of living from whites as do the masses. In fact, those of them who are lucky enough to get jobs earn the same salaries as whites, giving them an enhanced economic status within the African areas. For some it could thus be advantageous to maintain the *status quo*. The nationalist movements – the A.N.C., N.D.P., Z.A.P.U. and Z.A.N.U. – recruited their followers by making them aware of their poor wages and poor land, the mere eight acres allocated to those in Tribal Trust Lands, and the small plots with poor water facilities in the African purchase areas, compared with the thousands of acres farmed by some Europeans. Much rich and well-watered land lay fallow waiting for white immigrants to come to buy it. On the social plane, Africans were not allowed in white schools, hotels, restaurants, cinemas or lavatories. Up till now, only Bulawayo and Salisbury have cinemas where Africans can be admitted. The A.N.C. had sought to end all these injustices by trying to expose the hypocrisy of the partnership policy, putting pressure on the Government through public meetings. The N.D.P. added propaganda and public demonstration to the rallies: by visiting the people in their homes and talking to them, it was able to make them aware of their plight. The A.N.C. stressed that the exposure of the U.F.P. policies would lead the Government to fulfil its promises of ending racialism. The N.D.P. sought to end all evils by constitutional changes which would bring about the representation of Africans in parliament.

The U.F.P., on the other hand, wanted the African élite to support their party, but were fearful of Africans swamping it. The white supporters of the U.F.P. believed that their aspirations were the same as those of the élite Africans, but different from those of the African masses; they saw the African middle-class as an ally against mob rule, which the nationalist movement seemed to be wanting to introduce. They reacted in a most hostile way when the 'élite' or 'moderate' African was subjected to racial discrimination, sending apologetic messages to calm the victim. Some Africans found themselves in a half-way house between the U.F.P. policies of paying lip-service to the multi-racial concept and that of non-co-operation championed by the African nationalist.

The announcement in the British House of Commons by C. M. A. Alport that the Africans of Rhodesia would be represented at the constitutional conference evoked enthusiasm among educated Africans. Those in Britain led the way in joining the N.D.P. Dr. B. T. G. Chidzero, Enoch Dumbutshena, John Shoniwa and W. Zengeni announced their membership, while in Rhodesia H. W. Chitepo and the Rev. N. Sithole joined.[16] The *Daily News* referred to the 'African intellectuals' joining the nationalist movement.

Within a few days Mugabe, Dr. E. Pswarayi, J. Bassoppo Moyo, Edward Ndlovu and others announced their membership. The arrival of the 'intellectuals' on the political scene had a great impact on the nationalist movement; it gave the masses a fillip, bringing courage and hope. The quality of the speeches at the meetings improved, and goals were better defined than before. Mugabe, with his easy oratory and straighforward nature as well as his experience in Ghana, was a gift to the movement. The Rev. N. Sithole's book *African Nationalism* had just appeared, and his appearance on the nationalist platform was also a great asset.

It was H. W. Chitepo who was 'the last straw that broke the back of partnership'.[17] All along, the white population had believed that he was supporting either the U.F.P. or the C.A.P., but this first speech delivered to an audience estimated at 2,000 people in the Harare Stoddart Hall[18] surprised many whites; it showed the spirit of the African continent at the time. Chitepo said that Africa was a continent in turmoil, and this was reflected in Southern Rhodesia. Africans wanted freedom and democracy in Central Africa; they were suspicious of the white man because he seemed to be finding unlimited excuses for continuing his rule. He dealt at length with the fears of the white people, which they express by saying Africans are incapable of ruling themselves, and declared: 'The truth is that the white man fears African vengeance. We have no desire to be revengeful at all and to build our country from the bitterness of the past'. He said that Africans wanted freedom without delay, as any delay was likely to be dangerous. The speech startled the white community. The C.A.P. reacted by accusing the U.F.P. Government of only concerning itself with white voters while ignoring genuine African grievances. The U.F.P. expressed bewilderment at the thought of middle-class Africans joining a mass movement, but trusted that their presence in the N.D.P. would avoid strife and bitterness, and that they would accept basic democratic principles.

Mugabe's first speech as an N.D.P. member, delivered on 11 June, emphasised the need for educated followers of the N.D.P. to be loyal to the leadership. He declared 'It will be necessary for graduates, doctors, lawyers and all others who join the N.D.P. to accept the chosen leaders even if these may not be university men.'

The speeches had a political impact, but they came too late. It is impossible not to look back to the late 1950s and not to wish that these learned gentlemen had joined Nkomo from the start, thus lending the movement respectability, and getting it to define its goals, at an early stage. Although the Rev. N. Sithole joined the N.D.P. in June, he did not take an active part in politics until after

26 August, 1960, when he resigned his position as a teacher and president of the African Teachers' Association. At this stage both the British and Southern Rhodesian Governments had accepted in principle that the Africans would be represented at the constitutional conference, but the problem of who among African leaders would represent the black community had not arisen.

As talks about the constitutional conference gained momentum, the U.F.P. became uneasy about the massive African meetings. Attendance at rallies was estimated at between 2,000 and 10,000 between April and June. Meetings were held in almost every township, and speeches were directed against all forms of injustice. Constitutional issues were left to the members of the executive and the new intellectual recruits. Although the U.F.P. Government had caused Macmillan to ignore Mawema and his colleagues in January, they were uncertain of scoring a similar success at the imminent constitutional talks due to be held at the end of the year. The temptation to suppress the N.D.P. by the 1959 laws which had banned the A.N.C. became strong. On 7 July, 1960, the N.D.P. headquarters in Highfields was raided by the police; correspondence and other documents were taken away. Twelve days later the homes of Takawira, Mawema and Samkange were raided, and the three leaders were charged under the Unlawful Organisation Act 1959.[19] The raids spread to the homes of leaders of the branches in all areas of the country, especially in urban areas where the N.D.P. was most active.

On the following day, 20 July, nearly all African workers stayed away from work. Two delegates were sent, with the support of 25,000 people who marched behind them, to see Sir Edgar Whitehead. Chitepo, Silundika and Nkala addressed the crowd, advising it to be steadfast behind their leaders. In the evening, 4,000 stayed to spend the night at the police station where the leaders were immured. A. E. Abrahamson, Minister of Labour, Social Welfare and Housing, and H. J. Quinton, Minister of Native Affairs, appealed to the strikers to go back to work, but their appeal was ignored. The confused situation was worsened by schoolchildren who rampaged through the townships, throwing dustbins on roads, and overturning and stoning police cars.

The significant factor in this strike action was that people who had become members of the N.D.P. less than a month before the strike took leading parts in various capacities. On the third day of the strike, Dr. Pswarayi, J. Bassoppo and R. Jamela, a trade unionist, went to see S. E. Morris, the Chief Native Commissioner, about ending the disorders in the townships. The N.D.P. stalwarts would not have gone to the Department of Native Affairs because they loathed it as intensely as they did the Police Department. The intention of the three delegates was not in accordance with the policy of the N.D.P., but their intentions in seeking the release of the leaders were praiseworthy.

The police panicked, used tear-gas and arrested Prof. S. Samkange (brother of the Samkange arrested on 19 July), Malianga and Nkala on 22 July. At the end of that week the strike spread to Bulawayo and other centres. In Bulawayo, industrial action in support of the action in Salisbury resulted in serious riots, looting, arson and blockading of the roads to keep the police away from the African townships. Bulawayo was in a state of siege for nearly a week. Contact between black and white was lost: troops were massed along Lobengula Street which divides the white from the African areas.

The Government admitted that twelve Africans were killed, while the N.D.P. made the number three times higher, claiming that the higher number had been obtained from Africans who had buried their relations.

Sir Edgar had been obdurate in refusing to meet the African leaders, but after the Bulawayo riots and the loss of life and property he was impelled to accept the release of the arrested leaders from prison, and expressed willingness to meet the N.D.P. leaders. At the same time he blamed the N.D.P., accusing it of being anti-white. In this tense atmosphere, the N.D.P. sent a telegram to Lord Home demanding that the British Government should use its veto powers, and in London, Nkomo and Todd sent a letter to Lord Home calling for the use of troops to end the bloodshed. Todd's letter provoked protests from his C.A.P., which resulted in his resignation from both party and leadership.

The N.D.P. had achieved recognition from the Rhodesian and British Governments the hard way. The N.D.P.-inspired strikes and riots brought a sudden realisation on the part of whites that the Africans in Rhodesia were as much affected by the wind of change as those north of the Zambezi. This realisation was translated into the *Indaba*, or national convention, which was held at the multi-racial Jameson Hotel in Salisbury. It was a non-political group composed of leading Africans who were keen to find a common solution to the political problems of the country; it was organised by the white Rhodesians of pioneer stock, led by Sir Charles Cumming. African clergymen, chiefs, schoolteachers, businessmen and M.P.s attended the *Indaba*, but the N.D.P. discouraged its supporters from attending. Its results were most encouraging to Sir Edgar. The *Indaba* had recommended the introduction of a Bill of Rights, abolition of the Native Affairs Department, the repeal of the Land Apportionment Act, legislation to end legal and social discrimination,[20] and representation of Africans in Parliament. The *Indaba* did not envisage more than five Africans in the Parliament of thirty M.P.s.

On the African continent, 1960 was the year of liberation from nineteenth-century European colonialism; it heralded the end of all the suffering the continent had undergone from slavery, imperialism, economic exploitation and racialism. The scene had been set by Harold Macmillan's 'Wind of Change' speech at Cape Town in February of that year. Rhodesian Africans were as keen as those in other parts of Africa to be rid of the colonial yoke, and they studied closely events in Kenya, Ghana, Nigeria and Tanganyika and the anti-colonial resolutions at the U.N.

The N.D.P. campaigned for change all through 1960. Political tension had been felt throughout the country. In May the women in Sakubva township, Umtali, rioted against night raids by the police, and increased rents.[21] Riots took place in Salisbury, Bulawayo, Gwelo and Umtali between June and October 1960; industrial strikes were almost a daily occurrence. The strength of the N.D.P. had been demonstrated, and it was in a position to step up its activities in preparation for the constitutional changes. The movement was gaining momentum and creating a working structure.

Almost all the N.D.P. policies were clear except on African representation in Parliament; there was no blueprint for a supposedly workable constitution to guide party members on what form it should take. They preached 'one man, one vote', but never showed how it would affect the system. No analysis was made of the economic system and how it could be improved to meet the new government structure under adult suffrage. The policy the N.D.P. published in a statement by Nkala on 25 August[22] to explain why it would not attend the *Indaba* stated that it would attend only if it were assured that the decision would be binding on the Government. It would have nothing to do with a General Election unless Africans were assured of twenty-five seats in an enlarged house of fifty M.P.s; a strength of only four or five M.P.s (as provided for by Sir Edgar's Bill to enlarge Parliament, passed after the recommendations of the *Indaba*) would bring in stooges again, as in the Federal Parliament. The same policy statement added: 'If the Government was keen on African participation in the future elections, they ought to give the Africans half the seats in order to enable our members to acquire experience. . . . I must assure you that if this does not happen, another Congo will happen here, because we shall assume power without political or administrative experience.' On the other hand, Mawema was prepared to see the N.D.P. contest the election.[23]

In retrospect, Nkala's approach can be seen to be in keeping with the thinking of the Africans. After his speech, letters and statements which appeared in the African press seemed to favour boycotting elections in which Africans did not have the opportunity to win twenty-five seats. The African Federal M.P.s were thought to be useless, having failed to influence the European power in the interests of the Africans. The racial situation, except for a few changes, remained as before 1953. The African hatred of the qualitative franchise and the desire to have 'one man, one vote' made any talk of trying to fight the election under the old system seem futile. Savanhu had become a parliamentary under-secretary, and apart from the obvious advantages of a new house in Highfields and travelling in a chauffeur-driven car, people did not see any advantage in having four or five black faces among forty-six white ones.

The problem of African representation was to remain vague until the constitutional conference in 1961. None of the leaders, not even the most fiery, ever thought that Africans would take over the administration of the country after the conference. Nkala alone referred to 1961 as 'the year of freedom'. Malianga repeated the concept of 'one man, one vote' in 1961 and Takawira spoke of the 25–25 formula in an enlarged Parliament. Most of the speeches made throughout the country at week-ends expressed detestation of the prevalent social injustices. Even after the congress which elected Nkomo as president of the N.D.P., the resolutions passed at various meetings did not envisage African government immediately after the conference. On 7 January, 1961, at the first public meeting which he addressed after his return from exile in Britain, Nkomo warned that Southern Rhodesia 'may find itself plunged into a period of strife and bitterness unless, as a result of the constitutional talks, Africans are given a full share in the government of this country.' This speech, made during a session of the constitutional conference, did not give the impression that Nkomo expected to see himself as President or Prime Minister after the talks.

At his press conference after the brief conference in London in December, Nkomo said that the N.D.P. did not talk of European, African, Asian or Coloured representation. His party's policy was to shape the electoral law so that no political party should manipulate it to its own advantage. The N.D.P., it appears, did not have any definite form of parliamentary representation in mind; it pinned its hopes upon universal adult suffrage, which would create an egalitarian society for all the social groups.

The result of the conference in February 1961 and the N.D.P.'s subsequent refusal to participate in the election under the 1961 Constitution exposed the African leaders, especially Nkomo, to ridicule outside Southern Rhodesia. But although most of West

Africa was free by 1960, Central and East Africa at that time were nowhere near freedom. Tanganyika alone appeared to be moving towards the freedom which she eventually obtained in December 1961, and Uganda was not far behind. Kenya and the three Central African territories of Northern and Southern Rhodesia and Nyasaland, all of which had considerable concentrations of white settlers, were all still far from freedom. The absence of this element in West Africa had made Britain more liberal towards the demand for independence. The agitation of the settlers' leaders such as Sir Michael Blundell in Kenya, Sir Roy Welensky of the Central African Federation, and the territorial leaders Sir Edgar Whitehead in Southern Rhodesia, John Roberts in Northern Rhodesia and Sir Malcolm Burrow in Nyasaland, made the freedom struggle for Africans more intricate than in West Africa. The Congo disaster complicated matters further.

This background created some sense of fatalism in the N.D.P. delegates to the 1961 Conference. What Nkomo and his colleagues appeared to have in mind was that even in Northern Rhodesia and Nyasaland, where the British Government was more sympathetic to African aspirations, the composition of the Legislative Councils were: Nyasaland, twenty Africans out of thirty-three members, and Northern Rhodesia nine Africans out of thirty members. They had some Africans in the Executive Councils also but in 1960 they were nowhere near freedom. The demand by Nkala for twenty-five African M.P.s in a House of fifty was regarded by the *Daily News* as 'a little too many at the initial stage; ten to fifteen would have been an ideal number.'[24]

Despite the evasiveness of the British ministers, there is no doubt that the N.D.P. put pressure on the British Government to accept the principle that Africans would be represented at any future constitutional talks on Rhodesia. The N.D.P. success was due first to the spirit of the time, which accepted that Africans should rule themselves, and secondly to the indefatigable campaign in Britain waged in Parliament and through public meetings by Labour M.P.s like John Stonehouse, Hilary Marquand, James Callaghan, George Thomson, Fenner Brockway and Hugh Gaitskell, then leader of the Opposition, and by Nkomo himself. Stonehouse, who had personally experienced being manhandled and deported from the Federation, led the way. His book *Prohibited Immigrants* wakened public opinion in Britain to its responsibilities for the African people of Rhodesia. Before his expulsion from Rhodesia, people had accepted the myth of Rhodesia's independence since 1923.

From C. M. A. Alport's statement about African representation made in Parliament on 9 May, the N.D.P. believed that the British

F

Government had in mind African nationalists – an assumption that would have been correct for the rest of Africa – but the Government of Sir Edgar Whitehead was thinking only of Africans accepted by the white population, not by other Africans. Over the sort of Africans that would represent the black population, Alport was evasive. When he discussed the political future of Southern Rhodesia he referred to the end of discriminatory laws and the rearrangement of land rights, and he told the House of Commons that Britain would not relinquish her power over the protection of Africans unless these two elements in the Rhodesian political impasse were discussed.[25] On the question of his visit to Southern Rhodesia Harold Macmillan did not explain convincingly why he had failed to meet African leaders as he had done in Ghana, Nigeria, Northern Rhodesia, Nyasaland, Swaziland, Basutoland and Bechuanaland. In South African and Southern Rhodesia he had met only those put forward for display by the Government.[26]

When pressed to ensure that the political aspirations of the Africans were met in Southern Rhodesia as in other African territories, Macmillan said vaguely that 'in the event of any change being made in the constitution of Southern Rhodesia, the interest of the Africans will of course be given full weight'.[27] The British Government always wanted to establish degrees of difference in their constitutional responsibility for Africans in Southern Rhodesia compared with what it owed to Africans in other African territories. No British government has ever explained satisfactorily why the constitutional provision for the protection of African interests has not been honoured. In 1960 Alport failed to give satisfactory reasons when the British Government had not vetoed the Southern Rhodesian legislation designed to stifle African political activities such as the Amendment of the Native Affairs Act 1959, Preventive Detention Act 1959, and the Unlawful Organisation Act 1959.[28]

When the constitutional conference had been announced, Sir Edgar was in a position to select the people he wanted as participants at the expense of the African nationalists. His own party, the U.F.P., was represented, as a party, with the D.P. and the C.A.P. An Asian, J. N. Patel, and a Coloured man, G. T. Thorncroft, were to represent their respective communities. The U.F.P. had European representatives, with four African supporters who included S. J. Moyo,[29] President of the Railway African Workers' Union. The D.P. had four Europeans, two delegates and two advisers. The C.A.P. also had two delegates and two advisers, one of them an African attorney, Walter Kamba. Sir Edgar led the Rhodesian Government ministers; thus the U.F.P. had two sets of delegates, at party and ministerial level. Africans in the rural areas were supposed to be represented by Chief Kayisa Ndiweni, but for all practical purposes he was part of the Government delegation.

The N.D.P. were at a disadvantage from the beginning. To start with, they were not even invited, so Nkomo, who had been received by thousands of people after his two years' exile abroad, found himself left out.[30] He returned to Britain to confer with Banda and Kaunda and to press for admission to the conference. It is difficult to understand how the strings were pulled, but the N.D.P. were finally admitted with two delegates and two advisers. Nkomo, the President, and Sithole, the Treasurer-General, were the delegates, while Silundika and Chitepo were advisers. At this stage, the Conference was about the Federation's future; Southern Rhodesia and the other territories were to be discussed individually later. Sir Edgar was still unhappy about the N.D.P.'s presence at the conference, and about having to explain the presence of African nationalists to the white electorate. When Banda, Kaunda and Nkomo walked out in protest on some procedural point, Sir Edgar used the opportunity to exclude all the N.D.P. delegates. This high-handed policy was being carried out in London in the presence of the British ministers, who claimed the legal right to protect the Africans. It is noteworthy that the Southern Rhodesian delegations were weighted in favour of the whites, yet the constitutional changes under discussion were to do with British trusteeship over Africans as provided for in the 1923 Constitution. If Nkomo and his delegation had been removed, only those Africans who belonged to the U.F.P., with one from the C.A.P., would have remained to witness the removal of powers meant to protect their own people. Even then it would have been fairer to have more Africans than whites in the conference, since the topics of discussion concerned them most closely. But despite the already unbalanced representation in the conference, Sir Edgar wanted to keep the N.D.P. out as unrepresentative. After an exchange of letters with Nkomo, Sir Edgar allowed the N.D.P. to return to the conference; Nkomo's expulsion had resulted in riots in Highfield, which must have influenced Sir Edgar's decision. Whether the British ministers intervened it is difficult to say, because their attitude towards the schoolboy treatment meted out to Nkomo by Sir Edgar was not made public.

The Conference reconvened in Salisbury at the end of January 1961. To start with, Sir Edgar was in the chair,[31] Duncan Sandys taking over later. Only the N.D.P. and the C.A.P. were prepared to recommend constitutional instruments which they believed would help create good race relations in the country. The N.D.P. put forward universal adult franchise, a bill of rights (Nigeria version) and a change in the Land Apportionment Act. On the bill of rights, the N.D.P. had the support of the C.A.P., Thorncroft and Patel. On this even some the U.F.P. delegates supported the N.D.P. policy.

The conference spent most of February 1 discussing the bill of rights. Sir Edgar himself was not fundamentally opposed to it; the *Indaba* had recommended it in their meeting in 1960, so he believed that the people wanted it. The N.D.P. further insisted on the inclusion of a clause guaranteeing citizens' right to private life. The D.P. opposed this aspect of N.D.P. policy, claiming that the guaranteeing of private life would encourage mixed marriages. The N.D.P. itself had been impressed by the way the bill of rights was working in the Nigerian Constitution, and even offered to bring Dr. T. O. Elias, then Attorney-General of Nigeria, to take over Silundika's place as an adviser on the bill of rights. Sir Edgar rejected that offer.

Dr. Claire Palley, then lecturer in law at the University College in Salisbury, was alarmed by the excitement of the N.D.P. over their achievement on the bill of rights, and wrote an article in the *Daily News*[32] with the warning that it had been found impotent in other countries. She said it was not the final answer. It had originated from the English philosopher John Locke, who had influenced the American Founding Fathers to include it in their constitution. After the First World War, European countries introduced it, and so did India in 1931, Nigeria, Pakistan, Malaya, Ceylon and Ireland followed, but various Parliaments in those countries later amended it, reducing its effect. The N.D.P. took no heed of Dr. Palley's advice. Even Chitepo, a barrister with experience of racialist judges, ignored her warning. The N.D.P.'s faith in the bill of rights is clearly shown by its satisfaction after the conference. At the press conference on 7 February, Mugabe, the N.D.P.'s Publicity Secretary declared: 'Several major features proposed in the Constitution have fallen into line with the demands that have been made by the N.D.P. since its inception. These have been the enshrinement of a declaration of rights, the outlawing of discrimination and the protection of the rights by the Courts.'[33]

Having won on the bill of rights, the N.D.P. pressed onwards with franchise. Discussion on universal adult suffrage took place on 1 and 2 February, bringing about a clash between Nkomo and Sir Edgar. The N.D.P. was supported by the Asian and Coloured representatives. The C.A.P. thought that the demand for universal adult suffrage was premature and were prepared instead to settle for a wider qualified franchise. Dr. Morris Hirsch intervened when the clash between Nkomo and Sir Edgar was threatening to break up the conference, and put forward a suggestion for fifteen special seats for Africans; the N.D.P. rejected the idea, claiming that it would keep them as a minority in Parliament. Sandys decided to have separate meetings with the N.D.P. on the question of representation, and in a private meeting he was told that the N.D.P. favoured staying out of Parliament and continuing the fight as before. The N.D.P. also rejected the U.F.P. suggestion for a second chamber as a substitute for the reserved powers, but indicated its willingness to consider it if the franchise was to be 'one man, one vote'. The Land Apportionment Act was discussed after the conference, and the N.D.P. boycotted this discussion in its last stage.

The other parties' contribution to the conference was confined to details. The U.F.P. policy of a second chamber failed and in its place was introduced the Constitutional Council, which was meant to be a watchdog over the bill of rights. It was hoped that its activities would prevent the enactment of discriminatory legislation. The U.F.P. succeeded in obtaining provision for fifteen special seats for African M.P.s. Their original intention of obtaining complete independence for Southern Rhodesia also failed.

On the other hand, the D.P.'s contribution to the conference was negative. It did not put forward a policy line designed as a blueprint for the future political life of the country.[34] Its aim was to oppose any measure which appeared to 'appease' the Africans. For example, it attacked the U.F.P. policy of providing special seats for Africans. Its leader, W. J. Harper, was violently hostile to this provision. He warned Britain that his party would be forced to use 'force to secure independence for this country'. At the time, Harper had only been in the country for thirteen years, having arrived in 1947. His claim that Britain would discover that the loyalty of some Europeans would soon disappear referred to those whose residence in the country was, like his, restricted to the period after the Second World War.[35] The D.P. claimed the inclusion of the fifteen Africans in Parliament was 'lowering standards'. Even Sandys was shocked by the D.P.'s negative attitude. He could not see why they wanted Africans removed from the vote, or understand their rejection of African political advancement and preoccupation with racial details. He pointed out that 'the 25 per cent vote means nothing to us at all'.[36]

In Britain, the results of the constitutional conference were regarded as a great achievement for Sandys. The newspapers praised him and criticised Iain Macleod, then Colonial Secretary, for taking a long time in settling the Northern Rhodesian Constitution, which appeared easier than that of Southern Rhodesia.

Nkomo and his delegation appeared satisfied with the results of the conference, although they did not succeed on the franchise, which was their main concern. The N.D.P. believed it had scored a great success with the bill of rights, but the jubilation felt was unfounded. No one in Rhodesia, or in Britain for that matter, ever believed seriously that 'one man, one vote' could be introduced in Rhodesia at the time, and more than ten years later, Britain and the Rhodesian whites still doubt the practicability of increased African representation in Parliament. At the press conference, Mugabe stated, probably wisely, that they had prevented the settlers from getting the independence they wanted; Southern Rhodesia remained a colony, and Britain retained overriding authority over the settler régime. The N.D.P. was at pains to prove to the world from the start that the provision of fifteen seats for Africans did not have its blessing. It felt itself trapped in the policy of racialism implied by giving Africans fifteen seats, because its policy was one of non-racialism based on the belief that human beings are equal. This equality is achieved by 'one man, one vote'. This was emphasised in the statement read by Mugabe on 7 February, 1961. He insisted that the N.D.P. would not move from 'one man, one vote' and 'therefore the annex on the franchise and representation is not related to the N.D.P.'[37] The claims made at the time and still circulating in books and journals, that the African leaders accepted the fifteen seats, are unfounded.

The way the N.D.P. fought in the conference was praised even by S. J. Moyo, who was with the U.F.P. delegation, and who said that the N.D.P. had done its best. The N.D.P. thought not about the fifteen seats but about the franchise. Nkomo appeared to believe that his followers would attack him for his failure to achieve the acceptance of 'one man, one vote', and he sought to demonstrate that the N.D.P. should not be blamed for not gaining the franchise. He insisted, as did Mugabe, that 'the operative word is "considered" '; his party had 'considered' the franchise, but not 'agreed' on it. Nkomo wanted his followers to make a distinction between the Constitution itself, the franchise and representation. He rejected the last two while accepting the first. He accepted the Constitution because, with the bill of rights, private citizens were protected by the courts against arbitrary arrest, and against discrimination; the courts would stop the country from becoming 'another South Africa'. The Constitution might be inadequate, but the courts would help. He added that a bill of rights 'will also be there as a yardstick for any government that is moral'. Even after a month of criticism from all over the world, Nkomo was still determined to defend his bill of rights. He told a meeting, after the special congress held in Cyril Jennings Hall on 19 March, that they had never agreed on representation and the franchise. He was bent on proving to his followers the utility of being protected by the courts against tyranny. He said: 'We were able to move the mountain which had been set before us an inch by getting the declaration of human rights and the protection of the courts enshrined in the new Constitution.'

Two basic errors clouded the N.D.P. approach to the problem. When Nkomo said, 'We lost nothing and achieved nothing,' he was right, but his error lay in placing too much faith in the courts acting impartially; the way the courts dealt with him and his right-hand men has proved that error. Their belief was that no one would in future be detained without recourse to the courts. They also believed that all racialism would end as soon as the Constitution was implemented. But it was the settlers who were deceived in believing that Rhodesia had become independent under the 1961 Constitution. This was discovered not to be the case after the 1962 General Election.[38]

Another reason for the N.D.P. opposing the Constitution was the fear that acceptance of fifteen seats would put them in the same boat as the Federal M.P.s, and that their followers would accuse them of being salaried stooges. Hence their determination to reject being associated with the seats right from the start, and not even to consider standing for Parliament.

The general public was kept briefed on all the proceedings of the conference. Someone within the N.D.P. delegation must have been releasing correct information to Nkala of what was happening after every session, and Nkala passed it to the *Daily News*.[39] The British delegates were upset at what they thought a betrayal of the secrets of the conference, and for this they blamed the N.D.P. The African people, however, did not react against the N.D.P. for its performance, and indeed they stood by their leaders until well into the year after several congresses had criticised the N.D.P. for the proposals.

The youth leader of the N.D.P., Samuel Gozo, a science graduate of the University College of Rhodesia, said that the youth were impressed by the fight put up by their leaders at the conference, but not by the franchise and representation in Parliament; however, the conference had not been concerned with those two facets of government only.

The decision to reject the entire Constitution as well as the franchise and representation was not taken lightly. A number of congresses were held between 11 February and 21 October, 1961, before the final decision was taken. At the meeting of the national council (the supreme body responsible for policy formulation), the delegates appear to have fared quite well. This can be inferred from the confidence of Nkomo, who went to London to discipline Takawira, Mushonga and Dumbutshena, who had sent a telegram denouncing the Constitution and accusing African delegates of selling the Africans down the river.[40] On 10 February, 1961, Chitepo and Silundika sent a statement to Sandys stating that Nkomo's press conference was not a repudiation of 'the whole Southern Rhodesian constitutional documents' but of the franchise. The same confidence seemed to be present in Nkomo after the special congress on 18–19 March. In his speech following the congress he referred to his delegation at the conference as generals who had to use every tactic in order to change the strategy. He wanted his audience to understand that the end of racialism in the new Constitution made their task of fighting for freedom easier. While in London Nkomo had two meetings with Sandys, and felt exonerated when the Minister gave him a letter acknowledging his disagreement over representation and the franchise.[41]

The first special congress, held four days after the conference, did not reject the Constitution, but instead put forward conditions which it wanted to be met so that the N.D.P. could participate in the referendum. The land question as a whole was to be settled to the satisfaction of the African people;[42] the N.D.P. should be allowed to hold meetings in the rural areas; the A.N.C. men still held in detention or under restriction were to be released; and the Federal Government should not interfere in the constitutional affairs of Northern Rhodesia. The special congress also indicated that people were unhappy with the constitutional proposals. Sithole, speaking at a rally in Harare, admitted: 'The decision taken at a two-day special meeting on the Southern Rhodesian talks now makes the previous January's proposals less acceptable.'

The N.D.P. reaction against the Constitution must have worried Sandys. Quite unexpectedly, he returned to Southern Rhodesia to 'discuss points of interest with people who attended the constitutional conference'. The N.D.P. met the Minister at the British High Commissioner's office[43] and requested a conference to discuss land rights. They objected to Sir Edgar Whitehead's chairmanship of the continuing conference. But Sandys rejected this request, a rejection which opened a new era of campaigning for the N.D.P., for it was at this meeting that it decided to reject the entire Constitution.[44] As time went on, the attitude of the N.D.P. became harder and more implacable. Another special congress of the N.D.P. to discuss the Constitution was called for 17–18 June in Bulawayo. At this congress decisions were taken to reject Sandys' white paper, to submit its own proposals to the British Government, to pass a vote of confidence in Nkomo as N.D.P. President and to conduct its own referendum of every adult.

In October 1961 the congress endorsed the decision which the leaders had made while in retreat in the Matopo Hills not to contest the fifteen seats. This congress, held in Macdonald Hall in Mzilikazi, was the last nationalist congress until that of 1963 after the split at Cold Comfort Farm.

Even before Takawira and his colleagues sent their telegrams of protest to Nkomo, criticism of the constitutional conference result came from the Bulawayo branch of the N.D.P. D. K. Naik of the Makokoba branch attacked the Constitution as 'wholly inadequate'; he believed that the two-roll system was 'highly discriminatory' and aimed at denying majority rule.[45] A. Mukahlera, also an executive member of the Makokoba branch, believed that the decision to compromise was negative because the leaders must have been influenced by the fact that South Africa has no African M.P.s, making the Rhodesian situation seem better in comparison. What they ought to have taken into account was that one country was a colony, while the other was independent. Africans could not give up British protection in exchange for fifteen special but useless seats. The same view was held by Mugabe. Although he read the first press statement immediately on behalf of the N.D.P. he did it only as a duty, and not from conviction; in private and in the party conference, he joined those at Bulawayo in criticising the delegates. In the first conferences, the Mugabe-Mukahlera group was weak, but in time it gained momentum. For nine months their ideas were not decisive. The most outspoken critic had been Mawema, a founder-president of the N.D.P., but by then only a member of the National Council. He was quick to criticise the N.D.P. delegation, accusing it of failing to represent the views of the African people. Mawema's criticism evoked a strong reprimand from the congress for abusing the leaders in public.

The Africans in the U.F.P. supported the Constitution as reasonable. Chenetsa, later a M.P., was irritated by the short-sightedness of those N.D.P. supporters who attacked the Constitution; they could help to success an irresponsible racialist element within the D.P. led by W. J. Harper.[46] Chenetsa's advice was not taken seriously because, as a U.F.P. supporter, he was regarded as a 'moderate'.[47]

The unrest among the people in the rural areas had spread to many districts. At the time the chiefs came to the conference, 600 people had been arrested under the Law and Order Maintenance Act of 1960 in these rural areas. A meeting on 6 March, 1961, called by the District Commissioner of Buhera, which was designed to report on the Constitution, ended in uproar: the people present were arrested and given prison sentences under the Law and Order Maintenance Act.[48]

The N.D.P. finally put the constitutional proposals to a referendum on 23 July to pre-empt the Government, but Sir Edgar did not want to repeat his provocative action of arresting leaders as in 1960. In spite of some minor administrative difficulties, the N.D.P. succeeded in organising their referendum. A total of 372,546 people voted 'No', while 471 voted 'Yes'. The figures were impressive in comparison with those of the official referendum which recorded 41,949 voting 'Yes' and 21,846 'No'.

The N.D.P. referendum encouraged the leaders to follow a militant line against the Constitution. They attacked it at every meeting they addressed, making Sandys the ogre of the situation. Thus the idea of the Party standing for election (under the 1961 Constitution) was collapsing.

Political tension was growing daily. The white people were alarmed, and their morale declined, after the N.D.P. referendum because they thought the African population was getting arrogant and difficult. Lack of progress in the settlement of the Federal Constitution, which was nearly nine months overdue, heightened the sense of uncertainty. In Nyasaland, the Macleod Constitution introduced in 1961 was tantamount to 'one man, one vote' Provision was made for a person who could read or write in any language to qualify for the vote if he had paid tax for ten years. Representation in Parliament was even more liberal, twenty seats being provided for Africans on the lower roll out of thirty-three, and eight provided on the higher franchise, which was mainly for Europeans with property, but not at the expense of the Africans. There was no devaluation of the voting power as was the case of the lower roll in the 1961 Constitution in Rhodesia. The Southern Rhodesian whites started to be alarmed lest a similar one might be introduced in their territory. Sir Roy Welensky, aware of the concern, assured miners and U.F.P. supporters that the outlook of the Federation was favourable, and that the Nyasaland constitutional formula would not be repeated in Southern Rhodesia.

When the Northern Rhodesian constitution eventually emerged, the formula was fifteen seats for whites, fifteen for Africans, and fifteen open to anyone. This led to an uneasy coalition between Kaunda and Nkumbula. It was the first black government in that territory, and it marked the end of colonial rule. Protests from Sir Roy and J. M. Greenfield, his deputy, ended in disappointment for the whites.

Iain Macleod's statement in January 1961[49] increased the uncertainty in the minds of the whites. He criticised the policy of the whites of keeping Africans from effective participation in politics by using a qualified franchaise. He ridiculed the notion that improvement in a man's education, housing and health standards could be a substitute for political rights, or could ever make him cease from demanding them. He thought economic and political advantages went together. The British political system he regarded as inappropriate on the one hand, and he rejected the idea, on the other, that a tiny minority could rule the majority indefinitely. Later he repeated the statement made in 1948 by Arthur Creech Jones, the Colonial Secretary in the Attlee Government, that the central purpose of the British Government was to guide the colonies to freedom from oppression from any quarter.

The white population construed these statements as pointing to the end of their rule in all the three territories. The whites in Southern Rhodesia put pressure on Sir Edgar to ban the N.D.P. and arrest Nkomo. This eventually happened on 9 December 1961, when Nkomo was attending the independence celebrations of Tanganyika. The N.D.P. had lasted one year, eleven months and nine days. Troops and policemen were massed all over the country, especially in areas where the N.D.P. was strongest. The leaders were restricted to the areas of their birth, or to where their registration certificates had first been issued. Some people found themselves in areas where they knew nobody, because they had been away for twenty to thirty years.

Despite the presence of troops, violence erupted in many parts of the country. Todd warned Sir Edgar that his policies would lead to racial conflict. Nkomo's and Chitepo's houses in Highfields were stoned and leaflets written by 'General Chedu'[50] were found on their windows, but Africans argued that this was the work of white police reservists who wanted to give the impression that Nkomo's supporters were turning against him. Nkomo conferred with Sandys in Dar-es-Salaam about the situation in Southern Rhodesia, and was told that the British Government did not have the power to intervene in the country's security matters.

Nkomo returned and, only eight days after the ban on the N.D.P., formed Z.A.P.U.

REFERENCES

1. Barber, op. cit., p. 63.
2. Barber, op. cit., p. 157.
3. For the first time in the six years of the Federation Sir Roy Welensky made attempts to implement the non-racial policy of the U.F.P. African post office clerks were allowed to serve people of all races, general post

office reforms were announced, the Land Bank gave loans to African farmers; and other banks employed African counter clerks. In the territorial sphere, Africans were allowed access to lottery betting and horse betting as well as all forms of liquor.

4. Mugabe, who had been a teacher in Ghana, returned home on leave and decided to enter politics on the side of the N.D.P.

5. *The Daily News*, 19 May, 1960.

6. *The Daily News*, 21 May, 1960.

7. Zvobgo soon left to study in the U.S.A.

8. *The Daily News*, 3 March, 1959.

9. The teachers knew that according to the Public Service Act 1930 they did not qualify for the privileges of a civil servant. Even its amended version of 1960 did not give African teachers all the advantages enjoyed by white teachers who were civil servants.

10. See arguments for the African Juvenile Employment Act 1926 and African Affairs Act 1928, Ch. III.

11. M. M. Hove, Lawrence Vambe and Jasper Savanhu were editors of African newspapers.

12. Founded in 1956 by African Newspapers Ltd.

13. *Daily News*, 28 February, 1959.

14. Mawema had said that Africans in Rhodesia would be represented at the future constitutional conference.

15. Section 53 (*b*) of the African Affairs Act as amended in 1959 was invoked. The section prohibits gatherings of more than twelve people to meet in the Tribal Trust Lands.

16. *The Daily News*, 6 June, 1960.

17. Editorial, *Daily News*, 6 June, 1960.

18. The audience shouted 'Long live Chitepo'. *Daily News*, 6 June, 1960.

19. The section under which they were charged stated: 'Any person who is an office bearer, official or member of an unlawful organisation or who shouts or utters any slogans or makes any sign, or contributes money to such an organisation, or anywhere takes part in its activity, or allows a meeting to be held in his house, shall be guilty of an offence. The maximum fine is £1,000 or a sentence of five years in prison or both.'

20. E. Mlambo, *Rhodesia: The British Dilemma*, p. 2.

21. *Daily News*, 14 May, 1960.

22. *Daily News*, 26 August, 1960.

23. Barber, op. cit., p. 61.

24. Leader in the *Daily News*, 26 August, 1960.

25. Debate in House of Commons, 9 May, 1960, *Hansard*, vol. 623, Cols. 31–7.

26. For the political leaders seen by Macmillan during his tour of Africa, see *House of Commons Debates*, 18 February, 1960, Vol. 617, Cols. 14–6–8.

27. *House of Commons Debates*, 18 February, 1960, Vol. 612. Vol. 1417.

28. Alport replied that 'the veto was not used because the Governor [in Rhodesia] did not recommend it.' *House of Commons Debates*, 10 May, 1960, Vol. 623, Col. 49.

29. Moyo was deposed by his union for going to the conference without their approval. He was subsequently elected Federal M.P. for Gwaai.

30. Nkomo had been unanimously elected as President by the N.D.P.'s first congress in October. He arrived in the country on 19 November, to test his popularity, and returned to London at the end of November to press for the representation of the N.D.P.

31. Nkomo, Malianga and Nkala protested to Sir Edgar against his chairing the first session of the conference. Their meeting lasted two and a half hours, and ended after the N.D.P. leaders were 'satisfied' with Sir Edgar's explanation.

32. *Daily News*, 31 January, 1961.

33. *Rhodesia Herald* and *Daily News*, 8 February, 1961.

34. The D.P. even opposed the removal of the word 'native' in the constitution, and they claimed that the word 'Rhodesian' would be confusing as it would refer to both races.

35. Only six Rhodesia Front M.P.s in 1962 had been born in the country; the rest were post-1945 immigrants. Ian Smith owes much of his strength to his Rhodesian birth; he is the only white politician who can speak Shona well.

36. *Rhodesia Herald*, 8 February, 1961.

37. Press statement made on 7 February, published in the *Rhodesia Herald*, the *Chronicle* and the *Daily News* on 8 February, 1961.

38. See Chapter IX.

39. The British documents on the conference agree with the *Daily News* reports. *Daily News*, 29 January, 1961. Silundika told a rally of the N.D.P. that the delegates would 'reject utterly any suggestion that there be any African seats' and added that followers must not expect miracles out of the constitutional conference.

40. The telegram read: 'We totally reject Southern Rhodesian constitutional agreement as treacherous to future of Africans. Agreement diabolical and disastrous. Outside world shocked by N.D.P. docile agreement. Signed L. Takawira, P. Mushonga, E. Dumbutshena.'

41. Sandys wrote to Nkomo that his party had reserved the complete freedom to press for its objective of 'one man, one vote', and went on to say that he had always understood the position of the N.D.P. on the franchise and parliamentary representation: 'The report which was agreed to at the conclusion of the conference does not imply that your party or any other party declares itself satisfied with the proposals. On the contrary, the report specifically states that having regard to their widely varying views and aspirations, it was not surprising that no group was able to secure agreement of the conference to the particular matter it favoured.'

42. The conference was due to resume on 15 May, 1961, to discuss the land question. The N.D.P. walked out because it wanted the whole land question discussed. Discussion centred on protection from discrimination, the electoral college, and the African land problem.

43. Nkomo, Sithole, Mugale, Malianga and Chitepo met Sandys on 30 May, 1961.

44. As a result of Sandys' refusal to reconvene the conference to discuss

the land question, the N.D.P. was no longer bound 'by our agreement even to the constitutional council and the Bill of Rights, matters on which we had expressed our approval'.

45. The *Daily News*, 9 February, 1961.

46. Many of Harper's followers were Afrikaners of whom there are about 20,000 in Rhodesia, concentrated in Hartley, Charter, Rusape, and Gwelo district – today Rhodesia Front strongholds. The Rhodesian Front régime, unprecedentedly, has brought Afrikaners into Parliament, and even the Cabinet.

47. U.F.P. supporters were referred to as 'moderates', a word that acquired the same meaning as 'Quisling'. Sithole once told an N.D.P. meeting that 'a moderate is one who says the European should always be up and the African who is prepared to sell his birthright. You must be perfectly ashamed of yourself if called a moderate.'

48. N.D.P. sent a telegram to Sandys saying: 'Your attention is drawn to a serious situation developing in the country as a result of your document which is unacceptable to the African people and your continued refusal to recognise the view of the majority people in Southern Rhodesia and your continued private discussion with the Southern Rhodesian Government on land.'

49. *Rhodesia Herald*, 3 January, 1961.

50. The militant youth wing of the N.D.P. used also to call themselves *chedu* (Shona for 'ours').

CHAPTER VII

THE INTERNATIONALISATION OF
THE RHODESIAN PROBLEM

(i) *The United Nations*

From 1957 onwards the Rhodesian African nationalist leaders made
international contact with other movements holding similar ideals.
The Southern Rhodesian A.N.C. had worked in co-operation with
the Nyasaland, Northern Rhodesian, and South African Congresses
and other independence movements. By 1958 Nkomo had become a
figure of international standing. In December of that year he
attended the All-African Peoples' Organisation in Accra and was
elected a member of its steering committee. In the latter capacity he
attended the Afro-Asian People's Solidarity Council meeting in
February when the A.N.C. was banned.

Nkomo's stay abroad after the ban on the A.N.C. gave him the
opportunity to meet many leaders of African, Asian, European and
American countries, contacts which brought him great prestige and
advantage at home. His election to the presidency of the N.D.P.
was based on the belief that his experience abroad would enhance
the prestige of the movement at home.

Up to February 1959, the problem of Rhodesia was almost
unknown in the outside world. Other than experts, few people
could have said whether Rhodesia was a colony or an independent
state. The 1923 Constitution had made the world believe that it was
independent; but it was not independent, because Britain retained
legislative powers over matters affecting African interests, the
Rhodesian Railways,[1] external affairs, international credits and
discriminatory legislation. Most important of all, the Colonial
Laws Validity Act of 1865 still applied to Rhodesia: constitutional
amendments required British approval. The country was not
considered a dominion under the Statute of Westminster of 1931,
which had defined dominion status; yet Rhodesian prime ministers
behaved as though they were independent.[2] Rhodesia was a
member of the Interim Commission of the International Tele-

communications Union, and was a contracting party to the General Agreement on Tariffs and Trade (G.A.T.T.).

The confusing aspect of Rhodesia was that it had its own civil service responsible to Rhodesia, an army, a police force and its own judiciary system. Although not internationally recognised as independent, she had a High Commissioner with an office in London, on a par with Canada, South Africa, India, Australia and New Zealand. Unlike India, with her less advanced constitution, she had not been a member of the League of Nations. In 1946, with the launching of the U.N., all countries were classed as nations, trusteeship territories and non-self-governing territories and so placed in the relevant chapters of the U.N. Charter. Rhodesia was the only country not mentioned or classified in any category.

The tide of African nationalism sweeping across the continent of Africa in the late 1950s and early 1960s created a climate in which the world began to study the status of every country in Africa. To understand how Rhodesia entered the international arena it is necessary to view trends in international politics in the early 1960s. The spirit of African nationalism found expression in the organs created by the U.N. to lead colonies to independence.

Chapters 11, 12 and 13 of the U.N. Charter were devoted to ways of solving questions connected with colonialism. From Africa only Liberia and Ethiopia were represented at San Francisco, as no other African countries had been members of the League of Nations. The then lack of nationalistic spirit in Africa and the prevalent attitude in the world that the African territories would remain under colonial rule for another ten years was responsible for the failure to realise that Southern Rhodesia was not numbered officially among the colonies. On the other hand, if Britain had been pressed to define the status of Southern Rhodesia, it is far from inconceivable that she would have said 'independent'. Since Britain was a strong member of the international community, she could doubtless have got away with it, and thereby legitimised Southern Rhodesia's independent status. The disadvantages of the country's remaining unclassified outweighed the advantages in the final analysis. Those who framed the Charter were, nonetheless, unaware that the political renaissance of the African peoples was near. Even though provision for the colonies was made in the Charter, it was the trusteeship territories taken from the defeated powers after the two World Wars that had their status most advantageously defined – with the exception of South West Africa.

Rhodesia was represented at the Conference of the Empire's Ministers of Finance in Canada in 1932. But out of the five Imperial Conferences of 1921, 1923, 1926, 1930 and 1937, she only attended that held in 1937. The 1930 Conference appointed a committee to set up legal principles of dominion status, and this resulted in the Statute of Westminster, which the British Parliament enacted in 1931. The Statute formalised Britain's surrender of the legislative powers that it no longer exercised. The Statute's implication was that Britain could only legislate at the request of dominion parliaments. A dominion parliament could legislate in contradiction to the British Parliament, because, in respect to it, the Colonial Laws Validity Act 1865 had been removed. The appeal to the Judicial Committee of the Privy Council in London was removed by all except New Zealand. The self-governing dominions of Canada, Australia and New Zealand, the 'older members of the Commonwealth' with which Rhodesia continued to identify herself, had constitutionally advanced to independence, so that in 1926 they became equal in status to the United Kingdom. But in spite of Southern Rhodesia's attendance at one Imperial Conference between the wars and several Commonwealth Conferences after the second, she was never equal in status with the other imperial members, and did not attend the conference which met in 1945 to ratify the U.N. Charter. She was never subject to international law in her own right, but depended on Britain's treaty-making power. She had diplomatic attachés in the U.S.A., Portugal[3] and West Germany under the British embassies. Twenty western countries were represented by consuls in Salisbury up to 1965 and France, the U.S.A., Norway, Switzerland and the Netherlands up to 1969, with the consent of the British Crown. When this consent was withdrawn after the Republic was declared in 1969, these countries pulled out.

When the founding members of the U.N. met at San Francisco in 1945, Africa was still a forgotten continent. South of the Sahara, only South Africa, Ethiopia and Liberia played any role in international affairs. The U.N. was unanimous in internationalising the former mandates of the League of Nations but there was resistance, especially from Winston Churchill, to discussion of the future of dependent territories. Of the three leaders who met at Yalta, however, both Roosevelt and Stalin were anti-colonial, and these two succeeded in persuading Churchill to accept some token form of international supervision of the non-self-governing territories. The colonies in Asia, especially India, were regarded as different from those in Africa. None of the leaders at Yalta believed that Africa would form independent national states in their lifetime, although Churchill in fact lived to see it.

The Yalta Conference provided for some form of supervision, which was later formalised at San Francisco in the Charter under

Articles 73 and 74 in Chapter XI. The less contentious mandates were put in Chapters XII and XIII with elaborate machinery for their administration.

Article 73 required the administrative power to be responsible for administering the people of the non-self-governing territories and for ensuring, among other things, their just treatment and protection against abuse, the development of self-government, and due account being taken of the political aspirations of the people.

These ideals were accepted by the British Government as applicable to all the non-self-governing territories except Tanganyika, Libya, the Cameroons and Togoland, which were mandates. Britain believed that Rhodesia did not qualify for inclusion among these non-self-governing territories or mandates, and she found herself covered on Rhodesia by Subsection (e) of Article 73, which required the administrative powers to supply information to the U.N. Secretary-General 'subject to such limitation as security and constitutional consideration may require'. The information in question was of a technical nature relating to economic, social and educational conditions; political conditions were left out. The ambiguous phraseology of the Section suited Britain's policy on Rhodesia; she was to invoke it in 1962 after the Africans had brought the case before the General Assembly of the U.N.

Rhodesia was to remain in that twilight position between independence and dependence up to June 1962, and indeed until the Unilateral Declaration of Independence in 1965. The debates over Rhodesia's status, and the legal, political and social viewpoints that have been argued, have skated lightly over one vital matter, namely that the administrating power, Britain, never had a political will to solve the problem. The lack of political will has been a symptom of successive governments, first Lloyd George's Liberal Government (the 1923 Constitution), then Ramsay MacDonald's Labour Government (the 1930 Land Apportionment Act) and Macmillan's Conservative Government (the 1961 Constitution). In each case the Africans came off badly by comparison with the settlers.

The facts and issues of the Rhodesian dilemma came to the surface after 1960 when the case was internationalised by the N.D.P. following the abortive constitutional conference. As shown above, the reaction of the N.D.P. office in London was one of shock at the party's 'docile agreement' to the 1961 Constitution. In June the Afro-Asian Solidarity Conference in Bandung passed a resolution to help Africans to freedom. According to the international community, freedom meant – and still means – the freedom to be ruled by universal adult suffrage. Southern Rhodesia had not got this by the 1961 Constitution, and was therefore one of the countries referred to by the Bandung Resolution. By July 1961 Nkomo received encouraging support from the Afro-Asian Solidarity Committee after the conference in Indonesia.[4] He received telegrams of support from the All-African People's Conference, of whose steering committee he was a member, the ruling party of the United Arab Republic, and Kaunda on behalf of U.N.I.P.; Kaunda's message was: 'Support your stand in rejecting the Constitution.' Similar encouraging messages were given to him in person at a meeting of the steering committee of the All-African People's Conference in Conakry, Guinea, in September 1961. Ghana was even more out-spokenly critical of the Constitution. Sir Edgar exposed himself to additional adverse publicity by banning the N.D.P.[5] on 9 December, 1961, just at the time when Tanganyika was celebrating its independence. The publicity given all over the world to movements and activities in Africa, including the violence that followed the ban, only helped Nkomo's cause against that of Sir Edgar. The embarrassment of Sandys, who was in Dar-es-Salaam at the same time as Nkomo, must have been considerable. He had told the world that his constitution was going to improve race relations in Rhodesia; then the ban on the N.D.P. by British settlers, while other African leaders were taking over responsibility for their countries, was difficult to explain to the curious international press. All Sandys could say was that the banning of the N.D.P. came under the security of Southern Rhodesia, and the British had no say in the matter. Nkomo met a number of world leaders who were attending the independence celebrations in Tanganyika, and was promised support. This came in February 1962 when the Special Committee on the Declaration on Colonialism (later called Committee of Twenty-four) was formed.

By the time the conference on the 1961 Constitution met in Salisbury, the attitude of the whole world towards colonialism had radically changed. The growth of an anti-colonial attitude had been encouraged by the Cold War since the early 1950s. By 1960 it reached a peak because Africans had capitalised on it all over the continent in their demands for freedom. A review of the growth of anti-colonialism in the international community is necessary in order to understand how the Africans finally focused attention on Rhodesia. Despite the ambiguity of Article 73, as shown above, the U.N. General Assembly was able to establish a 'Committee on Information' on the non-self-governing territories in 1946. The Committee was not as effective as the Trusteeship Council, where matters affecting the mandates were discussed, but it served the political purpose of persuading, prodding and criticising colonial administration into examining the information supplied. Its setting up was resisted by Portugal, Spain and Belgium. France and

Britain co-operated at the start. The British Labour Government, with its progressive Colonial Secretary Arthur Creech Jones, did its best from the beginning to co-operate with the U.N. on colonial matters. Rhodesia was under the Dominion Office, which became the Commonwealth Office in 1947 with Patrick Gordon Walker as Secretary of State. Although Rhodesia was referred to in the statute books as a colony, it found its place in Gordon Walker's office. It never occurred to Britain that she had an international obligation to supply information under Article 73 (e). This was emphasised by Sir Patrick Dean in June and in October 1962 by a British minister, Joseph Godber.[6]

The work of the Committee on Information was helped by Resolution A/742 of 27 November, 1953.[7] This Resolution established factors to be taken into account in assessing whether a territory was non-self-governing or not. The factors which put Rhodesia in its perspective were two Sections, (a) and (b). Section (a) dealt with the international status. A state was recognised as self-governing only if it was able fully to execute its international responsibility, was eligible for membership of the U.N., was able to enter into direct relations of every kind with other governments and with international institutions, and to negotiate, sign and ratify international instruments, and had the right to provide for its own national defence. Section (b) was concerned with internal responsibilities. A state was also regarded as self-governing if the people enjoyed freedom to choose the form of government they desired, if it was free from external control or interference by the government of another state, or if it had jurisdiction over its own economic, social and cultural affairs.[8] This resolution, which was passed when Winston Churchill had again become British Prime Minister, clarified the non-self-governing position of Rhodesia, as far as the international community was concerned. All Subsections of Section (a) applied to Southern Rhodesia, since the country had not obtained powers of treaty-making under the 1923 Constitution; the first two Subsections of (b) also applied to Rhodesia, as her people did not all enjoy the right to choose their government. Similarly, Subsection 2 clearly defined Rhodesia as non-self-governing, as it was subject to British intervention in all legislation under Articles 28–47 of the 1923 Constitution. The Resolution appeared as if deliberately designed to clarify the ambivalent position of Southern Rhodesia.

The Southern Rhodesian case remained in the background of international politics until France decided in 1959 to inform the Secretary-General of the U.N. that she would no longer submit information on her colonies since they had all become independent.

But the colonies had not yet been admitted to the General Assembly, and Ghana, India, Ceylon and Iraq accused the French Government of abruptly terminating the transmission of information under Article 73(e), thus not complying with GA/1051 XI.

The significant development subsequent to this French move was that Liberia, with the support of other anti-colonial powers, sponsored a Resolution which added a new paragraph to the preamble of Chapter XI, affirming the General Assembly's competence to decide whether or not a territory was non-self-governing according to the letter and spirit of Chapter XI. Liberia's clarification and expansion of the principles of Article 73 (e) helped to put Rhodesia in the same category as other colonies because she had not qualified for independence under the principles. The amendment was passed by the General Assembly as Resolution 1469 with fifty-eight votes to nil, with seventeen abstentions, on 3 December 1959.

By the time the Resolution was passed, Southern Rhodesia had become part of the Central African Federation of Rhodesia and Nyasaland. The British spokesman at the U.N. was at this time concerned with Federation, because, as a result of representation by petitioners such as the Rev. Michael Scott, who protested against Nyasaland's inclusion in the Federation, it was incurring U.N. disapproval. Whether the British Government would have supplied information on Southern Rhodesia after 1953 is difficult to say, but it is clear that it never considered doing so. It continued to behave as if Southern Rhodesia were self-governing.

The principles governing the procedure of conferring independence on non-self-governing territories were further reinforced by the establishment of the Special Committee of Six,[9] a forerunner of the present Committee of Twenty-four. After their meeting on 22 September, 1960, the Committee recommended for adoption by the General Assembly twelve principles, which further expanded on Articles 73 and 74,[10] to guide administering powers when conferring independence on a non-self-governing territory. Without knowing that it would be used against her on Rhodesia, Britain agreed with the other five members that there was a *prima facie* obligation to transmit information under Article 73 (e) on territories geographically separate and ethnically and/or culturally distinct from the administering country. The principles emphasised that whatever constitutional changes took place, the wishes of the peoples in the territories must be 'expressed through informed and democratic process, impartially conducted and based on universal adult suffrage. The United Nations could, when it deems necessary, supervise these processes.'[11]

Whether Britain was aware that the principles would be turned against her in the future, it is not easy to say. The British Representative clashed with his opposite number from Morocco over the interpretation of the desirability of using democratic processes of adult suffrage, stating that, while fully accepting the desirability in principle of universal adult suffrage, he believed that 'there might be circumstances in which full self-government could be achieved before it was practicable to implement this principle.' Britain's reaction was based on the belief that Morocco and India were concerned about the Central African Federation. At the time the Committee was meeting, the Monckton Commission Report had just been published, Sir Edgar Whitehead was introducing the notorious Law and Order Maintenance Act in the Southern Rhodesian Parliament, and the constitutional conference on Southern Rhodesia and the Federation had been announced.

When the twelve principles were put before the General Assembly, Britain continued to object to Principle 9, and this provoked a debate in which many former colonies participated.[12] Nigeria, which had become a U.N. member that year, argued that the British objection to Principle 9 would provide an escape-route for member states 'which refuse to transmit information on territories they administer',[13] under Articles 73 and 74, as was the case with Portugal and Spain. The principles were adopted by sixty-nine votes to two, with twenty-one abstentions in the General Assembly. The principles closed the loophole in the Southern Rhodesian case. Britain could no longer revert to the clause in Article 73 (e) which stipulated that information could be supplied 'subject to such limitation as security and constitutional considerations may require', or easily escape the obligation to supply information on Southern Rhodesia under the Article.[14]

The success of the anti-colonial states in getting the U.N. to pass Resolution A/1514 should be seen in the context of the changing spirit of the times.[15] At the end of the 1950s the world had suddenly changed its opinion over colonial matters. No one any longer envied the colonial powers, as in the period between the Congress of Berlin and the Second World War; rather these powers were made to feel guilty about their colonial possessions. Universities were teaching against colonialism, an increasing number of institutions specialising in African Affairs were being founded in the U.S.A., Britain, continental Europe, the U.S.S.R. and elsewhere. The advent of African states to the U.N. brought a great deal of anti-colonial opinion which had always existed but had not had the vote. The creation of the Committee of Twenty-four further increased anti-colonial pressure.[16] The Cold War, and the African states' resistance to being dragged into it, gave these states influence over the super-powers.[17]

In 1960 the anti-colonial attitude at the U.N. was magnified by circumstances: the clash between the U.S.A. and the U.S.S.R. over the U2 spy plane; the collapse of the summit conference between the U.K., the U.S.A., the U.S.S.R. and France; the Sharpeville massacre in South Africa, and the Congo independence disaster. The last-named became a Cold War issue as it gave rise to speeches by the U.S.S.R. and U.S.A. designed to win the non-aligned nations; the U.S.S.R. put a resolution through the General Assembly designed to end colonialism immediately, while the U.S.A. called for a 'combined United Nations effort to assist the new African countries'.

In this perspective Rhodesia, despite her ambiguous constitution, could not continue to remain undiagnosed as a colonial disease in a world atmosphere that was inimical to colonialism. The Afro-Asian nations loathed both the racial and the colonial nature of the Rhodesian situation. Colonialism and racialism are linked because these two evils dominated the peoples of Africa and Asia from their first contacts with the peoples of Europe.

The consideration of Rhodesia as a problem came to the fore in February 1962 after the formation by the United Nations of the Committee of Seventeen, later known as the Committee of Twenty-Four.[18] Britain tried to prevent the Committee from taking up the Rhodesian problem, on the grounds that it was not a colonial one, but the move was defeated; this was the first humiliation Britain suffered in connection with her policy on Rhodesia. The racial nature of the problem had not yet been exposed; Britain could still count on the support of twenty-three nations, but these later deserted her when it was revealed that Rhodesia was not independent and that Britain had encouraged the development of a situation which violated the Declaration of Human Rights. Most important of all, Rhodesia did not meet the specifications of the declaration regarding non-self-governing territories (Resolution 1514), the principles embraced in Resolution A/742 VIII, and the twelve principles of Resolution 1541. The British delegate could not refer to any provision of the U.N. Charter which would fit Rhodesia as a state, and the British reversion to the Clause (e) of Article 73[19] was soon weakened by the principles of the resolutions above.

In the early stages of the case several countries were confused about the legal status of Rhodesia. Britain benefited from this confusion and obtained the support of almost all the western bloc, including the Scandinavian countries. Most of the Afro-Asian countries voted for the consideration of the Rhodesian case, and they were joined by the Soviet bloc. No amount of legalism could succeed in convincing them; their criterion of independence was universal adult suffrage. This did not apply in Rhodesia, which had all the symptoms of colonialism such as minority foreign rule and racialism. The anti-colonial blocs were joined from Latin America by Cuba and Haiti; Japan, Ireland, Thailand, Malaya, Laos, Israel and Nationalist China abstained together with the other Latin American nations. Twenty-one other western nations voted with Britain, apparently accepting the British view that Rhodesia was self-governing. The states shifted their position considerably after the report of the Committee of Twenty-four.[20]

The British policy was even more exposed after a Subcommittee of the Committee of Twenty-four, under the chairmanship of the Indian diplomat C. S. Jha, had conferred in London with four British Government ministers: Lord Home as Foreign Secretary, R. A. Butler as Minister responsible for the Central African Federation, Reginald Maudling as Colonial Secretary and Duncan Sandys as Commonwealth Secretary. The Conference was like a lecture by the British ministers to the U.N. delegates on colonial policy. Reginald Maudling was gentle in his approach to the problem, but Duncan Sandys, the Commonwealth Secretary and architect of the 1961 Constitution, was determined to end what he believed to be U.N. meddling in British colonial policy in general and in the Rhodesian case in particular. After expounding the constitutional position of Southern Rhodesia, Sandys accused the U.N. delegates of 'listening to one set of petitioners' and pointed out that the U.N. should not be irritated by the monetary and educational qualifications for the franchise in Rhodesia, because Sir Edgar Whitehead would raise salaries to make it possible for Africans to qualify.[21] He also stated that the British ministers had decided never to refer the matter to the U.N. in their negotiations. He told the Subcommittee that Sir Edgar had predicted majority rule in twelve years. Sandys also referred to the constitutional safeguards requiring a racial referendum of four groups – Africans, Europeans, Coloureds and Asians – who would vote separately, and all have to register a positive vote before constitutional changes could be made; he argued that this was a guarantee against the subjugation of any race. The British Government has not subsequently referred to that racial safeguard, despite the fact that this was the basis of the constitutional changes in 1961. These were the obstacles against the constitutional amendment which forced Smith to declare independence, because he could not test the country by using the provisions. Even the famous Five Principles shied away from referring to this safeguard in testing acceptability, because both the Smith régime and the British Government were aware that the Africans do not support the régime's policy.

The Subcommittee, made up of Jha of India, Sory Caulibaly of Mali, N. Rifai of Syria, N. Swai of Tanzania, T. Slim of Tunisia and Ignacio Silva Sucre of Venezuela, showed itself better informed on the constitutional problems than the British Government had expected. It argued that Rhodesia was non-self-governing, the Constitution of 1923 having been given to the territory without the knowledge or consent of the indigenous people; that the Constitution had not endowed the territory with an acceptable measure of self-government, and had not met the requirement of Resolutions A/742 VIII and 1541 XV. The Subcommittee expressed alarm at the introduction of the 1961 Constitution, which utterly ignored the expression of world opinion in Resolution 1514 XV. They rejected the claim of Sandys, pointing out that Sir Edgar had said the Constitution would last 300 years: the educational and monetary provisions would prove Sir Edgar correct. The Subcommittee explained to the British ministers that the franchise was central to the Rhodesian problem and no amount of constitutional safeguards could solve the problem as long as those responsible for the administration glossed over the franchise.

They discussed the Land Apportionment Act,[22] the banning of political parties, the imprisonment of African leaders and the absence of justice and equality, accompanied as it inevitably was by racialism. The British ministers ended their discussion by threatening to withdraw their co-operation if the U.N. continued to interfere in British colonial policy.

The report of the Subcommittee to the full Committee of Twenty-four and to the General Assembly in June 1962 destroyed the British standpoint on Rhodesia. The claim that the territory was independent was exposed as a fiction;[23] furthermore the arrogance with which Sandys had lectured the Subcommittee had not helped the British position. When Rhodesia was discussed in the General Assembly in June 1962 'as a matter of urgency', Britain started to lose friends.[24] Her attempt to kill the two June Resolutions and so prevent the inclusion of Rhodesia on the agenda failed. The two October Resolutions came after the ban on Z.A.P.U. and the arrest of Nkomo and other leaders. Delegates had come to believe the testimony they had received in February from Nkomo and other leaders; by October 1962 support of the British stand appeared tantamount to condoning the repression of Africans. A sense of rejection impelled the British Government to send Sir Edgar to the U.N. with the British delegation, but the move was not efficacious because most members had shifted from their February positions. Those that had opposed the first Resolution decided to settle for neutrality by abstaining. Only South Africa and Portugal stuck to the original standpoint. The Afro-Asian members had increased their majority from fifty-seven in February 1962 to over eighty in October.[25] As the problem dragged on, nations grew impatient with British policy. Even the most friendly, such as Canada, New Zealand, and the U.S.A., spoke out against the policy designed to leave power in the hands of a minority.

The political chasm between Britain and the majority of U.N. members widened between 1962 and 1965 after Britain had persistently denied to the U.N. the right to define the status of Southern Rhodesia. Annual resolutions were ignored as a nuisance. The Afro-Asian states were the more shocked when they understood that a British Labour Government could resort to the same tactics as the Conservatives.

(ii) *Rhodesia at the Commonwealth Conference*

Rhodesia's ambiguous constitution enabled her to be represented at Imperial and later Commonwealth Conferences, especially those on economic problems such as those in Ottawa in 1932 and London in 1946, 1948 and 1951.[26] Her presence at these conferences was not a concession to her independence, nor was it ever implied that she was included as of right.[27] Apart from the conferences on economic matters, Rhodesia attended the British Empire Conference from 20 to 27 May, 1944, for consultation purposes because her troops were engaged in the War. Sir Godfrey Huggins and Sir Firoz Khan Noon, representing Rhodesia and India respectively, sat in the conference as observers. This conference was the first where Rhodesia participated in political matters, but she was not invited to the conference which took place from 13 April, 1945, to present a united front on behalf of the British Empire at San Francisco. India was invited as of right, her constitution being regarded as much more advanced than Rhodesia's. She had also, unlike Rhodesia, been a member of the League of Nations. At the full Commonwealth Conference in London on 23–30 April, 1949, Rhodesia was again not represented, because the conference was concerned with international politics, and Rhodesia was not independent over matters of foreign relations. India, Pakistan and Ceylon attended as independent dominions. The conference agreed that the Commonwealth members would be represented abroad by high commissioners with ambassadorial status. At the conference on defence matters which took place on 8–15 September, 1951, Rhodesia was not present because, although she had had an army and an air force since the 1920s, she had never had a minister of defence. This had remained the preserve of the Governor, under the control of the British Government. At the conference on the balance of payments in the sterling area held on 6–13 June, 1953, Rhodesia was represented, as were several other colonies including Northern Rhodesia. The Federation of Rhodesia and Nyasaland attended the conferences of the 1950s.[28] Ian Smith, who had now succeeded W. J. Field as Rhodesian Prime Minister, was refused an invitation to the conference of 1964. This conference was the first following the collapse of the Federation, and Smith had expected that, since the Federation had been attending the conferences during the 1950s, Rhodesia would take its place after its demise.

The policy adopted by Sir Alec Douglas-Home of consulting the Commonwealth countries on the question of whether an invitation should be extended to Rhodesia originated from the fact that Rhodesia had never sat as a dominion at the Commonwealth Conferences. There was suspicion in Britain and in several other Commonwealth countries that Smith was intending to capitalise on the attack of the Afro-Asians at the conference and walk out, as Dr. Verwoerd had done in 1961; he would then declare himself independent, pretending that he had been forced. Sir Alec did not want to afford him this opportunity of passing the buck. He sent a letter to member-states asking their approval for Smith to attend the conference from 25 July to 1 August, 1964; at the same time he told Smith to ask for an invitation to attend according to precedent. He explained this policy ot the House of Commons, saying: 'It has long been recognised that the only persons who attend these meetings as of right are the prime ministers of the fully independent countries of the Commonwealth.' The British Government felt the need to be satisfied that other member-states accepted the situation if a dependent territory was to attend. This policy was supported by the Leader of the Opposition, Harold Wilson, who emphasised in the debate that 'independence should not be agreed by the United Kingdom without provision for democratic rule in Southern Rhodesia.' By 'democratic rule' Wilson meant 'majority rule'.

As might have been expected, the replies from the Commonwealth countries were discouraging to the supporters of Smith's régime. No country saw the point in inviting Rhodesia. The reply from Ghana expressed shock that the British Government should ever have considered the desirability of inviting the Smith Government which, as a mere colony, had 'no basis in law or precedent'; Kwame Nkrumah accused Southern Rhodesia of practising racial discrimination and oppression. Jawaharlal Nehru's reply took the toughest line of all. He could not see why the representation of a country which followed racialist practices, suppressed civil liberties and arrested popular African leaders should be desirable.[29] At the time Sir Alec was receiving replies to his letter sent in April, the special Committee of Twenty-four was in London in May to warn the British Government that it should not grant independence unless there was universal adult suffrage, and that it should demand the release of Nkomo.[30]

After receiving letters from the Commonwealth leaders that were all negative, the British Government informed Smith that he could not attend the conference. This exasperated him, and he replied through a press conference on 7 June, saying he was 'naturally extremely disappointed'. He was the more upset in that his case was not judged on its merits; he was being rejected because 'the Commonwealth has outgrown itself, and there is no longer room for us among the motley of small countries which have recently acceded to independence and been admitted to the Commonwealth without regard to their adherence to the ideals and concepts of the association.' Smith's statement ignored the fact that the older Commonwealth countries were marching with the ideals of the time; Canada and New Zealand, for example, are highly respected by non-white nations inside and outside the Commonwealth because of their non-racial policies. South Africa's departure owing to her racial policies was also ignored. Despite Smith's remonstrances, the Commonwealth nations conferred without him on the planned dates.

The attitude of the Commonwealth nations on U.D.I. was made abundantly clear. While they appreciated Britain's policy of trying to create sufficiently representative institutions before independence was given, they gave due warning that they would not recognise U.D.I. All except Britain and Australia declared that majority rule was a prerequisite of independence. All detainees should be released and a constitutional conference held for the creation of representative political organisations.

Smith's argument that it was a motley of small countries which opposed his racial policies was proved false. No country supported him. Canada, the oldest member, was firmly behind the African countries, and India led the Asian members in attacking the policy of trying to obtain independence under a restricted franchise. New Zealand and Australia sat on the fence because they could not justify their support of Smith's policies. Their silence was in deference to the British Government rather than out of sympathy with Smith, but it was misconstrued as support. Their refusal to support U.D.I. clarified their stance.

In any case Sir Alec Douglas-Home replied that the British Government would consider all the views expressed. Smith protested that the convention of not discussing the internal affairs of a member-state had been broken because Rhodesia had been discussed in his absence; he believed it was contrary to precedent and to principles of justice as he understood them. But when his own institutions sit in judgement on Africans who are not represented, it does not appear to Smith as contrary to the justice that he understands.

(iii) *The Commonwealth and U.D.I.*

The unity of the Commonwealth was put to the test by U.D.I. At the Conference of 1965, pledges had been made not to recognise U.D.I. if it took place, and indeed it had been clearly demonstrated that the Commonwealth was averse to Smith's racial policies. The failure of the British Government to take decisive action against the rebellion caused dismay throughout the world, but the U.N., the O.A.U. and the Commonwealth were the only international organisations capable of expressing disapproval of British policy. The O.A.U. Council of Ministers met in December 1965 and made recommendations – which were then ignored by member-states. Some states, such as Ghana, Algeria and Egypt, were inclined to take military action even without the O.A.U.'s support.

What induced the Nigerian Prime Minister, Sir Abubakar Tafawa Balewa, to call a special Commonwealth Conference in Lagos, the first ever to be held outside London, is not clear. The conference met on 10 January, 1966, nearly two months after U.D.I., and discussed only Rhodesia. Harold Wilson's attitude was defensive, and more hostile to Africans than had ever been shown before at such a conference by a British Prime Minister. His very attendance at the conference was only due to pressure from the British High Commissioner in Lagos.

The conference insisted that the rebellion should be ended by the use of force. All suggestions designed to end minority rule in Rhodesia were rejected by Wilson. Instead he placated the critics of British policy by promising that, according to the expert advice available to him, the cumulative effect of the economic and financial sanctions might well bring the rebellion to an end 'within a matter of weeks rather than months'. At the conference Nigeria submitted a far-reaching seven-point plan for action against Rhodesia, while Sierra Leone demanded the use of force under Article 42 of the U.N. Charter.

This statement on the supposed future outcome of sanctions bought time for Wilson. Even leaders who doubted the sanctions policy changed their attitude to one of 'wait-and-see'. They decided to support the idea of forming a committee which would act as a watchdog over the effects of sanctions on the Rhodesian economy. The Sanctions Committee submitted to the Commonwealth Conference in September 1966 an analysis of the economic situation in

Rhodesia, which pointed out that the sanctions begun in November 1965 and the oil blockade of Beira from April 1966 had depressed the economy, but were unlikely to achieve the desired political ends. This report led the heads of Commonwealth Governments to realise that Wilson's assurance in Lagos was based on unreliable information. While they bowed before Wilson's promise of another attempt at settlement before the end of 1966, the majority were convinced of the need for stronger, mandatory sanctions under Chapter VII, Articles 41 and 42, of the U.N. Charter, covering both exports and imports.[31] Those favouring a mild approach preferred sanctions on a selection of important Rhodesian commodities. The conference was unanimous that there should be co-operation among member-states of the Commonwealth to solve the problem. Zambia and Malawi were both to be helped by the Committee to stave off the effects of sanctions on them. When the *Tiger* talks collapsed, the Sanctions Committee met on 5 December, 1966, and recommended action to provide for effective and mandatory selective sanctions as outlined at the Commonwealth Conference. The Resolution which was introduced by George Brown at the U.N. Security Council had been agreed between the British Government and the Sanctions Committee.

The history of these events leads again to the conclusion that the British Government had no political will to end the Rhodesian régime. All the punitive action taken was meant to save the Commonwealth from breaking up. In the House of Commons debate on mandatory sanctions, Wilson said: 'They [the Opposition] feel that the issues are such that we should break our obligation to the Commonwealth. If this is their attitude, let them say so. I know that if we had not [taken punitive action], the Commonwealth would have been destroyed.'[32]

In order to relieve tension at the conference, Lester Pearson, the Canadian Prime Minister, recommended that countries of the Commonwealth should take over the responsibility of helping the Rhodesian African to obtain education. Consequently a scholarship scheme was set up. But this was a decision made in ignorance of the situation. The Africans in Rhodesia are better educated than they are in several independent African countries, and the number of educated Africans outnumbers the white population. The scholarship scheme had emanated from the belief that the Rhodesian whites were sincerely prepared to accept majority rule based on a system of meritocracy.

The communiqué, issued after three days of discussions on Rhodesia, 'reaffirmed that the authority and responsibility for guiding Rhodesia to independence rested with Britain, but they acknowledged that the problem was of wider concern to Africa, the Commonwealth and the world.'

The conference reconvened in London in September 1966, by which time the régime had consolidated itself. The threat posed by African states had been shattered, to the delight of the minority régimes. A coup had taken place in Nigeria one day after the conference; and Nkrumah, who had not attended the conference, was overthrown only a month later. So Nigeria and Ghana, the two most powerful African Commonwealth countries, were in a state of chaos. Smith and his supporters inside and outside Rhodesia could relax.

The states which attacked Britain's Rhodesia policy at the conference in September 1966 were led by Zambia. S. M. Kapepwe, then Zambian Foreign Minister, angrily told Wilson that his attitude was 'imperialistic' and 'racialistic'. His anger was due to the near-destruction of Zambia's own economy because of the senseless policy of sanctions. Wilson's approach was condemned by nearly all states, the exceptions being Malawi, Australia and Mauritius. New Zealand sat on the fence, while Canada reiterated its previous attitude. The Commonwealth had been shaken to the core.[33] To save a complete breakdown, Wilson promised to try to solve the problem by peaceful means before the end of 1966; he assured the conference that it would be his last attempt, and that if it failed, the British Government would withdraw all its previous proposals for settlement. This could have meant the cancellation of the notorious Five Principles, which Wilson knew were unpopular throughout Africa. The withdrawal would mean that Britain would introduce NIBMAR (No Independence Before Majority Rule.) This was a ploy designed to achieve two objectives: it would please the people of Africa, and at the same time it would be used as leverage to compel Smith to accept a settlement for fear of NIBMAR. To frighten Smith it was further agreed that the British Government would sponsor in the Security Council before the end of 1966 'effective' and 'selective' mandatory sanctions.

Wilson revealed for the first time at this conference the extent to which his policies on Rhodesia were dictated by Britain's relationship with South Africa, saying that mandatory sanctions should not involve all Southern Africa. 'In international politics, and for Britain's economic future, this is a crucial rider.' The conference eventually accepted a policy that would not develop into a confrontation, economic or military, involving Southern Africa as a whole: it was believed that such a confrontation would dwarf the Rhodesian problem. However, the conference made Wilson promise that the British Government would 'withdraw all previous proposals for a constitutional settlement which have been made; in particular, they will not thereafter be prepared to submit to the British Parliament any settlement which involves independence before majority rule.'[34]

It is difficult to tell what communications were taking place between Salisbury and London before the conference. But there is reason to think that Wilson knew that Smith was out for a deal. This resulted in the *Tiger* talks in December 1966, but the *Tiger* settlement, although involving a sell-out of the Africans, was rejected by Smith and his régime. The promises made to the Commonwealth in September then immediately fell due for fulfilment, and Britain was compelled to go to the U.N. with a resolution for selective mandatory sanctions.

At the Commonwealth Conference in January 1969, Wilson's attitude was one of resistance to the use of force against Rhodesia, insisting that it would cause a bloodbath in Southern Africa, and heavy loss of life in Rhodesia. No British Government would entertain such an adventure. The *Fearless* proposal would remain, together with NIBMAR. Wilson's defiant attitude in 1969 won him sympathy from the British public, as, before the conference, the public had come to believe that the Commonwealth was no more than a forum for regular indictments of the British Government.[35] A similarly hostile attitude was taken by Edward Heath at the Singapore Conference in January 1971 over the sale of arms to South Africa, with similar public acclaim.

(iv) *The Commonwealth Sanctions Committee*

The Sanctions Committee of the Commonwealth Secretariat, composed of seven member-states, was responsible for all the stiffer resolutions that were passed at the U.N. after 1966. The Labour Government, when it first introduced sanctions in 1965, earnestly believed that the Smith régime would fall as a consequence within weeks. By the middle of 1966, this belief and the political will to solve the problem had died away.[36]

It was the Sanctions Committee which forced the British Government to continue the fight against Rhodesia through the U.N. It recommended the commodities for sanction by Britain after it had satisfied itself that Britain would not be harmed (hence the British refusal to blockade Lourenço Marques for fear that it would affect her trade with South Africa). In June 1969, following the introduction of an apartheid constitution, the Committee examined the possibility of severing cable, telephone, postal and radio links with Rhodesia: Britain refused to recommend this to the U.N. so it was never included in the sanctions list. On 24 September, 1969, the Committee noted that Rhodesia still traded with many countries apart from South Africa and Portugal, which had declared at the U.N. that they would apply sanctions. It recommended to the U.N. practical steps to be taken 'to improve the vigilance against sanction-breakers, and other additional measures'. Some of these recommendations became part of the General Assembly Resolution passed on 21 November, 1969. Like all other international organisations, the Commonwealth has come to the conclusion that sanctions are useless.

(v) *Rhodesia at the O.A.U.*

Unlike the U.N. and the Commonwealth, which had equivocated over whether Rhodesia was independent or not, the O.A.U. was clear over Rhodesia's status. Its founding occurred in May 1963, after the U.N. had ruled that Rhodesia was a colony according to the Charter. Some of the O.A.U.'s founder-members, such as Ghana, Nigeria and Ethiopia, had sponsored resolutions at the U.N. challenging the status of Rhodesia. The most important criterion had been that elections were not held under universal adult suffrage. The policy of banning African political parties, which Sir Edgar Whitehead had followed since 1959, met with intense disapproval from African states. When the O.A.U Conference in 1963 discussed the Resolution on Decolonisation, Rhodesia was included among the colonies under consideration. The Resolution called upon Britain 'not to transfer the powers and the attributes of sovereignty to foreign minority governments imposed on African peoples by the use of force and under cover of racial legislation'.[37]

The same Resolution assured the African nationalists in Rhodesia of 'effective moral and practical support' for bringing majority rule to Zimbabwe. After the Resolution, Rhodesia was included among the African problems to be brought under annual review. This was done at Cairo in 1964 and at Accra in October 1965.[38] At the latter conference, held while Wilson was in Rhodesia, the O.A.U. heads of state passed a Resolution condemning the settlers' intention to declare independence. Their plan to deal with U.D.I. was firm. Among the details were refusal to recognise the U.D.I. Government, recognition of a government in exile, an emergency meeting of the O.A.U. Council of Ministers with a view to involving the U.N. in Rhodesia, reconsideration of the O.A.U.'s relations with Britain, and treatment of the Rhodesian whites in the same way as those of South Africa. These plans were put on paper, but no contingent plans were made for the eventual confrontation. The settlers were aware that, apart from Egypt, none of the African countries was in a strong position to tackle the régimes in Southern Africa; so as soon

G

as they felt satisfied that Britain herself would not use force,[39] they declared independence. The O.A.U. Council of Ministers met on 3–5 December, 1965, and decided that all African states should sever diplomatic relations with Britain if the rebellion had not been brought down by 15 December. It simply endorsed the heads of state Resolution and plan made at Accra two months before, without realising that passing a resolution is different from actual fighting. The Accra Conference was ignored, and only a few countries observed the Resolution.

At the Kinshasa Conference in September 1967, the O.A.U. changed its strategy. Here there was a realisation that empty threats of military action were futile, and a decision was taken to arm, train and assist the Zimbabwe freedom fighters. This would be accomplished by the 'committee of experts' composed of seventeen nations,[40] which would operate with the help of reports supplied by the following: the permanent commissions of information and administration, general policy and defence, and finance, by liberation movements, and by the Council of Ministers of the O.A.U. The Committee is supposed to meet to review the struggle and co-operate with the military commanders of the liberation movements, trying to improve the movements' fighting capabilities.

The O.A.U. expressed its lack of confidence in the British sanctions policy, but once the sanctions were imposed, most of their member-countries observed them. The Secretariat kept close vigilance on countries outside Africa that broke sanctions. The O.A.U. Conference in 1969 decided to put diplomatic pressure on companies in West Germany, the Netherlands, France and Japan which broke sanctions, and to make representations to N.A.T.O. powers that were supplying arms to the minority and racist régimes in Southern Africa.

Both Z.A.N.U. and Z.A.P.U. have had a fair share of the £700,000 O.A.U. Liberation Fund. O.A.U. members have been successful in prevailing on some non-African U.N. members to provide funds for liberation movements via the O.A.U. for arms, medicines and transportation. But the O.A.U. has not been successful in uniting Z.A.N.U. and Z.A.P.U. In September 1968 a committee comprising Kenya, Zambia and Tanzania sought to reconcile the two nationalist parties, but failed. Instead, Z.A.P.U. decided to form an alliance with the African Independence Party of Portuguese Guinea and Cape Verde Islands (P.A.I.G.C.), the Popular Movement for the Liberation of Angola (M.P.L.A.), the African National Congress of South Africa (A.N.C.), the South West Africa Popular Organisation (S.W.A.P.O.), and the Movement for the Freedom of Mozambique (Frelimo). Z.A.N.U. has been left to choose friends among the weaker splinter movements of the areas from which Z.A.P.U. has drawn its allies. The O.A.U.'s desire to unite Z.A.N.U. and Z.A.P.U. has not been particularly relevant to the struggle.

REFERENCES

1. The Rhodesian Railways Act 1948 removed the railways from the 1923 Constitution. The Attlee Government altered the legislation to provide for the Rhodesia African Railway Workers' Union as an organ for the Africans.

2. Sir Godfrey Huggins attended Dominion Conferences which comprised Canada, Australia, New Zealand and South Africa and, after 1947, India and Pakistan.

3. In 1965 Harry Reedman was appointed to represent Rhodesia in Portugal, without British approval.

4. Telegrams were published in the *Daily News*, 21 July, 1961.

5. The N.D.P. had lasted one year, eleven months and nine days longer than any other African nationalist organisation in Southern Rhodesia. (The A.N.C. had lasted one year, six months and fourteen days, from 12 September, 1957, to 26 February, 1959, and Z.A.P.U., formed on 17 December, 1961, was to last only nine months to September 1962).

6. Godber's statement in the General Assembly on 29 October, 1962. A/C 4/570–1364.

7. It was strengthened by Resolution GA 1051 XI of 20 February, 1957, requiring the administrative power to supply details on how a territory was to attain independence.

8. GA Resolution 742, 27 November, 1953.

9. Countries on the Committee of Six were the United Kingdom, the Netherlands, the U.S.A., Mexico, India and Morocco. See GA Res. 1467 XIV, 12 December, 1959.

10. The Special Committee had agreed that the Charter, as a living document and obligation under Chapter XI, must be viewed in the light of the changing spirit of the time. *Yearbook of the United Nations*, New York, U.N., 1960, p. 504.

11. Principle No. 9.

12. In 1960, thirteen former African colonies were admitted to the U.N. as independent members.

13. Resolution of 15 December, 1960, GA 1541. For full debate see A/AC 100/2, 1.2.

14. The influence of the Afro-Asian states had become strong enough to cause the amendment of Articles 23, 27 and 61 of the U.N. Charter.

15. 'Although the Charter was essentially sympathetic to aspirations of the colonial peoples for national freedom, the votes were not available before 1960 to ensure that these sympathies found practical expression in

resolution.' A. G. Mezerik, *Colonialism and the United Nations*, International Review Service, (U.N., New York, 1964). Vol. X, No. 83, p. 4.

16. Alex Quaison-Sackey, *Africa Unbound*, Praeger, New York, 1963, p. 135.

17. T. Slim, 'The Work of the Committee of 24', *Annual Review of United Nations Affairs 1963–4*, New York, Oceana Publications, p. 16.

18. The General Assembly passed Resolution 1745 XVI on 23 February, 1962, by 57 votes to 21 with 24 abstentions, authorising the Committee of Twenty-four to investigate the status of Southern Rhodesia under Article 73 (*e*) of the Charter.

19. Specifying that information could be supplied subject to such limitation as 'constitutional consideration may require'.

20. Up to the time of U.D.I., Britain was left with Portugal and South Africa.

21. A/5124. Subcommittee's report on the question of Southern Rhodesia.

22. The British ministers promised that the Land Apportionment Act and other racial restrictions would end 'by the end of the year'.

23. Sandys had declared that the territory was not independent, but that it *was* independent from Britain in all the aspects under discussion.

24. In February 1962, before Nkomo and Mushonga gave evidence, the western nations were in doubt about the actual issues which caused friction. But after the African evidence to the Subcommittee and the latter's report, U.N. members drifted to the Afro-Asian side. For example:

		For	*Against*	*Abstentions*
(*a*)	23 February, 1962, members voted	57	21	24
(*b*)	22 June, 1962, ,, ,,	53	35	13
(*c*)	28 June, 1962, ,, ,,	75	1	23
(*d*)	12 October, 1962, ,, ,,	83	2	11
(*e*)	31 October, 1962, ,, ,,	81	2	19

25. Important resolutions were A/1747 XVI, whereby the status of Southern Rhodesia was that of a non-self-governing territory. Britain should supply information under Article 73 (*e*) of the Charter. A/1760 XVIII requested the British Government to suspend the 1961 Constitution and extend the vote to the whole population without discrimination.

26. These were attended not only by Rhodesia but by other non-self-governing territories, as in 1946 when Pakistan, India and Ceylon were represented, although they were not yet independent.

27. Ian Smith told a press conference on 7 June, 1964, after he had been told that he was not invited to the Commonwealth Conference: 'We are not excluded now because we are no longer loyal to the Crown or to the ideals on which the Commonwealth was founded.'

28. The Constitution of the Federation was much more advanced than that of Rhodesia in international politics. There were departments of foreign affairs and defence. Provision existed for high commissioners in Commonwealth countries under the control of the British Government. Trade attachés under the British embassies existed in non-Commonwealth countries such as the U.S.A., West Germany and Japan.

29. Nkomo had just been arrested and taken to the concentration camp at Gonakudzingwa, where he is still held up to the time of writing. Replies to Sir Alec's letters are found in the *Keesing Archives*, April to June 1964.

30. At this time, the Labour party were still champions of freedom. Arthur Bottomley attacked the Government and called upon the minister to go to Rhodesia to see that the Africans had their rights.

31. This point was suggested by Sierra Leone at the Lagos Conference.

32. *The Times*, London, 9 December, 1966.

33. Wilson told Parliament on 5 December, 1966, after the collapse of the *Fearless* talks, that the Commonwealth had been close to breaking up in September. He had risked its very existence for the right to make a last attempt at agreement with Mr. Smith, and he would risk it no further. (*The Times*, London, 6 December, 1966.)

34. Section 10 of the communiqué issued after the conference in September 1966.

35. See Edward Heath's article in *Foreign Affairs* (Washington, D.C.), October 1969.

36. Commonwealth Relations Office officials, led by Sir Duncan Watson, were sent to Salisbury for 'talks about talks' with Rhodesian Government officials.

37. Section 3 of the Resolution on Decolonisation.

38. Zdenek Červenka, *The Organisation of African Unity and its Charter*, C. Hurst, London, 1969, pp. 184–90.

39. Arthur Bottomley told a press conference in Accra on 6 August and in Lagos on 10 August that Britain would not use force because it would lead to a Congo-type situation, and Zambia would suffer. Harold Wilson made a similar announcement to a press conference in Salisbury on 30 October.

40. Červenka, op. cit., p. 187.

CHAPTER VIII

AFRICAN RESISTANCE TO MINORITY RULE 1963–1970

(i) *Origins of Resistance*

Its decision not to fight an election under the 1961 Constitution meant that the N.D.P. had to fight to achieve its goal of majority rule by using extra-parliamentary pressure. This was no easy choice, nor was it regarded as a wise one by its friends – or by its enemies. The decision held the N.D.P. and Z.A.P.U. together, despite the formation of the Zimbabwe National Party (Z.N.P.) by Patrick Matimba and Michael Mawema. These two leaders failed to attract support or to divide the N.D.P. If Nkomo had decided to stand for election, the militant youth might have gone over to the Z.N.P. because he would have been accused, like the African Federal M.P.s, of wanting to make money for himself and his friends.[1]

The announcement that they would fight for majority rule outside Parliament alarmed Sir Edgar Whitehead's Government. Its suspicions concerning nationalist activities increased, and its vigilance became intensified. The N.D.P.'s policy of stepping up its campaign outside Parliament was interpreted as meaning terrorising the African population into supporting it; large numbers could thereby be organised and used for committing violence. The thousands who attended nationalist meetings were said to have been intimidated into doing so. The word 'intimidation' was used so often that it came to mean very much the same as African nationalist activity. No person who came to the nationalist meetings was believed to have come of his own accord. The fact that the N.D.P. had a membership of 250,000 and that 372,546 people had voted in its referendum was not proof enough that African nationalist leaders were genuinely popular with the African masses.

The story put about by settlers, and canvassed overseas, was that the Africans in Rhodesia accepted white rule, and thus were unlike those in West and East Africa who wanted majority rule. A few African U.F.P. supporters were sent to Europe, especially to Britain, to state that Rhodesian Africans preferred multi-racialism, which was almost the same as saying that they preferred European rule.

Similarly, police tactics were used to demonstrate that the Africans were forced into supporting N.D.P. and its successor Z.A.P.U. The police would either arrest people whom they suspected of recruiting members, and charge them with intimidation under the Law and Order Maintenance Act 1960 or place them in detention. Canvassing for a meeting, distribution of leaflets or party literature, even reminding a neighbour about a meeting, were regarded as intimidation. The manner in which the police handled 'intimidators' often caused riots, in which the police then fired indiscriminately, killing and wounding Africans. This became frequent after the British Government had announced that it would promulgate the 1961 Constitution as an Order-in-Council on 6 December, 1961.

The N.D.P. stepped up its meetings and its opposition to the Constitution. Sir Edgar began to fear that Britain might be impelled to withdraw the Constitution due to African pressure, so police dealt with meetings with increased ruthlessness and determination. In November, following the N.D.P.'s decision on 21–2 October not to fight the election, police provocation was intensified. A meeting held at Mufakase in Salisbury on 12 November ended in rioting. Police claimed that they had identified 'intimidators' among the crowd of several thousands, and fired tear-gas at people who were going home after the meeting. Provoked by this police action people rioted, with the result that several people were injured and others arrested. In Bulawayo a similar example of police aggression caused riots, and three Africans were shot. The police claimed that they had opened fire to defend themselves against stoning by the youth leaders; but it was the use by the police of tear-gas and their firing at peaceful crowds that had caused the riots which culminated in Africans stoning beer halls, the police, white-driven cars and houses belonging to 'stooges' (sometimes unjustly so described). In all, seventy Africans were arrested. This had all been in reaction to police attack and had never come unprovoked, as the police, the press and the whites in Rhodesia wished the world to believe. On 3 December, 1961, the N.D.P. meeting held at Highfield and, attended by between 10,000 and 12,000 people, was subjected to the same police aggression as that held at Njube in Bulawayo a week earlier.

The protests against the 1961 Constitution was intensified with the participation of women. In the time of the A.N.C. and during the early days of the N.D.P., women had not been active in nationalist politics. But with the growing African determination to obtain a constitution which would provide for majority rule, women felt spurred to take part. Two hundred women sat at Compensation House (the offices of the Rhodesian Government), protesting against the 1961 Constitution, and arrests were made. Six hundred others joined the first two hundred and went to prison with them, refusing to be given bail. The following day, hundreds of other women assembled at Highfields and Harare police stations demanding to be arrested. Although these women were practising tactics of passive resistance without weapons, the police were frightened into opening fire, killing one person and wounding fourteen. In all, eighty-six people were arrested under the Law and Order Maintenance Act (1960). To demonstrate the strength of his Government, Sir Edgar requested the Federal Government for troops, and on the same evening as the disturbances (6 December, 1961), two companies of the Rhodesia Light Infantry were deployed in Harare and High-fields to control all entrances and exits. The soldiers were reinforcing the police and the special constabulary that had been active since the first disturbances at Mufakose on 12 November. Demonstrations continued with vigour, despite the presence of the troops which had turned African townships into military garrisons. Tear-gas was used on 8 December to disperse a crowd of 1,000 who had gathered in Cecil Square near the Houses of Parliament. Twenty-five women were arrested at Sir Edgar's office as they protested against the 1961 Constitution.

African U.F.P. members in the townships were concerned at the pressure being put on the African community. On 3 December, 1961, 150 of them who attended a heavily guarded meeting in Harare passed a Resolution for the formation of a special constabulary to act as home guards to counter intimidation. The presence of the Federal M.P., Sydney Sawyer, led non-U.F.P. Africans to believe that the Resolution had been put into the mouths of the Africans by the U.F.P. headquarters; no African could have risked the possibility of reprisals from African nationalists by forming a constabulary. In fact, despite Sir Edgar's immediate endorsement of the Resolution, no constabulary was ever formed. Instead, the Resolution was used by the Government to amend the Law and Order Maintenance Act to deal with 'intimidators'.

The protest resulted in the Salisbury City Council banning all open-air N.D.P. meetings in Harare until the leaders had given a written assurance that they would prevent disorderly behaviour. Similar restrictions were imposed by the Bulawayo City Council at Njube. The Government spokesman issued a statement that these decisions emanated from the Councils themselves, and that the Government had not put pressure on them. However, the truth of this statement was doubtful in view of the fact that it was Sir Edgar and the Government, and not the Councils, that were worried about the opposition. In fact, only a day after the statement was made, the N.D.P. was banned.[2]

This ban on the N.D.P. on 9 December was followed by the immediate formation of Z.A.P.U. on 17 December, 1961. The executive of the new party was composed mainly of the old N.D.P. officials except for Dr. Samuel T. Parirenyatwa, who had resigned his post as a medical officer to become a politician. During its ten months' existence it followed N.D.P. tactics. Although the ban on the N.D.P. had revealed to the Africans that the whites were determined to retain power by any tactics, even including terrorism, the Africans were still hopeful that the British Government would play the role of an honest broker between black and white. Both Duncan Sandys and R. A. Butler, who succeeded him with special responsibility for Central Africa, had been evasive in replying to African protests. Butler told Nkomo on 20 March, 1963, that while Britain had the power to legislate for Rhodesia, there was a long-standing convention that she would not do so without the consent of the Southern Rhodesian Government. This statement was misleading: Britain had never exercised this power because successive British Governments had approved all the Bills that had become law in Rhodesia. The laws were as British as they were Rhodesian. The convention referred to had only been recognised officially as a sop to Sir Edgar for his acceptance of the 1961 Constitution. Before this date, all the Bills passed by the Rhodesian Parliament had been discussed by the British Government representative in Salisbury before they became law, controversial ones being sent straight to the Commonwealth or Colonial Office for scrutiny.[3]

Even in the bitterness over the ban of the N.D.P., Nkomo said at a press conference in Dar-es-Salaam that his party had no intention of forcing the immigrant races out of the country, but 'they must accept the authority and the sovereignty of the people.' The British Government had continued to ignore the representations from the African people over the 1961 Constitution. The Duke of Devonshire, then Minister of State for Commonwealth Relations, had told Nkomo that Southern Rhodesia was too well developed economically to be handed over to untried African hands. This statement reinforced the growing belief among Africans that the country could not be won back peacefully, as had happened in West and East Africa. None the less, Z.A.P.U. was formed while Northern Rhodesia, Nyasaland and Rhodesia's other neighbours were still under colonial rule. The Africans in Rhodesia had not lost hope in 'British fair play'. In any case the leaders of the nationalist movement were at pains to convince the young militants of the merit of achieving their objectives without violence.

The belief in mass rallies was still supreme in the plans of the leaders; Z.A.P.U. meetings were attended by crowds running to tens of thousands. A crowd of 20,000 Africans met Nkomo at the airport when he arrived from New York where he had been to petition the U.N. Special Committee on Colonialism. The police showed their disapproval of Nkomo's activities by marshalling a strong force: riot squads armed with rifles and shotguns surrounded the crowd. Even the *New York Times* reporter in Salisbury admitted that 'police force displayed was one of the strongest for a long time'.[4] Nkomo was forced to travel on foot all the way from the airport to the African township.

Despite their non-violent policy Z.A.P.U. meetings sometimes ended in riots in the same way as those of the N.D.P. had done, but this was often due to the actions of the police. The Law and Order Maintenance Act empowered the police to order speakers at a rally to get off the platform if they thought their utterances were subversive. Since the word 'subversive' could be interpreted in many ways to cover statements unpalatable to the Government, the police often declared statements subversive if they were too critical of the Government. After ordering his squad monitoring the meeting to take position with tear-gas, rifles and shotguns, the police commander would order the speaker to be quiet and get down from the platform. This was clearly calculated to offend the crowd. Reactions of shouting or jeering at the police as they ordered the speaker to climb down from the platform often caused the police to fire at the crowds, because jeering was regarded as undermining the authority of the police and exposing them to ridicule – an offence under the Law and Order Maintenance Act. Many people were shot and killed after such provocative behaviour on the part of the police. Riots developing from such police behaviour would be blamed on Z.A.P.U., which became the polecat of the reactionary towns Hartley, Gatooma, Rusape, Macheke and Umvuma. Its rallies were virtually banned there by the local authorities. In the Tribal Trust Lands, District Commissioners prohibited meetings under Section 53 (*b*) of the African Affairs Act (as amended) of 1959, which prohibited a gathering of more than twelve people. This was done to lessen Z.A.P.U.'s influence among the peasant population.

The popularity of Z.A.P.U. in the middle of 1962 made the white population believe that Africans were taking power. White businessmen even consulted Nkomo after the U.N. General Assembly had passed Resolution 1747 XVI,[5] believing that he would be the next ruler after Sir Edgar. Their aim was to get to know Nkomo's economic policy in the independent Zimbabwe. Constitutional changes in Northern Rhodesia, Nyasaland, Kenya and Uganda were showing a movement towards government under majority rule. The people who saw a similar trend in Southern Rhodesia were conditioning their minds to majority rule. It was not unusual to see white people joining and paying their subscriptions to Z.A.P.U.

A meeting called by J. T. Maluleke of the Southern Rhodesian African Trade Union Congress to protest against working conditions and lack of freedom of speech and assembly ended in riots. This resulted in strike action during May 1962. Police used tear-gas first and then shot into the crowds, resulting in Salisbury in the killing of three people and the wounding of ten. In Umtali, fifteen demonstrators were wounded. All this happened while R. A. Butler was on a fact-finding tour of the Central African Federation. Although it did not appear that the British minister was unduly concerned over these events, no doubt the white population was uneasy. Sir Edgar Whitehead was forced to throw his weight into the situation and decided to ban Z.A.P.U. on the 19 September, 1962.

The A.N.C. and the N.D.P. had been banned while the leaders were in ignorance of what was happening; however, Z.A.P.U.'s intelligence service knew of the ban well in advance, and its assets were taken out of the country several days beforehand. Their knowledge of the ban was implicit in the announcement of the Zimbabwe Liberation Army issued by 'General Chedu', whose name (Shona for 'ours') symbolised the desire to get the country back. On 12 September he declared a revolution, and called on all Africans to join the army within seven days. On 13–14 September, action started with the cutting of the telephone lines of the F.B.C. Petrol bombs were thrown at the homes of whites, and at white farms. This marked the beginning of African nationalist militancy and determination to take the country by an armed struggle, as all attempts at independence through peaceful, constitutional action had failed. From now on, African nationalists started recruiting men for military training, for which they found bases in African and other friendly countries. It is difficult to say who was responsible for the army, but most of the later leaders of the guerrilla movement, both in Z.A.P.U. and Z.A.N.U. were in the militant youth wing of Z.A.P.U. in 1962.

(ii) *The Banning of Z.A.P.U.*

The reaction to the ban on Z.A.P.U. was a country-wide wave of violence, the burning of schools, government buildings and the British South Africa Company forests and plantations at Melsetter, and riots in Karoi, Darwendale, Hot Springs, Penhalonga, Concession, Marandellas, Nkai, Melsetter, Silobela, Bindura, Mrewa, Salisbury, Bulawayo and Gwelo. It is difficult to identify the facts concerning the riots, looting and burning which took place after the ban. The Government blamed all on Z.A.P.U., but since its leaders had all been silenced, the party was unable to reply to the accusations. It is certain that the Africans were frustrated by the bans which had been placed on their movements since 1959, and that they were provoked by police and army arrogance and brutality. Police, police reservists and the army searched the houses of leading Africans who had not been arrested. Schoolteachers were searched in classrooms in front of their pupils. C. G. Msipa, President of the African Teachers' Association, was beaten up; Dr. M. A. Wakatama was treated by police with extreme rudeness; J. M. Chinamano was ordered by the police to say 'Yes, Sir' in answer to questions. Road blocks were set up on all major highways, buses carrying Africans were searched and those without passes were arrested at gunpoint. Police and the army found 700 home-made weapons. In all, 1,600 people were arrested for alleged strikes, protests, arson, malicious injury to property, carrying firearms and explosives and cutting the Rhodesia Railways central control system near Salisbury and Gwelo. This included 300 leaders who were restricted for three months. About fifty-five people sought by the police escaped arrest by going into hiding.[6] Police brutality was, and is still, felt most ruthlessly in rural areas where there is no press, and Africans are less well educated and less equipped to protest.[7]

The publication of details of these crimes by the Government was meant to provide the U.N. with reasons for the banning of Z.A.P.U., yet before September 1962 Sir Edgar Whitehead had been telling whites that the Africans were happy and contented with the Government. The paradox of it all is that the Africans' grievances were known by people abroad, and not by the white people in Rhodesia.

After the ban on Z.A.P.U. there was a lull in political activity until June 1963, when the split took place in the Z.A.P.U. executive, precipitated by the decision of Sithole and other Z.A.P.U. leaders to depose Nkomo as leader and form a political party under Sithole's leadership. Nkomo's reaction to this was to suspend Sithole and the leaders involved in the plot. Nkomo had the advantage of dealing with his colleagues politically because he was in the country while they were in Dar-es-Salaam. As the rift developed, the word 'intellectual' was used pejoratively by their opponents of Sithole's followers, who now returned home and campaigned for support within the country. Sithole, the leader of the breakaway group, formed Z.A.N.U., and Nkomo organised under the People's Caretaker Council (P.C.C.). The split introduced an element of fighting among rival parties never known previously in the history of Rhodesian African politics, although it had long been taking place in colonies such as Kenya, Northern Rhodesia and Nyasaland. The campaign became intensified in July 1963, and revived the protests of the Z.A.P.U. days.

This split between Nkomo and Sithole was used as a weapon against the Africans in Rhodesia. After the referendum of 1964, Ian Smith told a press conference that Africans in Rhodesia did not fight for their rights peacefully, as was the case with the Irish people. Of course, this showed laughable ignorance of the history of the political struggle in Ireland. The violence of the Africans in Rhodesia shows nothing to equal that of Ireland; or of Kenya's Mau Mau, or that in Jordan, India and Pakistan during their independence struggles. On the other hand, there are some people, especially in the independent African countries, who believe that the Africans in Rhodesia are not prepared to fight for their freedom as they themselves did. Apart from Kenya and Algeria, no African country has had to fight for its independence as hard as Rhodesia has already. And the struggle has barely begun.

This chapter includes as many cases of violence as possible; these were published in the papers by the Government of Sir Edgar Whitehead and by the present régime. But what is published is probably only half the story: where it is reported that three people were killed, there could very well have been ten times that number. Although the Africans burying their relatives who had been shot at a rally or on allegation of violence sometimes knew that more people had died than was reported in the press, they had no means of correcting the information through the press. Violence and sabotage preoccupied the political activists in 1963 and 1964, and they had been rife even before the split. As noted earlier, this emanated from the belief that Rhodesia could not win independence peacefully as other territories in West and East Africa had done.[8] The leaders made no secret of their new methods. Pressure for militant action from the young was irresistible after September 1962. Some young men were recruited and sent out of the country, while others were used within the country to throw petrol bombs and hand grenades. In three months between 13 September and 18 November, 1963, eight plastic bomb attacks were made, directed at the railways, electricity installations and sometimes at private homes. On 15 August a train was nearly derailed near Bulawayo. An organisation called 'The Voice of Women', consisting in fact of young men, was responsible for planning and co-ordinating information. Riots such as the one which took place on 16 January following police harassment of the crowd which gathered to greet Nkomo at Harare were no longer impressive to the young.[9] One of the actions which shook the population was when a bomb exploded at a sports meeting in Bulawayo attended by W. J. Field, then Prime Minister, on 17

February, 1964. In March a train was derailed near West Nicholson in Gwanda district. When Nkomo was put under restriction on 16 April, 1964, 120 women demonstrated, and 105 of them were arrested and sentenced on 28 April either to pay a £20 fine or to three months in prison.

The youths followed a different form of protest. Twenty or thirty of them attacked European customers at a supermarket, the O.K. Bazaars, in Salisbury. In Bulawayo the news of Nkomo's restriction was followed by attacks on public buildings. Up to 100 people were arrested in Bulawayo alone from 18 to 19 April. Clifford Dupont, then Minister of Justice, Law and Order, reported that a total of thirty-two white-driven cars were heavily stoned between 16 and 21 April.

(iii) *The Courts – a Crisis of Confidence*

The violence against white supremacy was sometimes directed against Africans of Z.A.N.U. or Z.A.P.U.–P.C.C. The purpose was not to press members into Z.A.P.U.–P.C.C. or Z.A.N.U., as was claimed by white propagandists. Z.A.P.U.–P.C.C. believed that the people who joined Z.A.N.U. were 'sell-outs' or, to use another popular term, 'Tshombes'. Z.A.N.U. itself somehow failed to convince the people with the reasons for its break-away. To claim that it broke away because Nkomo's leadership was weak, and at the same time to say he was a dictator, seemed contradictory. On the other hand, Nkomo's claims that Z.A.N.U. was formed with the encouragement of foreign powers who were hostile to the liberation of Zimbabwe was taken seriously. Nkomo had the advantage in that most of the leaders who broke away had not been in politics for as long as he, and those who remained with him, such as J. Chikerema, G. B. Nyandoro, J. Msika and J. Z. Moyo, had been. In reality, most Z.A.N.U. leaders are as much nationalists as those of Z.A.P.U. The Z.A.P.U. youths mostly attacked Z.A.N.U. followers in the belief that they were following a foreign-sponsored organisation. What the contestants actually believed is difficult to establish, but nine months of intense rivalry followed, from September 1963 to June 1964, which was later exploited to the detriment of the African cause. Those who accepted the story put about by Smith's régime about African violence failed to appreciate that far more Africans were killed by the régime's police and the army after 1960 than ever died in the party clashes. The Z.A.P.U.–Z.A.N.U. conflict was confined mainly to Highfields or the Salisbury area. Other areas had little, if any, experience of inter-party clashes.[10]

Until U.D.I. Africans believed in the impartiality of the judicial process in Rhodesia. It was not unusual to see leaders fight their cases through from the magistrates' courts to the appeal courts. In the heyday of the A.N.C., G. Nyandoro was constantly victimised by the police under the Public Order Act of 1955. Chikerema was also tried in the High Court for criminal defamation because he had attacked Sir Patrick Fletcher, a minister in Todd's Government in 1958. Enos Nkala, Mawema, A. Mukahlera, D. Dabengwa and several others submitted to trial and, in some cases, received heavy sentences under the Whitehead laws of 1959 and 1960. After U.D.I. the African nationalist attitude changed, defendants with few exceptions refusing to plead.[11]

Faith in the courts was later enhanced by the declaration of rights provided in the 1961 Constitution, the basic purpose of which was

> to ensure that every person in Southern Rhodesia enjoys the fundamental rights and freedoms of the individual, that is to say, the right, whatever his race, tribe, place of origin, political opinions, colour or creed, but subject to respect for the rights and freedoms of others and for the public interest, to each and all of the following, namely (a) life, liberty, security of the person, the enjoyment of property and the protection of the law (b) freedom of conscience, of expression and of assembly and association; and (c) respect for his private and family life.

These provisions were, on their face value, praiseworthy and could have safeguarded every citizen's civil rights if they had been sanctioned by courts which were backed by public opinion. But in Rhodesia, the composition of the judiciary reflected the structure of society with its bias in favour of the white population. This eliminated nationally based public opinion, and as a result the ideals of the Declaration of Rights and other statutes were interpreted to suit the interest of white public opinion. The African attitude could safely be ignored because it was not backed by power to threaten the interests of the rulers.

African belief in the impartiality of the courts in Rhodesia was due mainly to an underestimation of the impending confrontation between black and white. Except for the 1914–18 land case, no significant constitutional case had ever appeared in the Rhodesian courts. The behaviour of the régime and the failure of some of the judges to make clear-cut decisions in cases with political consequences were responsible for the waning prestige of the Rhodesian courts. The Law and Order Maintenance Act (1960) was amended almost annually up to 1970, becoming progressively more severe. Nkomo, Sithole, Chitepo and Silundika lived to regret their naïvety in assuming the impartiality of the courts at the 1961 constitutional conference. The history of the Supreme Court of the United States' decisions on the Declaration of Rights should have taught them what courts can do under racial pressure.[12]

The Rhodesia Front was determined to silence African political opposition, and as soon as it gained power in 1962 it made sure that the white man's strength was felt through the police force, public utterances and the courts.[13] Courts were reorganised partly to accommodate the legal institutions of the defunct Federation, but also to increase the powers of the magistrates. Stringent penalties, such as a mandatory death sentence for petrol-bombing of either people or property, were introduced into the Law and Order Maintenance Act.

Accused at Umtali of 'untrue statements about torture by the police' which were likely to bring the police into 'contempt', 'ridicule' or 'disesteem', Nkomo was charged under the Law and Order Maintenance Act, and given a sentence of six months. On appeal, the sentence was reduced to a fine of £50 and three months of hard labour suspended for three years. The sentence was imposed even when Nkomo proved his claim by producing people who had suffered electric shocks, 'electric snake' torture and beating at the hands of the police.

On 9 February, 1963, Nkomo was charged at Rusape with contravening the Law and Order Maintenance Act by leading an illegal procession of 3,000 people to welcome ex-detainees. He was acquitted on this charge, but found guilty of resisting arrest and assaulting and obstructing the police. He appealed and won; but then he served a prison sentence in Gwelo where he had been found guilty of inciting racial violence when he spoke of prisoners-of-war who had come to settle on the land in Rhodesia. After that, he and sixteen other P.C.C. leaders were served with detention orders under the Preventive Detention Act. Nkomo had served two and a half months of a nine-month sentence originally imposed on him for a 'subversive' speech in Gwelo in August 1963, when he told a meeting that Africans were displaced from their land by the Germans and Italians whom they had defeated and brought to Rhodesia as prisoners-of-war. After an appeal, Mr. Justice Young confirmed the sentence but suspended seven and a half months of it for three years. But there was truth in what Nkomo had said: all the Germans and Italians who had come as prisoners are wealthy, enfranchised and no less arrogant than other white people. The houses at Beatrice Cottages, Salisbury, in which they lived as prisoners were given to 'emergent' Africans.

In his appeal against a conviction for a subversive speech at Inyarzura on 20 October, 1963, Nkomo, with twenty-five leaders of the P.C.C., challenged, under the declaration of rights, the legality of their restriction at Gonakudzingwa. Mr. Justice Dendy Young ruled on 26 June, 1964, that the orders of restriction were invalid, noting that the Preventive Detention Act obliged restrictees to notify the police of their movements and left them otherwise as free as any citizen resident in the area. He was convinced that Nkomo and others did not have such freedom – in effect, the liberty of the individual had in their case been reduced almost to vanishing point. D. W. Lardner-Burke, Minister of Law and Order, appealed to the Appellate Division of the High Court and left the restrictees living in the conditions which they had challenged. The Appellate Division heard the case in November 1964.

Mr. Justice Dendy Young's verdict was confirmed by the Chief Justice, Sir Hugh Beadle, on 12 November, 1964, but as the régime was planning a U.D.I., it could not afford to comply with the decision. Sir Hugh ruled that the Preventive Detention Act as amended contravened the Declaration of Rights in the Constitution, and that the Government did not have the right to extend the Act beyond its expiry as it had done in April 1964. Lardner-Burke then appealed to the Privy Council on 20 November, 1964, claiming that the release of the detainees 'might jeopardise the security of the state'. This was simply a plan to buy time to prepare for U.D.I. without any interference from Nkomo. Nkomo's ban came only two days after Ian Smith was made Prime Minister, when Winston Field had been forced to resign because of his diffidence over U.D.I. The release of Nkomo, as the court had ruled, would have made the contingent planning for U.D.I. nearly impossible, hence the appeal to the Privy Council. The appeal remained dormant for over a year until it was dropped by Lardner-Burke in 1966, by which time his U.D.I. plan had been accomplished. At the time the decision to appeal was made, Nkomo and his sixteen colleagues were in prison in Gwelo under detention conditions, having been removed from the camp at Gonakudzingwa. They were later allowed to return to the latter place, but detention conditions were imposed on them there too when U.D.I. was approaching.

The leaders of Z.A.N.U. had also believed in the fairness of the courts. The Rev. N. Sithole was arrested at Fort Victoria under the Law and Order Maintenance Act for urging Africans to oppose U.D.I. The magistrate dismissed twelve of the thirteen charges made against him: as Sithole had clearly urged people to oppose an unlawful fact, he saw no case to be answered. However, Sithole was found guilty on the charge that he had called on his followers to be ready to oppose U.D.I. with axes, bows and arrows. The magistrate claimed that it was tantamount to fostering a private army, and sentenced him to twelve months hard labour, with six months' suspended for three years. This time the Government was bent on screwing down the political offenders, so Sithole was not allowed bail while appealing to the High Court. Takawira was sentenced to six months for a subversive speech at Umtali in 1962. Edson Zvobgo was sentenced to eighteen months for being an official of a banned organisation outside the country, and served this sentence. Enos Chikowore, Z.A.N.U.'s secretary for Youth and Culture, was sentenced to one year for public violence over a clash with a P.C.C. supporter. The African leaders thought at that time that the courts were prepared to judge fairly in all cases, but after U.D.I. they realised that decisions on political crimes were regulated by the political tone of the country.

After the victory of the Rhodesia Front in 1962, the *Daily News* dropped its paternalistic policy over Africans and adopted a new approach designed genuinely to express the Africans feelings.[14] When the split in the nationalist movement took place in July 1963, it first supported Z.A.N.U. policies. This provoked protests from Nkomo's P.C.C. Mrs. R. Chinamano led a delegation of women to remonstrate on the matter with the management. The *Daily News* was also subjected to a serious boycott, together with commercial companies suspected of being pro-Z.A.N.U. Nkomo thus demonstrated that the masses were behind him, and after admitting that the split and the subsequent formation of Z.A.N.U. were a 'tragic abortion', the *Daily News* thereafter supported Nkomo and the P.C.C.

Supporters of Z.A.N.U. were infuriated by this change of sides. One Z.A.N.U. supporter was sentenced to death for attacking its premises as a protest against its pro-P.C.C. stance. It could not be accused of being a propaganda newsheet for the P.C.C., but all the same it started to expose police brutality over the schoolchildren who were often beaten for boycotting schools as a protest against increased fees. It published stories of harrassment of people over the pass laws, of unemployment, poverty, reactions to the restriction of Nkomo, and conditions in the restriction camps. Pictures of Nkomo, Mr. and Mrs. Chinamano, Msika and other first inmates of the camps often appeared in the press. The *Daily News* no longer vacillated in its opposition to the Rhodesian Front Government as it had done with the Whitehead Government.

Lardner-Burke decided to ban the *Daily News* together with the P.C.C. and Z.A.N.U. on 26 August, 1964. By that time both parties were virtually leaderless, for the leaders were in prison, detention or restriction camps. In moving an order in Parliament to ban the party, Lardner-Burke argued that the *Daily News* had kept the images of Z.A.P.U. and Nkomo alive, and had contained African nationalist propaganda of the most blatant kind, with editorials against Europeans[15] and sensational headlines to excite attention, photographed police action to foster hostility towards the police, and sown disaffection among sections of the population.

African Newspapers Ltd., the company which ran the *Daily News* as part of Lord Thomson's newspaper empire, applied to the High Court for the revocation of the ban. Their lawyer argued that Section 18 of the Law and Order Maintenance Act, under which the paper was banned, contravened the Declaration of Rights. The Court ruled on 23 September, 1964, that the ban was valid.

It is true that party rivalry between P.C.C. and Z.A.N.U. caused a great deal of concern among Africans, but the authorities did not care as long as the European public was not affected.[16] Dupont's visit in February 1964 to Harare Hospital to see the children of Chifamba, a leading P.C.C. official, who had been burnt in a Z.A.N.U. attack, was purely to find ways of legitimising the brutal reprisals that followed.

Two amendments to the Law and Order Maintenance Act approved by Parliament on 7 December, 1964, made the possession of a bomb punishable by death or imprisonment for up to twenty years, and possession of any offensive weapon other than a bomb by a maximum of twenty years. The second amendment adopted by Parliament without a vote on 19 March, 1965, extended the maximum period of restriction under the Act from one to five years.[17] As soon as Lardner-Burke, who had taken over from Dupont as Minister of Law and Order, armed himself with these repressive laws, he lifted the state of emergency in Harare on 4 April, 1965, and Highfield on 21 May, 1965. He had detained 1,936 people from these two townships and banned others from entering them.

The first target of repression was Nkomo, because, of the two leaders – Sithole and Nkomo – Sithole was first regarded as a better devil.[18] Against Nkomo the full weight of all the repressive laws was directed. He was banned from entering or staying in any Tribal Trust Land for fear of his influence over the peasants in the country,[19] and was later charged with not obeying this ban. The order banned him even from going to his home district, where he had been restricted in 1962 after the ban on Z.A.P.U. Later he was banned from entering the area within a fifteen-mile radius from the centre of Salisbury.[20] Before these two bannings, Nkomo and his P.C.C. had been prohibited from convening or attending public meetings,[21] and on 9 February, 1964, the ban was extended to cover any gathering other than a religious one for three months.

Dupont explained to Parliament that he had banned Nkomo because there had been violent disturbances after his meetings;

Nkomo had not denounced violence in the way Sithole had, but had allowed his followers to act irresponsibly. His public appearances, Dupont claimed, provoked intimidation and violence. He could not reveal the reasons for banning Nkomo because of their 'confidential nature'.[22] Dupont said he disliked the P.C.C. policy, which was designed to boycott shops that were practising discrimination, to boycott schools as a protest against fees, to instil fear into the Europeans so as to compel them to emigrate and discourage new immigrants, and to frighten overseas investors by creating an overall picture of an explosive situation in the country. Yet Dupont's draconian legislation was not effective. Banned as he was, Nkomo continued to meet people at religious gatherings. A day of prayer for Zimbabwe organised by African church leaders brought thousands to a meeting at Barbourfields addressed by Nkomo as well as the religious leaders.

The P.C.C. was organised into cells of every fortieth house in townships: Nkomo met the leaders of these cells in ones and twos. By mid-February, Dupont had not allayed the fears of the whites, which grew for as long as Nkomo was at large. The number of people arrested in possession of bombs and other lethal weapons was increasing.[23] The fears became near-panic when the P.C.C. announced the programme of the 'Book of Life', with 500,000 Zimbabwe registration cards. The intention was to enrol P.C.C. supporters officially. This represented a contradiction of policy because of the struggle between the P.C.C. and Z.A.N.U. At its inception the People's Caretaker Council was supposed not to enrol members; it was said to be a people's movement in which all people who were born, or lived, in Zimbabwe could be members without registering or paying a subscription. The arguments as to who had a larger following, Nkomo or Sithole, must have driven Nkomo to introduce the 'Book of Life'. Z.A.N.U. had its members registered so it could make a public claim to 100,000 supporters. Their failure to turn up at meetings, which were often attended by fewer than 300, was attributed to P.C.C. 'intimidation'. On the other hand thousands turned up at P.C.C. meetings, but could not be produced as members on paper.

By February 1964, the P.C.C. felt it was time to register its members in the hope of declaring itself a party at a suitable time. A total membership of 500,000 was anticipated, and a day was set aside for the registration of people in centres established all over the country. The settlers were alarmed at the programme, which appeared 'sacrilegious' because the name 'Book of Life' referred to the Book of Revelation: 'And whosoever was not found written in the Book of Life was cast into a lake of fire.' The Government thereupon banned the 'Book of Life' and confiscated all the cards.

Dupont soon also announced his plan to *restrict* persons under the Law and Order Maintenance Act, because 'not all offenders can be brought to court, mainly because of intimidation and threats against witnesses.' He told Parliament at the end of February that he had signed restriction orders for 144 people, with forty-eight pending. On 19 March, 1964, Dupont told Parliament in desperation that the situation was continuing to deteriorate and that in the past nine months ten primary schools and one secondary school had been closed following boycotts to enforce the non-payment of fees. Dupont's threats were for white consumption, for no one was restricted or detained until April 1964. The reasons for his inaction, even after making the threats, could have been Field's resistance. Although he had introduced a mandatory hanging clause into the Law and Order Maintenance Act in early 1963, Field did not regard it as sensible to detain people without trial, and had told the electorate in 1962 that he would not detain people outside the courts. This policy was consistent with his belief that the hanging clause would be deterrent enough against what appeared to whites as 'intimidation'. Furthermore, Field's preoccupation with the independence issue made him cautious towards the policies that could be used by the British Government to deny Rhodesia independence. This policy made Field lose his leadership of the Rhodesia Front, because he was unsuccessful in both directions.

The Africans disliked Field for bringing about the Rhodesia Front victory, but he was not viewed with the same awe as Sir Edgar Whitehead and Ian Smith. He was rather likened to the paternalistic Huggins. As soon as he was replaced by Smith on 13 April, 1964, Dupont struck. On 16 April, Nkomo, J. Chinamano and his wife Ruth, and Joseph Msika were restricted to Gonakudzingwa, and they were immediately followed by 141 other P.C.C. supporters. The *Rhodesia Herald* on 16 April criticised as 'an act of insanity' Dupont's restriction of Nkomo, because it unnecessarily made him into a hero. Dupont replied that he had no choice; he had acted to forestall Nkomo's policy which was designed to bring about black nationalist rule, and added that the P.C.C. had turned to 'Communism'. To soothe the consciences of his supporters he absurdly claimed that Nkomo's following was less than one per cent of what he claimed, because more than half the African population were children. Dupont did not realise that he was implying that all adult Africans supported Nkomo – and one per cent of the adults made a substantial following in Rhodesia in comparison with the whites whom Dupont represented.

The Todd and Whitehead Governments, like all minority governments, were often in conflict with nationalist leaders, as was Field, but with the Rhodesia Front under Smith, the conflict became intensified into a military confrontation. The present opposition between black and white is blamed on the lack of foresight by African leaders, and Nkomo is singled out for attack. In the British press and in books he is characterised as a colourless monster. Young describes him as an 'extremist', a 'minority leader' and 'the fat and obdurate leader'.[24] John Day writes of 'Nkomo the traveller',[25] and criticises him strongly without any appreciation of his efforts to bring acceptable rule to the country. The British Conservative Governments of Macmillan and Douglas-Home blamed the collapse of their 1961 Constitution and the victory of the Rhodesia Front on Nkomo. In fact there is no evidence to prove that without him the Rhodesia Front would not have come to power. Both Nkomo and Sithole have their weaknesses, like all world leaders, but the problems they have had to face are more serious than is admitted by those who criticise the African leaders in Rhodesia.

The *Central African Examiner* of December 1962 published a letter from J. B. Chikanya who, in reply to a letter in the previous issue, said that the country had not yet produced any leader with massive African support and with 'the ability and personality needed for the job'. The author of the letter was repeating a contention frequently seen in the European press. Nkomo was often regarded as weaker or less dynamic than Banda, Nyerere, Kaunda or Kenyatta. Both he and Sithole, however, compare well with all the leaders of Central and East Africa. Nkomo's experience is longer than that of any leader in Central and East Africa except Kenyatta. Nyerere, Banda, Seretse Khama and Kaunda, who are leaders of their nations today, became political figures long after Nkomo; so too did Milton Obote. Chikanya's reply put the position of Nkomo clearly:

> No leader in Central Africa or Tanganyika or Kenya or Uganda has been confronted with as tough an imperialist–colonialist problem. No leader in Central Africa has been able to keep the common touch; readiness to accept criticism and benefit from it; to keep abreast of and capture the spirit of the times; above all ability to keep in step with the feelings and aspirations of the people as Nkomo has done.

He is a speaker with the power to sustain the interest of large audiences, often running to between 30,000 and 50,000 people. Among his shortcomings was a failure to realise that the settlers in Rhodesia were desperate and would do anything, beyond the bounds of legality, to retain their privileges. Over the 1961 Constitution, he put too much trust in the British Government. The intricacy of

Rhodesian politics can be blamed not on Nkomo or any one of the African leaders, but on the British Government's failure to execute the trusteeship over the Africans conferred on them by the Constitution of 1923. The split of 1963 was the after-effect of frustration resulting from lack of progress towards majority rule which most African territories had achieved by that year. The breaking-point had been reached. Z.A.P.U. would have split under any leader so long as progress was not in sight.

Sithole too is a good leader. Like several other educated African leaders in Rhodesia, he arrived too late in politics, joining the N.D.P. after 26 August, 1960, but his contribution to the consolidation of African nationalism was immense. The split was unfortunate in the sense that people who were making one of the finest teams in Africa turned to tear each other's throats, incurring bad publicity which was to be used by their enemies in the Rhodesia Front to justify repression of the Africans and by British Governments to justify delaying progress towards majority rule. The violence which took place during the early days of the split was deplorable. But it was not unique and should be viewed together with what has occurred in other parts of Africa – the Mau Mau violence in Kenya, the activity of U.N.I.P. and A.N.C. on the Copperbelt, and the friction between the two African parties in Nyasaland in 1959 led respectively by Dr. Banda and T. D. Banda.

As has been shown, Africans believed up to U.D.I. that courts were competent to interpret the laws without racial prejudice, but they failed to take account of the fact that courts, like all human institutions, can only act justly if the laws themselves are just. In Rhodesia, the legislation manufactured by the fear-ridden minority is unjust, because it is made outside the rule of law. The attitude of the whites is that they are fighting for survival. The judges who dissent and made decisions which seem to appease the Africans are branded as traitors. This became apparent in the cases which challenged U.D.I. The judges who took the unpopular point of view decided to leave the country.

Two detainees, Daniel Madzimbamuto and Leo S. Baron, challenged their continued detention by a régime that had become illegal after U.D.I.[26] Their lawyer was armed with a certificate from the British Secretary for Commonwealth Relations, Arthur Bottomley, stating that Britain did not recognise U.D.I. He had evidence from Prof. W. L. Taylor, former professor of economics at the University College of Rhodesia, and adviser to UNESCO and the World Bank, who argued that the long-term effect of economic sanctions on the economy would be 'disastrous',[27] and from the

Bishop Skelton of Matabeleland, who pleaded in person for the release of the detained men on Christian moral grounds. The régime produced affidavits from twenty-two 'leading Rhodesians' who argued that Rhodesia would successfully overcome sanctions. The decision of the Court which came on 9 September, 1966, came as a thunderbolt to Africans, but gave great satisfaction to the white population.[28] It was ambiguous, as the whole political situation in Rhodesia has always been. The decision stated that the 1965 Constitution and its Government were illegal, but went on to bless the existence of the illegal régime by saying that to avoid chaos and a vacuum in the law, the court ought to give effect to measures of the effective government 'for the sake of peace', 'good government', and 'law and order'. The choice of these terms was unfortunate, because they are part of the special white vocabulary which has no meaning among Africans. Worse still was Mr. Justice Lewis' dismissal of Arthur Bottomley's testimony because it came from 6,000 miles away. He then admitted: 'I am unable to hold that the 1965 Constitution is the legal constitution of this country. I would be false to my judicial oath to apply the law; I would also be false to my oath of allegiance to Her Majesty the Queen.' Thus, while dismissing the testimony of the Queen's Secretary of State, he recognised the Queen, to whom he had taken an oath, and who was also 6,000 miles away. The subsequent split in the Judiciary over this appeal of the condemned prisoners in 1968, which led to the resignation of Justices Dendy Young and Fieldsend, was a self-indictment of the integrity of the courts. The judges' refusal to attend the new session of the Rhodesian Parliament because they did not 'consider it proper' no longer impressed anybody. The advocate Sydney Kentridge argued in the Privy Council that the judges had failed to decide fairly due to political considerations.

The guerrillas no longer either pleaded or answered questions at their trials, to signalise their loss of confidence in the courts on the one hand, and their non-recognition of the régime on the other. This attitude was revealed at the trial in Salisbury of seven guerrillas on 22 June, 1966, for attempting to sabotage the Beira–Umtali pipe-line. They told the court that they had declared war on Smith's illegal government; their fight was an attempt to set up a legal government. To this the judge replied that theirs would have been an illegal government as well. A group of Z.A.P.U.–A.N.C. guerrillas who were captured in the 1967–8 incursions refused to plead, maintaining that they did not recognise the courts, and stating that they accepted the sentences of death imposed on them as if it were part of life. Some of them said they were prisoners-of-war and were prepared to be shot rather than stand a mock trial.

Another factor which corroded the prestige of the Rhodesian courts was the Law and Order Maintenance Act 1960. From the time it was introduced, Africans believed it to be intended exclusively for them as a form of racial persecution. On its introduction, Sir Robert Tredgold, then Chief Justice of the Federation, resigned in protest because it was 'savage' and 'primitive'; and, indeed, it does infringe the Declaration of Rights. The Constitutional Council and the International Commission of Jurists commented adversely upon it. The amendment by Act 12 of 1963, which introduced Section 33 (a) to provide for mandatory hanging for anyone found in possession of grenades or petrol bombs, hastened the decline of the courts' prestige in the eyes of the Africans, for they knew that only they would be subjected to it. Of the 4,910 cases which came to court under the Act in 1964, none involved a white defendant. Only three whites have been tried under the Act after U.D.I.: sentences were given to J. A. Conradie and J. G. Dixon for possession of hand grenades and to George Brind for publishing a statement outside the country likely to spread alarm and despondency among the white population.

Sentences under the Law and Order Maintenance Act

Date[1]	Death	Life Imprisonment	Imprisonment for over ten years
17. 3.65	19	—	6
14.12.66	70	—	—
23. 9.67	82	—	—
10.12.68	92	25	292[2]

[1] Dates when the figures were published.
[2] The total number sentenced since 1963.

The fact that the number of sentences passed is increasing instead of declining, reveals that the régime is not achieving its intention of stopping opposition.

All those who have been sentenced to death and to periods of imprisonment up to life have been Africans, except for one white man, J. A. Conradie. They have been accused of political crime of various kinds, from shouting the slogans of banned organisations to bringing 'arms of war' into the country and fighting. In September 1967 the régime introduced an amendment of the Law and Order Maintenance Act which inserted Section 48 (a), imposing a mandatory death penalty for persons bringing in arms of war with intent to endanger the maintenace of law and order in the country and in neighbouring territory. Those arrested in battle decided not to plead at their trial.

Three Africans were hanged on 6 March, 1968, and another two on 11 March, although the Queen reprieved them. The Appellate Division of the High Court rejected the men's application to appeal to the Judicial Committee of the Privy Council in London, and confirmed the régime's right to execute them. This provoked a protest throughout the world. The régime's self-confidence was shaken, and no more have been hanged. Some guerrillas captured in battle have had their death sentences commuted to life imprisonment. There is suspicion among Africans that the captured guerrillas are executed secretly after they have been sentenced to death, which is part and parcel of the deep suspicion that exists anyway between black and white in Rhodesia, but we do not claim that it is necessarily true. The facts of the situation are that those guerrillas who stand trial and receive death sentences stay for years in death cells, or in some cases the Executive Council, under the chairmanship of C. W. Dupont, commutes the sentences to life imprisonment. It is believed that the trials of the Nazi leaders at Nuremberg haunt the minds of the present régime, and no one wants to be hunted down in Latin America like Eichmann. Defiance of world opinion has its limitations.

(iv) State of Emergency without End

Officially, states of emergency are declared to restore law and order, yet in reality one is often declared to restore the morale of the white community when it believes that the country is drifting into the hands of the Africans. This was noticeable in 1959 before the ban on the A.N.C. and in 1961 and 1962 when the N.D.P. and Z.A.P.U. respectively were banned. Correspondence in the white press often reflects the state of panic in the minds of the European population when the African nationalist organisations appear to be heading for victory. The high rate of white emigration when African organisations are at the zenith of their activity indicates the fluctuation of the white morale.[29] If Africans attend meetings in large numbers, or an African leader makes a strong speech suggesting that the Government is oppressive, that is enough to demoralise the white population. This is reflected in the laws which make it almost impossible for Africans to say a word of criticism of the system without being prosecuted under the security laws for causing despondency. The same security laws rarely if ever apply to the white people.

A state of emergency means that the police and the army have the power to make arrests without warrant, to order persons out of the emergency areas, to prohibit them from entering it or taking photographs, to ban controversial statements and those from people in detention or restricted areas, or those likely to cause alarm and despondency or affecting the security movements of troops and police. The Minister of Law and Order has the power to establish camps for the accommodation of persons so detained. When the P.C.C. and Z.A.N.U. were banned on 26 August, 1964, Wha Wha restriction camp was converted into a prison and people were detained there. The Rhodesia Front believes that in order to achieve complete subservience, terror must be instilled into the minds of the Africans as has been done in South Africa. A state of emergency is the best instrument for inflicting terror.

In 1964 five state emergencies were declared in Highfields, Harare and Mrewa. In Highfields the army used a cordon of barbed wire to surround 80,000 residents during the night. The police moved in, searching homes thoroughly and arresting, detaining and restricting those found, especially if they were unemployed. The same was done in Harare in October 1964, when Smith was gradually moving towards U.D.I., which had been intended for that year, but was postponed to make the preparations more careful. In Mrewa, a great demonstration of official power was given in the villages in December 1964. The police, army and air force were deployed to deal with 'an outbreak of intimidation and violence'. Lardner-Burke told Parliament on 3 December that damage had been done to property in the area, 'especially through arson and maiming of cattle', and then returned to the contradiction which is so typical of settler politics: he assured Parliament that the country was quite calm – yet much had happened during the year to prove the very contrary: political parties had been banned because of 'unrest', states of emergency had been declared as noted above, the *Daily News* had been banned, and African leaders had been detained. On 11 August, when asking Parliament to extend powers of restriction under the Law and Order Maintenance Act, he said there was a threat of a breakdown in law and order, but then revealing that two ex-chiefs, one headman, one ex-headman, and thirty-five kraal heads and ex-kraal heads were among 2,000 people detained and restricted under the state of emergency regulations because of 'unrest'. He told Parliament on the same day about the general tranquillity of the country.

The repression which came with the state of emergency did not curtail the Africans' quest for freedom. They went in hundreds to visit Nkomo at Gonakudzingwa. At this stage he was living under restriction in that he could visit places up to ten miles away from the camp where[30] he could receive visitors and sometimes eat food provided by his hundreds of guests. This was also the case with Sithole at Sikombela. A detention order was issued in 1965, a few days before U.D.I., to keep Nkomo and others in strict detention surrounded by barbed wire and under armed guard.

Even before this detention was imposed, the 'pilgrimage' had been proscribed for three months by a state of emergency declared on 28 May, 1965, in the whole Nuanetsi District.[31] Another was declared in Lupane, north-west of Bulawayo, because of 'unrest'.[32] The two areas were sealed off by police, troops, and the air force. The reasons given were that the state of emergency was necessary to stop a new method of 'intimidation' with 'witchcraft and magic' introduced by Nkomo's followers 'among the simple tribesmen in Nuanetsi'. The police removed 450 visitors to Nkomo, and sixty-seven people were arrested for an illegal meeting.

Heavy rains had fallen in the area after many years of drought. May is often a dry month in Rhodesia, and it appeared extraordinary that rain should come in torrents in a drought-stricken area at unusual times of the year. Stories spread that it was due to the presence of Nkomo in the area: God had decided to give him water to drink. This gave a stimulus to the 'pilgrimages', a thing which terrified Lardner-Burke and made him deploy the armed forces to knock the stories out of the peasants in the area while making a false claim that Nkomo was using witchcraft to gain support.

The police and the armed forces had instructions to detain in the Gonakudzingwa area any person they found in possession of articles like headgear or a walking-stick which resembled those articles worn or carried by restrictees which were reputed to signify membership of a banned organisation. Such persons would be found guilty of an offence and imprisoned for up to six months.[33] Lardner-Burke told Parliament that one of the reasons why the state of emergency was declared in the Nuanetsi area was to restore chiefs' and headmen's control over their people which they had lost as the result of 'pilgrimages' to Nkomo.

A victim of the Nuanetsi state of emergency was T. G. Makombe, a Z.A.P.U. official, one of the first graduates of the University College of Rhodesia. He had been restricted to Gonakudzingwa for a year. On the expiry of his restriction he took a train for home in possession of one of the 'walking sticks', and was arrested on the train only a few miles from Gonakudzingwa, tried at Nuanetsi magistrates' court, and sentenced to six months' imprisonment with hard labour. He served his prison sentence under most onerous conditions, sleeping in rooms with bugs, which are sometimes allowed to flourish to make prison conditions worse.

The state of emergency declared on 5 November, 1965, was to pave the way for U.D.I. and to create an atmosphere of war, which continues up to the present day.[34] In order to get the Governor to sign it, the ministers told him that it was intended to enable the Government to deal with incursions of trained guerrillas sponsored by Z.A.P.U. and Z.A.N.U. ready to strike any day from Zambia. The evidence of the arms produced in court during the trials between January 1963 and October 1965 made some well-meaning settlers believe the story put out by ministers. Smith was compelled to deny publicly the suggestion that the state of emergency was intended as a prelude to U.D.I.

The sweeping powers given to the Commissioner of Police and the regulations that came with the state of emergency left no doubt in the minds of those who had studied Smith's policies since 1964 that U.D.I. was round the corner. The Commissioner of Police was empowered to appoint officers and charge them with specific duties in some areas, with power to control the movement of individuals, seize private vehicles, and prohibit the possession and distribution of newspapers, magazines, pamphlets and other printed matter in areas where they were in charge. The inclusion of regulations dealing with the press made this state of emergency different from its predecessors because those were meant to deal with Africans. The regulations on printed material *ipso facto* included the white people, who had never before been affected by states of emergency, because the printing industry is in their hands.

The methods of terrorising Africans by states of emergency, such as the ones going on in Nuanetsi and Lupane Districts at that time, spread to all corners of the country. A total of over 40,000 armed troops from the regular army, trained reserves, police and ordinary police reserves and an air force contingent of 900 were stationed all over the country at that time, with heavy concentrations on the Zambia border and the Kariba Dam. African townships were like garrisons, and all the main roads were heavily patrolled. Armoured cars mingled with Africans going to work on bicycles. Suspects, or any persons who had ever associated themselves with Nkomo or Sithole and their parties, were rounded up and placed behind bars. There were house-to-house searches at night in the African townships – police moving in while the soldiers blocked the exit roads. They moved in on different townships on different nights. The six days before U.D.I. were worst for the Africans in the main townships: people collected at night were herded into barbed-wire camps at the nearest police stations, and were sorted out at leisure. Those who failed to answer interrogation satisfactorily were held back for further questioning. The detention prisons used were Khami for Bulawayo, Kentucky prison for Salisbury and district, Marandellas for Umtali, and Wha Wha for Gwelo. The standard reply one got from wives and children whose husbands and fathers had been arrested was '*uthethwe*' (Sindebele for 'he's been taken') or '*vatorwa*' in Chishona. The cell structure which Nkomo had attempted to construct in the P.C.C. before being rusticated to Gonakudzingwa was disorganised by the time of U.D.I.

A Thursday was craftily chosen as the day for U.D.I. because it was realised that most workers received their weekly wages on Friday. The temptation to defy a call for strike action would thus be enormous. This turned out to be a wise calculation on the Government's part. The University was deeply involved in examinations, U.D.I. having come when the first examination papers were being written.

The effect of military and police operations between 5 and 11 November was to leave Africans in Salisbury without any form of resistance. They had, after all, experienced the Highfield and Harare purges in 1964, and the terror of these kept Africans in a state of fear throughout 1965.

Que Que, Bulawayo, Gwelo and rural areas managed to organise some form of resistance. Farmers were affected, especially in the tobacco belt of northern Mashonaland and on the cattle ranches in Matabeleland. In Bulawayo, the *Vukandoda* method ('wake up, man') made the strike a success. Men within a cell – that is, a row of forty houses – decided to spend a night all sitting in one of the forty houses. The men would visit or patrol their homes by turns, making sure that none left the group. The result was that no members of a cell went to work. The police also helped to make the Bulawayo strike a success. When they received information about the existence of these cells, they collected all the forty wherever they could find them and marched them with their hands up to the nearest police station. The result was that on Wednesday 15 November, 1965, the barbed-wire camps were full. So full were the prison cells in Bulawayo that it was impossible for anyone to sit down. Inmates slept in relays day and night to provide sleeping room for others. It was impossible to get a bath. J. Ntutha, a Bulawayo businessman, stayed for twenty-eight days without a bath in a cell intended for six to eight people, which he shared with fourteen others. Naison Ndlovu, a Bulawayo teacher at Jairos Jiri school for the physically handicapped, spent twenty-one days in a similar situation before he was vetted for Gonakudzingwa. Cases of assault by the police were innumerable. The main reason was not that the police were particularly bloody-minded, but that there were too many detainees to deal with and provide accommodation for during those gruesome November days. It was sickening in these conditions to hear Harold Wilson talk of sending troops if there were a breakdown of law and order.

In theory, all the stringent laws and regulations that apply in states of emergency apply to every citizen of Rhodesia, but in practice they only affect the Africans. Only in rare cases like those of Nicholson and Gallacher (see page 9/18) do they affect whites. The police and the army, like all whites, know that the oppressive laws are designed for the African people. If they were strictly impartial and applied to both sections of the community, they would not be passed in Parliament.

People were too frightened even to go outside their homes. While thousands were in the barbed-wire camps, others stayed in their homes for the rest of the week. The failure of Salisbury to resist U.D.I. weakened the resistance of other towns, and the claim of Z.A.P.U. and Z.A.N.U. leaders outside the country that trained freedom fighters would come only served to destroy the morale of those who were resisting U.D.I. when nothing happened. If the guerrilla fighting of 1967 and 1968 had come at U.D.I. Smith would have been arrested by the white people themselves. Some known white liberals were also exposed to terror. As soon as Smith announced U.D.I. at 1315 hours, young white thugs known as 'Young Rhodesians'[35] attacked whites who were in the company of Africans. Chester Woodall, an economics student from Birmingham at University College, was beaten up when he was seen in the company of African students. Some white liberals had their lives threatened over the telephone. The Palleys slept with their telephone off the hook.

There was a general state of war in the country. When, on 2 February, 1966, Lardner-Burke asked Parliament to extend the state of emergency, on the grounds that 500 Communist-trained 'terrorists' were waiting to enter the country, C. Hlabangana, M.P. for Mpopoma, did not agree. He believed that the emergency was a smokescreen behind which the régime hid ugly things in the country; it was a naked form of intimidation of opposition without which there would be civil war. This was a correct assessment. The state of emergency declared in urban areas of Highfield and Harare was mainly to root out the element that was likely to rally the African people to oppose U.D.I.; officially, it was to get rid of 'the thugs and intimidators' who made life intolerable for 'law-abiding Africans'. Lack of leadership at that crucial time left the Africans in a state of bewilderment.

(v) *Guerrilla Warfare*

Guerrilla warfare started, as has been shown, in the early 1960s with crude methods of protest including petrol bombing of government buildings and the homes of government stooges or other agents.

The decision to fight was made after the ban on the N.D.P. and Z.A.P.U. in 1962, accompanied as it was by violence on the part of the soldiers. Africans then realised that Rhodesia was another Algeria. Freedom could not be won, as in other colonies, by political pressure alone.

The first step towards the implementation of the new policy became apparent in February 1963, when Bobylock Manyonga was tried in Bulawayo for bringing weapons into the country. The plan had been to stock ammunition all over the country in bases. The trials that took place between 1963 and 1965 give the impression that there was no desire to fight before U.D.I. Trained guerrillas returned into the country unarmed, to settle and train the people in the art of warfare in readiness for U.D.I.[36] On 7 February, 1965, twenty-two Z.A.P.U. guerrillas were tried for training between March and October 1964 in Moscow, Nanking and Pynongyang, North Korea, in the use of explosives and arms. Another group of twenty Z.A.P.U. intelligence officers returned in October 1965 from training, also in Russia, China and North Korea. They were arrested and tried in May 1966.[37]

The progressively more sophisticated weapons brought into the country included dynamite, T.N.T., sub-machine-guns, machine-guns, pistols, Russian high explosives and thousands of rounds of ammunition. When fighting broke out with intensity in 1967, the range of weapons was again more sophisticated than what had been discovered and produced in the courts in 1963–5. These included machine-guns, bazookas, T.N.T., booby-traps, radio communications and rockets.

The second stage of the fighting involved sabotage.[38] As with the bringing in of ammunition, evidence of this plan was seen in the trials of people caught before U.D.I.[39] Even at U.D.I. the first reaction was to destroy property and not life. The delay in attacking must have been due to the belief that the British Government was serious in its intention to end the rebellion. After its failure to meet the African people's expectation, Z.A.N.U. guerrillas decided to strike, and on 29 April, 1966, their men confronted the Rhodesian armed forces in a battle at Sinoia. Seven Z.A.N.U. supporters had already been captured at Umtali and Fort Victoria on 13 April, 1966, heavily armed. Fighting was reported at intervals throughout 1966 at Chirundu, Karoi and on the south bank of the Kariba Dam. Z.A.N.U. continued the struggle until about June 1967. Z.A.P.U. forces did not strike until 1967, although a good number of them were in the country earlier.

The first incursions of 1966 made little impression on the settlers, and the Rhodesian forces were able to account for all the guerrillas their intelligence services had reported. The settlers' attitude changed considerably after the announcement by Oliver Tambo, A.N.C. Vice-President, and J. R. Chikerema, Vice-President of Z.A.P.U., of an alliance between the A.N.C. and Z.A.P.U. on 19 August, 1967. This came in the middle of heavy fighting in various parts of the country, at Karoi, Kariba, Sinoia, Lamagundi, Wankie, Dett, Lupane and even Figtree, which is only twenty-three miles from Bulawayo. For the first time casualties among the Rhodesian security forces were admitted, and the presence of South African forces in Rhodesia was made public. Africans had always believed that these forces were aiding their Rhodesian counterparts during states of emergency, and sharing military and intelligence information. In May 1967, T. G. Silundika had already told the U.N. special Committee of Twenty-four that there were 3,000 South African troops in the area where their presence was subsequently admitted. The reason why the South African and Rhodesian régimes revealed their existence must have been the fear that if some died in Rhodesia, as later happened, without the public knowing of their presence, it would have brought embarrassment to the South African Government. The presence of the A.N.C. guerrillas offered an opportunity of divulging their presence in Rhodesia.

The battle in Wankie Game Reserve on 27 August, 1967, was the toughest ever fought by the Rhodesian and South African forces, lasting over six hours. The Rhodesian operations headquarters reported that six of their men had been killed and thirteen wounded. They claimed they had killed twenty-four of the guerrillas and captured an unspecified number. They also acknowledged the guerrillas' bravery and skill. However, they never mentioned the number of wounded guerrillas, and the guerrillas on their side have never reported the number of white troops they captured. The skirmishes went on until October 1968. J. Howman, Minister of External Affairs, said on 26 December, 1968, that a total of 160 guerrillas had been killed between 1966 and 1968 and an unspecified number captured, while twelve Rhodesian troops were killed and nine wounded.[40] The guerrillas have claimed that they killed large numbers of white troops. The facts are difficult to ascertain.

The confrontation with the guerrillas had a great effect on the morale of the white population. There was an unpublicised protest by the army in 1967 after the first report that some of their number had been killed. Representations were made for the laws on the armed forces to be changed to cover the dependents of the soldiers who died in the battle, and better wages were called for. All this came about in 1969 with the passing of a new law designed 'to keep pace with the ever-changing pattern of new conditions'.[41] It intro-

H

duced new disablement benefit and pension regulations, and created a liaison system with the University, schools, colleges, commerce and industry to keep manpower at full capacity when the armed forces were in action. New immigrants are drafted on arrival. The endemic nature of malaria and bilharzia has necessitated the drafting of young doctors to serve in the army medical corps for six months before they start full practice.[42] Boards to deal with drafts and conscientious objectors have been established throughout the country. In 1969, twenty-four whites refused to serve in the army for religious reasons. Some young men are leaving the country due to fear of serving in the Zambezi Valley.

The hot weather in the Zambezi Valley is a great advantage to the guerrillas. In psychological terms, the guerrillas can claim a victory because the Rhodesian security forces are on the defensive. They have to keep guard at all times, yet the guerrillas strike when it suits them to do so. Settlers are worried about guerrilla warfare because it is on the increase, especially when they consider that even a concentration of heavy armament does not scare away the freedom fighters. The attack on Victoria Falls Airport and the death of the South African soldier in the January–February 1970 operations left an impression that the guerrillas are determined to fight on regardless of the strength of troops massed in the 'sensitive' areas. The Report of the Secretary of Defence revealed the attitude of several white people:

> There can be absolutely no room for complacency, and the army must look forward to continuous deployment to meet and defeat the terrorist threat.[43]

When he wrote, the fight had not reached such intensity as it did in 1967, 1968 and 1970. Since U.D.I., 1969 has been the only year without reports of heavy fighting.

There is evidence that Africans are determined to have freedom in the country of their birth, whatever the cost.[44] One waits to see the results of the policy of infiltration which has been substituted for that of confrontation in battle. Many factors place the guerrillas at an advantage: the population explosion, poor economic growth, unemployment, the Smith Government's racialism, and, of course, the climate and poor water and bathing facilities in the Zambezi Valley which have been a great health hazard for young white men.

REFERENCES

1. For detailed reasons why the Africans did not stand for election under the 1961 Constitution, see Harold Wilson, *Labour's Years in Power*, chapter on Rhodesia.

2. Nkomo was banned by the Chief Native Commissioner 'from entering or remaining in any reserve or other tribal area, unless travelling through such reserve or area along a public road'. Another ban was signed by the Minister of Justice, A. R. W. Stumbles, prohibiting Nkomo from attending any public gathering in magisterial districts for three months.

3. See Gordon Walker's reply to the A.P.S., Chapter V.

4. *New York Times*, New York, 15 April, 1962.

5. The Resolution was passed by 73 votes to 1, with 37 abstentions, on 28 June, 1962.

6. A Government white paper listed crimes committed by Z.A.P.U. as 17 criminal offences, 33 petrol-bomb attacks, 14 attacks against Africans, 18 schools and 9 churches burnt down, 24 cases of blocking roads, 11 attacks on policemen and 16 attacks on Europeans.

7. See Nathan M. Shamuyarira's account of his encounter with the police at a road-block near Kutoma Mission in the *Central African Examiner*, October 1962.

8. Nkomo told the special Committee of Twenty-four on 25 March, 1963, that Rhodesia was explosive and potentially another Algeria. He repeated this in a personal interview with U Thant. In Dar-es-Salaam he told a press conference that Z.A.P.U. would make a complete reappraisal of methods and strategy in the national struggle, and intensify and redirect the efforts to achieve its goal through vigorous positive action.

9. Looting and arson followed. Thirty people were arrested. On 2 January, 1964, crowds stoned buses and the homes of 'stooges'. On 28 January, 1964, when Nkomo was sentenced at Umtali, buses and cars and individual whites were stoned. On 29 January, eighty Africans were arrested for violence. A call for a strike failed.

10. Deaths caused by party rivalries: One P.C.C. official was killed on 13 June, 1964; one died of burns on 18 June, 1964; a house set on fire in Highfields; Z.A.N.U. official killed in Highfields; one African died after being shot by the police, 26 June, 1964; one European factory worker killed, 4 July, 1964, near Melsetter; P.C.C. official died of stab wounds, 9 July, 1964; two children burnt in Highfields; one police reservist killed near Salisbury, 17 July, 1964; J. Masola, M.P., died of injuries received in attacks by nationalists. These are the casualties on record resulting from the split. Compare these with the deaths caused by the police and by court hangings for political offenders after 1960.

11. N. Sithole, tried in early 1969 on a charge of plotting the murder of Smith and other ministers, did plead, to the annoyance of many Africans, including his supporters.

12. The U.S. Supreme Court upheld the judgment in the case of *Williams* v. *Mississippi* (1898), saying the provision which required Negroes to show

proof of literacy and understanding of the Constitution was not discriminatory. The courts failed to enforce the 13th, 14th and 15th Amendments
to the Constitution of the U.S.A. because there was no public opinion to
encourage their enforcement. The Civil Rights Act 1875 was in fact frustrated
by courts in 1883; the case of *Plessy* v. *Ferguson* (1896) brought the doctrine
of 'separate but equal' educational facilities, which was reversed by the
Brown v. *Board of Education of Topeka* decision in 1954. See Ebenstein,
Pritchett, Turner and Mann, *American Democracy in World Perspective*, Harper
and Row, New York, 1967, Ch. 9.

13. Frank Clements, *Rhodesia: The Course to Collision*, Pall Mall Press,
London, 1969, p. 218.

14. The *Daily News* supported the Whitehead policy that 'Africans could
best hope for progress under white leadership and guidance.' Clements,
op. cit., p. 208. The newspaper was owned by the consortium of Anglo-
American Corporation of South Africa, Rhodesia Selection Trust, the
British South Africa Company and Imperial Tobacco, but in 1962 it was
bought by Lord Thomson of Fleet.

15. The Editor, Eugene Wason, and all other senior staff were Europeans.
A few Africans occupied junior posts such as representing and distributing
the paper.

16. Clements, op. cit., p. 217.

17. These laws were being passed while the appeal about the right to
detain and restrict people was pending in the Privy Council.

18. Clements, op. cit., p. 218.

19. *Rhodesia Herald*, 16 January, 1964.

20. *Rhodesia Herald*, 8 November, 1963.

21. *Rhodesia Herald*, 20 January, 1964.

22. *Rhodesia Herald*, 30 January, 1964.

23. On 17 February, 1963, a court trial revealed that a truck full of
weapons with instructions in a book entitled *People's Revolution* and *The
People Against Imperialism* had been brought into the country. More cases
of a similar nature occurred later.

24. K. Young, *Rhodesia and Independence*, Heinemann, London, 1967, p.
190.

25. John Day. *International Nationalism*, Routledge and Kegan Paul,
London, 1967, p. 112.

26. The detention of these men was not legal in the first place because the
decision of the High Court on 26 June, 1964, and the Appellate Division
on 12 November, 1964, had declared detention illegal under the Declaration
of Rights.

27. *Keesings Archives*, 1965–6.

28. Smith, who was at the Royal Show at the time the decision was
made, was jubilant. He told a meeting at the show: 'The Court said that
the present Government of Rhodesia was in complete and effective control
and was the *de facto* government. This is very good news for us. It is an
important milestone in our road. It is gratifying to know that we have this
decision from the courts of this country, which are renowned for their
standards and impartiality.'

29. In the 1960s Rhodesia lost 88,210 through emigration, while gaining 82,170 newcomers. Hence only 141,000 out of the present 230,000 whites lived in Rhodesia before 1960.

30. There are no villages or human dwellings within a ten-mile radius of Gonakudzingwa because it is a game reserve. Even before these laws were passed by Smith, laws introduced during the premiership of Sir Edgar Whitehead were used against the leaders in 1963 and 1964, in defiance of the Declaration of Rights.

31. Rhodesia Government Notice 366 of 1965.

32. Rhodesia Government Notice 367 of 1965.

33. Rhodesia Government Notice 582 of 1965.

34. Rhodesia Government Notice 736 of 1965, declared under the Law and Order Maintenance Regulation 1965 to cover the whole country.

35. Bodyguards to prominent Rhodesia Front political leaders at their public meetings. The police largely turn a blind eye to their para-legal activities, which are similar to those of the National Front in Britain.

36. On 18 August, 1964, Oliver Bwanya, P.C.C. Youth Chairman for the Salisbury District, was sentenced to sixteen years for arranging a meeting to train people in the use of grenades.

37. Some of these had secondary education up to 'O' or 'A' level. One of them, John Marsh-Rice, had been a headmaster in the Fort Victoria District since 1959.

38. Lardner-Burke told Parliament on 22 July, 1966, that since 11 November, 1965, there had been eighty acts of sabotage. He added: 'We may see an intensification of the efforts of the enemies.'

39. Six P.C.C. supporters were sentenced in Bulawayo on 10 March, 1965, for attempting to sabotage the Bulawayo–Salisbury railway line.

40. If one puts together all the numbers published in the papers between 1966 and 1970, one gets 1,229 guerrillas killed, 241 captured and no trace of wounded ones. The Rhodesian Forces' losses make a total of nineteen killed, 42 wounded and none captured.

41. Report of the Secretary of Defence, 31 December, 1969.

42. Report of the Secretary of Defence, 31 December, 1970, says 10 per cent of the army was affected by bilharzia.

43. Report of the Secretary of Defence, 31 December, 1966.

44. See 'A Smuggled Account from a Guerrilla Fighter', *Ramparts*, October, 1969.

CHAPTER IX

REINFORCEMENT OF WHITE SUPREMACY BY THE RHODESIA FRONT

(i) *The Rhodesia Front's Political Philosophy*

The basic philosophy of the Rhodesia Front is embedded in the expediency of preventing Africans from taking over power in the country at all costs. While the Afrikaner nationalists adhere to doctrinaire segregation policies, the settlers of British stock in Rhodesia believe in attaining the same ends as the South Africans, but without preaching about it. It is the practice or implementation of the policy that they regard as important, not the ideological approach or a clear commitment to doctrine. The Afrikaner nationalists produced theoreticians of apartheid such as Dr. D. F. Malan, J. G. Strijdom, Dr. W. W. M. Eiselen, Dr. H. F. Verwoerd and M. D. de Wet Nel; but the Rhodesia Front has no intellectual equivalent of these figures. The Universities of Stellenbosch, Pretoria and Potchefstroom have shaped the segregationist doctrine, but the attitude of the University of Rhodesia is, in general, one of intense hostility to the Rhodesia Front. Even a man like P. K. F. van der Byl,[1] a well-educated Afrikaner, does not flavour the Party's political attitude with intellectualism of the Nationalist type.

The Rhodesia Front's policies are most clearly reflected in the laws it has passed since it took power in 1962. These laws have as their primary intention (*a*) to strengthen European domination of the administrative and legislative machinery of government; (*b*) to perpetuate European political power indefinitely; (*c*) to confer economic benefits on whites at the expense of Africans; (*d*) to maintain police control in order to curtail African political resistance to the *status quo*; and (*e*) to reintroduce social segregation between the races in places where they have contact.

Of all the five principles of the Rhodesia Front's policy, that of perpetuating power in 'civilised' hands obsesses them. This is their bulwark against the advance of African nationalism. The development of African political institutions on the continent frightened most settlers in Africa into taking action to resist the passing of power into African hands. Macmillan's 'wind of change' speech in February 1960 and the British Government's announcement that there would be a constitutional conference on Rhodesia frightened them even more. In May 1960 they formed an organisation known as the Southern Rhodesia Association, with a basic philosophy on the lines of the present Rhodesia Front policies. The founders were D. W. Lardner-Burke, M. M. H. Partridge, A. McCarter, John Scott, R. Patterson, B. H. Mussett and George Rudland, all of whom are ministers or M.P.s in the Rhodesia Front régime. Their aims at the time were to persuade the Dominion Party and the U.F.P. to unite on a non-political basis to 'stop power from being handed to uncivilised hands'. They were not anti-Federation, but if Banda seceded, Rhodesia too would have to break away. The Southern Rhodesia Association preferred the Portuguese *assimilado* policy. McCarter, who was in the chair on the day the Association was founded, made an emotional speech which depicted African nationalism as a black monster whose only purpose was to destroy nascent civilisation in Africa. He declared that 'the lights of this huge continent are going out one by one as black nationalism sweeps down from the north destroying everything in its wake.'[2]

When the 1961 constitutional conference was taking place in Salisbury, the Association held a meeting attended by 1,500 people, the largest-ever attendance at a white meeting since the election of June 1958, which had been fought largely around the issue of African advancement. The meeting was full of emotion and hot air, and dominated by fear of an African government; it could have been broken up, and several speakers arrested, under the Law and Order Maintenance Act, if it had been organised by Africans. Even the *Bulawayo Chronicle* remarked that there was little difference between the African meetings and that of the whites. Sir Edgar was accused of 'bending to African nationalists like a broken reed'; he was not master in his own house, and had no backbone. One of the speakers quoted Nkomo's speech which had forecast early African government. The audience yelled back, 'No! No! No!' The S.R.A. was hostile to the very idea of a white prime minister sitting side by side with African leaders to decide the future of the country. This was regarded as an act of appeasement to be avoided at all costs. Branches of the movement were opened in several parts of the country.

Sir Edgar was as determined as they were to retain the government 'in European hands' and had also threatened to secede from the Federation if Nyasaland and Northern Rhodesia attained majority rule. This did not impress them because he was prepared to sit with Nkomo in the constitutional conference. Their chairman claimed that Africans in Bulawayo had approached him in connection with the formation of their own branch of the S.R.A., because they too feared 'to suffer under the majority rule of black demagogues'. The S.R.A. was repeating the tactics of most European political parties, which often make the mendacious claim that their policies are in the interest of Africans. In the end, they never formed an African branch, nor do they now trouble to try to recruit Africans into the Rhodesia Front. Their claim to have 'sympathy' for the Africans was hypocritical in practice. Their eventual merger with the D.P. to form the Rhodesia Front on 2 June, 1961, was prompted by a determination to fight the provision of fifteen seats under the Electoral Districts system, which were likely to introduce African M.P.s for the first time into the legislature. They believed that once Africans were allowed a certain amount of power it would be difficult to stop them from demanding, and obtaining, more.

W. J. Field was the automatic choice for the leadership of the organisation which now called itself the Rhodesia Front (meaning a front line in the battle against African nationalism). Field had been the leader of the right-wing D.P. in the Federal sphere since the mid-1950s. His experience as a farmer and leader was greater than that of other Rhodesia Front members.[3] Field's approach was to attack the fifteen 'B' seats and Sir Edgar's attempt to repeal the laws which discriminated against Africans. He argued that he was not against African advancement, but he did not think it was wise to accelerate it. On discrimination, he said he was prepared to see responsible Africans getting a square deal, but did not believe it was wise to force racial integration. In view of the laws that the Rhodesia Front have enacted since it came to power, it is clear that Field's policy permitted systematic discrimination against Africans. The expressions 'responsible Africans' and 'African advancement' were used to make people abroad, especially in Britain, believe that the Rhodesian settlers do not follow discriminatory policies and practices as in South Africa. This has brought them dividends. Some British politicians, mostly in the Conservative Party, continue, even after the settlers have broken the constitution introduced by Macmillan's Government and declared themselves a republic, to believe that the settlers represent a civilising mission. The true reason for their reluctance to see African advancement is that it would bring their rule, influence and privileges to an end.

No one who had analysed the tactics of the S.R.A. and its successor, the Rhodesia Front, was surprised by its victory in 1962. However, the British Government, Sir Edgar, and other 'liberals' were shocked when the election results of the 14 December turned out in favour of the Rhodesia Front. They had believed that the overwhelming results of the 1961 referendum in favour of the Constitution had indicated that the settlers preferred the U.F.P. policies to those of the Rhodesia Front, contesting the 1961 Constitution. This was a misinterpretation of the behaviour of the settlers in Rhodesia. The 1958 results showed that they were bent on returning to power a right-wing party which could deal ruthlessly with the African nationalists; Sir Edgar was saved then by Africans in the ten constituencies that cut across African residential areas.[4] The U.F.P. failed to appreciate that the result of the referendum was influenced by the belief of the whites that the 1961 Constitution had conferred independence on the country; they feared that if they voted against it, they would give credence to Nkomo's own policy of opposition to it, and that to do so would be tantamount to conceding majority rule. The world-wide opposition to the Constitution which came only a day after it was announced further persuaded the settlers into accepting it. It is a general characteristic of Rhodesian politics that what the Africans like the Europeans oppose, and vice versa.

   The Rhodesia Front's policy of outright resistance to majority rule turned out to be an advantage to them at the 1962 election, which Sir Edgar and other U.F.P. leaders did not foresee. The policies put forward by the Rhodesia Front at their annual congress in September 1962 were so obviously attractive to the settlers that observers could not doubt that they were heading for victory at the coming general election. These policies assured the settlers of the perpetual maintenance of their privileges, which Sir Edgar seemed to be allowing to go by the board. The policies defined all major aspects of interest to the settlers, and they have been doggedly adhered to even under the strain of U.N. economic sanctions. The Rhodesia Front's attitude on the Federation, separate development, land, majority rule, employment, law and order, education and local government – which was going to be put before the electorate – was approved by the congress.

(ii) *Foreign Policy*

The Rhodesia Front believed that the Federation was about to collapse. The British Government's policy was tending towards the end of Federation, so the Rhodesia Front planned that if it eventually did collapse, it would seek sovereign independence for Southern Rhodesia within the Commonwealth under a suitable constitution while striving for harmonious relations with other territories and states for the promotion of trade and mutual security. This policy was formulated in the belief that Britain was going to concede independence freely to the settler minority, undeterred by the racialist overtones of the Front's policy statements.

This belief was rather naïve in view of the bad year Britain had had at the U.N. in 1962 over Rhodesia. Never before had she been subjected to such virulent attack over matters of colonialism. The banning of Z.A.P.U. while the Rhodesia Front congress was actually taking place provoked such vehement protests all over Africa and such strong pressure against Britain's Rhodesian policy in the U.N. that Sir Hugh Foot (now Lord Caradon) felt compelled to resign as the British Government's representative on the Trusteeship Council. African leaders such as J. M. Chinamano, N. M. Shamuyarira, E. Dumbutshena and N. Sithole appeared before the General Assembly to petition against the British Government's policy. The Government of Sir Edgar counteracted the African nationalists by sending a multi-racial group under A. D. Butler, later opposition leader in the Southern Rhodesia Legislative Assembly. This group included three African supporters of the U.F.P. who later became M.P.s.

In the event, the group spoiled its case. The Africans were poorly informed about the spirit of the U.N., and their calibre and intelligence were no match for that of the African nationalists who had appeared earlier. The British Government was upset by the poor performance of the multi-racial group, and decided to ask Sir Edgar himself to join their delegation in October. Its main concern, it appears in retrospect, was to get Sir Edgar to state the policies which are currently embodied in the Five Principles, and so help it regain the support of its allies, the U.S.A., Canada, New Zealand and the Scandinavian countries, which were becoming reluctant to vote with Britain on the Rhodesia issue. Only South Africa and Portugal continued to give Britain unfailing support – unwelcome friends indeed, as Britain had been arguing that the situations in those countries were different from that in Rhodesia. *The Economist* even remarked that 'Britain's policy in Southern Rhodesia has brought it into unhappy near-isolation.' She was still accepted 'by such friendly, if embarrassed, powers as the U.S. and France'.[5] Resort on Britain's part to non-participation in the voting did not prevent her from being charged by the majority of nations with complicity in racialist policies.

From the start, the Rhodesia Front's policies on the independence of Southern Rhodesia were bound to face serious obstacles. U.D.I. came as an inevitable result of failure to appreciate the world's hostility to racialism. Similarly their racial policies were bound to conflict with Pan-Africanist states like Zambia and others north of the Zambezi.

In 1963 and 1964, the African states initiated the expulsion of Rhodesia from the I.L.O., UNESCO, and other international organisations.[6] In Britain, a Labour Government was in power; Kenya and Zambia, the East and Central African states which had suffered under settler politics, now had Pan-Africanist governments; and, most significantly, the O.A.U. had been founded with an anti-colonial attitude. The U.N. adopted a militant attitude towards all forms of colonialism and racialism, and the Rhodesia Front régime was viewed no differently from that of South Africa. Britain could no longer defend it with the same vehemence as she had done for Sir Edgar, who had at least shown willingness to end racialism and had accepted the advice of experienced British ministers. In fact, the Labour Government was prepared, until U.D.I., to co-operate with the U.N. over Rhodesia.

The Rhodesia Front reacted to world pressure with reckless stubbornness, branding every opponent as a 'communist' whose sole desire was to 'eliminate Christianity and civilisation'. Communists were to be found at the Commonwealth Conference, the O.A.U., the U.N. and UNESCO. Parliament debated for hours the presence of 'Communists' (UNESCO professors and lecturers) at the University College in Salisbury.[7]

They were surprised to see that Zambia rejected all overtures of 'co-operation', 'promotion of trade' and 'mutual security'. Instead, she was prepared to co-operate with international organisations and the British Government in promoting the cause of majority rule. Malawi did not give comfort to the Southern African redoubt until after ministers such as K. Chiume, O. Chirwa and H. B. Chipembere had quarrelled with Dr. Banda and left the country. The Rhodesia Front Government felt insecure from the start, and by August 1965 its policy on independence had changed from negotiation to U.D.I. Ian Smith's presidential address to this Party's congress at that time clearly indicates the trend. He told the delegates that an independent Rhodesia would not join the Commonwealth because (a) the Afro-Asian bloc would impose difficulties on the negotiated settlement; (b) Rhodesia could not join an organisation 'which seemed to be embracing Communism[8] and whose member-states were prepared to train saboteurs;' (c) if necessary, Rhodesia was prepared to take things into her own hands and (d) she had far more sympathy and support, and even a guarantee of official recognition, from certain other countries. On the claim by Arthur Bottomley, the British Commonwealth Relations Ministers, made in West Africa in August 1965 that Britain had averted U.D.I., Smith said that he knew that his Government was not ready; and if independence had been declared twelve months before, 'it would have been disastrous.'

Smith was correct on most of his points, but on the matter of recognition he was deceived, because, up to the time of writing this book, six years later, not one country has recognised his régime.

(iii) *Laws embracing Foreign Policy*

As soon as the Rhodesia Front took power, it introduced a series of security laws designed to protect the country from 'external and internal subversion'.[9] The Rhodesia Front had won power on the plank of resisting majority rule, so it was determined to prevent such a state of affairs from being imposed either from within or from without; and the first security laws it manufactured were to prevent external subversion.

In March 1963 it introduced the Preservation of Constitutional Government Act, no. 14 of 1963. Clifford Dupont, then Minister of Law and Order, told Parliament that the legislation was designed to protect the Consitution from being undermined from without. The Act would stop infiltration into the country by subversive elements similar to the Sudeten Germans before the Second World War. He also cited the cases of Algeria and Angola, and claimed that Sithole had made a subversive statement on Radio Cairo and at the Afro-Asian Conference at Moshi, Tanzania. The Act carried a maximum penalty of twenty years, imprisonment for anybody engaged in activities aimed at overthrowing the constitutional government. Dupont said: 'To all intents and purposes this is really treason.'[10] The irony of his speech was that his own government had committed treason by overthrowing a constitutional government by a U.D.I. in November 1965. Clause 2 of the Act makes it an offence for people residing in Rhodesia to overthrow a constitutional government, and not unnaturally, the régime has been careful to avoid trying anyone, even guerrillas, under it. Instead, the Law and Order Maintenance Act has been used to deal with freedom fighters, reinforced by the Foreign Subversive Organisations Act no. 29 of 1963, whereby the Rhodesia Front intended to make other 'friendly states' co-operate in prohibiting the formation of a nationalist government-in-exile in their territories.[11] The Rhodesian Government would reciprocate by doing for other countries what they would do for Rhodesia. The Act was passed only two months after the establishment of the O.A.U., as it was feared that the new organisation would help the African nationalists to form a government in one of the neighbouring states. Dupont must have known that the O.A.U. would not sponsor a government-in-exile in any country that would co-operate with Rhodesia, which in effect could only mean South Africa and Portugal. Pan-

Africanist states would not reciprocate, so the Act was essentially useless. No government-in-exile has been formed, but not because of the Act. The guerrilla movement has not reached an appropriate stage, and hence the atmosphere has never been right.

The Departure from Southern Rhodesia (Control) Act, no. 25 of 1964, was passed to supplement the two Acts of 1963 to control the manner in which citizens of Rhodesia left the country. This was, in fact, designed for Nkomo who had sometimes left and returned to the country in 'mysterious ways' during the time of the Federation. The country's frontiers were too large for the liking of the settler governments. With Federation behind it, the Rhodesian Government was determined to close all the possible areas through which people could leave the country. Another aspect of the policy behind the Act was that it assisted 'the preservation of public security' by making it an offence for anybody to travel outside the country without travel documents. This was the point where it involved Nkomo, because at that time Dupont had decided to withdraw his passport. Yet at the same time he was afraid that Nkomo could still travel without papers. The Act would make such movements impossible.

The guerrilla warfare which involved A.N.C. freedom fighters from 1967 to 1968 led the Rhodesian régime to introduce a law entitled Witnesses Compulsory Attendance Act, no. 13 of 1969. The Act provides for extradition of a person wanted as a witness for the trial of another in a 'friendly country' and compels a Rhodesian citizen to travel to that country and participate as a witness in the trial of the accused. A South African-born person in Rhodesia could easily be sent back to his country under the extradition laws if he were wanted for a crime, but it was not then possible for a Rhodesian-born person to be similarly despatched to another country. The Act makes it possible for a Rhodesian-born person to be sent to South Africa. The background of the law is that the Rhodesian authorities found themselves in an awkward position if a Rhodesian guerrilla were needed as a witness in a case involving A.N.C. guerrillas being tried in South Africa. This law enables the two régimes to exchange witnesses or prisoners without difficulty.

Before U.D.I., Rhodesia was not constitutionally qualified to make laws which involve her relationship with independent states. Up to the end of 1963 the Federation had powers to legislate on foreign affairs, but from 1964 it was the British Government which was supposed to control external affairs. However, the Rhodesia Front government passed three Acts designed to deal with extra-territorial matters. Two of these were enacted even before the Federation was declared defunct; those were illegalities which the settlers were allowed to get away with. The Act passed in 1969 could be regarded as different as the régime pretended to be independent following U.D.I.

After U.D.I., foreign policy activities were confined to the promotion of trade by clandestine means in European countries.[12] With the help of 'Friends of Rhodesia' – pressure groups formed in white countries – and international companies, Rhodesia was able to sell her products below world prices in several European countries and in Japan. The Ministry of Information continued to run an office in McGill Terrace, Washington, D.C. Its pamphlets, which were circulated all over the U.S.A. and Canada with the help of racialist organisations, especially in the Southern United States, carried a message on the back cover stating that registration under the United States' Foreign Agents Registration Act 'does not indicate approval by the United States Government.' This statement sought to absolve the U.S.A. from the opprobrium of recognising or helping an internationally-outlawed régime. Yet it is the U.S.A. which the régime's foreign policy was designed to win as a friend. Soon after U.D.I., Smith offered the U.S. 'Government troops' to fight 'Communists' in Vietnam, to demonstrate that Rhodesia was with the U.S.A. in her fight against 'Communism'. This offer of troops was later used by the pro-Rhodesian lobby, led by Southern senators and congressmen, as well as a former Secretary of State, Dean Acheson, to prove that Rhodesia was an ally of the U.S.A. The offer was repeated several times, in 1966 and 1967. In reality, it was never seriously believed, either in the U.S.A. or in Britain, that Smith meant to do anything more than make propaganda. He needed more troops than he possessed to fight guerrillas in Rhodesia: the presence of South African troops there is a clear indicator of Rhodesia's overwhelming need for troops.

The other proof that Rhodesia was in a desperate hurry to win the sympathy of the U.S.A. was when J. R. Nicholson and Trevor Gallaher were arrested and sentenced for spying on sanctions on behalf of a 'friendly western country'; the country was never officially named during the secret trial in December 1969. It was left to the press to guess that it could only be the U.S.A., because Nicholson was found to have banked £9,000 in New York. When the régime decided to declare the country a republic, despite protests from the U.N. and Britain, it was found imperative to retain some association with twenty western nations that had residual missions in Rhodesia. The U.S.A. was the key nation to win, because if she maintained her mission the rest of the western countries would do the same. The régime immediately released the sanctions spies on 15 January, 1970.[13] Their sentences had in any case been lenient in comparison with those imposed on Africans for political offences. The press again speculated that the régime hoped that the U.S.A. would recognise its republic. Smith told his followers that the release was necessary in the interests of Rhodesia. On the eve of the republic, the U.S.A. and the remaining western powers withdrew their consulates from Rhodesia, and up to the time of writing only South Africa and Portugal continue to give comfort to the régime. The decision of the U.S. Congress in November 1971 to import Rhodesian chrome for military purposes, in defiance of U.N. sanctions, gave Smith unexpected moral support during his crucial negotiations with the British Government.

Rhodesia did not cease to have connections with France, West Germany, Italy and other European countries with the help of Rhodesian businessmen and citizens of European and other countries who stayed on in Rhodesia. Settlers born in Britain, Australia, New Zealand, the Netherlands, Cyprus, Malta and elsewhere returned to their countries of origin and renewed their old passports from those countries which they used for travel in Europe promoting trade and speaking on behalf of the régime to foreign governments. A Dutchman, Nicholas Spoel, earning £12,000 a year, was responsible for selling meat in Switzerland, Germany and other European countries. A Cypriot resident in Rhodesia, known as John Maltas, was responsible for promoting trade in the Mediterranean countries, including France. Thus the régime's foreign policy, although following an unorthodox and surreptitious pattern, enabled it successfully to resist the sanctions war for five years.[14]

The policy of giving moral and material support to the régime's nationalist enemies, enshrined in the Security Council Resolution 253 of May 1968, which has resulted in some western governments and churches giving aid to the guerrillas of Z.A.P.U. and Z.A.N.U., has confused the Rhodesia Front. All along they had made their supporters believe that African opposition to their régime was Communist-inspired. Weapons captured from guerrillas were given wide publicity to prove the complicity of 'Communists'. Lardner-Burke expressed shock at the governments of Canada, Denmark, Holland, Norway, Sweden, Israel and West Germany giving financial assistance to guerrillas. The position of non-state organisations was regarded as understandable, because the Rhodesia Front believe that in western countries these are run by 'Communists'.[15] Lardner-Burke accused these organisations, as did the Rhodesian and South African churches, of encouraging people of all races to engage in 'terror and murder'; he argued that this could not be justified on moral or Christian grounds. Noteworthy is his insincere use of the phrase 'all races': it is the white people he has in mind, who elected and supported the Rhodesia Front government which is the target of the freedom fighters and those who support them.

(iv) *Entrenchment of White Supremacy by Constitutional Manipulation*
The Rhodesia Front was elected to power under the Constitution which Britain had introduced to Southern Rhodesia in 1961. The constitutional conference took place with a view to transferring to the colony the exercise of Britain's residual powers over Rhodesia. After the conference the British Government produced a white paper which implied that all the reserved powers had been removed, and that the Rhodesian Government could amend its own constitution. The reserved powers were exchanged for the Declaration of Rights and the Constitutional Council, which became a watchdog to ensure that the Declaration of Rights should not be transgressed. The referendum on the Constitution was held on 26 July, 1961,when most whites were convinced that Rhodesia had become independent. Sir Edgar even boasted that it was the first time independence had been given to white politicians in Africa since South Africa received it in 1910. This belief, together with the settlers' fears of Nkomo's opposition to the Consitution, led them to vote overwhelmingly 'yes'.

The settlers – rather, the most intelligent among them – were shocked to see the Constitution, in the Order-in-Council of 6 December, 1961, as completely different from what they had been led to believe at the referendum. The most shattering blow was Clause 111 under Chapter IX, which left the power to amend the Constitution with Britain. The clause stated:

> Full power and authority is hereby reserved to Her Majesty by Order-in-Council to amend, add to or revoke the provisions in Sections 1, 2, 5, 6, 29, 32, 42 and 49 and this Section and any Order-in-Council made by virtue of this Section may vary or revoke any previous order so made.

This clause was the key to the whole constitutional struggle between the Rhodesia Front Government and British governments in the negotiations that followed and which culminated in U.D.I. The shock of the settlers was expressed as follows by Dr. Morris Hirsch:

> It was with dismay and deep concern, therefore, that one noted after the Referendum in the Order-in-Council, setting out procedure until the constitution came into full effect, that the Secretary of State was entrusted with specific power to amend the agreed constitution.[16]

These powers were originally embedded in Article 61 of the 1923 Constitution. Lawyers such as A. J. A. Peck were indignant about the British and believed that Britain was dishonest and lacked integrity in cases where black and white conflicted.

Peck's argument was that Britain should have conceded independence to the whites entirely because they were their own kith and kin. He found it inconceivable that Britain would ever contemplate giving power to the Africans at the expense of the whites.

Before analysing the whites' reaction to British 'dishonesty', it is necessary to view some of the safeguards in the Constitution. The right of the British Government to veto discriminatory legislation was substituted for safeguards entrenched in the Constitution. The Rhodesian Parliament had power to alter the Constitution by a two-thirds majority of its total membership. The specially entrenched clauses involved a different procedure. A two-thirds majority of the total membership of Parliament was required as a first stage; the second stage was a referendum of all four principal races (Africans, Coloureds, Asians and Europeans) or alternatively the Queen's assent to the amendment.

The entrenched sections of the Constitution which referred to the Declaration of Rights[17] concerned appeals to the Privy Council, the Constitutional Council, the Judiciary, franchise qualifications, civil service pensions and the boards of trustees of Tribal Trust Lands.

The Consitution did not give any immediate advantages to the Africans, such as were being introduced in other colonies. None the less, it was unpleasant enough for the settlers because of the entrenched clauses. Only Sandys can say whether or not the accusations in the books of Peck and Hirsch are justified. But what is obvious from outside Whitehall is that if the British Government did not keep to the promises made at the conference (namely that Rhodesia would become independent under white rule) it was due to international pressure; opposition from the newly independent countries and at the Commonwealth Conference must have made the British Government think again. Sandys discovered within a few days of the conference that Africans were dead against the new constitutional proposals, and he lost the confidence he had earlier reposed in Sir Edgar due to his failure to attract a large African following in various campaigns. By December 1961 the N.D.P. had successfully demonstrated its rejection of the Constitution. On the other hand, the growing agitation of the Southern Rhodesia Association, which later merged with the Dominion Party to form the Rhodesia Front, must have hammered home the point that Sir Edgar was not going to be Prime Minister after December 1962.

All these factors would account for the inclusion of Article 111 in the Constitution.

The racial pride of Rhodesia Front supporters was deeply wounded at the discovery that the franchise, the Tribal Trust Lands and the Declaration of Rights had been entrenched in the Constitution, because this meant that the country would rapidly drift into the hands of Africans. At the 1962 congress of the Rhodesia Front, resolutions were passed to the effect that the intention of the new Constitution was to bring about premature African dominance, which must be avoided; therefore the Front would seek appropriate amendments to the Constitution. The entrenchment of the key provisions implied the total impossibility of any constitutional changes without resorting to illegality.

There is no doubt that the entrenched clauses were responsible for U.D.I. In no circumstances could the Rhodesia Front hope to achieve their land-segregation policies, known as separate development, nor, especially, could it prevent majority rule within the legal framework of the 1961 Constitution. The laws they have passed since U.D.I. clearly point to their reasons for the declaration. Since U.D.I. the Smith régime has changed the franchise, the laws on land and the Tribal Trust Lands, the Constitutional Council and the Declaration of Rights, and all the safeguards regarded by the Macmillan Government as sacrosanct were systematically emasculated to enable the Rhodesia Front to achieve its racial policies with fewer obstacles.

(v) *Constitutional Development Policies*

Although the Rhodesia Front was irritated by the franchise laws of 1961, it preferred not to make a great issue of them until it attained power. In the policy blueprint published after the party congress of 1962, the desire to amend the franchise was not clearly spelt out, except that there was the implication that an appropriate amendment would be made to the Constitution. Some of the candidates stated during the election of 1962 that the Rhodesia Front would rather operate under the 1961 Constitution; but that was inconsistent with their avowed desire to prevent majority rule, because the 1961 Constitution could have resulted in the achievement of that goal after many years. The period of time involved could have been longer than that envisaged by Sir Edgar and Duncan Sandys.[18] This explains why it was condemned by world opinion even before it was implemented.

Because the qualification for the franchise was so high, the Rhodesia Front were not much concerned about that aspect. Most of the Front's supporters, who are white workers and not only farmers as many people believe, earned such high wages that there was no chance of Africans swamping the voters' roll for a long time. What worried them most was the cross-voting, which had led to their failure to be returned to power in 1958. They knew that the growth of African votes could gradually eliminate them from power.

After the Rhodesia Front had thrown W. J. Field out of the leadership in 1964, it prepared a policy statement to tell its followers the form of the Constitution which would govern Rhodesia after U.D.I. The elemination of cross-voting was at the top of the list of items to be dealt with. Following on from this were: the extension of the 'B' roll franchise to include all African taxpayers; ten more 'A' roll seats and three 'B' roll seats to be filled by four chiefs (one from the existing fifteen seats); a law to restrict the vote to Rhodesian citizens; the removal of the restriction on the number of cabinet ministers; a fade-out clause for the 'B' roll seats; the amendment of the Declaration of Rights to allow preventive detention; and an alteration of the procedure for amending the specially entrenched clauses so that these could be amended simply by a two-thirds or three-quarters majority. The Rhodesia Front decided to make these ideas public in the 1965 General Election after they had failed to negotiate independence or to carry out a U.D.I. in 1964. Smith discussed the policy with A. D. Butler, then Leader of the Opposition on 25 March, 1965.[19]

The policy revealed in the 1965 General Election showed the determination of the Rhodesia Front to implement the racial policies that had led to their victory in 1962. The 1961 Constitution, with its non-racial spirit, had made it impractical to introduce racial laws because of the Declaration of Rights and the surveillance of the Constitutional Council. For example, the policy of Separate Development over land, local government and education could not be translated into legislation. The racial policies were achieved by administrative decrees. But even then the Constitutional Council made several adverse reports on the old racial laws like the Land Apportionment Act, which the Rhodesia Front wanted to retain. At its 1965 congress, the Rhodesia Front had decided to make laws to regulate the use of the Tribal Trust Lands in order that there should be opportunities for white enterprise in them. This was finally achieved by the Tribal Trust Land Corporation Act no. 47 of 1968 and the introduction of legislation to give powers to chiefs to try criminal cases in their courts, a policy eventually formalised in the African Law and Tribal Courts Act no. 24 of 1969.

The Rhodesia Front claimed that the new Act recognised a very long-established institution of African customary law and rules of procedure. The chiefs and headmen should be invested with appropriate legal powers of punishment, and these powers were to be supported by other courts. The real purpose of the Act, however, was to try to win the loyalty of the chiefs by giving them some punitive sanctions over the Africans. This would give them a sense of power, which in reality was ephemeral, and depended on the relationship between the chief and the District Commissioner in the area. If the chief 'misbehaved' – for example, by questioning authority, like Rekayi Tangwena – he would lose his power and find himself tried under stiffer laws in the District Commissioner's court. Government officials are exempt from trial by these chiefs' courts, which leaves them with the freedom to transgress any tribal law as they feel inclined, without fear of sanctions from the chiefs. No reason for this was given by the Minister, but the Constitution puts the police, government messengers and other government employees on the same level as chiefs for the purpose of maintaining order in the country.[20]

Soon after U.D.I., expression was given to the Rhodesia Front policies. The 1965 Constitution, often referred to as the U.D.I. Constitution, significantly altered the spirit of the 1961 Constitution by opening avenues for new legislation which would encompass the Front's policies. Its Sections 78 A and 78 B neutralised the effect of the Declaration of Rights by proclaiming in advance that no Acts could be inconsistent with the Declaration.[21] After 1966, the Rhodesia Front was – and is – able to introduce racial laws in all aspects of life, whether constitutional or social. Passing such laws would previously have required a racial referendum or the consent of the Queen. Having removed these obstacles, the Front found it easy to provide two legal systems, one exclusively for Africans and another for both races. While the whites are not affected by the laws for blacks, Africans are not accorded the same exemption from laws made for whites.

(vi) *The Republican Constitution*

It is curious that, even after amending the 1965 Constitution by passing the Constitution Act no. 1 of 1966, the Constitution Amendment Act no. 49 of 1966, the Constitution Amendment Act no. 58 of 1967, and the Constitution (Amendment) Act no. 43 of 1968, which were detrimental to African political advancement, the régime was still uncertain whether or not it had thwarted majority rule indefinitely. In the second reading of the Bill of the Constitution of Rhodesia Act no. 42 of 1969, Lardner-Burke told Parliament that the 1965 Constitution, like its predecessor, would lead inevitably to African majority rule. It contained no guarantee that Government would be retained in 'resonponsible hands'.[22] (The Anglo-Rhodesian constitutional settlement proposals of November 1971 did not alter the basic tenet of the Rhodesia Front embedded in the Republican Constitution. It simply modified some aspects of it.) The basis of the Rhodesia Front's fear of African rule was revealed in detail in one of their information sheets, which explained the reasons for the new constitution.[23] Lardner-Burke pointed out that the reasons for the republican constitution stemmed from 'the uncertainty, particularly among Europeans, because they have seen, near at hand in other African countries, what has happened to the European standards and civilisation which had been built up in the countries. They have been dismayed and saddened by the reversion to savagery, chaos and violence when European influence has been removed.' With majority rule, the Shona would subjugate the others, and tribal wars would ensue.

When the Rhodesia Front talk of 'European standards and civilisation', they mean white privileges, which in Africa can be found only in Rhodesia and South Africa. The Rhodesia Front supporters depend on the Government for protection from Africans by means of job reservation and artificially inflated salaries which they could not earn anywhere else in the world. Successful whites in the professions and business continue to be happy in the former British colonies of Kenya and Zambia, which had settlers like Rhodesia, and where a large number of whites continue to give invaluable service in the development of the countries. Those with non-professional posts such as prison guards, gang supervisors on roads or irrigation works, etc., drifted into Rhodesia and South Africa when the former colonies became independent. Yet, weakening the Rhodesia Front argument, many whites have gone to Kenya and Zambia since they became independent. In Rhodesia itself between 1950 and 1960 two-thirds of the white population were post-1945 arrivals in the country. In the 1960s, the country lost 88,210 through emigration, while gaining 82,170 newcomers;[24] only 141,790 out of 230,000 whites were in the country in 1960.[25] The average length of residence of immigrant settlers in Rhodesia hardly exceeds thirty years. W. J. Harper, former leader of the D.P. and Smith's rival for leadership between 1965 and 1968, has now left the country for South Africa. Sir Edgar Whitehead, the former Prime Minister, returned to England after staying in the country for thirty-one years. Most of them are in Rhodesia to earn easy money and enjoy high living standards. But they retire to their countries of birth. In England they are often found in the coastal towns or the Isle of Wight; Malta is a favourite haven, and many go to Durban or Cape Town in South Africa. The claim that 'they know no other home' applies to South Africans but not to Rhodesian whites. The Rhodesia Front passed the Citizenship of Rhodesia Act, no. 11 of 1970, to withdraw citizenship from those whites who oppose them. One of these, Guy Clutton-Brock, had his revoked after being in the country for twenty-three years. Only four of the Rhodesia Front cabinet ministers were born in Rhodesia. Lardner-Burke has lived there for forty years, but the rest are post-Second World War immigrants, including Clifford Dupont, their President, who came in 1949.

When Lardner-Burke talks of 'the Europeans' he is talking about immigrants who have spent fewer than ten years in the country. The claim that the Shona will subjugate others is a manoeuvre designed to put a wedge between the two African groups and so cause a feud, which would bring in the Rhodesia Front as a peacemaker. Tribal differences are not a major factor among Rhodesian Africans. Even during the days of internecine rivalry between Z.A.P.U. and Z.A.N.U., clashes were confined to the Salisbury area which is largely Shona, while Bulawayo, with a mixed population of Shona and Ndebele, had less of it. In any case, no African state has ever introduced racial laws since independence to oppress other races or tribes. There have been unfortunate experiences like these of the Congo and Nigeria. But the patently sincere desire of the African leaders of these countries to solve their problems cannot be compared with the negative attitude of the Rhodesia Front, whose policies are meant for one-twentieth of the population.

Another feature of the 1969 Constitution was a racial provision built on the view that the Westminster parliamentary system could not be exported,[26] although it works in Britain because majorities and minorities cannot be identified by race, religion or tribe. Events in Africa show that 'there can be no prospect of a multi-racial state in which differences of race do not play major roles in the political field.' The Rhodesia Front analysis of differences between peoples in other parts of the world is fascinating. They evidently regard as futile attempts by Britain to ignore differences between Hindus and Muslims in India, Turks and Greeks in Cyprus, Ibos and Hausas, etc. Lardner-Burke told Parliament in September 1969 that the régime's policy is based on the philosophy that ensures that European society and African society do not encroach on, or conflict with, each other. This justifies the provision in the 1969 Constitution for Parliament to be composed on a racial and tribal basis – for example in order to make each of the three tribes – namely Shona, Ndebele and whites – feel secure, seats were to be allocated according to the size of the income-tax contribution of the tribe. The allocation stood in this order in the House of Parliament:[27]

THE SENATE

A 23-member chamber consisting of:

(a) ten whites elected by an electoral college of whites;
(b) ten African chiefs elected by the Council of Chiefs;
(c) three persons of any race appointed by the Head of State (i.e. by the chief of the white tribe).

THE HOUSE OF ASSEMBLY

A 66-member chamber consisting of:

(a) fifty whites elected by the European electorate;
(b) eight Africans elected by registered African voters;
(c) eight Africans elected by four tribal electoral colleges.

The franchise was intended to eliminate the influence of the cross-voting, which had worried the Rhodesia Front since 1962; this was one of the first changes the Rhodesia Front introduced after U.D.I., early in 1966. The main reason is that a cross-vote makes it necessary for the Rhodesia Front to be accountable for their policies to the Africans, a concept of democracy that goes counter to its philosophy of white supremacy. To grovel to Africans for votes is something beneath its dignity. It prefers an old system which dominated Rhodesian politics before the 1950s, when the rulers pretended that Africans did not exist.[28] In the republican election of 1970, no Rhodesia Front candidates ever bothered to explain their policies to Africans. When African students heckled Smith near the University, he sang an Afrikaner song which implied that Africans were baboons and that they should join their fellow-beasts on the mountain.[29]

The Franchise under the 1971 settlement proposals stuck to racial divisions. Taking the place of the 'A' Roll, introduced in the 1961 Constitution, is a European Roll requiring an income of £900 p.a. or property valued at £1,800 – or an income of £600 p.a. or property valued at £1,200 and four years' secondary education. On the African Roll, income must be £300 p.a. or property valued at £600; or income of £200 or property valued at £400 and two years' secondary education. Africans increase their seats by two when their voters equal 6 per cent of the total of white voters (see Appendix C).

It is often claimed that Africans contribute little to the revenue of the state, to justify bad service rendered to the African community. However the African contribution could equal that of the whites. White families with five children who earn the average income pay only £1.35 per month, an insignificant figure compared to western countries. In all, 68 per cent of white Rhodesian bread-winners earn between £1,750 and £2,500. In Britain, only 5 per cent, and those mainly in the professionals, are in the same income bracket – in Rhodesia the professions earn even higher salaries.

Direct taxation in 1969 produced a total of £76.5m. of which income tax, derived from both Europeans and Africans, accounted for £12m. The fact that African workers, who are by far the largest contributors numerically to the labour force, earn very little from the companies distorts the income tax figure. If the Africans were paid by the companies at the rate that is morally their due, they would be paying more income tax than the whites. Settlers often say that African education and social and health services are paid for with their money. But they ignore other indirect sources of revenue which cannot be quantified on a racial basis, such as customs and excise duties, sales tax, vehicle taxes, investment revenue, post and telecommunications, pension contributions and court fees, schools, hospitals and other services. These sources accounted, in 1969, for £123·5m. out of a total revenue of £191·6m.

The Minister of Finance, J. J. Wrathall, was asked in Parliament by N. Gandanzara, M.P. for Manica, to state the amount contributed in taxation by Africans from sales tax, income tax, licence fees, hospital fees, and grain, cattle and other levies.[30] Wrathall replied that it was impossible to analyse taxation on racial lines[31] – a reply which highlights the double-thinking of the settlers when they try to justify their perpetual clinging to power.

(vii) *Land Policies and Laws*

The entrenched clauses of the 1961 Constitution created obstacles for the Rhodesia Front when they came to implement their land policy. At their congress in September 1962, the Front had pledged itself to retain the racial division of land as in the Land Apportionment Act 1930. Its statement pointed out that 'as the people of Southern Rhodesia differ in many respects, the pattern and principles of racial differentiation in the ownership, use, and tenure of land established in the Land Apportionment Act must be maintained.' This would be done both in urban residential and rural areas. Land should be preserved for specific races, though some zoned industrial and commercial land – and, in special circumstances, some residential land – could be used by persons of any race.

Since U.D.I., laws have been passed to give legal expression to this policy, and these have affected African land ownership and resident status in the towns and cities. The land policy was enshrined in the Land Tenure Act 1969, which collects together, with various modifications, the segregatory laws such as the Land Apportionment Act, the Tribal Trust Land Act, the African Land Husbandry Act, and the 1965 Constitution's version of the Tribal Trust Land Act.

ELECTORAL MAP OF RHODESIA

I. White constituencies (50). There were 82,852 voters at the election of 10 April, 1970.

II. Urban African constituencies (8) and **tribal electoral colleges** (8). (The names of the urban constituencies are in capital letters.) There were *circa* 8,000 voters at the election of 10 April, 1970. Electoral colleges are formed by chiefs, headmen and members of tribal councils. Elections are held under the supervision of the six Provincial Commissioners.

239

During the debate on the Land Tenure Act, Lardner-Burke told Parliament that the existing laws gave rise to 'a sense of injustice and insecurity among a large number of [European] people'. According to the 1961 Constitution (which the Rhodesian Government tore up in 1965), Tribal Trust Land was entrenched and reserved for Africans, yet European land did not have the same security. He declared: 'What is unjust is that no corresponding protection is afforded the European against the reduction of the acreage of his land.'

The purpose of the Act was to classify land into European areas, African areas and National areas (e.g. parks, game reserves, archaeological sites, etc.); to establish a board of trustees for European and for African areas and to prescribe its functions; to provide for the transfer of land from one area to another, and to regulate the ownership, leasing and occupation of land. Section 5 of the Act allocated the land proportionately to the two main races.

DISTRIBUTION OF LAND 1969

	acres	%
African land	44·94m.	47
European land	44·95m.	47
National land	6·00m.	6

The Rhodesia Front believe that they have been very fair to Africans in giving them nearly the same amount of land as Europeans – the area of African land has risen from 29m. acres in 1930 to 44·94m. in 1969. At the same time, they believe that they have relieved Europeans of a sense of insecurity. The white fear of rapid growth of the African population has been removed because they can no longer lose their land to Africans. The protection of both races has been entrenched in the 1969 Constitution. To give less than a quarter of a million people as much land as the 5¼m. majority, who are the true owners of the country, can never be called fair. More preposterous is the fact that there are about 918,000 Africans living in the 44·95m. acres of white land. These Africans are officially regarded as non-existent because they are in the areas developed by European enterprise. This, of course, is not a sound economic argument. Development was achieved by the use of the invaluable African labour force. Of the three factors of production – land, capital and labour – the Africans provided the two major ones, land and labour. Capital can be employed without bringing its owner on to the spot and indeed the greater portion of the land which the Rhodesia Front calls European is owned by people who do not even live in the country.[33] What is more, out of the total of 96,519,500 acres comprising the whole country, 6·6m. acres have been allocated as national land – game reserves (Wankie, Matopo and Gonakudzingwa), national monuments and municipal parks. These are in effect facilities for Europeans and tourists, and forests for industry, afforestation and conservation purposes. Municipal laws have been amended to make it difficult for Africans to use parks in towns: in the town of Fort Victoria, notices were put up in the parks banning all Africans with the sole exception of girls in charge of white babies. Of the unreserved land, 5·3m. acres were reallocated as European land. A total of 630,000 acres of Tribal Trust Land has been given over to parks and wild life, while African purchase land was reduced by 865,000 acres by re-assigning land along the shore of Lake Kariba. It was divided in this way:

302,000 acres to National area
148,000 acres to European area
415,000 acres to Tribal Trust Land.

These changes have left 19,755 African families exposed to possible removal from these areas.

The Land Tenure Act was drawn up with the same attitude of mind as led to the introduction of the Group Areas Act in South Africa.[34] The Minister of Lands, P. van Heerden, an Afrikaner himself, claimed in Parliament that the Act would avoid friction and discord between the communities, especially in residential areas. Section 24 (4) of the Act admits the possibility of segregation between the Shona and Ndebele.[35] The assumption is that there is a cultural difference between the two groups of peoples. This same argument was used in South Africa to justify the creation of bantustans for the Zulus, Xhosas, Sothos and Tswanas.

As already mentioned, the Act provides for a board of trustees in both African and Europeans areas. The chairman, the Chief Justice of Rhodesia, presides at both meetings. The members are appointed by the President for their 'suitability', a word of which the meaning differs according to the race referred to. In a European, it means knowledge and ability to carry out functions prescribed by the Act. In the case of an African it means someone acceptable to the régime on account of his docile attitude. The boards often meet jointly, and in that juxta-position it means that African interests are represented by two out of six people.

Section II makes it impossible for an African to buy or lease European land, yet Section 34 authorises the Minister to permit a European to occupy African land on lease. According to Section 42, the Government can acquire African land for mineral development,

defence, communications and other public purposes after consultation with the board of trustees. The acquisition is accomplished
without compensating the Africans. In reality the Africans do not
own land apart from the 6,852 who own it in the Purchase Areas.
The Land Tenure Act does not provide for Africans owning Tribal
Trust land. It is now easier to expel Africans from communally
held land under the Act than it was before.

The régime has been actually embarrassed by the case of Chief
Rekayi Tangwena, who is being charged under the Law and Order
Maintenance Act for subversive statements made in a conversation
in October 1970 with a university lecturer, Dr. A. McAdam, who
spoke to him in connection with his refusal to leave the area where
he lived because it had been defined as European land. Tangwena
had claimed that the people recognised by Smith are not chiefs and
that he could have earned £60 a month if he had accepted recognition by Smith and then obeyed the order to leave the area where his
ancestors had lived. Tangwena lives in an area in which his people,
the Manyika, have lived for several centuries; indeed they have
traded with the Portuguese since the sixteenth century in the very
area where they are today. Tangwena's portion of Manyikaland had
become a European farm, and he and his people were asked to
leave. Tangwena refused and encouraged his people to do the
same. He argued: 'A chief has to be a chief with the support of his
people, and a man is not a chief unless he listens to his people.'
This attitude he maintained even in court.

(viii) *Tilcor*

The Tribal Trust Land Development Corporation Act no. 47 of
1968 – established the Corporation of that name, otherwise known
as Tilcor. This body purports to have as its object the development
of the Tribal Trust Lands for the benefit of the inhabitants. 'Tilcor's'
purpose is to plan, promote, establish and run industrial, agricultural,
forestry and commercial undertakings, including banking. This is
achieved by companies and subsidiaries formed for the specific
purpose of developing the tribal areas.

The directors of 'Tilcor' must be appointed or dismissed by the
Minister of Internal Affairs. The scale of development is given as
six pence per acre per year by the Government as aid. The development is not restricted to government enterprise; large private
companies are also allowed to operate. The Associated Chambers of
Commerce of Rhodesia sponsored a research foundation, headed
by J. D. Cameron, to examine the possibility of investing in the
Tribal Trust Lands.[36] The Act has in practice opened African areas,
previously protected, to ownership by white entrepreneurs. Since

it is difficult for Africans, through lack of capital, to form the companies to exploit the areas, private companies run by whites will eventually benefit at the expense of the Africans.

The current chairman of 'Tilcor', W. A. Bailey, is a theoretician on African cultures similar to South Africans of the school of Dr. W. W. M. Eiselen and M. D. de Wet Nel. Bailey still adheres to the old theories regarding African migrant labour and the culture of 'bright lights': namely that African movement from the rural areas is caused by the desire to be near the cinemas, entertainments, sports amenities, etc., found in the cities, which do not exist in the rural areas. In Rhodesia, Bailey believes that the movement can be arrested (a) by the introduction of ingress or egress control to keep Africans in the Tribal Trust Lands; (b) by developing the Tribal Trust Lands and making available there the amenities found in the cities; (c) by providing vast housing projects in cities; and (d) by repatriating non-productive people from cities to the Tribal Trust Lands. In this policy Bailey has the support of the Director of African Administration in Salisbury, R. C. Briggs.[37]

The African M.P.s argue that the scheme is extremely unpopular with Africans because of its apartheid overtones; no African company has ever emerged since the scheme started. L. J. Mahlangu, M.P. for Mpopoma told Parliament in August 1971 how strong were Africans suspicions over the scheme. He was supported by Lewis Ndlovu, who questioned the wisdom of employing young Europeans as managers in these schemes, when these often left after only six months. Chiefs and others can continue to promise the people that the Government will provide work, schools, hospitals, etc., in particular areas. But the development has the overriding purpose of keeping Africans from taking an interest in national politics and looking for salvation to the freedom movements.

(ix) *African Urban Life under the Rhodesia Front Regime*

Like all the other major facets of the Rhodesia Front's policy, that concerning local government was formulated in September 1962. The Front passed a Resolution at that time that 'legislation will be introduced to enable local governments to pass by-laws recognising separate facilities and amenities for the various communities.' Like other aspects of the Rhodesia Front policy, this could not be translated into legislation without contravening the 1961 constitutional safeguards against racialism. So before U.D.I., the Front passed the amendment to the Local Government Areas (General) Regulations 1964, varying the regulations dealing with African lodgers and imposing a charge of fifteen shillings per year for their registration. From time to time the Minister introduced stricter administrative decrees but could not introduce racial legislation because of the Constitution. These decrees included the prohibition of African domestic workers from living with their children in the European suburbs; the workers were removed to African areas without further accommodation being provided. Hence thousands of people arrived in already over-crowded townships. An African school started by some well-intended Europeans to provide schooling for the children of domestic workers in a Salisbury domestic suburb was closed down under the Land Apportionment Act early in 1966. No school was made available as a replacement. As the nearest school was nearly ten miles away in the African township, the children were left without schooling.

The African (Urban Areas) Accommodation and Registration Act, introduced in 1946 and amended several times, was again amended in 1966 'to strengthen powers of control and to permit increased service and supplementary charges, and a policy of strict enforcement of the Act was adopted'.[38] In 1968, by ministerial decree, it was imposed on all willing and unwilling Europeans and on town management boards.

In 1966–7 a group of Salisbury whites, led by a M.P. of Greek origin, Dennis Divaris, agitated for the introduction of a Bill that would protect prices of European property because of encroachment by non-whites into the European suburbs. The protest was aimed against Asians, who are recognised as Europeans in the Constitution. Africans can never hope to move into the suburbs – partly because of their pegged incomes, which make it impossible for them to buy expensive houses, and also because the Land Apportionment Act – and now the Land Tenure Act – would not allow it. A pressure group led by Divaris forced the régime to introduce a Property Owners (Residential Protection) Bill, which at the time of writing, hangs fire in Parliament until the 1971 settlement proposals have been accepted.

The Municipal Amendment Act of 1967 was the first Act which overtly introduced segregation according to the 1962 Resolution quoted above. Using this legislation, municipalities could provide regulations or by-laws providing for racially separate amenities. Segregation could be reintroduced in parks, places of recreation, sports and athletic grounds, public lavatories and swimming baths. Before the passing of this Bill, the Minister of Education, A. P. Smith, had banned racially mixed sports, after personally explaining before a meeting of European headmasters why he did not recommend sporting activities between black and white schools. The major reason was that there would be difficulties in allowing black pupils to use white school toilet facilities. If children of both races used the same toilet facilities, he argued, race relations would be jeopardised.

(x) *Segregation in other Spheres*

Over employment and salaries, and in education and social life, segregation has been reinforced with ruthless vigour. The Rhodesia Front is a group of men dedicated to maintaining 'the Rhodesian way of life', which means upholding discriminatory practices which were threatened by the liberalism of Garfield Todd and Sir Edgar Whitehead. Although these two tried to fight discrimination, their impact, especially that of Sir Edgar, was only beginning to be felt when they were thrown out of power. Sir Edgar's legislation was half-heartedly introduced because his ministers were not liberals; he was also afraid of the electorate, which continued to be impressed by South African methods of suppressing African nationalism. It cost the Rhodesia Front little effort to introduce measures involving segregation in place of the few desegregation measures achieved in the years before they took power. The Rhodesia Railways had opened both first- and second-class travel and its railway restaurants to people of all races, and African apprentices could be taken into railway workshops as fireman and ticket-inspector trainees. The Rhodesia Front quietly abolished these 'freedoms' by ministerial designation.[39] In July 1971 the African teachers who were earning the same salaries as whites, based entirely on qualifications, were shocked to find that the Rhodesia Front régime had introduced racial scales. European teachers were now earning more than Africans.

	Old scales for all races £	New scales African £	European[40] £
Men: 3-year-trained			
non-graduates	1,030–2,304	1,134–2,418	1,500–2,850
graduates	1,332–2,304	1,398–2,418	1,770–3,330
Women: 3-year-trained			
non-graduates	840–	882–	978–
graduates	1,008–2,304	1,058–2,418	1,230–3,024

Africans were naturally upset by this discrimination, and made strong protests against it, but the reaction of the régime was one of calculated, almost sadistic indifference. The reason is that although there are over 20,000 African teachers, nearly all of whom are potential voters, the régime is not concerned because it knows that it gets its power from Europeans. More importantly, the more it is subjected to attacks by Africans, the more firmly its white support is consolidated. Africans are thus being deliberately provoked for the sake of the white vote.

The most effective techniques for implementing segregation are psychological. If people's failures, weaknesses and shortcomings are referred to often enough, they seem to have become facts. Such techniques were used by Josef Goebbels to vilify his enemies, the Jews and the Communists, and they are used by the Rhodesia Front. History is distorted to make Africans feel that they have no past achievements to look back upon with pride. The archaeologists Peter Garlake and Roger Summers were forced to resign from their posts as museum curators because they published writings stating that Africans had built the Zimbabwe complex. Attempts are being made to sustain the earlier view that it was built by a mysterious people, as yet unidentified. The history of the country is distorted to convey an impression that both Africans and Europeans are settlers: it is said that the Shona came first, followed by the Ndebele, and then by the white settlers. If all the people inhabiting Rhodesia are settlers, then there is nobody with a greater right to be there than anybody else. The Shona were in fact already in what is today Rhodesia, and trading with Asia and the Arab world, by A.D. 922.

The laws that have been enacted by the Rhodesia Front since U.D.I. have reversed the trend of African advancement and brought it nearer to the situation that prevailed before the 1950s. It will take many years, with all the good will in the world, to improve the situation to the level of the African countries north of the Zambezi.

REFERENCES

1. Van der Byl's father has been a United Party M.P. in South Africa for many years.

2. Mlambo, *Rhodesia: The British Dilemma*, 1971, p. 5.

3. Field's team in the new organisation included Lardner-Burke, C. R. Pockett, L. B. Fereday and C. A. Bott. Ian Smith had resigned from the U.F.P. and tried unsuccessfully to form his own organisation. He then decided to join the Rhodesia Front. Smith had the longest parliamentary experience of all.

4. The results in the first vote were: D.P. 18,142; U.F.P. 16,840; U.R.P. 4,663. There were 2,000 Africans on the voters' roll, and 1,224 cast their second vote for the U.F.P., giving Sir Edgar an additional vote which ended in victory for his U.F.P. with 17 seats, while the D.P. had 13 seats, and the U.R.P. none.

5. 'Two's No Company', *The Economist*, 13 October, 1962.

6. Report of the Secretary for External Affairs, 1964.

7. Commonly referred to as 'the Kremlin on the Hill'.

8. Rhodesia Front settlers have no understanding of Marxist ideology. They only seem to be aware that it has caused revolutions in other parts of the world and that the western powers are its opponents.

9. Like the word 'Communism', 'subversion' is used to mean any form of African opposition. The Secretary of Law and Order, A. M. Bruce-Brand, traced 'subversion' to 1957, when the A.N.C. was re-formed (see his Report of 1967). Dupont traced 'subversion' to 1936 when the Sedition Act was passed by Huggins to suppress the Watch Tower movement (Jehovah's Witnesses).

10. *Southern Rhodesia Parliamentary Debates*, Vol. 52, Col. 1245, 12 March, 1963.

11. Ibid., Vol. 53, Col. 627, 26 July, 1963.

12. See below, Chapter XI, pp. 271 ff.

13. The spies were charged and tried under the Official Secrets (Southern Rhodesia) Act 1914, carrying a maximum sentence of five years and alternatively under two sections of Emergency Powers (Counter-Espionage) Regulations passed in August 1969.

14. Articles on the breaking of sanctions were published in the *Sunday Times*, London, 28 August, 1967, and 3 September, 1967, in *The Observer*, London, on 17 March, 1968, and in the *Sunday Telegraph*, London, 1 February, 1970.

15. Lardner-Burke named the following private organisations in Parliament on 10 June, as responsible for encouraging 'terrorism' against his régime: the Defence and Aid Fund (U.K.); the Movement for Colonial Freedom (U.K.); the Anti-Apartheid Movement (U.K.); Oxfam (U.K.); the Afro-American Institution (U.S.A.); the Black Power Movement (U.S.A.); the World University Service (based in Switzerland); the Friedrich-Ebert Foundation (West Germany); the Social Democratic Party of Sweden; the Lutheran World Federation (based in Switzerland); Lund University (Sweden); the World Council of Churches (based in Switzerland); and the Joseph Rowntree Trust (U.K.).

16. M. I. Hirsch, *Focus on Southern Rhodesia*, Bulawayo, Stuart Manning, 1964, p. 33.

17. The Declaration of Rights is regarded by the Rhodesia Front as unnecessary because it interferes with parliamentary sovereignty and it repeats features of common law – e.g. the right to personal freedom and to meet and speak freely. The régime decided that Parliament would be the custodian of the Declaration of Rights, and the legal committee of the Senate would take the power of the Constitutional Council.

18. Sir Edgar told the U.N. General Assembly on 30 October, 1962, that majority rule could come in twelve to fifteen years. In Rhodesia he claimed that the Constitution would last three hundred years. The British mission in New York told the U.N. in June 1964 that if Africans had registered, there would have been 100,000 of them eligible to vote.

19. The chairman of the Rhodesia Front, N. A. F. Williams, issued a statement on 27 April, 1965, reiterating the policy on constitutional matters.

The policy followed the lines of the current Rhodesia Front legislation.

20. The African Law and Tribal Courts Act no. 24 of 1969 was made of bits and pieces after the repeal of (a) African Law and Courts Act, Chapter 104; (b) Amendment of Sections 10 and 29 of the Magistrates' Court Act; (c) Amendment of Section 9 and substitution of a new section for Section 14 of the African Affairs Act.

The Rhodesia Front claimed that it was emphasising the difference between African and European law. The courts would deal with African law in matters such as seduction or adultery, the custody or guardianship of children, African wills, rights to commercial lands, and marriages. In cases where white as well as black persons are involved, the chiefs are not supposed to try.

21. Sections 67 and 67 of the 1961 Constitution outlawed discrimination on grounds of race, tribe, colour or creed.

22. *Rhodesia Parliament Debates*, Vol. 75, Col. 1044.

23. *Rhodesia Case*, Government Printer, Salisbury, February 1970.

24. In a period of ten years the emigration almost equalled immigration. The latest recruits are peasants from Spain, Italy, Greece, Cyprus and Turkey. L. J. Mahlangu, M.P. for Mpopoma, attacked the régime's policy of decrying the African birth-rate while importing into the country 'useless innocent souls who cannot even speak two sentences of English'. *Rhodesia Herald*, 1 July, 1971.

25. *Economic Survey of Rhodesia*, Government Printer, Salisbury, April 1970, p. 23.

26. *Rhodesia Parliamemtary Debates*, Vol. 75, Col. 537, 2 September, 1969.

27. This remains unchanged in the 1971 Anglo-Rhodesian settlement proposals.

28. Philip Mason, *The Birth of a Dilemma*, Oxford University Press, London, 1956, p. 280.

29. The song starts: '*Bobbejaan, klim die berg*' ('Baboon, climb the mountain). See *The Times*, London, 10 April, 1970.

30. In 1963, 69 per cent of Post Office savings deposits were owned by Africans.

31. *Rhodesia Herald*, Salisbury, 5 August, 1971.

32. There are only 6,000 white farmers who own most of the land.

33. Only 3–5 per cent of the European-owned land is under cultivation. Prominent members of the Anglo-Rhodesian Society such as Sir Archibald James, who lives in Essex, have farms in Rhodesia.

34. B. Bunting, *The Rise of the South Africa Reich*, Penguin, 1964, p. 145.

35. See articles by Claire Palley in *Race*, Vol. XII, July 1970. No. 1, and Vol. XII, October 1970, No. 2.

36. Section 105 of the 1969 Constitution allows other races to invest in the Tribal Trust Land.

37. *Rhodesia Herald*, 6 August, 1971.

38. C. Palley in *Race*, October, 1970, p. 143.

39. Rhodesia Parliament Debates, Vol. 74, Col. 96, 27 June, 1969.

40. *Times Educational Supplement*, 16 July, 1971.

CHAPTER X

RHODESIA: BRITAIN'S DILEMMA

(i) *The Labour Party's Record*

Africans believed that in the Labour Party they had an ally against British imperialism. Their policies appeared to be designed to raise up the exploited within Britain itself, and to fight the exploitation of non-white peoples in Asia and Africa. It was the Labour Party under Ramsay MacDonald that released Mahatma Gandhi from what Winston Churchill described as his 'commodious internment' and in the 1930s prepared India for self-government. It was Attlee's Labour Government which pressed forward the post-war decolonisation in Asia and even succeeded in retaining the Asian states within the Commonwealth, an example which was later followed in Africa during the period of Conservative government in the 1950s.

It was Arthur Creech Jones, Colonial Secretary in Clement Attlee's Government, who laid the foundation for decolonisation in Africa. In the 1950s, socialists such as Fenner Brockway, Barbara Castle, Denis Healey, George Thomson and Judith Hart were leaders in promoting the anti-colonial cause. The Fabian Society, the Movement for Colonial Freedom, the Anti-Apartheid Movement and Amnesty, all of which were managed by socialists, were known for their anti-imperialism, anti-racialism and indeed for their humanitarian attitude to all peoples. This was consistent with the Labour Movement's traditional opposition to the exploitation of human beings by international capitalism, which advocated the colonisation of Africa and other parts of the world. Racialism in Africa today is its by-product.

In their struggle for independence, African leaders pinned their hopes for freedom on the leading socialists. Some Labour leaders even boasted of the prestige which they had gained as a result of their fight against colonialism in Africa. Denis Healey wrote in *Africa Report*, after the British General Election of 1959 in which the Labour Party was unsuccessful, and expressed the general dismay which the African leaders felt as a result of his party's defeat. He wrote:

In all the African territories where Europeans had settled in large numbers on the land, the British Government [Conservative] tended to take the side of the whites against the black. Although the official policy was racial partnership, the Tories seemed content that the settlers should decide the pace and direction of the political evolution. Labour defeat sent a wave of despair over Africa.[1]

This accurately described what Africans *later* felt about the policy followed by the British Government in which Healey himself was a leading minister. The African leaders came to realise that Britain was not to be trusted where black and white are in conflict, even when the blacks are morally or legally on the right side.

In the debate on Rhodesia at the U.N. in June 1962, Henry Ford of Liberia castigated William H. Barton of Canada for defending the British decolonisation policy. Ford questioned the intentions of those who sought to persuade the world to support Britain in her decolonisation without making it clear that Britain had been successful only in West Africa. While in West Africa, where there were few white settlers, Britain allowed a large measure of freedom, in East and Central Africa 'African exploitation and discrimination were the rule'. This analysis of British policy was shared by the Ethiopian delegate, who said it was unfair to compare Britain's policy in Central Africa with that she had pursued in 'West Africa, on which she wants to be judged'.

The Labour Party's approach on Rhodesia up to the time it assumed power in 1964 appeared to be more respectable than that of the other parties; this had been the case ever since the struggle for responsible government in the early 1920s.[2] The efforts of John Stonehouse saved the Rhodesian Africans from a complete handover to the settlers in 1961. Until John Stonehouse was manhandled by the police in the Federation in 1959, the British Government had been evasive over its responsibility for the trusteeship of Africans enshrined in the 1923 Constitution. Stonehouse was soon joined by the Leader of the Opposition, Hugh Gaitskell, and other Labour leaders. The Labour Party contributed in 1961 to the Conservative Government's decision to hold a constitutional conference, and later to its refusal to concede independence to the minority régime at the break-up of the Federation by pressing the then Commonwealth Secretary, Duncan Sandys, and Sir Alec Douglas-Home, when he was Prime Minister in 1963–4, to take a tough line with Smith after he replaced W. J. Field.

But, going even further than forcing a tough approach over the settlers, the Labour Party under Harold Wilson succeeded in making the Government change from a state of vacillation to a definite policy on Rhodesia; the absence of a clear British policy in 1962 and 1963 had brought immense frustration to the African people. All the colonies, except Rhodesia, had had clear indications by that time regarding their future independence. The leaders of Z.A.P.U., who had been banned by Sir Edgar Whitehead in 1962, appeared to be at a loss as to their next step. With the encouragement of their friends in the Anglo-Rhodesian Society, led by Lord Salisbury, the settlers were determined to put back the clock in regard to African advancement. The impasse of that time was summarised by *The Economist*, which warned that this entire part of Africa 'is a dangerous political minefield . . . an explosion could go off in any part of it at almost any time. Such an explosion would not time itself to the convenience of the British Government. The world in the shape of the U.N. does consistently carp at British policy in Southern Africa. Again, in the Rhodesias, African nationalists are, at the moment, in a mood to see every British action as a Machiavellian design to retain white influence in southern Africa.'[3]

While the Africans were in a state of confusion and frustration over British policy in Rhodesia, Harold Wilson was elected Leader of the Opposition early in 1963 following the death of Hugh Gaitskell. His first notable speech on Rhodesia has been quoted in several books that have reviewed British policy on Rhodesia; curiously, he ignored it in his own book.[4] Maybe he was afraid of tarnishing the clear record he wanted to display in the book. Wilson harried R. A. Butler, then Minister responsible for Central Africa, over the Rhodesia issue. On 11 April, 1963, he cross-examined Butler over the problem, wanting the British Government to state categorically that independence would only be conceded to Rhodesia under universal adult suffrage. 'Will he [Butler] give the House a clear assurance that there will be no question of granting independence to Southern Rhodesia until the country has a constitution which enables the mass of people to govern themselves? Is he aware there should be no question of granting independence under a constitution where 250,000 have the right to rule three million people?'[5] In the same month Wilson told Joshua Nkomo that a Labour Government would change the 1961 Constitution and provide independence under universal adult suffrage. While Wilson was putting pressure on Butler, independence for Southern Rhodesia under the 1961 Constitution was being demanded by Field and C. W. Dupont, backed by Sir Roy Welensky, who had become bitter over the Conservative Government's decision to dissolve the Federation.

Wilson's task of pressing the British Government to give independence to Rhodesia under majority rule was made easier when the leadership of the British Government had been taken over by

Sir Alec Douglas-Home in 1963. During a debate on the Speech from the Throne in November 1963, Wilson exerted pressure until the Prime Minister announced in the House on 12 November that the Government had accepted the principle of self-determination without qualification, with majority rule and protection for the minority, and that this policy would be applied to Southern Rhodesia. The whites in Salisbury, led by Charles Olley, were outraged by Wilson's pressure on Sir Alec, and responded by sending Wilson letters of protest. Africans, on the other hand, were deeply impressed by the definition of a policy which for the first time acknowledged the Africans' birthright to shape their own destiny – the principle about which successive British Governments had been so evasive. African students at the University College in Salisbury sent congratulatory telegrams and letters to Wilson, to which he replied assuring them of his unfailing support. A similar assurance was given in writing in a letter to Dr. E. Mutasa, a member of the Committee Against European Independence in Salisbury. Wilson wrote on 2 October, 1964: 'The Labour Party is totally opposed to granting independence to Southern Rhodesia so long as the Government of the country remains under the control of a white minority.'[6]

The political affinity that had existed between the African independence movements was greatly enhanced by all these speeches by Wilson. African leaders pinned their hopes for a solution of the Southern African problem even more fervently on the Labour Party. On the eve of the British General Election in October 1964, the African rank and file hoped for a Labour victory.[7]

As soon as it was in power, the Labour Party demonstrated its determination to cleanse Britain's name, besmirched by her Southern African policy. Lord Caradon was appointed as the Government's representative at the U.N., with ministerial rank; as Sir Hugh Foot he had resigned from the British mission at the U.N. in 1962 over British policy on Rhodesia (see p. 224). He was acceptable to African leaders as a man of good will with an understanding of African problems. The Labour Government co-operated with the U.N. and implemented the spirit of the Security Council Resolution of 7 August, 1963, on the South African arms embargo, an issue on which the Conservatives had abstained from voting. On Rhodesia Britain appeared between October 1964 and November 1965 to be co-operating with the U.N. and to appreciate African feelings. In October 1964, Wilson issued a strong warning to Smith over U.D.I. after he had sacked General John Anderson as commander-in-chief of the Rhodesian armed forces, on account of his opposition to U.D.I.

Before reviewing the Labour Government's mismanagement of the Rhodesian problem, it is necessary to examine the reasons for African optimism. Some observers of British policy believe that in essence British foreign policy is not partisan. The difference in style of the two Parties is in the way money is spent to achieve policy goals. If these involve too much expense, Labour would rather withdraw from a commitment, whereas the Conservatives would hold on at all costs. This, rather than human considerations, prompted the decolonisation of Asia. In Africa, the Labour Governments do not have a clean record.[8] It was Attlee's Government which banned Sir Seretse Khama from going back to his country in 1948 because he had married a white woman. From 1946 it supported Smuts' policy over South-west Africa, and it ignored India's protests over racialism in South Africa during the early days of the Declaration of Human Rights. In the early days of African nationalism, it put Nkrumah in prison.

Its record in Rhodesia is even grimmer. As Colonial Secretary under Ramsay MacDonald, the eminent socialist and reformer Sydney Webb (Lord Passfield) laid the foundations of the present racialism in Rhodesia by providing the country with the infamous Land Apportionment Act of 1930, although as a young civil servant in the Colonial Office in 1890 he had protested to his seniors at their permitting Rhodes to acquire land in Mashonaland without the consent of King Lobengula. In 1930 he saw fit to legalise the title to the same land that he knew to have been illegally appropriated many years earlier. He allowed the Moffat Government to pass an act giving the white people compulsory education while the Africans were relegated to the poorly financed area of missionary education. The Civil Service Act was passed in 1930 with a clause that clearly excluded the Africans, and the Labour Government allowed it to remain on the statute book until it was repealed in 1960 at the instigation of the Conservative Government. When Labour took power in 1929, the notorious Native Affairs Act 1928 was not yet a year old. Since the Party had attacked it from the opposition benches, the A.P.S. hoped that it would repeal the Act under the powers conferred on the Secretary of State by Article 61 of the Southern Rhodesian Letters Patent of 1922, to repeal within twelve months laws that discriminated against Africans. Although the Labour Government took office within this period, it rejected the A.P.S.' pressure to repeal the Act. In 1946 Attlee's Government allowed Rhodesia to pass the Native Urban (Registration) Act with a pass system which harassed the Africans, and the Native Land Husbandry Act 1951, which provided for forced labour. Harold Wilson's Government of 1964-70 finally destroyed the illusion that an affinity existed between African socialism and its European counterpart. While it had always appeared that the two movements believed in the vote as a right, the Labour Government's policy on Rhodesia soon revealed how easily the British Party could borrow the language of capitalism. While in Rhodesia in October 1965, Wilson spoke the language that Disraeli and (the earlier) Lord Salisbury had used in the nineteenth century; he called the vote a privilege to be achieved by 'hard work', and claimed that progress to majority rule would not be measured by calendar time or the clock but by achievement. Wilson forgot that majority rule comes from universal adult suffrage, which is achieved not by hard work but by birth. He added that he had been out of political power for thirteen years, and urged the African leaders to follow his example and work within the framework of the 1961 Constitution instead of waiting for Britain to solve the problem by means of military power. To compare his position in opposition to that of the African leaders who were in prison, and to expect the latter to achieve their birthright by merit, was blindness. If he had spent the thirteen years in jail he would have been a different man, and would have understood that only the vote could end the oppression of the masses, as had been the case in his own country. His assertion from the Opposition benches that over Rhodesia Britain should not vote with' the discredited imperialist powers' was quickly forgotten.

The Africans who had hoped for the support of the Labour Government out of the Southern African impasse failed to appreciate the background of the Labour Party. Despite its Southern African lobby, and the pamphlet *Labour and Southern Africa*, many of its members are lukewarm on colonial matters. They are, of course, aware that the problem is caused by British investment and trade interests in Southern Africa. As President of the Anti-Apartheid Movement, Mrs. Barbara Castle told the U.N. Special Committee on Apartheid in April 1964 that 'British businessmen who invest in South Africa are providing the economic sinews of apartheid'; yet, as a minister in the Labour Government, she was pushed by these same people to pursue a discreditable policy on Southern Rhodesia. When members of the London Stock Exchange toasted the republic of Clifford Dupont on 3 April, 1970, Mrs. Castle satisfied herself by denouncing their action as 'treachery', but no government action was contemplated against such defiance designed to give comfort to rebellious settlers. The lobby that propagates the belief that investment in Southern Africa is indispensable for the British economy and brings wealth to the country has done its work supremely well.

Another aspect of the British Labour Party that the disappointed

Africans had failed to take into account was the fact that the Party is like a federation of various ideologies. The radical element, which forms the anti-racial and anti-colonial pressure groups lobbied by African nationalists, is only one wing among several. It is well represented by the authors of the Transport House pamphlet *International Briefing*, which suggested a British policy for Southern Africa. The group, which includes some ministers in the 1964–70 Governments, succeeded in 1970 in getting the Labour Party National Executive to accept the principle of providing financial aid to the liberation movements of Southern Africa, a move which provoked many protests among the white settlers there. J. H. Howman, a minister in the Smith régime, condemned the financial aid as an affront to 'civilised government'.[9] This decision gave the liberation movements the impression that the entire Labour movement in Britain was behind them, so that when the next Labour Government comes to power, there will be an expectation that the National Executive's policy will be carried out at ministerial level; but when the example of Wilson's policies on Rhodesia is repeated, the Africans will be disappointed again. They ought to realise, however, that the Labour Party, like the other parties, represents the British people, whose own interests take precedence over those of people outside their country. Rhodesia has affected the British people only in so far as their 'kith and kin' live there; to the vast majority of them, of whatever political persuasion, the interests of the settlers are paramount. The pressure from the U.N., the Commonwealth and the O.A.U., or from Africans inside the country had a moral dimension only, and few political decisions are made for moral reasons. Economic and political reasons are paramount, and in the Rhodesian case these favoured the settler's cause. At U.D.I. on 11 November, 1965, the Labour Government had a majority of a single seat in Parliament. A by-election was taking place in the constituency of Erith, and two Labour M.P.s, Reginald Paget and Desmond Donnelly, were not completely responsive to the Party whip. It was impossible politically for Wilson, with all the good will in the world, to make dramatic decisions such as sending troops to Rhodesia without risking his Government's downfall.

The Conservatives, under their new leader Edward Heath, condemned U.D.I., but erroneously believed that if Wilson had stayed a little longer in Salisbury it could have been avoided. The Conservatives chose deliberately to be vague in order to gain a political advantage at the expense of Wilson's miscalculations in dealing with U.D.I. They accepted a sanctions policy, but on condition that it was not 'punitive', and they pressed that force should not be used thus reflecting the prevalent British mood over

Rhodesia, which in turn was dictated by the racial nature of the problem. British public opinion could not help but support the settlers despite their being on the wrong side in law – something which, according to Tory tradition, should have been deplored. Any measure involving compulsion would have been resented, and in any case only the few Labour radicals, of which Wilson was not one, could contemplate the proposition that Africans in Rhodesia were ready to rule themselves in 1965. The use of force might have resulted in majority rule. Heath intended to exploit this political atmosphere and lead Wilson on to take steps that would result in the downfall of his Government and a subsequent general election, from which he himself would emerge as Prime Minister. Wilson, therefore, had to rule out the use of force in any circumstances. He has recorded that 'It is true, of course, that had we decided to intervene by force of arms, he [Heath] would have led a united party, and almost certainly won majority support in the country. But this was never on.'[10]

The second consideration which militated against decisive action by the Labour Government over Rhodesia at U.D.I. was the economic situation. One of the issues that had led to the victory of Labour in October 1964 was the Party's economic policy. Wilson appeared better equipped to cure the chronic imbalance of payments than his opponent Sir Alec Douglas-Home. The country had an overseas trading deficit of £800m. Any dramatic action on Rhodesia which involved further strains on the economy could not be contemplated.[11]

Although the second factor contributed to British vacillation, it had not the overriding strength of the political or racial considerations. (One factor which never seriously affected the Government's reckonings was morality.) Economic problems could have been circumvented by organising a Commonwealth or U.N. force. But even this could never have been contemplated because public opinion would have been horrified by the very thought of setting the world against people of British stock in Rhodesia. The possible inclusion of black forces would make the participation of Commonwealth countries unacceptable, and troops from the Soviet bloc would have terrified British business interests with investments in Southern Africa. Only fear of Russian or Chinese intervention and the break-up of the Commonwealth was responsible for the token sanctions introduced in November 1965. Wilson comments that the speed and direction of policy on U.D.I. was part of 'a battle for the soul of Africa'.

Racial considerations destroyed the political will to solve the problem, and the lack of political will was clearly demonstrated in the way sanctions were applied. Following the demand of the

Conservative Opposition that they should not be 'punitive', it was predictable that the effect of those that Wilson piloted through the Security Council would be minimal.

Sanctions were imposed in the hope that a large enough body of white people would rally behind a liberal or moderate leader, who would be acceptable to the Rhodesian Europeans and to the British Government, though not necessarily to the Africans. Of course, the two words 'moderate' and 'liberal' apply to European politics. Africans would never accept them, being too reminiscent of Sir Edgar Whitehead's days. Africans have nothing but terror to remind them of Sir Edgar's 'moderate' or 'liberal' leadership. The moderates are also disliked by Africans because they view the vote as a privilege according to the Rhodes formula 'equal rights for all civilised men'. The Africans consider the vote as a birthright, to which the concept of 'civilisation', whether real or mythical, is immaterial. So the British policy of seeking moderate white leadership is no more than an expression of paternalism; it has no bearing on current Pan-Africanist ideas, because Africans will never put up with it.

With the idea of creating white liberalism among the settlers, Wilson fought an economic sanctions war in three stages: 'voluntary' in November 1965, 'mandatory' in December 1966, and 'comprehensive mandatory' in May 1968.[12] The way the sanctions were applied made Africans doubt from the start the sincerity of the Labour Government's determination to end the rebellion. The implementation of the first Resolution, which called upon states 'to refrain from any action which would assist and encourage the illegal régime and, in particular, to desist from providing it with arms, equipment and military material, and to do their utmost in order to break all economic relations with Rhodesia, including an embargo on oil and petroleum products' could never have been seriously intended. The Resolution assumed the compliance of all the nations of the world which traded with Rhodesia. It also assumed that all international monopolistic companies would refrain from trading with Rhodesia when they were told to do so. But this was soon proved false as they not only persisted, but devised clandestine methods of trading under cover, especially after more effective resolutions were passed in 1966 and 1968. Continental European companies were never influenced by a political will to see majority rule, so none of these 'international spivs' (the phrase was used by George Thomas, then Minister of State for Commonwealth Relations) were ashamed of conducting underground trade with Rhodesia. Demands by Africans for the imposition of stringent sanctions were deftly waved aside while sterile measures were rushed through the Security Council.

Lack of political will was further demonstrated by the fact that even the stronger resolutions, S/232 of 16 December, 1966, and S/253 of 29 May, 1968, only followed events; the initiative came not from London but from Salisbury. The resolutions were guided through the Security Council, respectively, after Smith had rejected the *Tiger* settlement[13] and after he had illegally hanged African freedom fighters.[14] Even then it took all the pressure from both the Commonwealth and the U.N. for the Labour leaders to agree to move further measures against their kith and kin. The bitterness with which the debate on Resolution S/232 was conducted showed the mood of Africa in December 1966. Britain could only plead for time. She insisted that more time was necessary for sanctions to work. This remained her stand even when it was obvious that sanctions did not work.

Some of the critics of the Labour Government under Wilson argue that the Rhodesian issue was handled by the Labour Government in an amateurish way. They argue that the Conservatives would have achieved what Labour wanted to achieve with less strain on the relationship between the settlers and themselves. Tories, however, would have ignored the Africans; this, after all, is what even Wilson did, although this did not enable him to succeed in convincing the settlers that he had come round to the Tory policy of regarding a vote as a privilege.

The threat to British investments in South Africa due to the proximity of a crisis-torn Rhodesia must account for the advice given to Wilson against 'thoughtless action' aimed at appeasing African nationalists. This suspicion seems reinforced by Wilson's repeated blunders: revealing in advance that he would not use force against the Rhodesians in the event of U.D.I., telling the Lagos Conference of his 'expert advice' that sanctions would bite in 'weeks rather than months' and, most significantly, admitting publicly that he was afraid of a confrontation with South Africa. The removal of civil servants on the Rhodesia desk at the Foreign and Commonwealth office is curious. All those who had been involved with Rhodesia at U.D.I., except for a very small number, were transferred to other posts: Sir Maurice James to India, Sir Duncan Watson to Malta, J. B. Johnson to Nigeria, Oliver Wright to Denmark, and K. J. Neale and Mrs. Chitty to the U.N. in New York.[15] Also, the fact that Wilson clashed with the Labour Party Organisation over Rhodesia explains that factors not purely ideological were at stake.[16]

The first test of Labour administrative skill was over Harry Reedman's appointment by Ian Smith in 1965 to serve as his envoy in Portugal. Both Rhodesia and Portugal knew that as Rhodesia was not independent she could not have a representative who was outside the control of the British Embassy. Smith sent Reedman to Portugal, first to prepare for U.D.I. and secondly to test the reaction of the British Government. All Wilson did was to protest to the Portuguese Government about accepting Reedman as a Rhodesian envoy with independent diplomatic status. He took no action. This ought to have been a time to act decisively to stop Portugal from upsetting British policy. The British public would not have been averse to strong action against Portugal, who would not have risked her good relations with Britain for the sake of an Ian Smith's U.D.I. adventure. The Labour Government's inaction only encouraged Smith to pursue his plans towards U.D.I.

Wilson also allowed Smith and three of his cabinet ministers to return to Rhodesia after the two abortive meetings at 10 Downing Street on 7 and 8 October, 1965, when they had behaved with obvious contempt for British authority and had demonstrated that they were hell-bent on illegal action. That was the time for a strong warning. He could have told them that Britain would either use force against an illegal action, or would not defend them in the U.N. or the Commonwealth if they decided to rebel. Instead of strong action, Wilson decided to explain away some of the reports appearing in the press to try and convince the potential rebels that his Government was not at fault in the breakdown of talks.

His worse failure was in revealing that the only weapon that he would use against U.D.I. was a trade embargo. Wilson calculated that if the trade embargo hit tobacco farmers, miners and industrialists, they would organise a counter-rebellion, overthrow the Smith régime and rally behind the 'moderate' influence of the Governor and 'liberal' leaders who would sue for peace with the British Government. He was depending on the Governor, Sir Humphrey Gibbs. But Sir Humphrey was as much afraid of majority rule as any other white person in the country, and his attitude towards progress in that direction was obstructive rather than helpful. Wilson had the mining and tobacco industries in mind, as he believed that they especially would collapse in the face of a boycott, as Britain was the chief customer for those commodities. If the commodities were boycotted, the standard of living of the European community would receive a hard blow that might make them give up the idea of supporting Smith. This policy ignored the realities of the Rhodesian economy. While Rhodesia like most developing economies, depended on exports, more of Rhodesia's white population were employed in the nascent manufacturing industry which depended on internal markets than in the export-oriented sectors of the economy.[17]

In 1964, Rhodesian exports totalled £137·9m. while imports were

£109·6m. Britain imported £30·5m. of goods, while she exported £33·4m. Suppose Britain had managed an effective boycott, which she did not, Rhodesian exports could have been reduced by only £30·5m., a substantial but not crucial reduction.[18]

Another false belief was that Smith's support depended on the farmers – although he is strongly backed by them as well as by white workers. Of the 4,300 (1970) farmers, fewer than 3,000 are tobacco growers.[19] The rest are maize and cotton farmers and ranchers. These commodities are mainly for domestic use and would never be touched by sanctions. Since sanctions were founded on ignorance of the economic dynamics of Rhodesia, they were bound to fail.

The Labour Government's failure to recognise that once South Africa and Portugal refused to co-operate, sanctions would not work, led other people to believe that sanctions were a diversionary measure intended to silence African opposition. The Africans' suspicion of the Labour Government's intentions in Southern Africa was enhanced by their refusal to extend sanctions to Portugal and South Africa. The Rhodesian whites were aware that without South Africa's support their U.D.I. would not last a day. They were fortunate because, like themselves, South Africa distrusted Labour intentions. After all, while still in opposition, Wilson had expressed resentment at the Conservative Government's policy of complicity in racialism. He himself was a member of the Anti-Apartheid movement and had addressed meetings attacking racialism in South Africa. Even though they did not support U.D.I. when it was only contemplated, the South Africans were impelled, once it was a fact, to foil any stratagem such as economic sanctions intended to coerce governments to change their policies.

South Africa's refusal to implement the sanctions put Wilson's Government on the defensive, as if it were anxious to protect South African behaviour against world attack at the U.N. After B. J. Schoeman, Minister of Transport, had let it be known that South Africa would not only boycott sanctions but would take steps that would cripple Britain if sanctions were extended to her,[20] Wilson recoiled into utter submission. But the Labour leaders were not prepared to suffer the humiliation alone; they made other nations share it by resisting Afro-Asian pressure to impose sanctions on South Africa and Portugal for violating the British-sponsored U.N. sanctions.[21]

Articles, in the *Financial Times* of 22 November, 1966, and by Professor Alan Day in *The Observer* of 11 December, 1966, made it clear that South Africa's threat was an empty one because she depended more on Britain than Britain did on her. A study published in 1971 by Robert Molteno has demonstrated that Britain need have no fear in a confrontation between herself and South Africa because the latter is bound to suffer much more than Britain. After all, South Africa accounts for 9 per cent of Britain's trade with South Africa, whereas South Africa itself depends more on Britain than on any other country.[22]

However, having established this moral ascendancy over Britain, South Africa intervened on behalf of the whites in Rhodesia. Dr. Carel de Wet, then South African Ambassador in London, lobbied Mrs. Eirene White, then Minister for State for Foreign Affairs in the British Government, on 8 December, 1966, and Wilson on 13 December, on behalf of the independence demands of the white Rhodesians. On 11 December, 1966, Schoeman urged Wilson to give in to Smith's demands because the white man in Rhodesia was determined to 'fight to the death' to remain in power. If Wilson gave in he would avoid another Congo.

In 1967, following battles between the guerrillas and Rhodesian troops in the Wankie area, South Africa simply sent her own troops into Rhodesia, although in terms of international law Rhodesia remained British territory.[23] Even after this violation, B. J. Schoeman demanded that the Labour Government should confirm or deny an allegation (obviously false) made in the Rhodesian Parliament by a white M.P., J. A. Newington, that the British Government supported South African guerrillas. The following day, 6 September, 1967, the Commonwealth Office denied the allegation as 'completely untrue' and added that the British Government's opposition to all acts of terrorism had been repeatedly made clear. What was surprising to observers was that the British Government, which was on the right side in law, was placed on the defensive by South Africa, which was on the wrong side. South Africa then refused to withdraw her troops in Rhodesia following a diplomatic note sent to Pretoria from London in August 1967. Wilson sent a note also to Dr. Kaunda telling him not to support 'terrorists'. It was believed by the British Government that this attitude of apparent lack of partiality for Africans would induce the 'White South' to co-operate.

The worst case of maladministration was the failure by the British Government to make its blockade of Beira effective; i.e. it confined its attention to oil imports. If not only Beira but Lourenço Marques, an equally significant port of entry, had been blockaded militarily, Smith would have been brought to his knees 'in weeks rather than months' for the lack of vital oil. The supply that came to Rhodesia by road via Beit Bridge could not have kept the country going for the years up to the time of writing. Oil continued to enter the country via Lourenço Marques. This route as well as the Beira–

Umtali route, had always been used for oil before U.D.I., and this must have been known. Fear of South Africa made the British Government turn a blind eye to that route, resulting in the failure of their intentions – if in fact those intentions were genuine in the first place.

If the Labour Government had meant to end U.D.I. as quickly as it claimed, the Rhodesian civil servants could have been ordered to act decisively on the matter. All Wilson needed to do was to supply the Governor with the necessary funds for the salaries of all civil servants while instructing the forces to arrest the rebel ministers. If Wilson had not confused the civil servants by telling them to continue in their jobs while refraining from supporting the régime Smith might have collapsed. Up to the middle of February 1966, the settlers were not certain if force would always be ruled out. The effect of paying the civil servants via the Governor could have divided them between the diehard racialists and those who were, at that time, concerned with the illegality of what was going on, and their own future if Smith was finally subdued. The settlers who were in doubt were able to relax once more when Sir Duncan Watson and Oliver Wright visited Salisbury in March and April 1966 and conferred with Smith. It then became clear that Wilson was not treating the rebels as criminals; rather, the British Government was recognising their power and tenacity. The loyalists who had defied the régime felt let down and forlorn.

The argument that for 'historical and geographical' reasons it was impossible to conduct a military operation against Rhodesia, which is often repeated in Wilson's book, is untenable. His claim implies that Rhodesia is strategically the strongest country in the world. Does Wilson want the non-white world to believe that British armed strength, backed by its NATO allies, could not have succeeded in tackling Smith's forces, which depend on the volunteer army? Or are we to believe that Britain's refusal to allow U.N. forces to operate in Rhodesia was made in the belief that they would not have been defeated by the Rhodesian forces? Wilson sent British troops to Botswana to guard the B.B.C. radio sub-station there. Yet those very troops witnessed goods being carried by train to and from Rhodesia via Botswana. No attempt was made to intercept or discourage this illegal traffic.

It was due to a kind of paternalism that Wilson rejected Zambia's offer to allow her territory to be used for military operations against Smith. The Labour Government can only have concluded that Zambian leaders were not mature enough to realise that it was not in their national interest to use their country as a base against Smith. The Zambians knew that they would have suffered, but they also knew that that particular form of suffering would have come to an end; instead they live perpetually under the threat of attack from the 'White South'. A majority government in Rhodesia, even if its existence is brought about through terrible sufferings, is safer for Zambia than continuous racial tension across its frontiers. It was the paternalistic attitude implied in this decision which prompted Simon Kapwepwe to accuse Wilson of racialism in September 1966. Most Africans appreciate that the Labour ministers are not racialists, as are some of the Tory leaders, but it is evident that some of their policies on Southern Africa have been shaped by the activity of racialist pressure groups. If Wilson had admitted that he was a prisoner of these pressures, few could have accused him of racialism.

(ii) *The Conservative Party's Record*

Unlike the record of the British Labour Party, which consented to oppressive legislation being introduced in Rhodesia against Africans, that of the Conservatives was almost without blemish except for the Juvenile Employment Act 1926 and the 1961 Constitution. The 1889 Charter was undoubtedly based on a forgery, the Rudd Concession. The British Government in London knew this, but allowed Rhodes to occupy Mashonaland. It is inconceivable in retrospect that the part of Africa known today as Rhodesia could alone have escaped the attentions of the European imperialism of the time. The 1889 Charter, therefore, was a child of expediency, born out of contemporary imperialism. In Britain, most champions of imperialism were and still are in the Conservative Party. Colonialism was as fashionable at the end of the nineteenth century as it seems anachronistic today. Attempts by the African leaders of the time to resist in the uprising of 1896–7 resulted in a savage and ruthless suppression by British troops. World opinion approved of the reprisals meted out to the Africans who attempted to restore their own autonomy, believing civilisation in Africa to be at stake.[24]

The Tory-sponsored Constitution of 1898 showed realism in that its features continue to be used up to the present. Despite strong resistance from Rhodes, Joseph Chamberlain was able to build protective measures into the Constitution, which can be regarded as forward-looking for the time. Although Sir Richard Martin,[25] appointed to protect Africans on the spot on behalf of the British Government, failed to carry out his duties, this could not be blamed on the Conservative Government.

In 1926 Stanley Baldwin allowed the Rhodesian Government to pass the notorious Juvenile Employment Act despite the evidence brought forward in Parliament by Col. Josiah Wedgwood, which showed that the settlers were employing children in the open mines and farms.

Apart from these comparatively minor errors, the record of the Conservative Party on Rhodesia before the advent of African nationalism is more creditable than that of the Labour Party. The 1923 Constitution, like that of South Africa in 1910, was introduced by the Liberal Party. The fact that the Conservatives have not (up till the time of writing) sold out to the settlers in Rhodesia does not mean that their Rhodesian policies have been especially humanitarian. They have not happened to be in power at the time when there was a major decision to be made on Rhodesia. History shows that all the ruling parties in Britain followed similar policies on colonial matters before the end of the Second World War. The prevalent attitude to Africans as children, unable to stand on their own, was reflected in the Covenant of the League of Nations.[26] To anyone who is not British, it would appear as if the tendency of British political parties in power was to implement the policies of the opposition. Labour started the Central African Federation and the Tory Government completed it. A Tory Government first enunciated the Five Principles and a Labour Government embraced them in the *Tiger* and *Fearless* settlements.

While the racial attitudes of the other parties in Britain have changed considerably since the Second World War, that of the Conservatives has not. They are still in conflict with the Africans and basically in alliance with the settlers; there are, of course, many leading Tories who have moved a long way from the traditional Conservative attitude towards non-white people, an attitude that is generally paternalistic, still adhering to old beliefs about the white man's burden in Africa and his civilising mission. Among the Tory traditionalist M.P.s, in the Rhodesia case, are Sir Derek Walker-Smith, Patrick Wall, Evelyn King, John Biggs-Davison, Ronald Bell, Enoch Powell, Robin Turton, George Pole, Elspeth Rhys-Williams and Harold Soref.[27] These and several other Tories support the whites in Rhodesia, not on the merits of their case or on moral grounds, but entirely because of the traditional belief that black and white have not evolved in the process of 'civilisation' to a similar extent. This belief has resulted in an ambiguous use of terms such as 'civilisation' and 'race'. Sometimes these two are used interchangeably.[28] On 17 June, 1969, Lord Salisbury told the House of Lords that majority rule was not a moral principle because it was not covered by any of the Ten Commandments. It is rather 'a stage in the evolution of a nation from a primitive to a civilised society, and one which the great majority of the black Rhodesians have not yet reached.' Lord Salisbury, and others who view Africans as still in a primitive stage of evolution, seem unable to say when the Africans as a whole in Rhodesia would be likely to have reached its civilised stage; but they do believe that if an African is educated, his stage of civilisation is equal to that of the whites – without defining the standard of education which an African must attain to be called 'educated'. In the same debate, Lord Salisbury prescribed a solution to the problem of Rhodesia. He asked whether it might not be proposed that 'we and the Rhodesians should declare it our joint aim to make African education a central theme of our policy'.[29] The concept that an educated black man is equal to a white person, whether the latter is educated or not, originates from Cecil Rhodes' formula of 'equal rights for all civilised men', a dictum which has dominated Rhodesian politics since the introduction of the franchise in 1898. Horowitz writes that Disraeli's saying that the suffrage is not a right but a privilege 'reflected the Conservative tradition of the nineteenth century, a tradition that did not entirely disappear even when suffrage in Britain had become universal. This intellectual heritage, like many other traditional Conservative attitudes which could no longer be applied to British life, was still thought to be applicable to the colonial Empire.'

That the Conservatives still subscribe to these paternalistic ideas leads black people to believe that the party as a whole is racialist. This African belief is reinforced by, for example, a statement of Lord Hailsham that a degree of discrimination is 'not intolerable'. Other Conservatives talk of the discriminatory policy of multi-racialism as preferable to apartheid. The Heath doctrine of denouncing apartheid while supplying weapons that can be used by South Africa to enforce it opens Conservatives to attack from the non-white world and white states such as Canada and those in Scandinavia and Eastern Europe.

Guy Clutton-Brock, who lived for half his working life as a social welfare worker in the East End of London and the other half in Rhodesia, believes that the paternalism of the Conservatives is not entirely racial, but their attitude to people who are less well endowed economically is paternalistic regardless of race. References to Africans as 'lazy', 'ignorant', 'dirty', 'unreliable', and the claim that they 'steal', 'lie' and so on, which he had heard from whites in Rhodesia for twenty-three years, he had also heard used of inhabitants of the East End of London before he left for Rhodesia. The irony of this relationship is that some of the settlers were themselves East Enders and other underprivileged members of British society, who had emigrated to escape exploitation by British capitalists, only to become aligned with them when they were themselves in Rhodesia or South Africa.

The settlers in Rhodesia reacted with open jubilation at the victory of the Conservative Party in the British General Election on 18 June, 1970. Ian Smith told the press the next day that he wished the British people good luck; they had made 'the right decision' in electing a Tory government. W. J. Harper, one of Smith's former ministers, expressed the hope that his one-time master would co-operate with the Tory Government in reaching a solution of the Rhodesian impasse.

During his republican elections in March 1970, Smith told *Die Welt* of Hamburg that if the Tories won the election in Britain he would negotiate independence with them; after their victory he told the *Sunday Express* of Johannesburg in October 1970 that he was prepared to negotiate with Britain 'in the best interests of Rhodesia'. But he insisted that Britain would have to climb down further than Rhodesia for negotiations to start. However, Smith welcomed the speech Heath made in Parliament on 27 October, 1970, which appeared more watered down than the utterances of Labour ministers. The change of position by the Conservative ministers was also appreciated by Radio South Africa which stated (not quite truthfully) that 'the settlement is in the interests of the Africans more than the whites', and urged Heath to ignore the radical leaders in Africa who opposed it. Typically, Radio South Africa saw no contradiction in the idea that the settlement could be in Africans' interests and at the same time, opposed by Africans.

It was the Conservative Government under Sir Alec Douglas-Home's premiership that laid the foundations of the present independence crisis in Rhodesia. Under pressure from the Labour Opposition, especially from Harold Wilson personally, Sir Alec condemned all forms of racialism. On the question of granting independence to the colonies he told Parliament on 12 November, 1963, that his Government had accepted, at the U.N., the principle of 'self-determination without qualification'. He emphasised his Government's belief both that 'the majority should rule' and that 'minorities should be protected'. He went on to say that 'when we come to the question of Southern Rhodesia – we are not there yet – these questions will guide us in any decisions we may have to take in respect of the rights of the majority.' This statement was clear enough, and in a normal colonial situation not befogged with racialism, everyone would have understood what the Conservative premier was saying. But Wilson understood the truth – that African people could never put any trust in Sir Alec's policy statement. Something more explicit needed to be said in order to remove all the ambiguities in Britain's Rhodesia policy. Wilson demanded further clarification of the Government's policy: 'Will the Rt. Hon.

Gentleman [Sir Alec] now give a pledge that there will not be independence until there is a democratic constitution [majority rule]?' Sir Alec replied that the answer to this question had been implicit in his statement, but he reiterated his principles, adding that 'the second principle which I was enunciating was that it is the very essence of true democracy that minorities, whether black or white, should be protected. Therefore, as we proceed to consider the question of independence for Nyasaland, and Northern and Southern Rhodesia, these principles will apply.'

Like the Labour Party, the Conservatives had retreated from those principles, on the basis of which the Rhodesian problem could have been solved, to the invertebrate Five Principles,[30] which completely ignore the mood of the Africans in the country. These can be said to exist in order to offer a *pretended* solution to the problem, enabling the British Government to put on a bold face at the U.N. and the Commonwealth Conferences. Anyone familiar with the African attitude, in Africa in general and in Rhodesia in particular, could never contemplate a settlement that would leave power entrenched in minority hands, no matter how philanthropic the minority might be. But in fact the Rhodesian settlers have never disguised their motives and no honest politician could ever hope to eliminate Rhodesian racialism by imposing a policy stated in principles to which Smith and his colleagues are violently hostile.

Having created the Five Principles, the Conservatives, from opposition, pressed the then docile Harold Wilson to carry them out on their behalf. It was made impossible for Wilson to take any other course that would have produced equitable results between black and white. They mistrusted the U.N. because of the Congo experience and also because of fear of Soviet influence spreading to Southern Africa. Sir Harry Legge-Bourke believed that the U.N. should not be given supervisory powers. Even when it was obvious that Wilson would not allow the U.N. to go beyond supporting his sterile policies, the Tories insisted that Britain must always take sole responsibility for this matter above all others. They pressed Wilson to ignore the much larger number of Rhodesians, namely the Africans, who were disfranchised, and concentrate on the whites who had the economic and political power. This was called 'realism'.

The Emergency Resolution moved by John Tilney, M.P., at the Conservative Party conference in Blackpool on 13 October, 1966, opposed 'the handing over of this British problem to the U.N.' At the 1965 conference, Selwyn Lloyd had been the Party's spokesman on foreign affairs, and he introduced a Resolution on Rhodesia which would forestall any attempt to use force, on the part of either Britain or the U.N. The Resolution claimed that the use of force would bring suffering to both Europeans and Africans. The British press reported that the debate was bitter and full of racial emotions.

Reginald Maudling, who had visited Smith and Vorster in September 1966, told the Tory Conference in that year that Rhodesia was the last and toughest of Britain's imperial problems. He foresaw that it would be for Britain what Algeria had been for France. He opposed mandatory sanctions, he said, because they would harden the white attitude towards a settlement. He also feared that it would not be possible for Britain to maintain control of the situation once the matter had gone to the U.N. Mandatory sanctions could not succeed without South African co-operation and, most important, without the danger of a confrontation against Southern Africa as a whole, with political and economic consequences for the whole western world. The Tories believed that the Labour Government was being dictated to by the Commonwealth leaders, especially those from Africa and Asia. The stormy Commonwealth Conference of September 1966 was repeatedly referred to with resentment by Conservative politicians as well as by Smith. Undoubtedly, the Conservatives' attitude was responsible for encouraging Smith to defy the U.N. and the Commonwealth. It confused Harold Wilson and led him into the blunders he committed over Rhodesia. Because of this attitude, the Conservative Party earned the hostility of the whole non-white world.

The Conservatives thus forced Wilson to enfeeble his stand with the advance declaration that he would not use force even if the settlers took the law into their hands. When they immediately did so, he had to swallow his pride by opening 'talks about talks' even after he had told the House of Commons that the British Government would have nothing to do with the régime. Even after Wilson had humiliated himself by sitting down with Smith in H.M.S. *Tiger*, apparently forgetting about all the declarations he had made at U.D.I. to the effect that he would not talk with rebels, Conservatives continued to attack him for riding roughshod over the settlers. Even after the settlement made on board H.M.S. *Fearless*, which came after Smith had rejected the *Tiger* settlement with the utmost contempt, the Conservatives continued to accuse Wilson of not going far enough. They argued that the psychological handling of the Rhodesian issue by the Labour Government was 'appallingly bad' and that NIBMAR was responsible for consolidating right-wing opinion and had inhibited the emergence of any moderate opposition.

Lord Salisbury expressed horror over any move by the Wilson administration which appeared to take stern action against the settlers. He told the Tory Conference in 1965 that he was opposed to coercion by either Britain or the U.N. of 'a small, peaceful country which is not threatening anyone'. He was upset by the Conservative Party National Executive's apparent acquiescence in the Labour Government's abandonment of 'our friends and kinsfolk'. He could not see the reason why a British government should hand over, 'at a very early date, the fates of their kinsfolk and their wives and families to the tender mercies of men who, the Government must know, are as yet totally unfitted to conduct any free form of Government at all'. Lord Salisbury's fears over the horrors of majority rule are not shared by the white citizens of Kenya. Fourteen leading British settlers in that country expressed 'deep shock and dismay' at U.D.I. They blamed the Rhodesian whites for the racial tension that followed it in Kenya and Zambia. White people in Kenya and Zambia were not molested as a result of U.D.I., but after the hangings in 1968, the African rage could not be contained, and some whites in Kenya, Zambia and Rhodesia were stoned by Africans in protest.

The Conservatives' present policy on independence will never succeed because it is designed to deceive the world and the British public into thinking that a solution to the problem is seriously intended. However, the Africans are not deceived. They will not be obliged to honour any decision on a settlement reached without the participation of their leaders.

(iii) *International Socialism, U.D.I. and Sanctions*

Socialist parties all over the world, whether in government, coalition or opposition, expressed their horror at the usurpation of power by the white minority in Rhodesia. However, the reaction varied according to the extent of the particular country's involvement in African affairs. Socialists in Africa, Asia and the Scandinavian countries were prepared to support whatever stringent measures the British Government might take to end the Smith rebellion. The Socialists in major European capitals condemned the intention of the Smith régime to perpetuate power in the hands of a small settler minority, but those in coalition governments, even with influential cabinet positions, were not effective in their support for their socialist comrade Harold Wilson.

The reaction against U.D.I. in the Scandinavian countries was especially strong. The Swedish (Social Democratic) Government was the first in the world to announce that it would not recognise U.D.I., having long been a strong opponent of colonialism and apartheid. It had given financial aid to freedom fighters in Africa and Asia, basing its policy in this respect on the belief that disarmament and the relaxation of world tension cannot be achieved until all people are free. Racialism in South Africa and colonialism in Rhodesia, Mozambique and Angola are thus viewed as crucial obstacles. Sweden was the first country to withdraw from the Cabora Bassa scheme in support of the O.A.U. stand. The Swedish Prime Minister, Olof Palme, told the annual conference of the Tanganyika African National Union (T.A.N.U.) in September 1971 that his Government would increase aid to the liberation movements of Southern Africa in 1972, and expressed the hope that other European governments would follow his country's lead. After U.D.I. in Rhodesia, the Swedish Labour Organisation decided to support the Government's policies by refusing to off-load any ship it suspected of carrying Rhodesian cargo. This co-operation between government and workers was absent in other European countries.

In Denmark the Social Democratic Prime Minister condemned usurpation of power by 'a small minority, belonging to a specific race'. His Government supported the principle of majority rule in Rhodesia and immediately introduced sanctions in support of the British Labour Government. Denmark is one of the few countries where companies that violated sanctions have been prosecuted and fined. The Norwegian Labour Party was not in power at the time of U.D.I., but its paper *Arbeiderbladet* sympathised with the British Labour Government's plight over Rhodesia; it blamed the impossible Rhodesian problem on successive British Governments.

Scandinavian trade with Rhodesia in 1964 was infinitesimal by comparison with that of the larger European powers. In that year, Denmark imported tobacco to the value of £0·5m., Norway imported £0·2m. worth of tobacco, while Sweden imported £0·3m. of asbestos and £0·1m. of chrome ore. In all, Rhodesia exported commodities worth only £1·1m. to the three Scandinavian countries in 1964. The paucity of trade with Rhodesia, nevertheless, does not suggest that the Scandinavian countries would be insensitive to the anguish of the African people of Rhodesia if the trade were higher. On the contrary, the record of these countries in the U.N. and other international organisations has shown that they are consistently opposed to any form of oppression.

Socialists were members of coalition governments in six European countries, which were the main trading partners with Rhodesia. All their official newspapers condemned U.D.I. for various reasons, and in general they sympathised with the African cause. The Social Democratic Party of West Germany, which was in coalition with the Christian Democratic Union, expressed disgust at U.D.I. because it was going to encourage the spread of Communism from China and Russia. The S.P.D.'s official daily paper *Pressedienst* believed that the fear of Communism must have influenced Harold Wilson against initiating military action in Rhodesia. The S.P.D. understood the concern of African states over the plight of Africans in Rhodesia, and it hoped that the Federal Government would take into account the African struggle for freedom in their dealings with African states. The S.P.D.'s weekly paper *Vorwaerts* expressed the view that U.D.I. could mean 'the beginning of the end of white dictatorships in Africa'.

The Austrian Socialist Party, which was also in coalition at U.D.I., though it took power in 1966, expressed sympathy with the Africans' struggle for their birthright. Their paper the *Arbeiter-Zeitung* hoped, like the British Labour Party, that the business interests in Rhodesia would overthrow the *status quo* and establish a loyal government. Austria, like the Scandinavian countries, traded very little with Rhodesia at U.D.I.

In Italy the Social Democratic Party's official paper *Socialismo Democratico* supported Wilson's policy of sanctions. It disapproved of the 'extreme' measures which the U.N. wanted the British Government to take – namely, force – which it believed would compel reaction from the rebels in Salisbury, thus inevitably widening the conflict to the whole of Africa.

Le Peuple, the newspaper of the Belgian Socialist Party, regarded U.D.I. as an insult and a provocation to Africa, the Commonwealth and the U.N. It said that Smith had never sought to negotiate independence, but had always planned to grab it.

The Social Democratic Party of Switzerland likened the Smith régime's electoral system to that of Portugal, where the Government is always assured of victory. Its paper *Volksrecht* deplored Smith's claim that chiefs represented African opinion; chiefs were 'complete puppets of the white régime, and only by shameless distortion could their views be represented as the vote of the African majority.'

The only socialist parties which were neither in coalition nor in government were those in France and the Netherlands. Their reaction none the less was similar to that of other European socialists. They expressed their sympathy with the struggle of the African people while condemning Smith's intentions in Southern Africa.[31]

The countries which kept the Smith régime alive in 1966–71 were mostly in Europe, the two exceptions being Brazil and Japan. The most notorious were West Germany, France, the Netherlands and Italy. The Netherlands provided facilities for goods to be shipped to and from Europe by her vessels and at her ports of Amsterdam and Rotterdam, while the other three turned a blind eye to the surreptitious trade with Rhodesia. France gave official support to Rhodesia, supplying her with oil banned by the U.N.[32] France refused to co-operate with the U.N. because she believed

Rhodesia to be a colonial affair of Britain's, and in consequence a domestic one. She also argued that Britain had supplied Tunisia with arms during the Algerian war, knowing that they found their way into Algeria. This led France to turn a blind eye to a known sanctions-breaking racket being organised from Paris. Italy and West Germany traded as usual. West Germany took advantage of the clause in the Security Council Resolutions which only allowed trade in goods needed in Rhodesia on humanitarian grounds.[33] An interesting case in point was the conference on tourism held in Rhodesia in 1971, and attended only by European countries in defiance of the U.N. resolution of May 1968 prohibiting trade relations with Rhodesia. Rhodesia's tourist industry earned £11·7m. in 1970. This shows that thousands of white people continue to come into the country. Facilities exist for nationals of fourteen European countries, as well as South Africans, to enter Rhodesia without visas.

The presence of socialist ministers occupying key posts in various coalitions made African socialists hope for dramatic action against Smith such as that later taken by Asia and Scandinavian countries. When the mandatory sanctions were imposed in December 1966, the Social Democratic Party in Germany had just (in November) joined a 'grand coalition' formed between itself and the Christian Democratic Union. In the coalition there were seven S.P.D. ministers, four of whom held posts closely concerned with foreign affairs, which could have enabled them to support the policies of their comrade Harold Wilson. Willy Brandt, especially, as Foreign Minister and Vice-Chancellor, could have influenced German policy on African affairs, while Karl Schiller in the post of Minister of Economic Affairs was in a strong position to exercise surveillance over sanction-breaking firms. The West German firm Norddeutsche Raffinerie continued to import and refine copper from Rhodesia – copper which eventually found its way into Britain. Heinrich Plambeck of Hamburg imported Rhodesian meat. Rhodesian agents in Hamburg, Bremen and West Berlin organised the importation of tobacco and minerals into Europe via South Africa.[34] The Justice Minister, Heinemann, could have prosecuted the firms and agents who were breaking German trade laws against Rhodesia; but, like the first two ministers, he failed African and British socialists. Austrian firms co-operated with sanctions-breaking companies in Germany also without restraint from their Government, whose Foreign Minister, Kreisky, was a socialist. Not so directly involved was the socialist minister of Development Aid, Wischnewski; but with that portfolio he should have been aware of the intensity of African feelings against the racialist policies of Smith, and been expected to advise his colleagues against their *laissez-faire* policy on sanctions.

Italy, too, had socialist ministers in key positions in relation to the Rhodesian problem:[35] Pietro Nenni was Deputy Prime Minister, while two other eminent social democrats – Luigi Preti, Minister of Finance, and Roberto Tremelloni, Minister of Defence, were in positions to influence policy. Giusto Tolloy, a socialist but belonging to a different party from the latter two, was in charge of foreign trade. In this capacity he could have dealt severely with firms that persistently traded in Rhodesian products. Following the deliberate trading policy of the Smith régime, these products were being offered on the world market at greatly reduced prices. As in Germany, goods reached Italy from Rhodesia via South Africa; Genoa was the main port of entry from which goods from Rhodesia were distributed to other parts of Italy and to Switzerland. At the same time sanction-breaking was taking place, Italy was trying to create good relations with Zambia, the country which was under a constant threat from Smith, whom the Italian trade was strengthening. Weapons produced by a subsidiary of Fiat, Macchi, in South Africa found their way into Rhodesia; Fiat also competed with Japan, Germany and France in the car trade in Rhodesia. The socialists cannot be blamed for the continuity of trade between Rhodesia and Italy; however, their failure to act decisively in 1966 when they were in a position to do so deserves censure.

Belgium and Switzerland were also actively involved in breaking sanctions despite the presence of socialist ministers in their cabinets. The Dutch socialists were in opposition, but they put up a brave fight against the failure of their conservative Government to prosecute those who broke sanctions. Their spokesman on foreign affairs, Peter Danckerts, is well informed on Rhodesian matters and sympathetic to the African cause.

It is thus clear that European socialists, who, like their counterparts in Africa, are fighting capitalism, failed to deal with the clandestine activities of international companies in their countries. The Rhodesian case has demonstrated the sad truth that few socialists, in Europe or anywhere else, are prepared to resist compromise in any circumstances with even their most extreme political adversaries where national prosperity is involved.

REFERENCES

1. Denis Healey, 'The 1960 Revolution in Britain's African Policy', *Africa Report*, Vol. 5, No. 2, 1960, p. 3.

2. It was the Labour M.P.s of the 1920s, led by Colonel Josiah Wedgwood, who pressed the British Government to retain the principle of trusteeship over Africans in Rhodesia as in all African territories under the Crown.

3. *The Economist*, article entitled 'Behind the Golden Curtain', 16 November, 1963.

4. The speech, which is quoted in books by Dr. M. I. Hirsch, Paul Foot and Anne Darnborough, ran as follows:

We have said that no constitution is defensible which fails to allow the people of those territories to control their own destinies. We have bitterly attacked the Southern Rhodesian Constitution for that, and a Labour Government would therefore alter it . . . We've made that very, very plain. But we would go further. When these questions are debated at the United Nations, you would not find us voting in a collection of new, to some extent discredited, imperial powers.

5. Wilson's interest in Rhodesia was accompanied by ignorance of the exact facts of the situation. There were more than 4m. Africans and only 215,000 Europeans. In his book, he said that Sir Edgar Whitehead was defeated at the polls and replaced by the Rhodesia Front in April 1963, yet it happened in December 1962.

6. The letter was later used by Smith as a reason for declaring independence and refusing to negotiate with Wilson. Even after Wilson had scuttled away from that policy, the settlers continued to take him seriously whereas Africans had already seen that he had begun backsliding. (See Cmnd. 2807, November 1963–November 1965, p. 47).

7. The author was among the students at the University College of Salisbury who followed the British Election results all through the night of 15 October, 1964, listening to the results. For details on how African hopes were dashed, see Richard Hall, *The High Price of Principles*, Hodder and Stoughton, London, 1969.

8. Rhodesia is difficult for the British Government, because it combines the dimensions of foreign and domestic policy. Its colonial nature involves the British Government in controversies at the U.N., yet the presence of the British settlers makes it appear as parochial as a borough in an English city, like Bromley or Lewisham. The British Government has the problem of defending the behaviour of fewer than $\frac{1}{4}$m settlers who are 6,000 miles away, as though they were part of the home country.

9. *Rhodesia Herald*, 11 June, 1971.

10. Harold Wilson, *The Labour Government 1964–70*, Michael Joseph, London, 1971, p. 180.

11. Wilson listed four dimensions that his Government took into account in dealing with U.D.I.: public opinion (by definition white) in Rhodesia, the same in Britain, world opinion at the U.N., and the views of the Commonwealth countries.

12. See resolutions S/216 12 November, 1965; S/217 20 November,

1965; S/221 9 April, 1966; S/232 16 December, 1966; S/253, 29 May, 1968; S/277 18 March, 1970.

13. See Cmnd. 3171.

14. Of the five men executed, one was guilty of civil murder and had no connection with the political crimes of the other four – his presence was intended to deter possible protests. The strength of international protest, however, has deterred the régime from any further executions. In November 1971, there were forty-four men and one woman in death cells.

15. The ignorance of some of the leading civil servants about Rhodesia is amazing. Their information about what the Africans think is based on what they are told by 'liberal' Europeans from Rhodesia. Very little interest, if any, is shown in talking to the Africans themselves.

16. George Cunningham, later a M.P., was forced out of his post at Transport House because he called for the use of force.

17. Out of 87,000 whites employed in 1964, by far the largest majority were (a) in distribution 18,660; (b) in manufacturing 15,040; (c) in transport and communications 9,670; (d) in government administration, 8,980. Agriculture accounted for 4,530 and mining for 2,740. These were the industries likely to be affected by sanctions. Manufacturing could have been affected immediately if it had been feasible (as it was not) for Zambia and Malawi to boycott Rhodesian goods as soon as sanctions were imposed.

18.

RHODESIAN EXPORTS TO THE U.K. (c.i.f.)	£m.	U.K. EXPORTS TO RHODEISA (f.o.b.)	£m.
Tobacco	20·6	Motor vehicles and parts	6·2
Asbestos fibre	3·3	Machinery	1·6
Beef	1·2	Tractors	1·1
Corned meat	1·2	Railway locomotives	1·0
Sugar	1·0	Miscellaneous	23·5
Miscellaneous	3·2		
Total	30·5	Total	33·4

Exports in 1964	£m.		£m.
United Kingdom	30·5	West Germany	7·9
Zambia	30·8	France	0·7
South Africa	9·0	Netherlands	2·2
Malawi	5·6	Italy	1·3
Australia	1·6	Europe N.E.S.	7·2
India	1·0	Mozambique	0·7
Botswana	1·1	Angola	0·1
Hong Kong	0·5	Congo (Kinshasa)	1·5
Other countries in the sterling area	4·3	Other African countries	0·6
U.S.A.	4·0	Japan	5·6
Canada	1·4	Soviet bloc	0·9
Other dollar area countries	0·1	Other countries	0·7
		Total	118·3

19. Europeans owned farms with a total of 34,484,176 acres averaging between 2,501 to 5,000 acres.

20. Schoeman's speech on 20 November, 1966, reported in the South African press. Dr. H. Muller and J. B. Vorster made similar speeches on the same day.

21. The British representative at the U.N. told the Afro-Asian countries that 'to refuse to commit suicide is not immoral'.

22. South Africa's five main trading partners in 1968 were:

	Exports (£ millions)	Imports (£ million)
U.K.	629·3	666·5
U.S.A.	465·9	146·2
West Germany	355·2	141·8
Japan	173·5	286·2
Italy	109·3	60·1

23. The Southern Rhodesia Act 1965, Ch. 76, passed by the Wilson Government on 16 November, 1965, reaffirmed Britain's jurisdiction over the Colony. Section 1 says: 'It is hereby declared that Southern Rhodesia continues to be part of Her Majesty's dominions, and that the Government and Parliament of the United Kingdom have responsibility and jurisdiction as heretofore for and in respect of it.'

24. Contemporary approval is seen in the books written by the men who took part in suppressing the revolt in Rhodesia – D. T. Laing, who attacked the home of the author's grandparents at Belingwe Mountain, and F. C. Selous.

25. Sir Richard was present at the *Indaba* between Rhodes and the Ndebele leaders in September 1896. Rhodes deceived the Ndebele into believing that the war was over and that they and the white people would live together, without telling them that the very place where they held the *Indaba* in the Matopo had been declared his farm, and that they would be removed at the appropriate time to semi-desert areas in Nkai, Gwaai and Tsholotsho. He must have known this because he stayed in the country long enough to see the Ndebele evicted from their beautiful and rich areas – named 'World's View' by Rhodes.

26. Article 22 referred to people of the colonies as those 'peoples not yet able to stand by themselves under strenuous conditions of the modern world', to whom 'should be applied the principle that the well-being and development of such peoples form a sacred trust of civilisation.'

27. Most of these are members of the Rhodesia Committee of the Monday Club.

28. See Dan Horowitz's article in *Race*, Vol. XII, No. 2, October 1970, pp. 169–87.

29. When Ian Smith declared a republic in March 1970, Lord Salisbury resigned from the presidency of the Anglo-Rhodesia Society, whose purpose was to promote friendship between the British and Rhodesian people, in protest. He regretted that, for all his 'love for Rhodesia and his kith and kin', he could not approve this rejection of the Queen. Patrick Wall also resigned from the society.

30. These principles are: (i) Unimpeded progress to majority rule, already enshrined in the 1961 Constitution, would have to be maintained and guaranteed; (ii) Guarantees against retrogressive amendment of the Constitution; (iii) Immediate improvement in the political status of the African population; (iv) Progress towards ending racial discrimination; (v) and that the British Government would need to be satisfied that any proposed basis for independence was acceptable to the people of Rhodesia as a whole.

31. The French socialist spokesman on African affairs received vicious anonymous letters because of his articles opposing the Rhodesian régime.

32. Thayer, *The War Business*, p. 277.

33. The word 'humanitarian' was stretched to cover motor cars, supposedly exported for use by missionaries in the bush, and machinery for printing banknotes after Britain had confiscated a massive consignment of German-printed Rhodesian notes in 1966.

34. *The Observer*, London, 17 March, 1968.

35. In 1966 Italy had a coalition of four political parties in a Centre-Left Government.

CHAPTER XI

A RACIAL MATTER OR
A COLONIAL ONE?

(i) *The End of Trusteeship*

Legally, Southern Rhodesia remains a British colony as long as there is no constitutional settlement. The U.N. placed the colony under the supervision of its Special Committee on Colonialism as from 1962, and the Judicial Committee of the Privy Council confirmed in 1968 that in terms of British law Rhodesia was a colony. The Judicial Committee declared that all legislation and administrative decrees of the régime which were made after U.D.I. were illegal. Politically, much of the world regards Rhodesia as an African colony which the British would like to retain for their citizens. Only South African and Portugal believe that the settlers are right in defying the Africans as well as world opinion in clinging to power in an African country.

The British Government does not, on the whole, support the white settlers. But it finds itself in a dilemma, for it is aware that the settlers' claim to power in Rhodesia is no longer in conformity with international concepts of democracy and freedom. Yet Britain is seeking means of escaping from her admittedly heavy and thankless responsibility – hence the outcome of the Salisbury talks in November 1971.

The western world's attitude towards Africa developed in three phases: first, before 1914, whole-hearted approval of colonialism for the purpose of 'civilising' Africa; then, after 1918, the concept of trusteeship and the aim of protecting African peoples against exploitation by European speculators and adventurers was accepted; finally, after the Second World War, came the desire to grant political freedom. Only two nineteenth-century African colonies, one British (Rhodesia) and the other German (South West Africa, or Namibia), remain under foreign or European rule.

Rhodesia was in a sense unfortunate in that her first major constitutional development came in the second phase of colonialism between 1919 and 1923. It would have been inconceivable at that time for power to be given to Africans. Nonetheless, the British Government decided not to confer the attributes of independence

on the settlers. The reason for this refusal was clearly – and prophetically – stated by Winston Churchill in 1921 when he declared:

> It will be an ill day for the native races when their fortunes are
> removed from the impartial and august administration of the
> Crown and abandoned to the sea of self-interest of a small white
> population. Such an event is no doubt very remote. Yet the
> speculator, the planter and the settler are knocking at the door.

Churchill's attitude marked a change from the rigorous policy of
L. S. Amery, which was intended to concede all demands made by
settlers. As Under-Secretary of State for the Colonies, he repeatedly,
and prophetically, made it clear that it was 'to the views of the
white people in Southern Rhodesia that the Imperial authorities
would have regard in deciding the future form of government'.[1]
Without pressure from Colonel Wedgwood, a Labour M.P. of the
time interested in African colonial problems, the settlers would have
obtained a much more advanced constitution than they did.
Pressure from the churches, the A.P.S. and the Labour M.P.s
impelled the British Government to produce a constitution which
enshrined the concept of trusteeship in the interest of Africans, which
was the norm for all other African colonies. The spirit of trusteeship
was retained in the 1961 Constitution; but, since Rhodesia remains
a colony in law and according to the U.N. Charter, this trusteeship
would be abrogated by the legal independence which has been
negotiated between the British Government and the rebel régime.

Even Lardner-Burke acknowledged in Parliament that Rhodesia
remained a colony. He said: 'It is true that we had a measure of
freedom in the running of our internal affairs, but no one could
say that we were independent.' He listed six factors which limited
Rhodesian independence: the application of the Colonial Laws
Validity Act 1865; the convention of not legislating against Rhodesia
was political but not legal; the Governor was appointed through
consultation between the two Governments; the Governor had
certain powers, though these were limited; the Privy Council was
the final appeal court; and parts of the Constitution could not be
amended without the British Government's consent – in fact the
British Government refused in 1965 to allow the amendment of the
1961 Constitution to provide for the Preventive Detention Act of
1959.[2]

Rhodesia would be the second African territory, after South Africa,
to be given independence under white minority power. It can fairly
be maintained that when South Africa gained independence in
1910, even more than when Rhodesia was granted her Constitution
in 1923, the western world had never entertained the belief that a

K

black person was competent to run political institutions. In 1909, the Liberal Government of H. H. Asquith had felt bound to return power to the Boers, who were a focus for world sympathy at the time, just as Britain had been made to feel a usurper.[3] But today the international atmosphere overwhelmingly favours equality for all mankind. The U.N. Charter, the Declaration of Human Rights, and Resolution 1514 XV of 1960 spell out the details of how independence should be conferred on colonies. Over Rhodesia, Britain has ignored these world criteria for independence in preference for the political expedient of leaving power in the hands of the settlers. In other African territories, trusteeship was replaced by a vote.[4] The British Government's apparent intention to give independence to the white racialist régime in Rhodesia, despite world disapproval, has led the African people to believe that the moral principles of trusteeship have been sacrificed to racial expediency, and that the only way out of the situation is through a military confrontation.

(ii) Principles and Pragmatism

The Conservative Party's election manifesto in the election of June 1970 stated that Labour had failed to solve the Rhodesian problem 'to the detriment of all concerned'. It insisted that a Conservative Government would make a further attempt to find a solution according to the Five Principles which had been fashioned by Sir Alec Douglas-Home's administration in 1963–4.

The Conservatives believe that Rhodesia is too far advanced economically to be allowed to fall into untried African hands: the whites played a major role in building up the economy, and therefore it would be unfair to force them out of power or out of the country. The only method which can bring about political evolution is a calculated form of change, controlled by the whites themselves, which can be embraced in a constitution recognising the certainty that Africans will rule in the distant future. Reginald Maudling said on 13 January, 1968, that Britain had a responsibility for both Africans and Europeans; this necessitated planning for progress towards majority rule so that it did not entail the 'chaos, disaster and often bloodshed that has been so apparent in other parts of the African continent, and which quite rightly causes the Europeans of Rhodesia very real, deep personal concern.'[5]

The Conservatives formulate their policies on Rhodesia entirely on the basis of information collected from Rhodesian Europeans. They do not attempt to consult African opinion other than the chiefs introduced to Tory visitors by the Smith Government. If they did, Maudling would have been aware of the Africans' stated intention of not removing whites from the country once they take power, or of taking revenge. However no majority government could tolerate a situation in which a sector of the population as small as that which the whites form in Rhodesia had a standard of living higher than that of the U.S.A., the richest country in the world, while 96 per cent of the people lived in perpetual poverty. It is their awareness of this obvious contradiction that causes the whites to fear majority rule.

Africans do not deny Europeans the right to live in Rhodesia. None of their leaders ever advocated the removal of Europeans from Rhodesia in the way that Enoch Powell has demanded the removal of Commonwealth immigrants from Britain.[6] But they do regard as irrelevant Maudling's claim that power should remain in the hands of whites because they built economy. At the end of the Second World War, the U.S.A. helped many European nations, including Britain, to rebuild their economies. But Americans never thought of directly controlling political power in Europe to protect their investments. It is incomprehensible, therefore, that Britain should believe that Rhodesian Africans would tolerate oppression for the sake of economic progress which is, in fact, the preserve of the white population at the expense of the Africans.

Rhodesia is a country of great natural wealth, which is under the control and direction of fewer than 250,000 people, who benefit from 'cheap labour'. Maudling's argument is that whites in Rhodesia fear a repetition there of what has happened in other parts of Africa, namely Nigeria and the Congo. But this is a narrowly racial attitude: what it amounts to is that if any black state has had failures, the blame is to be laid on all other blacks. If Africans were to review the chaos brought about by European wars in this century, then it would have good reason to refuse settler rule. If Europeans in Rhodesia feel that majority rule is no good for them, they can always emigrate back to Europe, or to other areas ruled by whites. Where can Africans go, other than into exile, if they do not accept minority rule. The Europeans in African countries operating under majority rule are far happier than those in Rhodesia and South Africa. The statement of leading white Kenyans before U.D.I. in 1965 showed clearly that they were happier under majority rule than under colonial rule.

Conservatives believe that Wilson failed to solve the problem because there was distrust between Labour and the settlers, and that their own policy of settling will be in the interest of all. They conveniently ignore the African distrust in their own Government and argue, rather naïvely, that 'NIBMAR' consolidated right-wing opinion and inhibited the emergence of a moderate opposition in

Rhodesia. By this they are unwittingly admitting that both the right and the moderate groupings are against majority rule.

Soon after the Conservatives gained power in 1970, Sir Alec Douglas-Home made a further clarification of his Government's policy over Rhodesia at the Party's conference in Blackpool. He claimed that the principle which had guided the Government in resolving the Rhodesian impasse was to create the political conditions in which different racial groups within the country could live in harmony. The British Government had never intended to prescribe the nature of the majority rule which should eventually prevail after Britain had relinquished power; this was to be left to the discretion of the white electorate. The policy was designed to avoid any situation that might appear to let down the white people. As such it leaves power in their hands by pretending that a multi-racial solution has been found in which anybody of any racial group could rise to any political position with the support of people of all races. In Sir Alec's words, Britain sought a 'political solution': 'Under the Constitution, the majority which emerges from the ballot box rules, and the minority are at the same time protected under the law. That has been the essence of British policy. Our practice, therefore, has been the very antithesis of government by racial supremacy.' Sir Alec believes that Britain must devise a constitution which is fair to all races, and with genuine prospects for a 'multi-racial society'.

On its face value, the statement gives the impression that what is contemplated is the introduction of majority rule under universal adult suffrage, for it is only under this type of franchise that majority rule could emerge from the ballot box. The claim that British practice has been the 'very antithesis of government by racial supremacy' is equally praiseworthy, if it is not subjected to critical analysis. But there is no doubt that this language has two meanings, one for each of the main racial groups. To the Africans it is a way of trying to convince the British electorate and the world that Britain is concerned about the welfare of both races in Rhodesia. But to the ill-informed majority of the settlers it means what it says, no more or less than majority rule; hence they are scared of any settlement with Britain because of a suspicion that Smith and his colleagues might be deceived into accepting a constitution that would eradicate all manifestations of white supremacy. The settlers who have this attitude make settlement wellnigh impossible. The intelligent ones, who belong mainly to the (liberal) Centre Party, understand that British policy is a 'multi-racial one' designed to leave power effectively in white hands. The language, which appears to be at war with all forms of racialism, is nothing more than a reassertion of Huggins' policy of the horse and the rider. As far as Africans are concerned, no amount of sweet language will mollify their attitude.

The concept of a multi-racial society was embodied in the Central African Federation of 1953–63; to British ministers this concept means partnership between racial groups under the leadership of 'responsible' and 'civilised' men: in theory any person of any race can take responsible positions on merit alone. The policy of partnership is opposed to the idea of universal adult suffrage. A former Tory Colonial Secretary, Lord Chandos, maintained this stance in his memoirs, and other leading Conservatives such as Lord Hailsham have claimed that Britain requires the Africans not to frustrate the multi-racial concept by trying to use their numbers to obtain power. Robin Turton, a Tory M.P., argued that multi-racialism means 'constitution and franchise', which 'are by nature evolutionary'.[7]

The Tory Government was deeply upset when the Africans refused to support Sir Edgar Whitehead's policies of partnership at the 1962 General Election, in which he lost power to the Rhodesia Front. Up to now, people of the same opinion as Duncan Sandys have not forgiven Joshua Nkomo for letting them down over their policy of multi-racialism enshrined in the 1961 Constitution.

Examples of multi-racialism were to be seen in the 'multi-racial' Federal Parliament which had only six African as against twenty-nine white M.P.s from 1953 to 1957, and in the Southern Rhodesia Parliament with its fifty white and fifteen African M.P.s in 1962. The University College in Salisbury is regarded as the best multi-racial institution so far created in Central Africa, but educationally it has remained stagnant while the Universities of Malawi and Zambia, which came into being in the 1960s with non-racial policies, have moved ahead of it. The University in Salisbury is so controlled that Africans remain fewer than whites; if Africans exceed the numbers of whites, the policy of 'multi-racialism' is destroyed. Multi-racial sporting teams are sent abroad with at least one African. In the heyday of the Federation one often found 'multi-racial' cinemas with only one white worker (the projector-operator), while the rest were black; and in practice the audiences were always wholly black. Some cinemas had lavatory doors written 'Europeans only, multi-racial toilets upstairs'. Reduced to its practical form, the policy of multi-racialism left Africans occupying old and decrepit office and residential buildings which Europeans had used at the turn of the century. Old hotels such as the Northern Grand, Victoria and Waverley Hotels in Bulawayo were abandoned by whites and were then patronised almost exclusively by Africans. In Gwelo, the Midlands and Royal Hotels have bars which are left for Africans. In Salisbury, the exclusive Meikles Hotel provides a small room where Africans are squeezed in while whites enjoy the spacious rooms. The Jameson and Ambassador Hotels in Salisbury are genuinely non-racial, but prohibitive prices limit African custom.

With this concept of multi-racialism in mind, the Tories have reached 'an honourable settlement' with Smith. They claim that their ultimate aim is majority rule when Africans are 'ready'; it need not come tomorrow or even at the end of the 1970s, but it must be embraced in a clear formula such as the Salisbury settlement proposals that can be entrenched in the Constitution and so made 'honourable', so that it can be defended in Parliament, at the U.N. and at the Commonwealth Conferences.

The Tories want the world to believe that Smith could be made to respect an agreement made between the British Government and himself. The fact that Smith spurned the *Tiger* and the *Fearless* settlements gives Tory leaders cause for encouragement rather than the opposite; they argue that if Smith were a man who went back on his word, he could have accepted those settlements and amended them once he was in a position to do so; his rejection of them depicts him as an honest man who does not accept anything solely for the sake of settlement.

Because of Smith's objection to sitting down with African leaders, the Conservatives have made themselves believe that it is not necessary to consult the Africans at the stage of negotiation. Smith does not want to take a risk like Sir Edgar, who sat in conference with Nkomo in 1961 and lost the election in the following year. Tories believe what Rhodesian 'liberals' tell them about the 'docility' of Africans in Rhodesia. Sanctions are said by these liberals to be harming the Africans, with the result that Africans are looking forward to a settlement. Prospects of expanding the economy following a large inflow of investment, which sanctions have kept out of the country, will improve the African standard of living. Africans are also believed to be keen on education, so the British Government hopes to satisfy this keenness by providing funds for secondary and university education to produce a 'civilised' man of whom the white person will not need to be afraid. It believes in the sincerity of the white people who argue that they want to maintain 'civilised standards'.

The approach that ignores the presence of Africans is the one which is most welcome to the settlers. The way Heath confused Wilson over Rhodesian policy in 1965–70 impressed the settlers, as did the way he treated the O.A.U. arms delegation led by President Kaunda of Zambia. Heath's defiance of the Commonwealth opposition to arms sales to South Africa made the settlers in Southern

Africa believe that they have a representative in Europe. J. H. Howman, Smith's 'Foreign Minister', said at a press conference in Salisbury that the Conservatives were the sort of people with whom one could negotiate. He added: 'We have been impressed by the British Prime Minister, Heath's, conduct. His sincerity of purpose makes him more admirable.' Smith told a group with the title of 'American Crusade against Communism in Africa' that 'Heath's showing at Singapore was admirable'. In August 1971, while expressing satisfaction with the progress of 'talks about talks', Smith warned a by-election meeting in Salisbury that the Rhodesia Front would never accept any settlement that would undermine 'civilisation and the traditional Rhodesian way of life'. He claimed that such a settlement would not be acceptable to 'Rhodesians whatever their race, colour or creed.' In May 1971, he had said on the B.B.C. Radio that the Rhodesia Front could prove to any impartial observer that the vast majority of the African population was satisfied and contented, but he knows that the Africans would accept any settlement that would bring majority rule; hence, to say that people of any race would resist change that destroyed white privileges is like saying Africans would reject freedom. The speech in August 1971 was in sharp contrast to what he said a year earlier at Umtali. While he acknowledged the advantages of co-operating with the Tory Government, he stuck to his obdurate attitude, telling another meeting that Rhodesia was at 'open war' with Britain. Relations between Rhodesia and Britain had deteriorated to an extent which would not have been believed possible five or six years before. He had never believed the Five Principles were true principles, because 'they could be interpreted in different ways by different people and some conflicted with others, making it impossible to come to an agreement harmonious to all.' Smith's statement was even dismissed as dishonest by Jack Humphries, a white correspondent of the *Rhodesia Herald*.[8]

If all this were true there would be no friction. Africans would long since have got the vote but for the fear of African revenge, as the whites are fully aware of the Africans' dissatisfaction. Even the 'moderate' African M.P.s see that under the Rhodesia Front the situation is getting worse. R. C. Nakaya said 'Europeans in this country must not think that the Africans' political silence denotes that they are satisfied with everything that goes on. . . . It is idiotic to think that Europeans will for the foreseeable future decide things for Africans.' The same bitterness was expressed by Africans of the Centre Party, L. J. Mahlangu, M. M. Bhebe and S. Moraka after they were refused permission by the District Commissioner to address a meeting of African farmers at Lupanda Purchase Area.[9]

The Conservatives are keen, like the Socialists before them, to withdraw from Rhodesia. They have had enough of taking the rap on Smith's behalf at the U.N. and at Commonwealth Conferences. Their main desire is to gain the support of the 'moderate' Africans inside Rhodesia – mainly the African M.P.s and some businessmen; they are not concerned about the chiefs or the African nationalists. They believe (correctly) that the chiefs are government servants and cannot speak for the Africans, while they are equally suspicious of the African nationalists because they sabotaged the 1961 Constitution and because they scare the white population with their radical policies: some Conservatives genuinely believe that Rhodesian Africans plan to expel the whites from the country. Tory ministers argue that the nationalists lost their opportunity in 1961 by clamouring for the unattainable ,i.e. universal adult suffrage.

At the same time, a significant number of Tory M.P.s believe that the whites are digging their own graves. Among them are businessmen with interests in Africa north of the Zambezi, where they have been disturbed to find deep hostility towards Britain on account of her Rhodesian policy. These Tories are concerned over the unpredictable reaction to an unacceptable settlement of Kenya, Nigeria or Zambia, which carry heavy British investment. This factor merely reinforces the African conviction that it is largely to satisfy and protect business interests that Conservatives are so keen to arrive at a settlement with Smith.

(iii) *Franchise – Barrier to Power*

No settlement that leaves out universal adult suffrage will ever be accepted by the Africans. Britain's promise to give aid for African education, so as to produce an educated middle class ready to assume the responsibility of political power, is pure escapism. This is an attempt to give a moral façade to the problem, and so conceal its true nature before world opinion.

The reality of the political situation in Rhodesia is that Africans are excluded from the franchise by monetary qualifications and not by reason of education. Even if all Africans obtained Ph.D.s, other reasons would be found for denying them the vote and employment – Africans with Ph.D.s in science are unemployed while semi-literate whites from Greece, Spain and Portugal are drafted into well-paid posts.[10] Europeans qualify for the franchise because their salaries are deliberately inflated to a very high level while those of Africans are deliberately kept very low. If education were the criterion for the franchise, there would be more Africans on the voters' roll than whites. This can best be illustrated by reviewing the 1961 Constitution which was introduced into Rhodesia by a Conservative Government. The first one of its type in Rhodesia, this two-tier system with two electoral rolls, one white and the other black, was deliberately designed to leave the Africans out of European constituencies so that the Rhodesia Front candidates should not have to woo African voters. It is regarded as beneath a white man's dignity to appeal to black voters. The Constitution introduced into Rhodesia a concept of racial federation where races would follow separate political lines but with one parliament as a meeting-place. It would never allow the proportion of white M.P.s to black to be affected by the increase in the African population relative to the Europeans. The 1971 settlement left this idea intact, thereby sanctifying the racialism of the 1969 Republican Constitution.

The Electoral Act 1951 doubled the franchise qualification of 1912–51 from £100 to £240 p.a. Education was not regarded as important: all that was needed was to complete a simple form in English and provide evidence of income. The average wage of Africans in 1951 was £55 p.a., whereas at the same time Europeans' salaries were above £800 – which was the average of most European countries twenty years later. There were 6,812 African teachers, educated and responsible citizens, yet only 453 Africans were voters. Compared to their European counterparts, the African teachers received miserably low salaries. The education of these teachers was much higher than that of European workers who earned higher salaries and qualified for the vote.

The election of 1953, fought under the franchise qualification of 1951, returned Garfield Todd to power. Todd discovered in 1956 that out of the electorate of 52,180, only 560 were Africans. It was then argued that funds should be found to increase the salaries of Africans, or alternatively that the franchise requirements should be lowered to enable Africans (mainly the teachers, who numbered 13,700 in 1956) to qualify. The average salary for a teacher was £109 p.a. while the average for all African workers was £75 p.a.; by 1956 European salaries were averaging £988 p.a. Todd failed to obtain the funds necessary to raise African salaries, but as he believed that it was unfair to keep educated people from the vote because the the country paid them badly, he set up the Tredgold Commission, which decided that education and a certain level of income should qualify Africans for the vote. The Commission, which was manned by Rhodesian and Federal judges, believed, like most whites in Rhodesia at the time, that the vote was a privilege; hence it created two rolls, 'special' and 'ordinary'. The ordinary roll required an income of £720 p.a. As the salaries of the whites averages £988 p.a., it was easy for them to qualify for the ordinary roll. Since the Africans were earning low salaries, regardless of their educational standard, a concession was made: teachers, or others with similar educational qualifications, who earned £300 and had four years' secondary education, were to qualify for the special roll. People who earned £480 p.a. and had eight years' education (primary) or the Standard VI certificate qualified for the ordinary roll. The sum of £480 p.a. would appear a small income for Africans to attain, but still it was not easy. Africans who earned that amount were usually businessmen running buses, general trading stores or groceries. But the Standard VI qualification was meant to exclude the majority of African businessmen, many of whom in the 1950s were older people who had started work before the Standard VI course was introduced by Jowett in 1928. Thus, although many qualified by their incomes, most of them did not have full primary education. It is noteworthy that while the Africans sit examinations that are conducted publicly under strict rules throughout the country, similar to those in Britain for the G.C.E. examinations, the whites do not sit public examinations at a primary level to qualify for a certificate of eight years' education. They simply proceed to secondary education at eleven plus as in Britain.

The enrolment at primary level averaged 600,000 per year during the 1950s but is reduced by the primary examination to an average of fewer than 10,000 per year in the secondary schools. The same qualification that is used to obstruct African educational advance is used to curtail political advance by making it an additional franchise requirement. Yet despite the high educational standard required, there are more Africans with Standard VI certificates (eight years' education) than there are white inhabitants in the country: 304,470 were awarded between 1928 and 1969.

In connection with voting rights, the régime argues that those who obtain full primary education are not sufficiently educated because only with some secondary education can a person be so counted. This question arose in 1959 after Sir Edgar Whitehead had extended industrial apprenticeship laws to include Africans. The Committee set up to place Africans in various industrial sectors found complications in equating African with European education. It was finally agreed that the European school-leavers who joined the apprenticeship scheme should be equated with Africans with ten years' education and two years' secondary certificate (Rhodesia's Junior Certificate). These are often academically capable people because the stiff primary public examination would prevent poorly endowed children from ever going beyond eight years' education. Even then, limited places in secondary schools usually necessitate the taking of only those who pass in the first and second classes into high schools. It is therefore safe to assume that people who have two years' secondary education conform to 'civilised standards' and have 'responsible hands'.

Under the regulation of the Apprenticeship Act, they are accepted on the same level as white workers – although, of course, the white workers are intellectually inferior to their African fellows by virtue of the stiff examination which the latter have gone through, unlike the whites. Following the hypothesis that the whites in Rhodesia would accept an educated African on an equal basis, there would be 58,643 Africans on the voters' roll because that number of Africans in the country have the two years' secondary school certificate. The Minister of Education told Parliament on 14 November, 1969, that this number of Africans were seeking places as apprentices.[11] On the other hand, only ten Africans were currently employed on apprenticeship jobs.[12] This denial to Africans of the right to train for skills was attacked even by the leaders of industry who feared that the country's reservoir of skilled manpower was being dried up owing to the policy of reserving the jobs for immigrants who might not arrive after all. Since 1940, when teachers' training schools were introduced as post-primary education,[13] 126,717 Africans have obtained various forms of secondary certificates. The number of Africans quoted above slightly exceeds that of the white adult population, which is approximately 100,000.

As if to underline the fact that education is not the barrier to the franchise, the Rhodesia Front M.P.s are poorly educated compared to the African nationalist leaders of both Z.A.P.U. and Z.A.N.U. Todd was the last premier to preside over an educated parliament, in 1953–8. Sir Edgar Whitehead's followers were less well educated than Todd's but they were certainly better educated than the Rhodesia Front followers of Field and Smith.

There is evidence that Africans are sincere when they say that their policies follow a *non-racial* approach based entirely on merit.[14] This was demonstrated clearly in the General Election of 1962. Dr. A. Palley fought a lone battle against Sir Edgar's oppressive laws passed between 1958 and 1962, and won the admiration of Africans. In the 1962 election he stood against African candidates in the exclusively African constituency of Highfield, and on his parliamentary record, the African voters backed him. But an African candidate would never be tolerated by the white people in their domain, even in he were the most 'civilised' and 'moderate'. In 1962 they threw out any white candidates who followed a middle-of-the-road policy. For example, there was the case of John Gasson, a graduate of Cape Town University, an Oxford Rhodes scholar and a barrister of Gray's Inn, who was much respected by Africans in Bulawayo where he was born and had a legal practice.

He fought the 1962 election in the typical white constituency of Bellevue, in a suburb of Bulawayo. Gasson, whose grandfather had come to Rhodesia via South Africa after the Boer War, and whose father was a medical practitioner in Bulawayo, stood at Bellevue against the poorly-educated R. Patterson, one of the founders of the notorious Southern Rhodesia Association. Gasson canvassed on a policy of compromise with the Africans, while Patterson took Smith's current line of white supremacy for all time. Gasson lost the election by 865 votes to 674. Frustrated, he emigrated to Britain, where he works in the Lord Chancellor's office. There have been many similar cases.

Education is not all-important as a qualification for the vote if it is assumed that the voter is not going to upset the *status quo*. For instance, according to the Tory Constitution of 1961, any chief or headman could qualify for the vote on the 'A' Roll. Yet people with Form II or two years' secondary education were on the 'B' roll. Most of these chiefs are illiterate. Giving them the vote was intended to buy their loyalty to the white régime.

As we have said, Africans are kept from the vote by the monetary requirements. Most Europeans qualified for the 'A' Roll under the provision of 'an income of at least £795 for at least two years in succession or ownership of immoveable property worth not less than £1,650'. This carried no educational requirement at all. In 1961 white salaries averaged £1,154 p.a., while Africans earned £94 p.a., thus most white workers qualify. The immoveable property qualification is equally easy, because white people have no trouble in raising mortgages for house purchase. Most houses in the white suburbs sell at £4,000 upwards, and a total of 189,200 whites (79·2 per cent) live in the main towns. As for the Africans, their farms and houses have a pegged price calculated to weaken their advance to the franchise. Currently, only 146 Africans have houses valued at more than £1,000, and these are already voters by income. Over 4,000 houses are owned by Africans, but they sell for between £250 and £499. Out of a total of 6,852 farms owned by Africans, only *three* were valued at over £500 in 1961. The few Africans who qualify have got there through the eye of a needle.

As long as the vote is determined by financial qualifications which the white people set according to their convenience, then power will remain in their hands. Africans maintain that the qualified franchise in Rhodesia is a racial device of the settler minority to keep power for themselves in perpetuity: when the white people talk of 'civilised and responsible hands', in which power must remain they are talking of the European way of life. It does not matter how hard the Africans work. Africans know that it is they who build all the roads, dams, houses, schools and hospitals, perhaps under the eye of one white supervisor. The question inevitably arises: how necessary is it to have a white gang supervisor who earns a salary which is more than the total earned by twenty or thirty Africans who do the actual digging or building?

The racial nature of the problem, and the collusion of Britain in the racism of the sellers, has been shown in the British response to political refugees of different races. Following the Soviet invasion of Czechoslovakia in 1968, Britain made many Czechoslovak refugees welcome on her soil. But when two Rhodesian Africans, Nimrod Khumalo and Mthethwa, entered Botswana in July 1971 as political refugees, Britain, being legally responsible for Rhodesia internationally, ordered the refugees to go back. One of them, Khumalo, was tortured to death by police in a Bulawayo prison. The only public protest at this was made in *The Guardian*. Rhodesian whites travel in and out of Britain despite the blame they share for the 1965 treason. But Africans, who are victims of the régime run by emigrants from Britain, find it almost impossible to enter the United Kingdom. They are subjected to racial discrimination along with other non-white immigrants.

(iv) *The Growing Confrontation*

Since the Rhodesian problem was brought to the U.N. in 1962, support for the African cause has grown rapidly, and it is apparent that any settlement of the problem unacceptable to the Africans will not be accepted by the international community, and would cause a racial explosion of a much more serious nature than has taken place in Southern Africa so far.

In their own way of measuring success, the Rhodesia Front could claim up to 1971 that victory had been on its side. It has succeeded in making Britain defy world opinion by preferring to talk to the settlers at the expense of the African owners of the country. Economic sanctions have been discredited; although with diastrous effect to their economy, the settlers have introduced a constitution designed to entrench white supremacy for all time, they have South African forces patrolling Rhodesian borders, they have destroyed African education which the Africans themselves built with the help of the missionaries, and so on. To their supporters this is an admirable record. But, of course, their achievement is only temporary. International attitudes on racial oppression are not in their favour.

The settlers have held on to power in Rhodesia up to 1971 mainly because the Africans in the country itself hoped that Britain would maintain the role of honest broker that she played in Zambia and Kenya. The regrettable split between Z.A.P.U. and Z.A.N.U., contributed immensely to the settlers' temporary victory. Similarly the O.A.U. has placed reliance on the U.N. and not on itself in handling Southern African issues; it ignored the reliance placed by the settlers on the support of European countries which the African spokesmen at the U.N. were attacking. For example, the way that Britain and the U.S.A.[15] vetoed the Security Council Resolution on Rhodesia in April 1970 and ignored U.N. pressure to use force should have made the African leaders aware long ago that only their own skill and determination could solve this African problem; their reorganisation of the O.A.U. Defence Committee points to new attitudes and a growing appreciation that African problems should be solved by Africans. The growth of the support for the African cause against oppression in Rhodesia is due to the racial nature of the problem. While world opinion is opposed to colonialism, it is even more hostile to racialism.

Sir Alec Douglas-Home, when he was Prime Minister, repeated to the House of Commons on 12 November, 1963, the speech he had made to the Royal Commonwealth Society to emphasise his opposition to racialism. He said:

> I believe that the greatest danger ahead of us in the world today is that the world might be divided on racial lines. I see no other danger, not even the nuclear bomb, which would be so catastrophic as that. There is no doubt that racialism is rearing its ugly head in many places, and I hope the Commonwealth will watch this and guard against it.

The only unfortunate aspect of speeches like this is that they are made by people who have never suffered under racial oppression so they do not strictly know what racialism is. If Sir Alec were an African, he would not have followed such a speech with policies in Southern Africa that gave encouragement to people like Smith and Vorster.

The peoples of the Third World have clearly demonstrated their agreement with the principles enunciated by Sir Alec's speech by supporting the liberation movements of Southern Africa. At the U.N. and at the conferences of non-aligned nations, a great deal of time and effort is given to consideration of methods of ending colonialism and racialism, both of which evils are present in Rhodesia. At the non-aligned conference in Lusaka in September 1970, leaders of Asian and African countries decided to establish a Special Fund for the liberation of Southern Africa. Western countries and Japan were attacked for their support of Southern African régimes. A leading article in *The Guardian* acknowledged that the attitude of the non-aligned nations to the Southern African problem was due to the constant reminder which the area afforded of the humiliations of their own colonial experience.

The most heartening support for the African cause has come from the churches which have long been concerned over the misrepresentation of Christian principles by the white leaders in Africa. The claim by Smith and Vorster that their struggle was in defence of Christian civilisation put the church in a difficult situation in African eyes; the church was automatically identified with the oppression which is an integral part of white rule. The Rhodesian settler's constant use of terms such as 'the bastion of western civilisation against Communism' (a coinage of Josef Goebbels in 1937)[16] prompted the Anglican Archbishop of Central Africa, the Most Rev. F. Green-Wilkinson, to disclaim Smith's and Vorster's assertions on Christianity, which he called 'great lies'. He said that the church was concerned lest this falsehood compelled Africans to turn increasingly to atheism in disgust because Christianity appeared to be allied with the minority régimes of Southern Africa.

W. P. Kirkman, writing in *International Affairs* of October 1969, confirmed the church's fears over the Smith régime. He wrote: 'It may be argued that to liken the Rhodesian situation to the situation in Nazi Germany is to exaggerate, but the exaggeration is a matter of degree rather than kind.' He pointed out that the laws and attitudes of right-wing extremists are overlaid with racialism.

On the Land Tenure Act, the church fought for and succeeded in obtaining concessions, in that restrictions imposed on the mixing of races on the mission stations were lightened. In this fight, the Rhodesian churches had the spirited support of churches from Botswana, Lesotho, Malawi, South Africa, Zambia and Swaziland, which met in Salisbury in April 1970 and called for a positive stand against the Land Tenure Act. Their Resolution declared: 'There is a need for positive resistance against the action of the present régime.'

The radical proposals against racialism made by the Central Committee of the World Council of Churches at its meeting in London in May 1969 represented a significant attack on racialism. Its decision to support guerrillas in their quest for freedom in Southern Africa demoralised those who support the Smith régime for its 'Christian principles'. Their actual financial contribution to the O.A.U. for the purpose of supporting the families of those suffering under oppression was very small in comparison with what is needed to achieve final liberation, but the gesture alone contributes immensely to the liberation struggle.[17]

Clearly there are conservatives in the church who would continue to support the régimes in Southern Africa under all circumstances.

In South Africa the Dutch Reformed Church stands by the National Party regardless of its treatment of the non-white communities. The Anglican Church in Rhodesia is divided between those who look to Britain for continued support and who would like 'justice' done to the Africans, and those who believe that Britain is letting down her kith and kin. The latter support Smith at all times, and even speak his language. The Rev. Arthur Lewis wrote in a news-letter urging the Anglican Church to secede from the Province of Central Africa, which is headed by Archbishop Green-Wilkinson and includes Rhodesia, Boswana, Malawi and Zambia, to form its own Rhodesian province. He did so because the Bishop of Malawi had supported the World Council of Churches in its support of guerrillas and of Z.A.P.U. and Z.A.N.U. The Bishop of Mashonaland, the Rt. Rev. Paul Burrough, went further, claiming that Africans had appealed to him for help against the Z.A.P.U. and Z.A.N.U. leaders in Lusaka. He told an Anglican conference in Nairobi, Kenya, that Africans were being forced by their leaders to fight against whites, implying that Africans preferred white rule. When he found himself isolated, he walked out of the conference and returned to Salisbury, where his utterances are swallowed eagerly.

Even the Archbishop of Canterbury has shown signs of double thinking on Rhodesia. Before it took place he advocated that in the event of U.D.I. Britain should use force. But afterwards, and when it was obvious that Britain would not use force and that the African guerrillas would do it themselves, the Archbishop rejected the use of violence and did not support the World Council of Churches. This illustrates the double standards used in the relationship between black and white. If the Government uses troops it is called force, implying that it is legitimate, but when Africans use their own troops it is called violence, which suggests something horrible. White force is orderly and Christian. This vocabulary comes from people who have never suffered under oppression. An African knows that the white régimes in Rhodesia have been violent from the beginning up to the present day. African men, women and children whipped for having no passes, failure to address the District Commissioner with the 'right words' and for being absent from work has brought untold violence right into the lives of the Africans. Other Africans, like Nimrod Khumalo, actually die at the hands of the police. The Africans themselves are the only ones competent to decide on their destiny.

Church opposition to the Land Tenure Act should not be construed as meaning that the white Christian community has decided to throw in its lot with its black fellow-Christians. In fact the churches opposed those aspects of the Land Tenure Act which affected the church land. Very little attention was paid to the disproportionate distribution of land between black and white. The churches play the game of international politics according to their countries of origin. While in South Africa the Anglican Church takes an unrelenting attitude against racial oppression, in Rhodesia the task was left to the Bishop of Matabeleland, the Rt. Rev. K. Skelton. None of the other leaders has been able to see anything unjust without being apologetic about it. The Methodists in Rhodesia are led by an African, the Rev. Andrew Ndlela. But this does not mean that they would tolerate similar leadership in politics. Ndlela's leadership is carefully watched to ensure that it remains within acceptable limits.

No doubt socialists in various countries let the Africans down in 1965, but there is evidence that they want to correct the record. The support for the guerrillas on the part of the Church worried the Southern African white régimes, but that of the British Labour Party, announced in 1970, caused a traumatic shock. Vorster stigmatised the Labour Party for helping 'Communism', and Sir de Villiers Graaff, leader of the United Party, expressed 'a sense of profound regret'. South African leaders showed concern over their country's future relations with the British Labour Party, as a potential British Government. Harry Nicholas, General Secretary of the Labour Party, explained that the party had taken the decision because it was in 'danger of losing friends in Africa'. Labour had decided to go ahead with a programme designed to give financial aid to those fighting white régimes in Southern Africa. The decision was made by the Conference in 1970 and endorsed by the National Executive Committee in 1971, and it accords with the spirit of the U.N. Security Council Resolution S/253 of May 1968 on Rhodesia.

The U.N. and its international agencies have been of great use in making the African case known abroad. In March 1968 the UNCTAD Conference was taking place in New Delhi, India, when the Smith régime hanged the African freedom fighters in Salisbury. The conference expressed its deep shock. The African countries attacked South Africa, which happened to be represented at the conference, demanding the expulsion of its delegation because it was the South African Government that had enabled the régime to succeed through evading sanctions. In February 1971 the U.N. Commission on Human Rights charged South Africa, Rhodesia and Portugal with the commission of genocide. It had taken four years to investigate aspects of human rights in Southern Africa. The Commission stated that in Rhodesia genocide was carried out by forced removals, in South Africa by dumping people in barren areas, and in Portuguese territories by mass execution of the régime's opponents. (Earlier these actions would not have been classed as genocide; however, the definition reflects the sensitivity of the international community to human suffering.)

One reason why Britain is anxious to settle with Rhodesia is so that international pressures can be thereby deflected from herself on to the Rhodesian whites. She complains that today she is traduced by the world on Rhodesia, and yet she has not the power to influence events there. Of course, this is a naïve approach because in transferring attributes of legitimacy to the régime, which the international community faithfully outlawed for more than six years, she will influence events in Rhodesia to an unimaginable extent – though it is all too true that she will be unable to control them. It is the approach of Pontius Pilate. There is no doubt that Britain will be attacked over the Rhodesian question for a great number of years to come.

Another reason why Britain has decided to settle with Rhodesia is because the military power of all the African states put together is not powerful enough to upset the *status quo* in Southern Africa. The fiasco when the O.A.U. failed to implement its Resolution for member-states to withdraw their diplomatic missions from London if Wilson failed to suppress the rebellion by 15 December, 1965, is taken by the present British Government to indicate that unanimity of action does not exist among African states. On their own the African states would not tackle South Africa, which is likely to come to the aid of Smith if a racial war were waged against Rhodesia. However, the belief that African states are too weak militarily to mount an expedition for the liberation struggle in the South is based on out-dated military concepts. Increased support by African states for guerrilla warfare could have a powerful effect, and make life intolerable for those against whom it is directed. Egypt, Algeria and Nigeria are the only military powerful African states, but it is extremely unlikely that any of them would contemplate racial war in Southern Africa. The two Arab nations are much more concerned with their confrontation with Israel than they are with Southern Africa, and Nigeria, recently ravaged by civil war, is too weak to face another war, which she could not hope to win. However, the mounting of an expeditionary force has been contemplated.

As for the Africans inside the country, the British Government believes, influenced by the industrious Lord Goodman, that it is helping a weak and divided people who are in a dilemma. The argument of Smith that Africans are happy under white rule is held to be untrue, but what is regarded as reasonable is the idea that Africans should prefer economic advancement under a liberal white leader, and that this can be brought about by a settlement and with British help. The contradiction in Britain saying that she no longer has the power to influence events in Rhodesia, while in the same breath claiming that she can help Africans, is glossed over. The scheme to expand secondary and university education is for consumption by the public in Britain, who will be made to believe that the Government has been generous to the Africans. Again, it is hoped that nobody will question how Britain can control the way the money is spent if Smith, following the example of Sir Edgar Whitehead in 1962, decides to use it for such pressing needs as improving his armed forces or increasing white immigration.

The Africans are not deceived by all the tricks which the British Government and Smith are playing. There is only one criterion by which the Africans judge the sincerity of British sympathy – adult suffrage. A settlement which would leave power in the hands of the settlers is totally unacceptable; of this the British Government is well aware. This is why they will not resort to the testing of opinion by the racial referendum which they specified in the 1961 Constitution which they themselves fashioned.

Already the population explosion in Rhodesia has laid a foundation which makes the maintenance of the *status quo* nearly impossible.

Composition of African Population

Males (over 16 years)	1,278,000
Females (over 16 years)	1,223,000
Children (under 16 years)	2,429,000

Out of a total African population of 5·1m., 325,000 are immigrant labourers. The rest have been born in the country. The total annual increase is 200,000, which is 3·5 per cent. Of the African population, 49·6 per cent are under the age of sixteen. In eighteen years it will be double, making a total of over 10m. The social and economic problems which come with the African population explosion do not discourage Africans, but rather give them a sense of hope because of their intense revolutionary potential; even under an African government, the situation would spell disaster. The régime hopes to solve the problem negatively, by forcing Africans to pay higher fees for education, hospital treatment and other social necessities while blaming the population explosion on the ignorance of the Africans. Professor H. Philpott (1) of the University of Rhodesia quoted an African medical student as telling him: 'We have no guns but we make sure we have more babies.'

The Africans believe that under the Anglo-Rhodesian settlement proposals of November 1971, minority rule will remain in perpetuity. This belief triggered off an extensive campaign to oppose the proposed settlement by organising the African National Council (A.N.C.)

composed of religious leaders and former detained leaders of Z.A.P.U. and Z.A.N.U. In the present avaricious mood of the settlers, little attempt will be made to give Africans responsible posts, in the hope that more settlers will one day come from Britain. Other people believe that the high rate of unemployment in Britain (the official total was close to 1m. in 1971) will drive thousands of settlers to Rhodesia as after the Second World War. (Salisbury City Council made preparations for the reception of 50,000 settlers in 1972–3 as soon as the agreement of November 1971 was announced. But this too will cause an explosion as long as Africans feel a sense of injustice, as they are bound to do while other Africans living in states run by themselves are making progress. The likely consequence is that the young people who do not find employment will be recruited into the guerrilla movement.

The guerrillas will undoubtedly win the war of liberation in the end. It is true that in Rhodesia they have not often been effective, but this may have given them a useful lesson for the future. Even Lardner-Burke admitted in July 1970 that his régime expected worse guerrilla incursions to come in the future. Colin Legum has written that the guerrillas continue to operate actively despite the huge forces ranged against them. Their techniques are continually improving and their weaponry is becoming more sophisticated, sometimes matching that of the enemy. International involvement, too, is on the increase.[18] With the end of the war in Vietnam in sight, and world interest switching to Southern Africa, it is not difficult to foretell an intensification of the struggle between black and white in Africa.

In Africa north of the Zambezi, military strength is growing. Since U.D.I., the manpower of armed forces in sub-Saharan Africa has grown by 250,000 to 700,000.[19] In the latter part of the civil war, the Nigerian strength reached 150,000, and the forces of Congo-Kinshasa and Ethiopia have reached 40,000 each. The growth of the military in these African countries is concurrent with that of the population, whereas the white population of Rhodesia is static. It has to be admitted that as long as some leaders of African states are prepared to accept overtures from South Africa for a dialogue, the violent overthrow of the régime in Southern Africa will take a long time. But the younger people in the African states seem determined to end racial rule in Africa. The coming years will surely see great changes. The emotional revulsion and the ideological motivation are present among the Africans; all that is needed is for these two factors to be channelled into an actual confrontation with the white régimes.

The desire manifested in discussions during 1971 by the guerrillas of Z.A.P.U. and Z.A.N.U. to unite and fight together is another pointer to victory. Africans will certainly rule Zimbabwe in Smith's natural lifetime.

(v) *Solution of the Problem*

The first prerequisite for the solution of the Rhodesian dilemma is for the British Government and public to accept that encouragement of the settlers to defy the world must eventually lead to disaster. The effect of it will be felt in all parts of Africa where there is contact between black and white. The explosion will affect whites in Kenya and Zambia, and those scattered throughout other parts of Africa. To forestall a racial confrontation in Southern Africa, Rhodesia should never be given the attributes of independence under the present racial régime. If African wrath is to be contained it will be necessary to stick to the majority rule principle which applied to all former British colonies. While a just settlement of the problem is being worked out, all political prisoners – persons sentenced or detained in prison under the Law and Order Maintenance Act – should be freed. The white population believes that all the people arrested and charged under this Act are criminals. Africans admire, and regard as heroes, all those so arrested. Smith and his colleagues committed a more serious crime of treason but, because they are white and of British stock, they escaped without personal pains except for weak sanctions half-heartedly imposed.

The second step, to follow the release of political prisoners, would be a free election conducted on the basis of universal adult suffrage, with constituencies drawn according to the concentration of population, regardless of racial composition. This could be arranged so that it takes place in 1974 or 1975. The period between 1972 and 1975 could be used to transform the civil service. A civil service commisson would be created with equal representation of the races to ensure that the reorganisation of jobs does not discriminate racially as has been the case hitherto. Appointments would be made on merit alone. Some departments such as the Department of Internal Affairs, as created in 1898, would have to be eradicated and one established which would operate on a national instead of a racial basis. Similarly, the Department of African Education would have to go, and one of national rather than racial education established. One national budget, one syllabus and a unified system of primary and secondary schools and technical colleges would have to be introduced. The apprenticeship laws would be used to their maximum. One department of health would have to be established with facilities for all, not for separate races. Money and skills are often wasted through racially separate institutions.

300 RHODESIA: STRUGGLE FOR A BIRTHRIGHT

The racial laws should not trouble anybody, because as soon as the Africans get the vote, they will die a natural death, as happened in Kenya and Zambia. The British argument that racialism can be ended by means of principles is hard to understand, because people cannot be forced to adopt the principles of others. The British argument on principles suggests that Rhodesia was never ruled by people of principle. Harold Wilson found that Nkomo and Sithole were not treated in accordance with civilised standards – starved and penned inside hot jeeps surrounded by police, who except for their uniforms, could be mistaken for London bobbies. In this case Smith is right in saying that there are no principles at all.

Courts would have to be radically overhauled to provide initially, as a protection for the whites, an equal number of magistrates and judges from each racial group. If the country is won for the Africans by a revolution, as seems likely, all judges and magistrates will be African and undoubtedly the same system of 'justice' will be turned against those whites who remain in the country as is now in operation against Africans. No decent-minded African wishes to see revenge being directed against whites. But this situation could be saved through willing reforms that are assisted and directed by impartial bodies such as the Commonwealth and the U.N. The Africans can never accept the settlers as judges of their case.

These recommendations cannot be anything but repugnant to the settlers who have deceived themselves to the extent of claiming that they will remain in power for 300 years. Settlers of this outlook can be helped out of their worries if Britain were to make funds available to assist those who fear majority rule to leave the country and settle abroad – in a country where power will remain in 'civilised hands'. Britain could guarantee the sale of their property as well as paying their passages. This would be a more practical use of funds than providing Africans with education. The more education the Africans acquire, the more bitter they become. When the literacy rate was still low in Rhodesia, the whites were happy, but as it grew higher the struggle intensified.

These suggestions for a solution to the problem are far from being exhaustive. Some African opinion will regard them as too moderate, because they imply a compromise with the non-African in the country. However, they are necessary as a starting point in order to avoid a racial holocaust in Southern African and possibly in much of the world.

REFERENCES

1. Palley, op. cit., p. 206, or House of Commons Debates, Vol. 118, Col. 2336, 30 July, 1919.
2. Rhodesia, Parliamentary Debates, Vol. 75, Col. 1045, 2 September, 1969.
3. J. H. Hobson, *Imperialism: a Study*. London, 1902 (3rd ed. 1938).
4. Zambia, with a population of 4·5m has 1·6m. voters, whereas Rhodesia has only 100,000 voters out of a population of 5·5m.
5. *Notes on Current Politics*, Conservative Research Dept. Publications, No. 16, October 1968, p. 297.
6. Rhodesian whites invited Powell to open the Marandellas Agricultural Show. One white correspondent in the *Rhodesia Herald* rebuked Powell's admirers, reminding them that if Powellism were applied to Rhodesia, the whites would be forced to go back to Europe. *Rhodesia Herald*, 11 June, 1971.
7. Horowitz, op. cit., p. 171.
8. *Rhodesia Herald*, 22 May, 1971.
9. *Rhodesia Herald*, 4 August, 1971.
10. *Financial Times*, London, 3 June, 1971.
11. Rhodesia Parliamentary Debates, Vol. 76, Col. 1383, 14 November, 1969.
12. The progress of the apprenticeship training scheme under the Apprenticeship Training and Skilled Manpower Development Act 1968 has been as follows:

	Africans	Europeans	Coloureds and Asians
1962	6	477	10
1963	18	349	9
1964	19	364	8
1965	16	419	7
1966	3	368	9
1967	4	405	5
1968	2	466	17
1969	10	451	49

13. For details, see Palley, op. cit., p. 790, and add the latest figures compiled by the Central Statistical Office, Salisbury.
14. The difference between multi-racialism and non-racialism is that non-racialism recognises human merit, regardless of race; it is thus preferred by Africans. The policy of multi-racialism implies that Africans are inferior and primitive; and that their quality could only be improved through an evolutionary process presided over by white men. In other words multi-racialism tells the African not to struggle for the attainment of the standards enjoyed by whites until the whites are ready.
15. In the U.S.A., Smith has strong allies in the anti-U.N., anti-Negro and anti-Communist elements. An indefatigable supporter is Senator Thurmond of South Carolina. In 1967 the 'Friends of Rhodesia' in the U.S.A. had 122 branches and 25,000 members, most of whom see the

situation in Rhodesia as a simple confrontation between black and white.

16. *Rhodesia Herald*, 27 May, 1971.

17. The General Assembly of the Church of Scotland followed the W.C.C. and pleaded its support for the freedom fighters. Reported in the *Rhodesia Herald*, 21 May, 1971.

18. *New Society*, London, 6 August, 1970.

19. W. Gutteridge, *The Coming Confrontation in Southern Africa*, Conflict Studies Series, August 1971.

APPENDICES

APPENDICES

A

SHORT BIOGRAPHIES OF
AFRICAN NATIONALIST LEADERS

JAMES ROBERT CHIKEREMA

Educated at Kutama mission near Makwiro, and at Marianhill in Natal, where he did secondary education to junior certificate level. He formed the City Youth League with the help of Duduza Chisiza, a Malawian migrant who later became a minister in Banda's cabinet, Edson Sithole, Thompson Gonese, Henry Hamadziripi and George Nyandoro. On the merger of the League and A.N.C., Chikerema became Nkomo's vice-president, but was detained in 1959–63. He did not participate in N.D.P. and Z.A.P.U., but he was consulted during their lifetime while in prison. He was released in February 1963, only to be faced with the Z.A.P.U.–Z.A.N.U. split. He was able to leave the country before the detention of Nkomo in 1964. He led Z.A.P.U. in exile for Nkomo from 1963 until the split in 1970, and has been one of the founders of FROLIZI.

JOSIAH CHINAMANO

Born in Chinamora reserve, North-east Mashonaland. Was adviser to Nkomo on educational matters. He was a teacher at Waddilove Institute, where he studied privately for a B.A. degree with the University of South Africa. He instructed missionaries in London in 1953–4 before returning home to be headmaster of a Methodist school. He later founded a secondary school for children who could not otherwise find secondary school places. In 1964 the Smith régime banned the school for 'indoctrination', and sent Chinamano with his wife Ruth into detention, where they remained till 1970. He refused to see Sir Alec Douglas-Home during the 1971 talks, as he preferred to meet him in the company of Nkomo. He is now treasurer-general of the African National Council.

HUBERT CHITEPO

Born in Manyikaland near Umtali, and educated at St. August mission, in the same district, at Adams College, Natal, and Fort Hare College. He then studied law in London and was called to the bar by the Middle Temple, becoming the first African lawyer to practise in the Central African Federation in 1954. In 1962 the Tanganyika Government appointed him its director of public prosecutions. At the Z.A.P.U.–Z.A.N.U. split, he joined Z.A.N.U. which he has continued to lead from Lusaka.

ENOCH DUMBUTSHENA

Son of Job Dumbutshena, the old stalwart of the Industrial and Commercial Workers' Union of the 1920s and 1930s, he is a trained teacher and a barrister of Gray's Inn. He taught in South Africa and Rhodesia before turning to journalism and the law. He set up a legal practice in Zambia after the Smith regime had made it impossible for him to practise in Rhodesia. Enoch was president of the A.N.C. in Bulawayo in 1949 following the Revd. Samkange, with Stanlake as his secretary. Stanlake was not effective in his opposition to the Subversive Activities Bill in 1949, and this forced Enoch to resign in disgust at his secretary. These two were among the few university graduates in the country in the late 1940s.

MASOTSHA MHIKE HOVE

Educated at Mnene, Masase and Morgenster missions in Rhodesia and at Mpumula Lutheran mission in Natal. He taught at Masase in the 1930s and at Waddilove mission in the 1940s. He was appointed editor of the *Bantu Mirror* when Savanhu took over the *African Weekly*. Like Savanhu, he was recruited to the Federal Party by Huggins in 1953, and fought Matabeleland constituency against Nkomo, and won.

He is a man of integrity and talent. He supported the white-led parties because he believed in making the best of the situation as it was. Hove was appointed Federal High Commissioner to Nigeria in 1962, leaving in 1963 when the Federation collapsed. He joined the Bulawayo Municipal Services, where he works at present.

AARON JACHA

Founder of the first Bulawayo-based African National Congress in 1934, he later led the Rhodesian African Farmers' Union. He became a Federal M.P. under the U.F.P. in 1962.

MORTON MALIANGA

Born in Manyikaland near Umtali, and educated at Ohlange Institute near Durban, he qualified as an accountant. But like most Africans in this profession, he found it difficult to obtain employment. He was one of the founders of the N.D.P. and became vice-president to Nkomo from October 1960. His brother Washington was general secretary of Z.A.P.U. in 1961–2. Morton Malianga joined Z.A.N.U. when the split occurred. He is currently detained in Salisbury prison with other Z.A.N.U. leaders.

JOSIAS TERRY MALULEKE

Educated at Mnene mission, which he left after only seven years' education. He was secretary-general of the African T.U.C. and a committee member of the Harare branch of the congress. He was detained in 1959 and released in 1961. When the Z.A.P.U.–Z.A.N.U. split took place in 1963, he formed the Zimbabwe African Labour Organisation, which supported Z.A.N.U. He studied privately during his detention, obtaining the G.C.E. certificate which enabled him to enter the University of Rhodesia in 1964. In the same year he was restricted to Gonakudzingwa for challenging the ban on meetings at week-ends under the bill of rights. He was free in 1965 but detained again within months of his release. He escaped in 1966 to Britain where he has obtained a B.Sc.(Econ.).

MICHAEL ANDREW MAWEMA

Born in Victoria district, and educated at the Dutch Reformed Church, Gutu Mission. He qualified as a teacher, but left to work as a social welfare worker in the Rhodesia Railways. He became an active member of the Railway African Workers' Union. When the A.N.C. was formed in 1957, he was one of the few people sent by the party to study abroad; he went in 1958 to Israel to study the organisation of co-operatives. He returned at the end of 1959 and formed the N.D.P. in January 1960. He was detained in 1964, but was released after three years. He joined Edson Sithole and C.G.B. Msipa to present a petition to Sir Alec Douglas-Home on the independence talks in November 1971. He is at present organising secretary of the African National Council.

JASON ZIYAPAPA MOYO

Born in South-west Matabeleland, and educated at Mzingwane, where he obtained a certificate in building and carpentry. He was vice-president of the African Trade Union Congress, and vice-secretary-general of the Congress when it was banned in 1959. He stayed in detention until 1960, when he joined the N.D.P. on his release. He became a member of the N.D.P. executive, and treasurer-general of Z.A.P.U.

He joined Nkomo in opposition to those who split from Z.A.P.U. in 1963. He was abroad when the P.C.C. was banned and its leaders detained in 1964. He was one of the five leaders of Z.A.P.U. in exile who organised the fighting which took place after 1967. Moyo led those who opposed Chikerema in the Z.A.P.U. split of 1970. He retained the support of most of the guerrillas in Z.A.P.U.

JOSEPH MSIKA

Born in the Mazoe area of Mashonaland – his father was from Gazaland. He worked as a chief clerk in a textile factory in Bulawayo, and was chairman of the old A.N.C. in that city until 1957 when it merged with the City Youth League to form the Southern Rhodesia A.N.C. He became a committee member of the National Executive in 1957, and was detained in 1959. He was later elected to the National Executive of the N.D.P. and Z.A.P.U.–P.C.C. He was detained with Nkomo in April 1964 and except for a brief period in 1965 has remained in restriction ever since. He is Z.A.P.U.'s spokesman for foreign affairs. While in detention he has studied privately for a B.A. in sociology with the University of South Africa.

CLEMENT MUCHACHI

Born in Selukwe district and educated at Goromonzi school, he has been active in nationalist politics since 1960. He remained at branch level in the N.D.P. but rose to executive level in Z.A.P.U. When the split took place he remained with Z.A.P.U. and was given the post of Secretary for Youth. He had been in Gwelo prison since U.D.I., and is studying for a B.A. in sociology.

ROBERT GABRIEL MUGABE

Born in North-west Mashonaland, and educated at Kutama and Empanden mission. He left school with ten year's schooling, but did all his secondary education and part of his first degree privately, finishing his B.A. at Fort Hare University College in 1951. He later obtained two further degrees by private study. He taught in Rhodesia until 1954, leaving for Northern Rhodesia in 1955 and Ghana in 1956. In May 1960 he returned home to join the N.D.P. as publicity secretary, until Z.A.P.U. was formed in 1961. He joined Sithole in forming Z.A.N.U. at the split in 1963. He was arrested in that year for making a 'subversive speech' and detained in 1964 after he had served his sentence. Since his imprisonment in 1963 he has obtained two more degrees with the University of London.

WILLIE MUSARUNWA

Born near Sinoia in Zwimba reserve and educated at Kutama mission and Goromonzi school, he worked in African newspapers, rising to the editorship of the *African Weekly*. He joined politics after the Z.A.P.U.–Z.A.N.U. split and aligned himself with Nkomo, being appointed Secretary for Public Relations in the P.C.C. He was arrested and sentenced for an alleged subversive statement. After completing the sentence he was detained in Gwelo prison and still remains there. He studied privately and obtained a B.A. of the University of South Africa.

ENOS NKALA

Born in Filabusi district. His father Mzombi was one of those who resisted the removal of the Ndebele from Filabusi to Tsholobho in 1947–8. Nkala was one of the founders of the N.D.P. in 1960, and was unequalled for bravery and tenacity of purpose. This brought him into conflict with Sir Edgar Whitehead's Government, and resulted in his being sentenced to long terms of imprisonment. After the split he joined Z.A.N.U. and with other leaders of that party, he remains in Salisbury prison.

LAZARUS NKALA

Born at Filabusi, and trained as a builder at Mzingwani government school, he is a soft-spoken man with a deep understanding of human problems. He was detained in 1959 and since then has never been free for longer than a year. He is detained with Nkomo and Joseph Msika at Gonakundzingwa camp.

JOSHUA MQABUKO NYONGOLO NKOMO

Son of a teacher and evangelist in South-west Matabeleland, he was educated as Tsholotsho Government School, Adams College, Natal, and Jan Hofmeyr School of Social Work. He studied privately for a degree with the University of South Africa. He started his political career in 1947 as organising secretary of the Rhodesian African Workers' Union. His union represented railway workers in Rhodesia, Botswana and Zambia. This brought him in contact with men who are now ministers in the latter two countries.

Nkomo represented Matabeleland at the Federal Talks in 1952, and denounced the talks on his return to Bulawayo. He was then elected president of the All-African People's Convention started by Charles Nzingeli. After the establishment of Federation, people in Matabeleland persuaded Nkomo to fight the Matabeleland constituency; he lost the election to M. M. Hove, but was elected president of the old A.N.C. Between 1952 and 1957 the A.N.C. had become a social organisation with very little political role. In Salisbury, which had become a larger city than Bulawayo after the Second World War, the City Youth League operated independently of the A.N.C.; in 1956 Joseph Mskia campaigned for the unification of the A.N.C. and the City Youth League, which resulted in the formation of the A.N.C. on 12 September, 1957. Nkomo became its president, and later was president of the N.D.P. and Z.A.P.U.–P.C.C. He was banned and detained in 1964, and remains so up to the time of writing. He also remains the most popular leader in the whole country.

George Nyandoro

Born in South-east Mashonaland in the district where his father is a chief. He started his political activity by joining the Native Association in 1951. which started the campaign against the Land Husbandry Act of that year. In 1955 he joined the City Youth League started by Chikerema, Edson Sithole and Duduza Chisiza. In 1957 he was elected general secretary of the A.N.C. and was detained in the Central African emergency of 1959–63. After his release from detention, he went to London for medical tratement, thus escaping the detentions of 1964. He returned to Lusaka to join the military struggle with the Z.A.P.U. liberation movement. When that movement split in March 1970. Nyandoro joined Chikerema and Nathan Shamuyarira in forming the Movement for the Freedom of Zimbabwe – FROLIZI. Nyandoro had only seven years' schooling, but studied privately to obtain a certificate in accountacy.

Revd. Thompson Douglas Samkange

Took over from Aaron Jachs the leadership of the African National Congress, which was strong enough in 1948 to organise a strike which paralysed Bulawayo, demanding higher wages. The strike was ruthlessly suppressed, and followed by the introduction of the Subversive Activities Act 1950. Samkange's son, Stanlake, was secretary to the Congress.

The Revd. T. D. Samkange was among the leading Africans who opposed the granting of self-government to Southern Rhodesia in 1923, and the provisions of the Land Apportionment Act of 1930. He was associated with the radical missionaries A. S. Cripps and John White. He died in 1956.

Jasper Zengeza Savanhu

Like most African leaders in Rhodesia, he started as a teacher – at Salusi mission of the Seventh Day Adventists near Bulawayo. He later joined the African Newspapers as editor of the Bulawayo-based *Bantu Mirror*. He represented the Africans of Mashonaland in the pre-Federation talks in 1952, while Joshua Nkomo represented Matabeleland. Savanhu was an official of the Congress started by Jacha in 1934. When the Federation had become a *fait accompli*, Savanhu joined Huggins' Federal Party, and stood for Mashonaland, the only constituency of the Federal Parliament representing Africans. His membership of a European-led party enabled him to beat a strong African-backed candidate Stanlake Samkange. Savanhu was appointed parliamentary secretary to the Ministry of Home Affairs after the Central African emergencies of 1959. When the Federation was about to collapse, he resigned from the U.F.P., then led by Sir Roy Welensky, and took a militant stand for the African cause.

George Silundika

Studied at Marianhill, the University College at Roma, and Fort Hare University College. Both colleges expelled him for political reasons before he could complete his degrees. He taught at Empandemi Secondary School near his birthplace in the Plumtree area. In 1960, while working as a laboratory technician at the University of Rhodesia, he and other young men founded the N.D.P. He was one of the first leaders to press in 1960 for a constitutional conference, resulting in the conference that took place in 1961. At the Z.A.P.U.–Z.A.N.U. split, he stayed with Nkomo and escaped abroad to continue the struggle against minority rule.

Edson Sithole

Born in the Gazaland area of Rhodesia, but came to work in Salisbury. He left school after only four years' formal education, but studied privately to university level, and obtained LL.B. and LL.M. of the University of London. He was detained in 1959–63, and studied for his degrees during that time. He was again detained in 1964–70, and during this period commenced study for a Ph.D. in laws. He started politics with the City Youth League and later joined the A.N.C. when the merger took place. At the Z.A.P.U.–Z.A.N.U. split, he joined Z.A.N.U. in protest against Nkomo's leadership which he regarded as weak and indecisive. He joined M. A. Mawema and Msipa in a petition to Sir Alec Douglas-Home on the 1971 independence talks. Sithole is one of the three African lawyers practising in Salisbury (1971). He is now restricted to within three miles of Salisbury, and yet he continues to fight as publicity secretary of the African National Council.

The Revd. Ndabaningi Sithole

Leader of the Zimbabwe African National Union, who broke away from Nkomo's Z.A.P.U. in July 1963, and a minister in the American Congregational Church. He is the author of two books, *African Nationalism* and a novel, *Obed*. Like most African leaders of his time, he did his secondary and university education by private study. He obtained a B.A. degree with the University of South Africa, and Bachelor of Divinity in the U.S.A. He joined nationalist politics in 1960, and became treasurer of N.D.P. and later National Chairman of Z.A.P.U. He was sent to prison first on a charge of subversion in calling on his supporters to resist U.D.I. in 1964 with any means at their disposal. After completing the sentence he was sent to detention, remaining there until tried and imprisoned on a charge of plotting to assassinate leading Rhodesia Front ministers.

EDSON JONAS ZVOBGO

Born in the Victoria district, son of a Dutch Reformed Church minister who later left that church to form an African one. Zvobgo obtained secondary education at Tengwani School in Matabeleland, and went to the University College at Roma, Lesotho. He was expelled from there, and returned to become one of the founders of the N.D.P. in Janaury 1960. He left the same year for the U.S.A. and graduated at Fletcher School of International Law, Boston, Mass. Nkomo made him Z.A.P.U. representative at the U.N., where he successfully lobbied the Committee of Twenty-four. He returned to Rhodesia in the thick of the 1963 split. He joined Z.A.N.U. and was the first to be arrested and tried for being a member of a banned organisation outside the country. He was detained after serving his sentence and while in detention he has studied and qualified as a lawyer. He is deputy Secretary-general of the African National Council.

L

B

RHODESIA: PROPOSALS FOR A SETTLEMENT

Submitted to Parliament as a White Paper by the Foreign Secretary,
Sir Alec Douglas-Home, 25 November, 1971

I. THE TEST OF ACCEPTABILITY

The proposals set out below are conditional upon the British Government being satisfied that they are acceptable to the people of Rhodesia as a whole. The British Government will therefore appoint a Commission to ascertain directly from all sections of the population of Rhodesia whether or not these proposals are acceptable and to report accordingly to the British Government. It will consist of a Chairman, Deputy Chairman and a number of Commissioners. The report will be signed by the Chairman and the Deputy Chairmen. The members of the Commission will travel extensively throughout the country visiting in particular all centres of population, local councils and traditional meeting places in the Tribal Trust Lands.

In the period before and during the test of acceptability normal political activities will be permitted to the satisfaction of the Commission, provided they are conducted in a peaceful and democratic manner. Radio and television time will be made available to political parties represented in the House of Assembly.

The Commission will carry out its inquiries in public or in private as it deems appropriate. There will be immunity for witnesses heard by the Commission in respect of their evidence and freedom for persons resident in Rhodesia, whatever their political views or affiliations, to enable them to appear before the Commission. All Rhodesian Government employees will be permitted to express their views to the Commission. Persons in detention or under restriction will be similarly permitted. Arrangements will be made in London and elsewhere as necessary for Rhodesians resident abroad to submit their views to the Commission.

The Rhodesian Government will provide the Commission with such assistance as may reasonably be required to enable them to carry out their functions.

II. THE CONSTITUTION

The Constitution of Rhodesia will be the Constitution adopted in Rhodesia in 1969 modified in the following respects. The Rhodesian Government will introduce legislation to make the necessary modifications in the Constitution and related electoral legislation with effect from the date on which independence is conferred by the British Parliament.

(1) *The House of Assembly*

(*a*) The existing provisions governing the increase of African representation in the House will be repealed and replaced by provisions to give effect to the arrangements set out in the following sub-paragraphs.

(*b*) A new roll of African voters (the African higher roll) will be created with the same qualifications as those for the roll of European voters. The relevant means and educational qualifications are set out in Appendix I.

(*c*) Additional African seats will be created, in accordance with the arrangements set out in the following subparagraphs, with effect from the dissolution of Parliament following the date on which it is established that any such seats are due. The seats will be filled at the general election consequent upon the dissolution of Parliament. However, the first four additional seats will be created and elections held to fill them as soon as it is established that they are due.

(*d*) When the number of voters registered on the African higher roll equals 6 per cent. of the number of voters then registered on the European roll, two additional African seats will become due; when the number of voters registered on the African higher roll equals 12 per cent of the number of voters then registered on the European roll, a further two additional seats will become due; further additional African seats will become due two at a time, for each such proportionate increase of 6 per cent in the number of voters registered on the African higher roll, until 34 additional African seats have been created, thus resulting in parity in the numbers of African and European members in the House of Assembly. This arrangement will ensure that at parity there are approximately equal numbers of voters on the African higher and European rolls.

(*e*) The first two additional African seats will be filled by direct election for single-member constituencies by the voters registered on the African higher roll and the next two will be filled by indirect election by electoral colleges on the same basis as the existing eight African seats filled by indirect election. This sequence will be repeated in relation to subsequent additional African seats.

(*f*) For the purpose of giving effect to the above arrangement the Registrar-General of Voters will review the number registered on the African higher roll and European roll at not more than six-monthly intervals, and whenever additional African seats have become due he will issue a certificate to that effect to the President and the President will then be required to make an order providing for the creation of those seats as described above.

(*g*) The qualifications for the existing roll of African voters (the African lower roll) will be replaced by qualifications equivalent to those for the 'B' roll under the 1961 Constitution subject to the financial qualifications being increased twice by 10 per cent. The relevant means and educational qualifications are set out in Appendix II.

(*h*) The Rhodesian Government have agreed to a simplified application form for enrolment on the African lower roll, and to an amendment to the Electoral Act to provide that an applicant for the African lower roll shall, if he so requests, receive assistance from the registering officer in completing the form.

(*i*) A candidate for election to an African higher roll seat will have to be registered as a voter on that roll, and a candidate for election to an African lower roll seat will have to be registered as a voter on one of the two African rolls.

(*j*) Within one year after the holding of the general election at which parity is attained a referendum will be held among all enrolled African voters to determine whether or not the seats filled by indirect election should be abolished and replaced by an equal number of seats filled by direct elections.

The new seats will all be African higher roll seats unless the Legislature has before the referendum provided for up to one-quarter of the new seats to be African lower roll seats. The Legislature may also provide that a specific number of the extra seats should be rural constituencies.

Laws providing for any of the matters mentioned in this paragraph, including the procedural arrangements for the holding of the referendum, would not have to be passed in accordance with the requirements for amending the Constitution; the only special requirement would be that in the House of Assembly they must be approved by a majority of all the African members.

If the majority of voters at the referendum is in favour of the abolition of the indirectly elected seats, an election to give effect to the change will be held within one year thereafter. It will be possible for an election to be held for this purpose without the dissolution of Parliament. If this course is adopted the indirectly elected African members and the African lower roll members and also, if the number of African lower roll seats is to be increased, the African lower roll members; will vacate their seats on the date appointed for the nomination of candidates in the election and Parliament will be prorogued from that date until the completion of the election.

(*k*) Not later than six months after the holding of that election or, if the result of the referendum is that the seats filled by indirect election are retained, after the completion of the referendum, an independent Commission will be appointed to ascertain whether the creation of Common Roll seats in accordance with the constitutional provisions described in sub-paragraph (*l*) below is acceptable to the people of Rhodesia and, if this is not so acceptable, whether any alternative arrangements would command general support. The commission will consist of a Chairman who holds or has held high judicial office, and equal numbers of European and African members appointed by the Government after consultation with all parties represented in the House of Assembly. The Commission will be required to report to the Legislature within one year of its appointment. A law to give effect to any recommendation of the Commission would have to be passed in accordance with the requirements for the amendment of the Constitution.

(*l*) The Constitution will provide that, with effect from the dissolution of Parliament following the date by which the Commission is required to report, 10 Common Roll seats in the House of Assembly will be created. The Common Roll seats will be filled by direct election by the voters on a roll consisting of all the voters for the time being registered on the European roll and the African higher roll. Elections to these seats will be conducted on the basis that the whole of Rhodesia will form a single constituency returning all the Common Roll members, and that each voter will have or votes which he may cast as he chooses amongst the candidates.

(2) *The Senate*

The Senate will continue to be constituted as at present. As a consequence of the establishment (see paragraph (3) below) of a new Declaration of Rights enforceable by the courts the Senate Legal Committee will be abolished.

(3) *The Declaration of Rights*

The existing Declaration of Rights will be replaced by a new Declaration affording protection to the fundamental rights and freedoms of the individual and conferring a right of access to the High Court for the purpose of obtaining redress on any person who alleges that its provisions have been contravened in relation to him. The text of the Declaration and the provisions for its enforcement are set out in Appendix III.*

(4) *Renewal of Declarations of Emergency*

Section 61 of the Constitution will be amended so as to reduce the period within which a Declaration of Emergency requires renewal by resolution of the House of Assembly from 12 months to 9 months.

(5) *Amendment of the Constitution*

(*a*) The Rhodesian Government have given an assurance to the British Government that they will not introduce or support in the Rhodesian Parliament any amendment of the specially entrenched provisions of the Constitution relating to the composition of the House of Assembly or the specially entrenched provisions of the Electoral Act until the first two African higher roll seats have been created and filled or until three years have elapsed since the Constitutional changes provided for by these proposals have come into force, whichever is the sooner.

(*b*) Until the date by which the Commission referred to in sub-paragraph (1)(*k*) above is required to report, or the date on which it reports if that is earlier, a Bill to amend any of the specially entrenched provisions of the Consitution will require, in addition to the existing requirements of the affirmation votes in each House of the Legislature of not less than two-thirds of the total membership of the House the affirmative votes in the House of Assembly of a majority of the total European membership and of a majority of the total African membership.

(*c*) The existing provision to the effect that a Bill to increase the number of members of the House of Assembly without altering the proportion of African members to the total number of members shall not on that account be regarded as amending a specially entrenched provision will be repealed.

(*d*) The specially entrenched provisions of the Constitution will include:

(i) The new provisions to give effect to the proposals in paragraph II(1) above;

(ii) The new Declaration of Rights, including the provisions for its enforcement by the High Court;

(iii) The amended Section 61 relating to Declarations of Emergency.

(e) The following provisions of the Electoral Act will be subject to the same requirements as regards amendment as the specially entrenched provisions of the Constitution.

(i) Those prescribing the qualifications and disqualifications for registration of voters on the European roll and both African rolls;

(ii) Those prescribing the qualifications and disqualifications for candidates for election to the House of Assembly;

(iii) The provision for variation of the means qualifications for voters in consequence of changes in prices; and

(iv) The provisions prescribing the composition of the Tribal Electoral Colleges.

Section 26 of the Electoral Act, which provides for the gradual increase of means and educational qualifications, for the existing African roll so that when parity is reached, they are the same as those for the European roll, will be repealed.

III. REVIEW OF EXISTING LEGISLATION

The Rhodesian Government have intimated to the British Government their firm intention, within the spirit of these proposals, to make progress towards ending racial discrimination. Accordingly an independent Commission will be set up to examine the question of racial discrimination. It will be required to consider existing legislation and to make recommendations to the Rhodesian Government on ways of making progress towards ending any racial discrimination. There shall be included in the functions of the Commission a special duty to scrutinise the provisions of the Land Tenure Act and to consider the possible creation of an independent and permanent Land Board to preside over the long-term resolutions of the problems involved. The terms of reference of the Commission, which will consist of three members, one of whom will be an African, are set out in Appendix IV. Its membership will be agreed with the British Government. The Commission will be established as soon as possible after the test of acceptability has been completed. Its findings will be published.

The Rhodesian Government recognise that the findings of the Commission will carry special authority and have given an assurance that they will commend to Parliament such changes in existing legislation as are required to give effect to its recommendations, subject only to considerations that any Government would be obliged to regard as of an overriding character.

IV. REVIEW OF CASES OF DETAINEES AND RESTRICTEES

The Rhodesian Government stated that 23 detainees have been released since the end of March 1971, leaving 93 detainees and 2 restrictees (excluding 34 detainees who have been released on conditions). It is the Rhodesian Government's intention to release a further 31 detainees as soon as the necessary arrangements can be made.

Since the settlement will have created a new situation there will be a new special review of the cases of all detainees and restrictees to see whether, in the light of changed circumstances, they can be released or the restrictions can be removed without prejudice to the maintenance of public safety and public order. This review will be carried out by the existing tribunal of which the Chairman is a Judge of the Rhodesian High Court, as soon as possible after the test of acceptability has been completed. The recommendations of the tribunal will be binding on the detaining or restricting authority. For the purposes of this special review an observer appointed by the British Government in agreement with the Rhodesian Government will be entitled to be present.

V. LAND

In the African area there is at present approximately 5 million acres of unoccupied land which is available for settlement by Africans, $3\frac{1}{2}$ million in the Tribal Trust Lands and $1\frac{1}{2}$ million in the purchase area. Provision exists under which significant additional land can be made available and the Rhodesian Government intend to make it available as the need arises.

Both Governments agree that they will immediately devote a proportion of the aid referred to in paragraph VI of these proposals to the improvement of areas currently occupied or intended for occupation by Africans.

With the exception of certain forest and national park areas the development of which may involve the removal of a limited number of occupants without established rights, the only two cases in which the Rhodesian Government are considering the eviction of Africans from land in the European area are Epworth and Chishawasha Missions. The Rhodesian Government have given an assurance that they will not take steps to evict African tenants or other occupants from these two areas or from other areas in which they are living until such time as the Commission referred to in paragraph III above has reported and its recommendations have been fully considered.

VI. DEVELOPMENT PROGRAMME

The two Governments attach the greatest importance to the expansion of the economy of Rhodesia and, in particular, to stimulating economic growth in the Tribal Trust Lands. There will therefore be a development programme to increase significantly educational and job opportunities for Africans in order to enable them to play a growing part in the country's future development, and early discussions between the two Governments will be held to agree on this programme and the best means of implementing it.

The British Government will provide up to £5 million per year for a period of 10 years in capital aid and technical assistance to be applied to purposes and projects to be agreed with the Rhodesian Government to be matched appropriately by sums provided by the Rhodesian Government for this development programme. This will be in addition to the annual expenditure currently planned by the Rhodesian Government for African education and housing and for development projects in the Tribal Trust

Lands and African Purchase Areas. Part of this development programme will be devoted to the establishment of new irrigation schemes, intensive cultivation projects, industrial projects and the improvement of communications in the Tribal Trust Lands and African Purchase Areas. As regards education, the moneys will be used to improve and expand facilities for Africans in agriculture, technical and vocational training, teacher training and training in administration and for other educational purposes in the field of primary, secondary and higher education.

The parallel development of the two elements in this programme will thus help to ensure that new job opportunities for Africans will become available as the economy expands and additional educational facilities are provided for them.

VII. OTHER MATTERS

(1) As vacancies occur in the Rhodesian Public Service they will be filled according to the criteria of merit and suitability, regardless of race. The Rhodesian Government have undertaken to take steps to enable an increasing number of Africans to fit themselves to compete on equal terms with candidates of other races so far as appointments or promotions are concerned.

(2) Rhodesian citizens who have left Rhodesia for any reason will be allowed to return freely and without being subjected to any restrictions by reason of their past activities, but without amnesty in respect of any criminal offence.

(3) The Rhodesian Government wish to revoke the state of emergency at the earliest opportunity. In the absence of unforeseen circumstances they will do so after sanctions against Rhodesia have been lifted.

VIII. IMPLEMENTATION

As soon as the British Government are satisfied that the legislation referred to in paragraph II above has been enacted and steps taken to give effect to the proposals in paragraphs III and IV above they will introduce legislation to confer independence on Rhodesia as a republic and will commend this legislation to the British Parliament. They will also terminate their economic and other sanctions when this legislation takes effect. Both Governments will take steps to settle outstanding financial and other issues and to regularise relations between the two countries and matters affecting the personal status of individuals.

Nothing in these proposals shall be regarded as implying any change in the current attitude of either side to the present status of Rhodesia or of the 1969 Constitution.

The above proposals are acceptable to the British and the Rhodesian Governments.

24 November, 1971.

*Not attached.

Appendix I

EUROPEAN ROLL AND AFRICAN HIGHER ROLL QUALIFICATIONS

(*a*) Income at the rate of not less than $1,800 per annum during the two years preceding date of claim for enrolment, *or* ownership of immovable property of value of not less than $3,600.

OR

(*b*) (i) Income at the rate of not less than $1,200 per annum during the two years preceding date of claim for enrolment, *or* ownership of immovable property of value of not less than $2,000; *and*

(ii) four years secondary education of prescribed standard.

Appendix II

AFRICAN LOWER ROLL QUALIFICATIONS

(*a*) Income at the rate of not less than $600 per annum during the two years preceding date of claim for enrolment, *or* ownership of immovable property of value of not less than $1,000.

OR

(*b*) (i) Income at the rate of not less than $300 per annum during the two years preceding date of claim for enrolment, *or* ownership of immovable property of value of not less than $600; *and*

(ii) two years' secondary education of prescribed standard.

OR

(*c*) Persons over 30 years of age with—

(i) Income at the rate of not less than $300 per annum during the two years preceding the date of claim for enrolment, *or* ownership of immovable property of value of not less than $600; *and*

(ii) completion of a course of primary education of a prescribed standard.

OR

(*d*) Persons over 30 years of age with—

Income at the rate of not less than $430 per annum during the two years preceding the date of claim for enrolment *or* ownership of immovable property of value of not less than $800.

OR

(*e*) All kraal heads with a following of 20 or more heads of families.

Appendix IV

TERMS OF REFERENCE OF THE INDEPENDENT COMMISSION TO EXAMINE THE QUESTION OF RACIAL DISCRIMINATION

1. The Commission will carry out an examination of all aspects of the question of racial discrimination in Rhodesia. The Commission will review all existing laws (including subsidiary legislation and the administrative practices thereunder) to determine which such provisions or practices in its

M

opinion are discriminatory. The Commission may receive evidence from any relevant source and the Government of Rhodesia will ensure that its officials will co-operate fully with the Commission in this respect.

2. The Commission will make recommendations to the Rhodesian Government on ways of making progress towards the ending of any racial discrimination and its Report will be published.

3. The Commission is required to give special attention to the provisions of the Land Tenure Act. The Commission shall consider *inter alia*—

(*a*) the question of removing any restrictions on the entry into European areas of Africans wishing to attend multi-racial places of education or to be admitted to multi-racial hospitals, and any other restrictions on occupation;

(*b*) the question of removing any restrictions on the right of an African member of the professions to practise in a European area;

(*c*) in the light of the national interest, the question of the equitable allocation of land in relation to the needs of the respective section of the population; and

(*d*) the possible creation of an independent and permanent multi-racial Land Board to preside over the long-term resolution of the problems involved.

C

BIBLIOGRAPHY

BRITISH GOVERNMENT PAPERS

Africa, South: British South Africa Company. C.O. 417 series 1889–1924.
House of Commons Debates 1889–1971.
Southern Rhodesia, Documents relating to the negotiations between the United Kingdom and Southern Rhodesia Governments, November 1963–November 1965. Cmnd. 2807.
Report of the Advisory Commission on the Review of the Constitution of Rhodesia and Nyasaland, October 1960. Cmnd. 1148.
Rhodesia: Documents relating to Proposals for a Settlement, 1966. Cmnd. 3171.
Rhodesia: Proposals for a Settlement (*Fearless*), October 1968. Cmnd. 3793.
Southern Rhodesia Native Juveniles Act, 1926. Cmnd. 3076.
Rhodesia: Proposals for a Settlement, November 1971. Cmnd. 4835.

RHODESIA GOVERNMENT PAPERS

British South Africa Company, Reports of the Directors, 1889–1923.
Chief Native Commissioner's Reports, 1890–1962.
Reports of the Secretary for Internal Affairs, 1963–.
Annual Report of the Secretary for African Education, 1928–.
Annual Report of the Secretary for Local Government and Housing,
Annual Reports of the Secretary for Law and Order, 1957–.
Debates of the Legislative Council, 1899–1923.
Debates of the Legislative Assembly, 1924–.
Government Notices, 1928–.
Economic Survey of Rhodesia, 1970.

NEWSPAPERS

The Central African Examiner, Salisbury, 1960–4.
The Chronicle, Bulawayo, 1958–.
The Daily News, Salisbury, 1958–64.
The Economist, London, 1960–.
The Guardian, London, 1914–.
The New York Times, 1889–1969.
The Observer, London, 1958–71.
The Sunday Times, London, 1964–.
The Times, London. 1888–.

UNITED NATIONS PUBLICATIONS

International Review Service, 1960–.
Monthly Chronicle, 1962–.
Decolonization Reports, 1962–.
Yearbook, 1960–.

BOOKS

Anti-Slavery and Aboriginal Protection Society, *Mr. Podsnap and the Sacred Trust*, pamphlet, 1918.
Atmore A., and R. Oliver, *Africa since 1800*, Cambridge, 1967.
Barber, J. P., *Rhodesia: the Road to Rebellion*, London, 1967.
Bennett, G., *Kenya: a Political History. The Colonial Period*, London, 1963.
Bull, T., *Rhodesia Perspective*, London, 1967.
Bunting, B., *The Rise of the South African Reich*, Harmondsworth, 1964.
Churchill, W. S., *The Gathering Storm*, London, 1948.
Clements, F., *Rhodesia: the Course to Collision*, London, 1969.
Colquhoun Jollie, E., *The Future of Rhodesia*, Melsetter, 1917.
Davidson, B., *Which way Africa?* Harmondsworth, 1964.
Day, J., *International Nationalism*, London, 1967.
Ezera, K., *Constitutional Developments in Nigeria*, London, 1964.
Franck, T., *Race and Nationalism*, London, 1960.
Gann, L. H., *A History of Southern Rhodesia: Early Days to 1934*, London, 1965.
——and M. Gelfand, *Huggins of Rhodesia*, London, 1964.
Glass, S., *The Matabeleland War 1893*, London, 1968.
Gray, R., *Two Nations*, London, 1962.
Hall, R., *The High Price of Principles*, London, 1969.
Hodgkin, T., *Nationalism in Colonia. Africa*, London, 1956.
Keatley, P., *The Politics of Partnership*, Harmondsworth, 1963.
Leys, C., *European Politics in Southern Africa*, Oxford, 1959.
Madden, F., *Imperial Constitutional Documents, 1795–1865*. Oxford, 1966.
Mason, P., *The Birth of a Dilemma*, London, 1956.
Maxey, K., and M. Christie, *Rhodesia Outlook*, London, 1969.
Mlambo, E. E. M., *Rhodesia: the British Dilemma*, London, 1971.
Mtshali, B. U., *Rhodesia: Background to Conflict*, New York, 1961.
Murray, D. J., *The Governmental System in Southern Rhodesia*, Oxford, 1970.
Palley, C., *The Constitutional History ond Law of Southern Rhodesia*, Oxford, 1966.
Palmer, R. H., 'The History of the Land Apportionment Act 1890–1936,' Ph.D. thesis (unpublished), University of London, 1968.
Passmore, G. C., *Local Government Legislation in Southern Rhodesia up to 30th September 1963*, Salisbury, 1966.
——and M. T. Mitchell, *Source-Book of Parliamentary Elections and Referenda in Southern Rhodesia*, 1898–1962, Salisbury, 1963.
Quaison-Sackey, A., *Africa Unbound*, London, 1963.
Ranger, T. O., *The African Voice in Southern Rhodesia*, London, 1970.
Ranger, T. O., *Revolt in Southern Rhodesia, 1896–7*, London, 1967.

Rolin, H., *Les Lois et l'Administration de la Rhodésie*, Brussels, 1913.
Samkange, S., *Origins of Rhodesia*, London, 1968.
Seidman, A., *An Economic Textbook for Africa*, London, 1969.
Selous, F. C., *A Hunter's Wanderings in Africa*, London, 1881.
——*Sunshine and Storm in Rhodesia*, London, 1896.
Shamuyarira, N. M., *Crisis in Rhodesia*, London, 1965.
Sithole, N., *African Nationalism*, London, 1959.
Thayer, *The War Business*, New York, 1969.
Wallis, J. P. R., *One Man's Hand*, London, 1950.
Widstrand, C. G., *African Boundary Problems*, Uppsala, 1969.
Wilson, H., *The Labour Government 1964–70*, London, 1971.

INDEX